THE COMPLETE
GETTYSBURG GUIDE

~ SPECIAL CWPT EDITION ~

J. David Petruzzi

Maps and Photography by
Steven Stanley

THE COMPLETE
GETTYSBURG GUIDE

Walking and Driving Tours
of the Battlefield, Town,
Cemeteries, Field Hospital
Sites, and other Topics of
Historical Interest

J. David Petruzzi

Maps and Photography by
Steven Stanley

SB

Savas Beatie

New York and California

Cataloging-in-Publication Data is available from the Library of Congress.

ISBN 13: 978-1-932714-63-0

05 04 03 02 01   5 4 3 2 1
Third edition, first printing

SB
Published by
Savas Beatie LLC
521 Fifth Avenue, Suite 3400
New York, NY 10175

Editorial Offices:

Savas Beatie LLC
P.O. Box 4527
El Dorado Hills, CA 95762
Phone: 916-941-6896
(E-mail) editorial@savasbeatie.com

Savas Beatie titles are available at special discounts for bulk purchases worldwide by corporations, government agencies, institutions, and other organizations. For more details, please contact Special Sales, P.O. Box 4527, El Dorado Hills, CA 95762, or you may e-mail us at sales@savasbeatie.com, or visit our website at www.savasbeatie.com for additional information.

Cover Photo: "Early morning fog hangs in the Valley of Death." ©2009 by Steven A. Stanley

J. David Petruzzi

To my Mom,
Thank you for the lullabyes

Steven A. Stanley

To Kyrstie
For mending my heart and supporting my passion

To my daughters, Samantha and Ashleigh
For being my future

Table of Contents

Introduction

For most of my life, I have been in awe of the power of the written word.

I recall in my earliest memory lying on the floor of our living room one evening, when I was perhaps four years old. My father was watching television and I was drawing pictures with crayons and paper. For some reason, I wanted to see what my name looked like. I asked my father, "Daddy, how do you write my name?" He got up from his chair, laid down on the floor next to me, pulled out a black crayon and a fresh sheet of paper, and wrote my name in big letters along the top of it: D-A-V-I-D.

For a few moments I stared at those letters, tracing each with my finger and saying my name quietly as I did so. Somehow, in a way I didn't yet quite understand, these letters on the page — these unfamiliar shapes — made the sound of my name when spoken out loud. It was quite a concept for a little guy to grasp. My father handed me the crayon and I began tracing the letters just as my father had written them, one by one. My name was on that paper — my identity. It dawned on me that those shapes, in that combination, were unique to me. I recall feeling like I was somebody for the very first time in my young life.

After tracing the letters several times, I wrote each letter in order below the ones my father had written. Instead of creating simply the random scribbling and coloring of a young child, my crayons now had a purpose. I wrote my name that evening many, many times on that sheet of paper and on many more after that. I felt the power — nearly overwhelming to my young mind at the time — that this written name possessed. Before I could actually "write," before I actually understood the specific sounds that letters and combinations of letters made, I could spell out my name. I was able to put my identity and my uniqueness down on a sheet of paper for the world to see. By the time I began kindergarten the following year, I was an old pro at printing my name on my little assignments. While others struggled, mine flowed from my pencil as easily as it had done the night my father showed me how to do it.

Since then, I have always loved to write. The most enjoyable part of school was always writing book reports and essays, anything that demanded I put my own thoughts and opinions on paper. When I joined the debate team in high school, I always wrote out my prepared speeches beforehand — deliberately and in detail — before practicing them out loud. By the time the live event arrived, I could give each speech from memory without even glancing at my notes.

Given my love of the written word, it should come as no surprise that I have been collecting and reading books as long as I can remember. My parents taught me to read before I began school. After reading the standard children's books (often many times each), I moved on to the Hardy Boys series and others — especially books about American and world history. When I was about eight years old, my father bought the entire set of the Encyclopedia Britannica for the house, and I immediately began reading each volume cover to cover. I couldn't get enough of them; the world opened up to me through those volumes. I loved reading about history and other lands, far away places so unlike the world I knew.

Nothing, however, interested me as much as the history of America. I devoured anything in books, magazines, and on television about the Colonial period. The Founding Fathers were larger than life to me. I read every book to be had in our school library about Washington, Jefferson, Franklin, and Adams. The Revolutionary War and stories of the West fascinated me, but it wasn't long before I discovered . . . the American Civil War. When it became clear to me that many of the descendants of the men who fought in the Revolution and drafted the Declaration of Independence—men who, together, crafted this nation — fought each other during the Civil War, I developed an obsession with this period in history that has become a large part of my adult life.

After college, I began collecting books about the Civil War. Beyond the secondary works, both new and old, I hunted down books written by the participants themselves. I wanted to read for myself what they experienced, and find as many of those primary works listed in the bibliographies of secondary works as possible. As the years passed, I developed specific interests in the cavalry service in general and the Gettysburg Campaign in particular. As a result, my main concentration was anything dealing with the mounted arm and the Pennsylvania campaign. I began researching repositories, libraries, historical societies, and universities around the country, amassing a wide collection of material containing soldier letters, diaries, and recollections. Each spoke to me in a way secondary works never could.

The power of firsthand accounts intrigues me. Words penned by a rank-and-file soldier to a young wife back home can never be replaced by descriptions written by someone who did not live the events of which they write. There is as much to learn from descriptions in a letter or diary of the terrifying hell of battle and horror of death as there is in the details of endless weeks of boredom and day-to-day drudgery. For a soldier, each day away from his family is one day closer to the time when he will return to them. That emotion is always present, in its own unique way, in every letter and diary entry. This hasn't changed throughout history. Our troops serving overseas today feel exactly the same thing when they pen a journal entry, keep a blog, or send a letter to loved ones back home.

Because of my appreciation for firsthand accounts, I have always tried, inside my own writing, to let the soldiers and civilians speak for themselves. My first book, co-authored with my good friend and fellow student of cavalry Eric J. Wittenberg, was *Plenty of Blame To Go Around: Jeb Stuart's Controversial Ride to Gettysburg* (Savas Beatie, 2006). This volume details the trials and travails of the eight-day ride through Virginia, Maryland, and Pennsylvania by the Confederate cavalry prior to the battle of Gettysburg. Jeb Stuart's wide-ranging operation through the often-hostile countryside is one of the greatest examples of how war tests the mettle of men, animals, and citizens.

My second book, written with Eric and our good friend (and retired cavalry officer) Michael F. Nugent, deals with the retreat from the Gettysburg battlefield. *One Continuous Fight: The Retreat From Gettysburg and the Pursuit of Lee's Army of Northern Virginia, July 4-14, 1863* (Savas Beatie, 2008) unfolds the effort of Robert E. Lee and his Southern army to find safe ground closer to home, and the Federal army's determination to catch and destroy the Confederate invaders. We made it a goal to include as much pertinent firsthand material as possible in each book so that our readers might appreciate the perspective of the soldiers and civilians as much as we do. Our objective was to let, as far as possible, those who experienced the events tell the story themselves. Who can tell the story better than the people who lived through it?

All of this brings us to the book you now hold in your hands. I have long wanted to write a book like this. Firsthand accounts penned by participants mean so much more to us today when you experience their words on the ground where the recorded events occurred. Frank Haskell's account of Pickett's Charge at Gettysburg of July 3, 1863, offers a perfect example. Walk to the Federal position along the stone wall near the High Water Mark and read his words as you look out across the fields toward Seminary Ridge. Haskell's prose jumps to life and evokes a meaning that cannot be appreciated sitting in your easy chair hundreds of miles from the battlefield. When read on the historic ground, every recollection and account takes on a greater meaning that lingers long after you have left the field.

There are a number of field guides to historic places available, and those for Gettysburg are legion. *The Complete Gettysburg Guide*, however, is different. Instead of another standard tour of the high points of the battlefield and the town, I have included a host of obscure and often relative "unknown" places the vast majority of visitors miss completely. I have spent many years studying the battlefield and surrounding areas, and have learned to love these out-of-the-way places and little corners of the field, each of which were desperately important in the lives of people no longer with us. The famous Angle in the stone wall near the Copse of Trees is one of the most visited areas of the field, and has been so since the battle ended. Pvt. Augustus L. Coble of the 1st North Carolina

Infantry, however, likely never saw the famous umbrella-shaped trees shading the Angle during the battle, and certainly did not see the low stone wall that gives it its name. For Coble, a couple of large boulders at the base of Culp's Hill near Spangler's Spring was the most important piece of real estate in the world on July 2 and 3, 1863. It was there that he held his regiment's colors during some of the most brutal fighting of the battle. In 1913, when Coble attended the 50th Anniversary of the battle as an old man (perhaps with his wife Letitia along), he sought out the spot where he held the standard as a young man and endured hell on earth. He crawled between the boulders and carefully and deliberately, with some sort of tool taken there for the purpose, carved his name and unit in the Gettysburg igneous rock. It was as if Coble was proclaiming, I was here, this is where I became a man. This is where I lost my friends and where I prayed for victory and to live another day. This locale is worth visiting every bit as much as the Angle, Devil's Den, and Little Round Top. Sadly, Coble's carved words, fading now after so many years of exposure, will one day in the not-too-distant future be gone forever. During a recent visit to Coble's boulders I watched as a small boy crawled in among the rocks and traced Coble's name with his finger. That simple action propelled me back in time to my own days with crayons and paper as a young boy. Through his carving, Coble's name continues to live and speak in ways he could have never imagined.

Take this book with you to the Gettysburg battlefield and surrounding areas and visit the sites — famous and obscure — where events of major and minor consequence unfolded. Of course you should walk the ground where thousands "carved" their names into history during the massive assault on the afternoon of July 3 — but you should also stand and ponder the consequences of the "first shot" on the spot where a Federal cavalry officer opened the battle with the squeeze of a single trigger early on the morning of July 1. Stand atop the tumbled boulders of Devil's Den and imagine the carnage that swirled around these stones — but keep the reservation for your quiet walk among the graves where thousands of former soldiers rest beneath a statue that cries stone tears over them for eternity. Stand tall on the heights of Little Round Top like virtually every other visitor will as well — but don't neglect to kneel down at the edge of a lonely field where a young Federal was buried by his comrades, who when finished with the sad task took a few minutes to carve the deceased's initials into the rock at the head of his grave so his father could find his son and one day take him home.

It is often said that we determine our future by understanding our history. I cannot think of a better way to erect a bridge from our past to our future than to read the words of men long gone, walk in their footsteps where history was made, and ponder their willingness to serve a cause strong enough to convince them to shoulder a weapon, abandon their families, and possibly give up their lives.

Acknowledgements

Over the years, I have been fortunate to enjoy Gettysburg — the battlefield, the town, and its people — with a multitude of good friends and acquaintances. With apologies to those I neglect to name herein, there are a number of folks I wish to thank for their assistance, support, and most especially for teaching me about the hallowed ground of Gettysburg. In one way or another, each of these individuals has contributed to make this book better than it otherwise would have been.

First and foremost, co-author Steven Stanley has done more for this work than I ever dreamed possible. In my opinion, he is the premier cartographer of historical sites, and his maps and photographs that grace these pages make the battlefield come alive. The collection of "Steve Stanley Gettysburg Maps" between these covers is alone worth the price many times over. Thank you, Steve, for being the more talented partner of our team, and I know that everyone who uses this guide will appreciate your amazing craftsmanship. I believe it will educate generations.

I am likewise blessed that my good friend and Gettysburg National Military Park Ranger Eric A. Campbell agreed to write the Foreword. I have happily taken tours of the field conducted by Eric many times over the years, and have enjoyed every one. I have always been drawn by the magnetism of his zeal for the story of the common soldier and the battlefield itself, which is vibrantly evident once he begins speaking anywhere upon it. Thank you, Eric — celebrated historian, author, and friend — for inspiring more of us than you will ever know.

I am very fortunate to have friends in Gettysburg who allow me to use their homes as a base of operations during my many visits there each year. Dave and Carol Moore have opened their Herr's Ridge home to me more times than I can count, and I am grateful for their hospitality. Dave has long tried to teach me about Culp's Hill, and I hope some of it stuck. Duane Siskey, the first to spur my interest in Civil War reenacting and living history, always opens his Gettysburg address to me at a moment's notice. Dave Moore and Duane Siskey enjoy "battlefield stomping" as much as anyone, and I treasure the many hours I have spent with them on this and many other fields.

I have benefited from walking the battlefield, alone and in groups, with many Licensed Battlefield Guides and Park rangers. I am grateful for the knowledge given to me by guides Wayne Motts, Gary Kross, Tim Smith, Garry Adelman, John Archer, Mike Phipps, Joe Mieczkowski, Charlie Fennell, Lt. Col. Wayne Wachsmuth (ret.), and rangers Eric Campbell, John Heiser, Scott Hartwig, Greg Coco, and Troy Harman. If this guide — or any other source — sparks an interest in the reader in a particular action or part of the battlefield, there is no better way to explore it than by the side of a Licensed Guide or Park ranger.

My appreciation for the historical aspects of the town, the battlefield, the cemeteries, and Gettysburg's war-era citizens was sparked long ago by William Frassanito's wonderful books. I have used his *Gettysburg: A Journey in Time* (New York: Charles Scribner's Sons, 1975) and his subsequent books heavily throughout the years. They are widely known as essential works in any Civil War library. I have been fortunate recently to be able to get to know Bill fairly well; listening to him over a pint in the Reliance Mine Saloon is nearly as educational as walking the field itself.

I have probably walked Gettysburg and other fields more in recent years with my good friend Eric J. Wittenberg than anyone else. Eric shares my deep interest in cavalry operations, and together we have written two books thus far — each with the primary purpose of getting our readers out to "see the ground." The knowledge I gained over many years of walking the fields of Buford's July 1 defense, Farnsworth's Charge, East Cavalry Field, Hunterstown, and Fairfield with Eric has found its way into these pages in a wide variety of ways.

My dear friend Michael F. Nugent has given me more appreciation for cavalry and infantry tactics and logistics than any book ever could. A retired armored cavalry officer and descendant of a Civil War trooper, Mike always gives me much to consider when examining Civil War battlefields, and especially how specific conflicts began and why they developed as they did.

My friend Scott Mingus deserves special thanks for all his willing assistance over the years. Scott enjoys studying the events in Pennsylvania during the days leading up to the battle as much as I do, and I am grateful that he shared his knowledge of Confederate General John B. Gordon's June 26 advance on Gettysburg. Scott also knows the terrain and back roads surrounding Gettysburg better than most, and his insights are always invaluable.

My friend Dean Shultz's encyclopedic knowledge of the battle, the citizens, and the terrain of Adams County and beyond is something to behold. You are reading a guide made of paper and ink, but Dean is a "Complete Gettysburg Guide" on two legs that have traversed nearly every yard touched by the campaign. Things I have learned during our many hours on the field, back roads, and in obscure places important then — but where only the occasional lost squirrel would go today — have weaved their way into nearly every page of this book. Dean and his wife Judy have hosted many of us at their wartime home (formerly a battlefield hospital) many times. No trip to Gettysburg is complete without "checking in" with Dean.

I must thank several folks who have helped me better understand many specific battle actions that appear in this book. Long a favorite little battle to me, the July 2 cavalry fight at Hunterstown is finally receiving long-overdue recognition and preservation notice thanks to the efforts of Hunterstown Historical Society coordinators Laurie and Roger Harding. The Hardings own the historic Tate property, where President George Washington once relaxed in the yard and where dozens of Civil War cavalrymen fought their last fight. Their hospitality and willingness to assist me is deeply appreciated. Likewise, the work of local historian Linda K. Cleveland has been valuable, and the fruits of her research are found in the battle of Hunterstown tour herein. Kevin and Kim Bream, owners of the of the Marshall farm in the heart of the Fairfield battlefield, are wonderful stewards of their property. Kevin has eagerly assisted me in interpreting the battle and has helped me to better understand what this fight — which all but destroyed a Federal cavalry regiment — meant to the surviving veterans. My friend Sal Prezioso, the owner and steward of Gen. Charles Collis' Gettysburg battlefield home "Red Patch," gave me much information concerning Collis and his beautiful dwelling. I am also grateful to my friend Randy Drais, who put me in touch with Wendy Cecil, a descendant of Augustus Coble. Wendy provided me with many useful details regarding her ancestor.

I must also express appreciation to many friends with whom I have spent so much time on the Gettysburg battlefield. Their specialized knowledge, observations, and inquisitive natures have been learning experiences for all of us. My thanks go to Steve Basic, Jim Lamason, Rick Allen, Karl Fauzer, Stan O'Donnell, Pam Sparks, Tony Christ, Allan Shikhvarg, John Rincon, and Jim Cameron. All of these fine folks, and many more I am sure I have neglected (accidentally) to mention, have taught me more than they will ever know. I extend my gratitude to my researcher, Bryce Suderow, who constantly comes up with primary source material that few have seen and no one has used.

I owe more than I could ever hope to repay to my publisher Savas Beatie LLC, and its Managing Director Theodore P. Savas. This is my third book with Savas Beatie, and Ted has always been a gentle but firm guiding force along the way. Ted is the partner whose name does not appear on the front cover of this book. His vision and skillful editing made our work better, and if not for him I may have never gotten much further than crayons and paper. I owe Ted so many steaks and pints of dark beer that I probably should just buy a herd of Angus steer and a brewery. I would be neglectful if I did not mention that it is always a pleasure to work with Savas Beatie's staff: Marketing Director Sarah Keeney, an extraordinary and knowledgeable organizer and publicist, and Tammy Hall and Veronica Kane, who field my calls, answer my questions, and keep the ship running smoothly. All three wonderful ladies have helped make all this effort worthwhile.

Special thanks to my daddy, who with but a simple example gave me an appreciation and an understanding of the awesome power of words.

My final, and most important, appreciation is humbly offered to my wife Karen. Although she understandably rolls her eyes when I bring new books or mountains of papers home to my library, the smile she gives when she sees my work is all I'll ever need to continue studying, learning, and telling the story of this sanguinary period in the growth of our nation. Her patience, support, and encouragement are a blessing every bit as rich as the day she looked me in the eyes and told the world she would be mine.

J. David Petruzzi
Brockway, Pennsylvania

When I finally sat down to thank everyone who has helped to make this book a reality, I came up with a nice list. Some of them directly assisted me with the work, and others helped indirectly over the years. Please forgive me if I leave anyone out.

First, I want to thank my co-author J. David Petruzzi. Without him this book would never have been created. J.D. came up with the idea of this guide book and after formulating it with his publisher, Savas Beatie, brought me onto the project. I later learned that J.D. had me in mind to create the maps all along, and that he felt this book could not reach its potential without my involvement. For that I am very grateful and humbled. He has helped me get my feet into the world of publishing, something I have dreamed of for many years. But my thanks to J.D. go beyond that. I wish to thank him for all the hard work he has put into the text of this project – decades of studying, walking the field, and listening to guides, rangers, and many friends. His insight into the battle is marvelous and without him this would be just another book full of maps and photographs. His words help my photographs and maps herein make sense to the reader. His knowledge of the battle is impressive, and he has truly helped me to put "on the map" the phases of this battle that are overlooked by all but the most astute visitor. Before I met J.D. and started working on this project, places like the June 26 skirmish at Marsh Creek and the Witmer Farm meant nothing to me.

I also express my deep appreciation to Theodore Savas, the managing director of Savas Beatie LLC. J.D. asked Ted what he thought about using my talents for this project, and Ted was very enthusiastic about having me on board. When J.D. and I were deciding how the book should look, Ted asked me if I wanted to do the layout for printing. That is rarely done in the publishing world – layout is typically performed by the publisher. I accepted, and for that I am not sure I want to thank him or curse him! This book was a labor to design – consuming many late nights and long weekends but always a labor of love. I only hope that I have lived up to his expectations. Again Ted, thank you!

In reality, this book is many years in the making. We did not start it back when J.D. had a full head of hair, but many years ago while living in the Fredericksburg, Virginia area, I became involved in a local battlefield preservation organization, the Central Virginia Battlefields Trust (CVBT). Because of that involvement, I began to find my niche in life – historic cartography. While working with the board of directors of the CVBT on a preservation project, I was asked if I could create a battle map showing the fighting on the parcel of battlefield they were trying to save. After that project, I caught the attention of the National Park Service and was asked to work on other mapping projects for them. So for helping me get my start into work that I love, I want to thank the founding board members of the CVBT, especially Dr. Mike Stevens. Mike was and still is a great fan of my work, and while serving with him on the board of the CVBT, Mike was somewhat of a mentor. As we sat in his office a while back, Mike asked me, "Could you please one day draw maps to help me make sense of the fighting in the Wheatfield?" Mike, I hope I was able to accomplish that.

I would be remiss if I did not thank the board of directors, staff and members of the Civil War Preservation Trust (CWPT). Nearly ten years ago, I was asked to produce a map for one of their upcoming land preservation appeals – land on the Cross Keys battlefield in Virginia. The response to the map was so great from their membership, that I have been producing battle maps for the CWPT ever since. Several of the CWPT staff have been extremely influential in the creation and evolution of my battle maps: David Duncan, Director of Membership and Development; Jim Campi, Policy and Communications Director; and Kim Davenport, Production Coordinator. All three have kept me busy and hopping over the last ten years or so but none more so than Kim. She points out little mistakes on the maps as she proofs them, and in a sense has helped shape how I create my maps today. Thank you to all three of you.

I also must thank Mr. Dana Shoaf, editor of *America's Civil War* magazine and *Civil War Times Illustrated*. A few years ago, Dana took a chance on me after seeing some of the maps I had created for the CWPT. He brought me on board as the map illustrator for *America's Civil War*. Dana left the map designs up to me, usually only sending me an article to work from. Thank you Dana!

In creating the maps for this book, many people have helped out in one way or another and many times did not realize how much they have assisted. I am grateful for the kind words that Gettysburg National Military Park Ranger Eric A. Campbell wrote in the Foreword to this book. Thank you, Eric. I want to thank Gettysburg Licensed Battlefield Guides Tim Smith and Joe Mieczkowski; Chuck Teague, part-time ranger at the Gettysburg National Military Park; Scott Mingus, Sr., author of *Flames Beyond Gettysburg*; and *Gettysburg Magazine* cartographer Phil Laino of Shoreham, NY. All of them at one time or another looked over maps for this project and offered their much appreciated criticism and advice.

And last, but definitely not least, I thank the love of my life, Kyrstie. She understands my passion for my work and my love of the Civil War so much that when I mentioned to her that I wanted to move to Gettysburg, she did not hesitate: "Yes, let's do it." She has put up with my tramping around the battlefield in all kinds of weather, and at all times of the day, just to "get that perfect photograph." She understands that creating a map is not something that can be done on a time schedule, and she puts up with my late nights at the computer – because I still haven't got that map just right. Thank you for understanding.

Steven A. Stanley
Gettysburg, Pennsylvania

Foreword

"*H*ow do you tour the battlefield?"

Having worked as a park ranger-historian at Gettysburg National Military Park for the last twenty-two years, I have probably heard that question thousands of times. My standard answer usually involves explaining the various battlefield tour options, which include self-guided tours, CD audio tours, bus tours, or a personalized tour with a Licensed Battlefield Guide. While each of these options has its own advantages and disadvantages, the major drawback of each is that they are designed to take only about two hours. A comprehensive tour of the Gettysburg battlefield could — and should — last at least an entire day, and realistically visitors can spend days, weeks, and even years on the field and still not see it all.

The Gettysburg battlefield is truly a national treasure that is not only sacred ground, but also contains thousands of sites and stories that can literally take a lifetime to explore and learn. The main thing any visitor needs to begin this journey is time. The second most important need is a good source of knowledge to provide the necessary background and information to get started and point the visitor in the right direction. In my opinion, *The Complete Gettysburg Guide* by J. David Petruzzi and Steven Stanley provides that necessary knowledge and direction.

This guide not only provides an overview of the main Gettysburg battlefield, but includes background information on the Gettysburg Campaign, explaining not only how the armies arrived at Gettysburg, but why — thus properly placing the battle within the context of the entire war. This book also includes tours of lesser known areas and sites including the town itself, hospital sites, rock carvings, the Soldiers' National Cemetery, the town's Evergreen Cemetery, and outlying battlefield sites (including the opening skirmish on June 26, 1863, and the cavalry clashes at Hunterstown, East Cavalry Field, South Cavalry Field, and Fairfield). I am confident that all readers — from well-informed "students" of the battle to novices and those just beginning their tramps over the fields of Gettysburg — will find this book educational, constantly useful, and endlessly interesting. It is perfectly suited for long use, over and over again, for each future return visit to Gettysburg.

Already well known for his scholarly articles and books on Gettysburg and the Civil War, J. David Petruzzi carries on his good work in the text for *The Complete Gettysburg Guide*. He not only does a good job relating the major strategic movements of the opposing armies and an overview of the tactical combat that followed, but also reveals the human element of the war by relating numerous stories of individual soldiers and the impact the battle had on them, their families, and the nation as a whole. *The Complete Gettysburg Guide* is very easy to use and the narrative is well written and easy to follow.

Steven Stanley's maps compliment the main narrative. Steve is already considered one of the premier Civil War cartographers today. The maps he created for this guide are simply superb and make this book even more valuable. Steve was also provided wide latitude by the publisher to design and format the entire book — an uncommon partnership in the world of publishing. His work here will surely justify his high standing in the Civil War community.

Together, the text and maps contained in this work create one of the most useful and comprehensive guides of America's largest and bloodiest battlefield available today.

Eric A. Campbell
Park Ranger-Historian, Gettysburg National Military Park

Helpful Hints for Using the Tours and Maps

The tours in this book will take you to many places that most tourists — and even serious students of the Gettysburg battlefield and area — rarely if ever visit. Please note than many of the areas we will visit consist of private land and dwellings. Please do not trespass, and be courteous to private property owners. Many property owners may be happy to give permission for you to examine particular sites, but always seek that permission first and honor the wishes and privacy of the owner and residents.

When you are on the main battlefield and Gettysburg National Military Park property, you are encouraged to leave your vehicle and explore. Sadly, most visitors see the battlefield almost exclusively from their car window or a tour bus. Take time one day and walk the rolling land of Pickett's Charge! Or, if you are in good physical condition, "charge" up the western slope of Little Round Top and experience a bit of what many Confederates of General Longstreet's Corps endured on July 2 (without the shooting, of course). Walk the winding path to the summit of Big Round Top, a wonderful nature trail of quietude and beauty that belies the savage fighting that took place below and around its slopes in July 1863. Wherever you go, take some time to get off the Park roads and explore. Let the ground and stones speak to you through your shoes, and try to imagine what it was like for the common soldier who marched in the ranks beside members of his family and neighbors, hoping he would survive another day of bloodshed.

Each of the numbered "stops" in the tours is keyed to a corresponding "stop sign" icon on the accompanying maps. Even on maps that detail smaller parts of the field, each stop within that field is shown on the map to help orient you to your exact destination. A compass might be beneficial to help figure out exact directions when other landmarks are not readily visible, but it is not something you will need to enjoy the tours in this book. Note also that existing Gettysburg National Military Park roads appear on applicable maps in order to assist you in locating various stops, important terrain features, etc. You can stand at any of the stops, orient yourself on a map of the area, and "see" the action as it unfolds around you through the bold color of these original maps. You will also find many of cartographer Steven Stanley's beautiful full-color photographs sprinkled throughout the text to show not only the vistas afforded at various stops on the field, but to showcase the Park in all of its seasonal glory. Also throughout the text are select historic photographs of the battlefield and town. The following are the source citations to be found with each: Library of Congress (LOC), National Archives and Records Administration (NARA), Gettysburg National Military Park (GNMP), and the Adams County Historical Society (ACHS).

Above all, we want you to enjoy each experience at Gettysburg. Make sure and dress for the weather and be careful when venturing off the roads and established trails — especially when hunting for many of the rock carvings shown herein, or while walking through the woods to obscure spots. For the more out-of-the-way locations we have included Global Positioning System (GPS) coordinates to help you find them. They are easily used with vehicle-mounted and hand-held GPS and navigator devices. You can even pre-load coordinates into your GPS device to guide you right to a particular location.

It is our hope that this guide will encourage you to seek out more detailed sources on the battlefield and those particular aspects of the fighting that interest you. Many of the tours and sections feature a handful of suggested titles for further reading, and the bibliography in the back of this book should be consulted as well.

The world-class Gettysburg Visitor Center and Museum, located at 1195 Baltimore Pike in Gettysburg (717-334-1124) is an excellent place to begin your tour. Park Rangers and Licensed Battlefield Guides are deep wells of information, and they live to help you enjoy your Gettysburg experience. Tours of the field in general, or specific aspects thereof, can be easily reserved inside the Visitor Center. Audio tours that you can use in your vehicle at your own pace are highly recommended (and many of them fit well with the main battlefield tours found in this book). The museum bookstore inside the Visitor Center carries a large number of Gettysburg-related books to help you learn about virtually any aspect of the battle and the men who fought it. Several privately owned bookstores throughout the town are also well stocked with good books. Please support these stores with your purchases.

Guided historic walking tours of the town of Gettysburg itself can be secured through the services of a Licensed Town Guide (717-339-6161). Guides are available daily April through November, and their expertise will enhance your experience of all the town has to offer.

Be sure to visit our website, **www.completegettysburgguide.com** for updates, supplements, and many other interactive features!

(Opposite page) A detail from the restored 1883 Cyclorama of "The Battle of Gettysburg" on display at the Gettysburg National Military Park Visitor Center. (GNMP)

Overview of the Battle and Campaign of Gettysburg

"I wish I could get at those people . . ."

About 7:30 a.m. on July 1, 1863, an officer of the 8th Illinois Cavalry crouched behind a rail fence in the yard of the Ephraim Wisler home about four miles west of Gettysburg on the road to Chambersburg. Surrounding him were his cousin Pvt. Thomas B. Kelly, Pvt. James Hale, Sgt. Levi Shafer, and others who were manning the advance picket post of Brig. Gen. John Buford's Federal cavalry division on the road. Lt. Marcellus E. Jones raised Shafer's carbine, rested in on a rail, and fired a shot at the approaching column of Confederate infantry approaching from the west. The troopers knew the shot would at least trigger a skirmish along the ridges leading to the small town behind them; it is doubtful that any of them had any idea that from that round would erupt the largest battle of the American Civil War. Two days later, at the end of July 3, some 50,000 men would be dead, maimed, or captured, and the landscape surrounding the town of Gettysburg was changed forever.

General Robert E. Lee's plan to take the fight out of war-ravaged Virginia and into Pennsylvania began in February of 1863, when Confederate cartographer Jedediah Hotchkiss was instructed to secretly prepare a map that encompassed the Shenandoah Valley of Virginia, and the south-central and southeastern territory of Pennsylvania. In mid-March, Lee discussed with Confederate leaders in Richmond his strategy to march his army north. Lee admitted to Jefferson Davis, "I think it all important that we should assume the aggressive by the first of May . . . If we could be placed in a condition to make a vigorous advance at that time I think the Valley could be swept of [elements of the Federal Army] and the army opposite me be thrown north of the Potomac."

Army of Northern Virginia commander Gen. Robert E. Lee. (LOC)

Following the Battle of Chancellorsville in early May, and the death of his able subordinate Lt. Gen. Thomas J. "Stonewall" Jackson, Lee again participated in meetings in Richmond concerning the upcoming Pennsylvania campaign. From that discussion, First Corps commander Lt. Gen. James Longstreet understood that "under no circumstances were we to give battle, but exhaust our skill in trying to force the enemy to do so in a position of our own choosing." Even if his recollection was accurate, events took a decidedly different turn.

Since Lee could not successfully attack the Army of the Potomac in its position north of the Rappahannock River, he determined to draw the Federals into Maryland and Pennsylvania where, he hoped, he could attack them piecemeal and defeat them. Lee calculated that he could feed his 70,000-man army from the rich and untouched farmlands of southern Pennsylvania, and thus take some of the logistical burden off Virginia in general and the Shenandoah Valley — the "breadbasket" of the Confederacy — in particular.

After Jackson's death, Lee reorganized his army from two corps to three. Longstreet continued to command his First Corps. The Second Corps was placed under the newly promoted Lt. Gen. Richard Ewell, while the new Third Corps was given to another recent promotion, Lt. Gen. Ambrose Powell (A.P.) Hill. The massive cavalry battle at Brandy Station, Virginia, erupted on June 9 when Federal cavalry commander Brig. Gen. Alfred Pleasonton took his horsemen across the Rappahannock to engage Maj. Gen. James Ewell Brown "Jeb" Stuart's Confederate cavalry. Although the Southerners were left in command of the field after the all-day slugfest, the Union horsemen earned a new-found respect from their antagonists. The fight delayed Lee's plans to move north by one day, and Ewell's Corps advanced into the Shenandoah Valley. On June 14 and 15, his soldiers roundly defeated the Federal command of Maj. Gen. Robert Milroy at Winchester, suffering fewer than 300 casualties while inflicting more than 4,400.

Longstreet's Corps, meanwhile, moved along the east side of the Blue Ridge Mountains, and Hill's men also advanced into the Shenandoah. By a plan of his own design and approved by Lee, Jeb Stuart took just more than one-half of his cavalry division across the river to repeat his storied

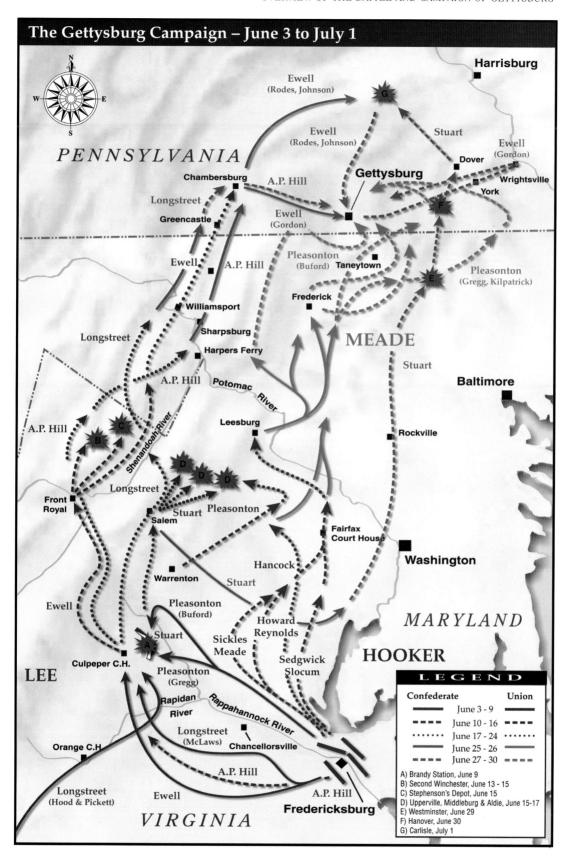

The Gettysburg Campaign – June 3 to July 1

Harrisburg

PENNSYLVANIA

Ewell
(Rodes, Johnson)

Ewell
(Rodes, Johnson)

Stuart

Dover

Ewell
(Gordon)

Chambersburg

A.P. Hill

Gettysburg

Wrightsville

Longstreet

York

Greencastle

Ewell
(Gordon)

Ewell

A.P. Hill

Pleasonton
(Buford)   Taneytown

Pleasonton
(Gregg, Kilpatrick)

Williamsport

Frederick

Longstreet

Sharpsburg

Harpers Ferry

MEADE

A.P. Hill   Potomac   River

Stuart

Shenandoah River

Leesburg

Baltimore

A.P. Hill

Rockville

C

B

D

D

D

Stuart

Front
Royal

Longstreet

Pleasonton

Salem

Fairfax
Court House

Hancock

Washington

Warrenton   Stuart

Ewell

Pleasonton
(Buford)

Howard
Reynolds

MARYLAND

A   Stuart

Sickles
Meade

Sedgwick
Slocum

HOOKER

LEE   Culpeper C.H.

Pleasonton
(Gregg)

Rapidan
River

Rappahannock River

Orange C.H

Longstreet
(McLaws)   Chancellorsville

LEGEND

Confederate		Union
——————	June 3 - 9	——————
- - - - -	June 10 - 16	- - - - -
··········	June 17 - 24	··········
——————	June 25 - 26	——————
- - - - -	June 27 - 30	- - - - -

A) Brandy Station, June 9
B) Second Winchester, June 13 - 15
C) Stephenson's Depot, June 15
D) Upperville, Middleburg & Aldie, June 15-17
E) Westminster, June 29
F) Hanover, June 30
G) Carlisle, July 1

Longstreet
(Hood & Pickett)

Ewell

A.P. Hill

Fredericksburg

VIRGINIA

ability to ride around the Federal Army. Once in Pennsylvania, after causing the Federals as much military indigestion as possible, Stuart was to link up with Ewell's command somewhere near the Susquehanna River. Lee's plan was as audacious as it was risky. By dividing his forces over such a wide swath of territory while advancing into enemy territory, he risked being caught flat-footed by an attack, unable to concentrate quickly enough, and defeated in detail. The commander of the Federal forces, Maj. Gen. Joseph Hooker, did not know Lee's plans, and the Federal cavalry's forays across the mountains to figure out what the Confederates were up to were met with sharp rebuffs. By the third week of June, Ewell's Corps had crossed into Maryland and was headed for Chambersburg, Pennsylvania.

On June 22, Lee sent a courier to Ewell with the message that the corps commander was to advance to the Susquehanna River and seize the Pennsylvania capital at Harrisburg if he were able to do so. Three days later, at his headquarters three miles east of Chambersburg, Ewell conferred with the commanders of his three divisions. Ewell decided to divide his own corps for the advance to Harrisburg. Ewell, together with his leading divisions under Maj. Gens. Robert Rodes and Edward "Allegheny" Johnson, would march to Carlisle with the cavalry brigade of Brig. Gen. Albert G. Jenkins clearing the way. Maj. Gen. Jubal Early, with Lt. Col. Elijah White's 35th Battalion Virginia Cavalry, would march his division directly east to York. Early was also instructed to cut the Northern Central Railroad and seize the Wrightsville Bridge over the Susquehanna as a prelude to capturing the capital.

On June 26, Early's Division crossed South Mountain and headed for Gettysburg with the cavalry deployed in the front, in the rear, and on the flanks. When he learned that local militia was guarding Gettysburg Early divided his own troops. He sent Brig. Gen. John B. Gordon's Brigade, with White's horsemen in the lead, directly to Gettysburg along Cashtown Pike, while he led the balance of his division on a northern route to approach Gettysburg from the north along the Mummasburg Road. Just a few miles west of town, White and Gordon met and dispersed the 26th Pennsylvania Emergency

Militia (including a company of Gettysburg students) and a local cavalry unit. Early triumphantly entered Gettysburg and demanded tribute from the anxious locals.

By the time Early entered Gettysburg, all of Lee's infantry (with the exception of one division) was in Pennsylvania. Stuart and three of his cavalry brigades were still in Virginia, riding hard for Maryland. Since he hadn't heard from his cavalry leader, Lee was inclined to believe that the Federal Army had not moved north of the Potomac River in pursuit. In fact, Hooker was already moving his army across the river; a dispatch sent the next day by Stuart advising Lee of this development would never reach the army commander.

On June 27, Ewell reached Carlisle, Hill's Corps was west of Chambersburg, and Longstreet's Corps was filtering into the Chambersburg area. Unbeknownst to Lee, the Army of the Potomac was now in Maryland, with its headquarters at Frederick. Three Federal cavalry divisions fronted the Federals' advance, with the veteran division of Brig. Gen. John Buford advancing toward Gettysburg.

About 3:00 a.m. on Sunday, June 28, Maj. Gen. George Meade, commander of the Federal 5th Corps, was shaken out of a deep slumber in his tent. Col. James Hardie of the War Department stood over Meade to inform him that he had brought "trouble" for the general. Meade immediately thought he was either going to be relieved of command or placed under arrest. Instead, Meade was informed that President Abraham Lincoln had removed Hooker and placed him in command of the 95,000-man Army of the Potomac.

That evening, Lee instructed Ewell to move on Harrisburg. Lee's plan for Pennsylvania was now in motion. Longstreet was to move in support of Ewell, and Hill's Corps would cross the Susquehanna River south of Harrisburg and seize the railroad leading to Philadelphia. Around midnight, Lee listened to a report from one of Longstreet's scouts, a ragamuffin spy named Harrison, that the Federals were already across the river and elements had reached the South Mountain range. Because he had not heard anything from Jeb Stuart, Lee was unable to discount the spy's warning. The army com-

On July 3 the Battle of Gettysburg culminated in the grand charge of Pickett, Pettigrew, and Trimble. This scene depicts Federal artillery repulsing the Confederate attack in the restored 1883 Cyclorama of the "Battle of Gettysburg" by French artist Paul Philippoteaux. (GNMP)

mander promptly countermanded his orders and instructed Ewell to return to Chambersburg.

By the morning of June 29, incorrectly deducing that the Federals were headed for the Cumberland Valley, Lee decided to take advantage of the South Mountain terrain and concentrate his army at the little mountain pass village of Cashtown. The disappointed Ewell received the orders to abandon his plans to take Harrisburg and countermarch southwest.

Army of the Potomac commander Maj. Gen. George G. Meade. (LOC)

By June 30, Lee still had not heard from Stuart. The cavalry leader and his horsemen were at this time heading for Hanover, Pennsylvania, just fifteen miles east of Gettysburg, actively in search of Ewell's command. Stuart probably assumed that his dispatch advising of the Federal advance three days earlier had reached Lee. Early that morning, Buford deviated from his direct ride to Gettysburg and had instead advanced toward Fairfield (about eight miles southwest of Gettysburg). On the way, he ran into an encampment of some of A. P. Hill's Third Corps infantry. Buford broke off the brief skirmish and countermarched to Emmitsburg, Maryland, where he likely consulted with the commander of the Federal 1st Corps, Maj. Gen. John F. Reynolds, before riding north to Gettysburg. At Hanover, Jeb Stuart battled all day with Brig. Gen. Judson Kilpatrick's Federal cavalry division before giving the Federals the slip that night and riding to Carlisle.

Buford entered Gettysburg about noon on June 30, and soon thereafter noticed Confederate infantry west of town on the road that led to Cashtown and Chambersburg. The men belonged to Brig. Gen. J. Johnston Pettigrew's Brigade, part of Maj. Gen. Henry Heth's Division, A. P. Hill's Corps. Some of the Southerners also spotted Buford's cavalry as it rode into town. Pettigrew was out on a foraging and reconnaissance mission, but when a squadron of Buford's 8th Illinois Cavalry galloped toward him, he wisely withdrew his brigade toward Cashtown. During the rest of that day and throughout the evening, Buford received solid intelligence that Longstreet's and Hill's corps were operating west of Gettysburg (along with Lee's headquarters), and that Ewell's Corps was marching toward Gettysburg from the north. In order to protect the important road network that pierced the town from several directions, Buford set up a chain of vedettes (the cavalry's equivalent of infantry pickets) to cover the environs of the town to the west and north. His experience told him that a Confederate advance on Gettysburg would probably come on Pettigrew's heels the following day, and the vedettes would thus act as an early warning system. If so, his pickets would kick into motion a classic *covering force action*, allowing Buford's dismounted troopers the opportunity to delay any enemy advance. Trading ground for time, the cavalrymen might hold on long enough for Federal infantry support to arrive.

Pettigrew reported the confrontation at Gettysburg to his superiors, but neither Heth nor Hill believed it likely that veteran Federal cavalry could be as far north as Gettysburg. It was more likely, they thought, that Pettigrew had spotted local militia. When Heth asked Hill if he had any objection to Heth's advancing with his entire division to Gettysburg the next morning (July 1) to scatter the military and requisition supplies, Hill replied "none in the world."

Early the following morning, about 6:30 a.m., Lt. Marcellus Jones of the 8th Illinois Cavalry aimed Sgt. Levi Shafer's Sharps carbine at an enemy officer atop a light-colored horse, held his breath — and fired. The few ounces of lead in that bullet was the first of tens of thousands of pounds of bullets and artillery shells that would be fired on this day and the two that followed. Buford's cavalry would fight stubbornly for the ridges west of Gettysburg, and just when his troopers were about to crack under the mounting pressure from Heth's infantry and artillery fire, a corps of Federal infantry under John Reynolds arrived to bolster the defense. Buford's lines along what became storied terrain features of the first day's battle — McPherson Ridge, Oak Ridge, and Seminary Ridge — were eventually

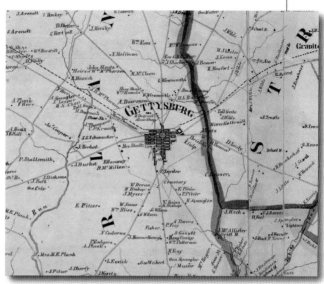

This 1858 map shows the extensive road network that helped to draw both armies to Gettysburg. (LOC)

held by two Federal corps until they, too, were defeated and shoved back through Gettysburg later that day and southeast onto the heights of the cemetery below town. Maj. Gen. Oliver O. Howard, commanding the Federal 11th Corps and the senior officer on the field, had chosen the eminence crowned by Evergreen Cemetery as the rallying point.

On July 2, when most of the infantry of both armies had arrived on the field, General Lee assaulted the long Federal flanks in an uncoordinated effort to roll them up and defeat the wounded Army of the Potomac. On the Union left, Longstreet's Corps (less Pickett's Division, which was not yet up) struck hard, driving back and collapsing part of the line and drawing in thousands of Federal reinforcements from other parts of the line. When the attack moved to the Federal left center, a few Confederate regiments managed to pierce the weakened center before being driven back. On the stripped down Federal right on Culp's Hill, Ewell's brigades managed to form a lodgment on the wooded slopes before darkness ended the fighting. The Federal line had held — just barely — and Lee realized he had come very close to another tactical victory. That evening, he believed one more day of assaults would defeat and dislodge the enemy.

Lee's plans for July 3 went awry before they even began. Ewell had orders to renew the attack on Culp's Hill, but a lengthy Federal spoiling bombardment and attack initiated before dawn threw back Ewell and ended the fighting on that end of the field before noon. Lee's main effort on July 3, however, was a massive infantry assault against Meade's right-center on Cemetery Ridge known to history as Pickett's Charge. Once about 12,000 infantry were in place, Lee's artillery opened a long barrage designed to soften the enemy position and make the task of his foot soldiers easier. As the infantry was advancing across nearly one mile of open ground to reach Cemetery Ridge, the cavalry of both armies battled. Jeb Stuart, who had arrived at Gettysburg the previous afternoon, fought a pitched battle with a Federal cavalry division led by Brig. Gen. David M. Gregg (augmented by Brig. Gen. George A. Custer's brigade) at the John Rummel farm three miles east on what is now called East Cavalry Field. Eight miles southwest near Fairfield, Maj. Samuel Starr's 6th U.S. Cavalry fought a cavalry brigade under Brig. Gen. William E. Jones after Starr attempted to attack Lee's wagons behind Confederate lines. Just as Pickett's Charge petered out along Cemetery Ridge, Brig. Gen. Wesley Merritt's brigade of cavalry Regulars, together with Kilpatrick's 3rd Division of cavalry, fought with infantry on Lee's right flank in the shadows of the Round Tops. Although Lee's last major effort was bloodily repulsed, Meade was reluctant to follow up his victory with an assault of his own. Although the participants did not know it, the battle at Gettysburg was over.

Rain fell most of the night of July 3-4 and continued the next morning. The heavy summer rain, broken occasionally by claps of thunder, was unable to muffle the screams of the wounded and dying. The maimed and mortally wounded were scattered by the thousands across the fields, in woodlots, in homes, and in nearly every outbuilding. Hastily dug shallow graves already dotted the landscape. Thousands of dead horses covered the ground, adding their offal to the putrid breezes. The remains of a pair of burned barns near the center of the battlefield still smoldered. One of them exposed the horrid remains of several wounded Pennsylvania soldiers who had sought shelter there, but were unable to crawl to safety when the structure was fired. In one woodlot, a badly wounded and exhausted Federal soldier had just spent the better part of the previous night beating off wild hogs with his bayonet; the beasts had feasted on his dead comrades all around him.

Lee began preparations to remove the battered remnants of his army from the field. Beginning on the night of July 4, he marched his soldiers and prisoners along both the roads to Fairfield and Cashtown. As many ambulatory wounded as possible were taken along in wagons. Although the fighting on the battlefield itself was at an end, the retreat to the Potomac River opened another round of engagements. The first major clash erupted about midnight when a fight under a pounding rain in the Monterey Pass of South Mountain broke out between Kilpatrick's Federal cavalry division and Lee's supply wagon train and guard. By the time Lee crossed his army over the Potomac on the night of July 13-14, nearly two dozen combats large and small had been fought south of Gettysburg and in parts of Maryland.

Once his army was safely across the river, Lee rested his men for a few days near Bunker Hill, in western Virginia. Meade made plans to cross the river and flank his adversary. As each army tried to outmaneuver the other along the Blue Ridge and in Loudoun Valley, small skirmishes erupted between the cavalry and infantry forces. Meade was unable to catch Lee or any sizable part of his force off guard, and by early August both armies had taken up positions on opposite sides of the Rappahannock River. They were in nearly the exact positions they had held in early June at the start of the campaign.

(Opposite page) This early 1900's view of Gettysburg shows the monument dedicated to the 26th Pennsylvania Emergency Militia. (GNMP)

Tour of the June 26 Skirmishes at Marsh Creek and Bayly's Hill

White's and French's Virginia Cavalry Rout the 26th Pennsylvania Militia and Bell's Cavalry

"They came with barbarian yells and smoking pistols"

At 7:00 a.m. on the morning of June 19, 1863, Gen. Robert E. Lee ordered Lt. Gen. Richard S. Ewell to march his corps into Pennsylvania ahead of the rest of the Army of Northern Virginia. Ewell was to advance his men toward the Susquehanna River on a broad front, and if Harrisburg (the state capital) "comes within your means, capture it."

On June 24, Ewell sent Maj. Gen. Jubal A. Early's Division, about 6,500 men comprising his right column, through Greenwood and on to Cashtown.

Greenwood is just east of Chambersburg and is today called Black Gap. Lt. Col. Elijah V. White's 35th Battalion Virginia Cavalry, about 250 troopers, and the 17th Virginia Cavalry under Col. William French, another 250 men, escorted Early. Early reached Chambersburg the following day and received orders from Ewell to march to Gettysburg and then on to York (where he was to cut the Northern Central Railroad and burn the Wrightsville Bridge across the Susquehanna). When that task was complete, Early was to join Ewell at Carlisle for a planned assault upon Harrisburg.

At 8:00 a.m. on the morning of Friday, June 26, Early and his men began marching under a cold rain toward Gettysburg. Two miles from their camp, they reached Thaddeus Stevens' Caledonia Furnace Iron Works, which they burned and destroyed. About five miles farther east, Early's column began passing through the Cashtown Gap. Three days earlier, an incident occurred in the gap that spilled Confederate blood a full week before the Gettysburg battle began.

Beginning on June 21, elements of the Confederate cavalry brigade of Brig. Gen. Albert G. Jenkins (ordered by Lee to scout ahead of his advancing army) had been foraging in and around Chambersburg. On June 23, members of Co. D of Jenkins' 14th Virginia Cavalry marched to Thaddeus Stevens' Caledonia Furnace Iron Works, appropriating nearly fifty horses and mules along the way. As

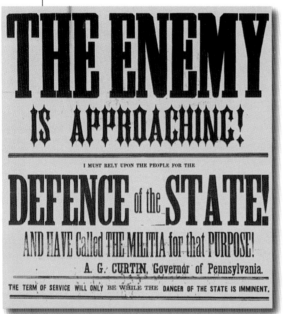

1863 poster warning the citizens of Pennsylvania of the impending Rebel invasion. (LOC)

they continued east, the troopers found the pike blockaded where it entered the Cashtown Gap. The blockade was manned by a few dozen armed Gettysburg area citizens, led by Capt. Elias Spangler and Lt. Hiram Lady, as well as militia troopers of Robert Bell's Adams County Cavalry Company. The Virginians charged at a gallop, sending the citizens and Bell's men skittering eastward. However, as the Southern troopers cautiously continued in the direction of Cashtown, a rude surprise awaited them.

Waiting for the Confederates at a rise known as Gallagher's Knob was a group of four local men, led by thirty-nine-year-old Henry Hahn. Hahn supported himself by hunting game with his shotgun and doing odd jobs for area farmers. When he learned that Confederates were advancing through the area, Hahn had hatched a plan to exact a measure of revenge for what Southern soldiers had done to him the year before.

Hahn's anger stemmed from an event that took place during the ride Confederate cavalry leader Jeb Stuart and his troopers had made into Pennsylvania in October 1862. Some of Stuart's men seized the mare pulling a wagon in which Hahn and his employer, Abraham Lentz, were riding on the pike between Cashtown and Gettysburg. Both men were left to walk several miles home on foot. Hahn vowed vengeance, and now he aimed to take it.

As the 14th Virginia cavalrymen approached, Hahn hid among rocks and brush along the south side of the road from the gap into Cashtown atop Gallagher's Knob. Beside him was David Powell. On the north side of the road opposite them, Henry Shultz and Uriah Powell waited. Only Hahn was armed. According to local legend, Hahn had scratched a line in the pike with the butt of his shotgun, and vowed to shoot the first Rebel that crossed it.

Perhaps whiskey from the nearby Willow Springs Hotel bolstered their sense of bravery; perhaps Hahn and his cohorts were simply foolhardy without artificial stimulation. The four watched as the Virginians rode into view on the pike. When the first Southerner, Pvt. Eli Amick, unknowingly rode his horse over the line, Hahn fired a load of buckshot into him. Hahn and his group scattered in the trees as the young cavalryman tumbled from his horse and slumped to the ground in pain. Capt. Robert Bruce Moorman, leading the Virginians, declared it was too dangerous to continue. The Confederates scooped up Amick and endured several more ambushes as they returned to the Iron Works. "This section of Pennsylvania seems to be full of 'bushwackers'," declared the 14th Virginia's Lt. Herman Schuricht.

Amick died at Greenwood, the first Confederate mortality so close to Gettysburg during the campaign. Fearing revenge, Hahn and his comrades kept their involvement a secret until after the war. When he was later exposed as the trigger man in the affair, the burden of guilt and remorse became too much for Hahn to bear, his health failed, and he died on March 2, 1879. According to local lore, he is buried in an unmarked grave in Cashtown's Flohr's Church Cemetery.

On June 26, a few miles west of Cashtown, Early received information that local militia were at Gettysburg. Early decided the best way to approach Gettysburg was to divide his force and hit them from both front and rear — just in case they put up a stubborn resistance. The division leader sent

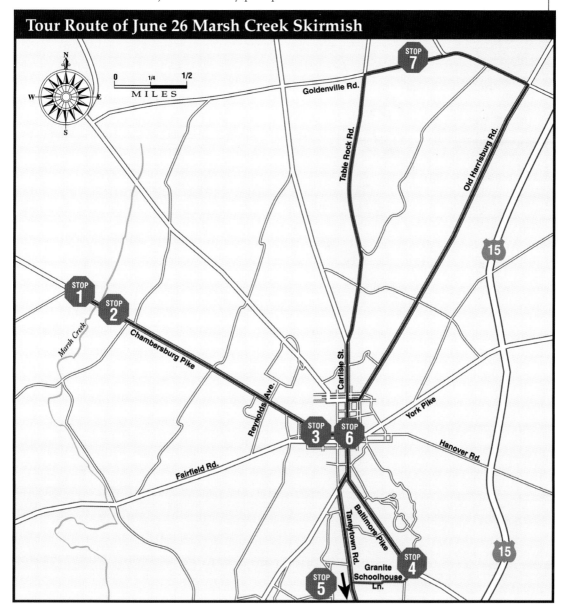

Tour Route of June 26 Marsh Creek Skirmish

the 1,900 men of Gordon's Brigade and White's troopers on the straight path to Gettysburg direct from Cashtown, while Early led the balance of his division and French's cavalry on a road to his left known as the Hilltown Road. Gordon had orders to engage any enemy troops on his front, while the rest of Early's men approached Gettysburg from the northwest on and perhaps in the rear of the right flank of the militia.

In answer to Lee's threatened invasion of the North, several Pennsylvania militia troops were mobilized in late June to protect the Cashtown Pass area and the Cumberland Valley. On June 18, the 26th Pennsylvania Emergency Militia mustered into duty 743 officers and men. Maj. Gen. Darius N. Couch, commanding the Department of the Susquehanna, dispatched the green regiment to Gettysburg where it arrived by train at about 9:00 a.m. on June 26. The regiment was commanded by twenty-four-year-old Col. William W. Jennings, and was made up mostly of soldiers from the central part of the state (with a few hailing from Maryland). One company consisted of fifty-six students from Pennsylvania (now Gettysburg) College led by Capt. Frederick Klinefelter, a graduate of the college and a seminarian. Capt. Samuel J. Randall's famed First Troop, Philadelphia City Cavalry, had arrived in Gettysburg five days earlier.

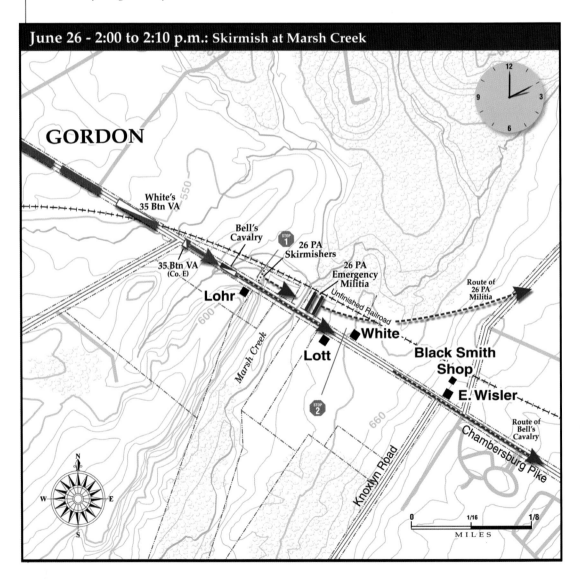

June 26 - 2:00 to 2:10 p.m.: Skirmish at Marsh Creek

A local cavalry unit, Capt. Robert Bell's Adams County Cavalry Company (which had fled from Jenkins' Virginia cavalrymen near the Cashtown Pass on June 23), was comprised of about fifty locals on their own horses and without uniforms. Bell, a thirty-three-year-old farmer with a home north of town, had formed the company on June 16. Bell's troopers joined the 26th Pennsylvania Emergency Militia and Randall's cavalry, and all were placed under the command of Maj. Granville O. Haller of the 7th U.S. Infantry, who was designated by Couch to organize the defense of the area. A few dozen men of the Gettysburg area, older citizens described as "armed to the teeth with old, rusty guns and swords, pitchforks, and pick-axes" made up the Gettysburg Home Guard and had been used by the major a few days earlier to barricade roads in the South Mountains. The Home Guard did not, however, join Haller's men this day.

At 10:30 a.m., completely unaware of the Confederates' advance on Gettysburg, Haller ordered Jennings and the militia infantry and cavalry to march west from town on the Chambersburg Pike. Haller wanted the green men to reconnoiter in the mountains and discourage any possible Southern advance from the west. Jennings, however, balked at the order, citing the inexperience of the troops. Haller insisted they march at once, so after detailing one company of the 26th Pennsylvania and all of Randall's cavalry to remain in town and protect the militia's baggage, Jennings marched the unsuspecting men along the pike through a fog and drizzling rain, with Bell's cavalry leading the way.

Let us now "march" in the steps of the green militia troops, and visit the site of their engagement with White's Confederate cavalry.

> *Leave Gettysburg by driving west on Rt. 30. When you reach the traffic light at the intersection with the Reynolds Avenue park road, set your odometer to 0.0. After 2.3 miles, you will reach the bridge over Marsh Creek. From the bridge, drive another .3 miles to reach a paved driveway on your left that leads to a large gray barn on a small hill. Turn into the drive, turn your vehicle around to face Rt. 30, and briefly pause where safe. Do not block the driveway since this is private property.*

. . . .

Tour Stop 1
White's Cavalry Routs the Militia

This is the area of the Samuel Lohr farm at the time of the battle. As you face Rt. 30, Lohr's home was located to the right of the driveway near the road. The dilapidated remains of the Lohr springhouse can still be seen in the brush a little farther to the east. Lohr's farm extended to the other (north) side of the road. Note that the present Rt. 30 in this area is not the wartime trace of the Chambersburg Pike. If you look across the road to the north, you can see the old trace of the roadbed. The newer part of the road was straightened and raised in the 1900s. You may carefully cross the road to examine the old road trace, but please be aware that the old road trace is now private property.

Jennings' militia column halted at the Marsh Creek bridge you just crossed and which you can see in the distance to your right. Jennings detailed forty of his "best" men of the 26th Pennsylvania across the creek to form a picket line with some of Bell's cavalry. This picket line was formed along a fence across the road from your location. Some of Bell's troopers advanced west (to your left) another 200 yards to watch the road. The rest of the 26th Pennsylvania militia set up camp on the right of the road in a clover field east of the creek. Most of that area is now covered with trees and thick brush, but you can see the area to your right just beyond the creek and to the north. Oblivious to the large force of Confederates now bearing down on them, most of the men pitched tents to shelter themselves from the rain.

Jennings and Bell rode back a few hundred yards to the top of Knoxlyn Ridge (as it is known today) to get a better view of the road to the west. You can see this hill in the distance to the east (to your right) toward town. It wasn't long before they spotted Gordon's infantry column, led by White's cavalry, descending a slight slope in the road about two miles away. One of Bell's cavalrymen rode into the camp yelling that the enemy was "quite near." Jennings had no intention of trying to hold back such a large column of veteran Confederate troops. The two officers rode back to the camp and ordered the soldiers to strike tents, roll their packs, and retreat east in the direction of Gettysburg.

The militiamen quickly gathered as much gear as possible and began scurrying northeast through farm fields. Bell's cavalry and Jennings' pickets, however, were ordered to hold their ground as long as possible to cover the rear. Within a short time White spotted the militia in the road ahead. White's troopers, led by Methodist preacher-turned-warrior Lt. Harrison M. Strickler and his Co. E, raised an ear-piercing Rebel Yell and charged into Bell's cavalry and Jennings' pickets in the road to your front. "They came with barbarian yells and smoking pistols, in such a desperate dash," the regimental historian of White's cavalry, Capt. Franklin Myers, wrote of his comrades' charge, "that the blue-coated troopers wheeled their horses and departed . . . without firing a shot. . . . Of course, 'nobody was hurt,' if we except one fat militia Captain, who, in his exertion to be first to surrender, managed to get himself run over by one of Company E's horses, and was bruised somewhat." White's cavalrymen captured nearly about forty of the infantry pickets. While a few pursued Bell's men who galloped toward town, many of White's troopers raided the infantry's camp of the items hastily left behind.

The men of the 26th Pennsylvania militia, hearing the shooting behind them, hurried their steps through the soggy fields east of Marsh Creek until they reached the modern-day Belmont School-house Road, which they followed north to the Mummasburg Road. Jennings followed the road back toward Gettysburg, where he intended to reach the railroad east of town and follow the tracks to Harrisburg. Bell's escaping cavalrymen galloped east on the pike toward town. At the next stop, we will visit a small marker placed to commemorate the less-than-noble experience of the 26th Pennsylvania Emergency Militia.

> *Reset your odometer to 0.0, turn right onto Rt. 30 and drive east back toward Gettysburg. After .4 miles, turn left into the dirt road entrance for A & A Auto Salvage (77° 17' 08"W, 39° 51' 11"N). Without blocking the road, park your vehicle where safe, and be mindful that this is private property.*
>
> *Carefully walk out to Rt. 30, and walk to your right along the shoulder, being very careful of traffic on this busy road. After a short distance you will come to a small marker, placed here in 1912, to commemorate the skirmish of the militia with White's cavalry.*

Tour Stop 2
Marker of the 26th Pennsylvania Emergency Militia

From here, looking to the west, you can see the area of the encampment of the 26th Pennsylvania militia on the right of the road on your side of the creek. Walk back to the driveway where you parked (note this road did not exist in 1863). The militia fled through the fields and woodlots that were to the north, and upon reaching modern-day Belmont Schoolhouse Road, followed it north to the Mummasburg Road and then continued eastward.

After galloping through Gettysburg, Bell gathered the remainder of his men near Rock Creek on the Hanover Road and ordered them to their homes, saying "Every man for himself." Bell and some of his men, with Major Haller and Randall's Philadelphia Troop, rode on to Hanover, then to York and Wrightsville. All were able to escape except for one of Bell's cavalrymen, Pvt. George Sandoe, who was shot dead by one of White's troopers along the Baltimore Pike. We will visit the site of his death, and monuments placed at the location, as we continue the tour.

White's Confederate cavalry entered Gettysburg's town square (known then as the Diamond) about 3:00 p.m., firing their pistols and scaring the townsfolk, many of whom had packed their valuables on wagons and were attempting to flee to the east. Northeast of town, Colonel Jennings marched his militia to Henry Witmer's farm about four miles from Gettysburg along the Goldenville Road, where the exhausted soldiers threw down their packs to rest. After barely having enough time to get some food and water, the unprepared militiamen were fired upon and charged by French's wildcat cavalry, which had snuck up on them from the west. Following a short, disorganized skirmish, French's cavalry captured many of the Federals.

The 26th Pennsylvania Emergency Militia marker commemorates the June 26 skirmish. (Stanley)

(See the end of the tour if you wish to visit the Witmer Farm to examine the area of the skirmish there, also known as the Battle of Bayly's Hill.)

Return to Rt. 30, reset your odometer to 0.0, and turn left to drive west back to Gettysburg. After 2.8 miles, at the intersection with Springs Avenue, you will see the Statue Monument to your immediate right. You may wish to turn onto Springs Avenue to find a place to safely park and examine the monument.

Tour Stop 3

Statue Monument of the 26th Pennsylvania Emergency Militia

This monument to the emergency regiment, featuring the sculpture of a young lad looking perhaps more defiant than his comrades actually were on June 26, was dedicated on September 1, 1892. Edward L. Pausch of New York sculpted the statue. Samuel Pennypacker, who became governor of Pennsylvania from 1903-07, was a member of the regiment and present that day as a twenty-year-old recruit. When the statue was being designed, Pennypacker suggested that it should show the young soldier's trousers tucked into the bootlegs "to indicate the sudden change from peaceful life to the battlefield."

Continue straight on Chambersburg Street for .2 miles until you reach the traffic light at the intersection with Washington Street. Turn right, and drive .1 miles to the first traffic light at the intersection with Middle Street. Turn left and drive .1 miles to the first traffic light at the intersection with Baltimore Street.

Reset your odometer to 0.0 here at the light, and turn right. Continue on Baltimore Street (Rt. 97 South) for 1.4 miles and note the wartime home of Nathaniel Lightner on your right.

The Lightner home will be discussed shortly.

Continue for another .1 miles and you will see a monument on your left just behind the guardrail. On the right side of the road is a dirt area that you may pull into and park (77° 13' 07"W, 39° 48' 32"N).

Walk very carefully across the road to the monument.

Tour Stop 4

Site of Pvt. George Washington Sandoe's Death and Monuments of the 21st Pennsylvania Cavalry

The first Federal soldier killed at Gettysburg during the campaign was Pvt. George Washington Sandoe. (Deb McCauslin)

Much of it overgrown now, the area behind the monument was a field owned by seventy-seven-year-old James McAllister, who operated a mill along Rock Creek. After being ordered to their homes by Captain Bell, Pvts. George Washington Sandoe and William Lightner rode the low land along Rock Creek to reach the Baltimore Pike. It was about 4:00 p.m. William was the nephew of Nathaniel Lightner, whose home you passed on the way to this spot. Thinking they were safe upon reaching this road, they spoke for a time with Daniel Lightner, William's cousin. Unseen due to scrub trees that lined the road, a few of White's Confederate cavalry made their way down the pike and, upon seeing the mounted Sandoe and Lightner, ordered them to surrender. Sandoe quickly pulled his revolver and fired at the Southerners. Daniel (who may have also been riding a horse) quickly escaped, and William's horse was able to jump a fence and carry him to safety. Sandoe's horse, however, balked at the fence and he was shot in the head and left breast by one of White's men. Sandoe fell from his horse and lay dead in the road near this spot. Sandoe is often, therefore, referred to as "the first Federal casualty at Gettysburg," although the battle proper was not to start for another few days.

The Confederates took Sandoe's horse, left the young cavalryman where he lay, and rode back toward town. At the Evergreen Cemetery gatehouse further up the pike, Elizabeth Thorn was feeding some of White's hungry troopers. Thorn was acting as caretaker of the cemetery in the absence of her husband Peter, who was serving in the 138th Pennsylvania Infantry. The Confederates leading Sandoe's horse approached the gatehouse, and one of the Southerners there paused from wolfing down Thorn's bread and buttermilk and said to the arrivals, "Oh, you have another one." "Yes," the trooper leading the horse responded, "the ---- shot at me, but he did not hit me, and I shot at him and blowed him down like nothing, and here I got his horse and he lays down the pike."

Early that evening, James McAllister rode his wagon from his mill and came upon Sandoe's body lying in the road, but didn't recognize the young man. He placed the body in his wagon, and a neighbor identified the corpse. After being told that Sandoe lived near Mt. Joy, a few miles south of Gettysburg (in an area known today as Barlow), McAllister took Sandoe there – where his wife awaited her husband's return from his assignment in Gettysburg. George and Diana Caskey Sandoe had only been married a few months.

The monument here was dedicated on October 5, 1893 to mark the spot of Sandoe's death. Another monument, dedicated about a year later on October 14, 1894, is the regimental monument and can be seen about 100 feet to the right on a group of rocks along the road. Both monuments were placed by Co. B of the 21st Pennsylvania Cavalry, the regiment to which Bell's company was later attached. Note that Sandoe was never officially a member of this regiment, but they understandably claimed him as their own.

Reset your odometer to 0.0 and continue south on Rt. 97, the Baltimore Pike. After .1 miles, turn right onto Blacksmith Shop road. After another .2 miles, continue ahead on Granite Schoolhouse Lane.

Note the small monument here on your left at this intersection - it is that of the 4th New Jersey Infantry Provost Guard and Train Guard detail, and is seldom visited in this remote area. This detail guarded Federal Army wagons in this area.

After another .6 miles, you will reach the Taneytown Road (Rt. 134). Turn left here and reset your odometer to 0.0.

After 3.9 miles, the Mt. Joy Church and cemetery in Barlow is on your right. Pull into the driveway here and park near the cemetery fence.

Tour Stop 5
George Sandoe's Gravesite at Mt. Joy Lutheran Church Cemetery

After you walk through the cemetery fence gate, you will find Sandoe's grave in the fourth row of stones nearest the road, with a newer stone marking his final resting place. Several of his family members are also buried next to him. Likely, Federals marching along this road to Gettysburg a few days later noticed Sandoe's fresh grave. Three other members of Bell's company (and Co. B of the 21st Pennsylvania Cavalry) are also buried in this cemetery, along with a number of other Civil War veterans.

To return to Gettysburg and the square to discuss Early's ransom of the town, exit the Church parking lot, reset your odometer to 0.0, and turn left back onto Rt. 134. Stay on Rt. 134 and after 5.0 miles you will come to the traffic light at the intersection with Steinwehr Avenue. Turn right, and after .1 miles you will come to the light at the intersection with Baltimore Street. Turn left onto Baltimore Street and you will reach the town square after .4 miles.

Park in an available space in the square, or along one of its side streets from where you can easily walk back to the square.

Tour Stop 6
General Early Ransoms Gettysburg

Known as the Diamond then (Lincoln Square today), the square consisted of a hard-packed dirt surface, and a tall flagpole stood in the center. The original county courthouse stood in the very center of the square until it was demolished in May 1859.

"The advance guard of the enemy, consisting of 18 to 22 cavalry, rode in Gettysburg yelling and shouting …firing their pistols, not caring whether they killed or maimed man, woman or child…"

Professor Michael Jacobs of Pennsylvania (Gettysburg) College describing the appearance of White's cavalry in Gettysburg on June 26

Upon entering the town, White's cavalry looted and ransacked many of the homes while terrified citizens tried to hide their horses and valuables. Gordon's foot soldiers, escorting the captured militiamen, entered along Chambersburg Street and filed into the square. Southern bands played Rebel tunes to serenade the arriving Confederates. Toward evening, Gen. Jubal Early rode through the square to the courthouse, where the forty prisoners captured at Marsh Creek had been gathered to hear a stern tongue-lashing from the Virginian. "You boys ought to be home with your mothers and not out in the fields where it is dangerous and you might get hurt!" he rebuked them. They were then locked in the courthouse.

As he sat atop his horse, Early wrote out a list of demands from the town, including sixty barrels of flour, 7,000 pounds of bacon, 1,000 pairs of shoes and 500 hats. David Kendlehart, president of the borough council, consulted with the rest of the council and then invited Early to instead search the shops for supplies. Little was found however, so Early gathered his men and left east on the York Pike to march for York in the morning. But before leaving, several of General Gordon's men chopped down the flagpole in the center of the square, and others torched the covered bridge spanning Rock Creek. Most of Early's men camped near Mummasburg about three miles to the northeast, while Gordon's Brigade camped in fields along the York Pike east of town.

If you wish to visit the farm where nearly half of Jennings' militia force was captured by Early's command, turn right from the square onto Carlisle Street (Rt. 34) and reset your odometer to 0.0.

You will cross a set of railroad tracks, and on your right is the beautifully restored Gettysburg Depot (President Abraham Lincoln arrived here on November 18, 1863, to attend the dedication of the Soldiers' National Cemetery the following day).

Continue straight on Carlisle Street (note that you will pass the battlefield feature known as Barlow's Knoll on your right, and the prominent Oak Ridge is on your left). After a total of 1.0 mile, bear right onto Table Rock Road.

Note that 1.7 miles along Table Rock Road, the wartime farm of Jacob Kime is on your left. Kime's property was used as a field hospital during and after the battle.

After a total of 3.1 miles turn right onto Goldenville Road. After another .3 miles you are approaching the unmarked Witmer Farm battlefield as you descend into a valley.

Tour Stop 7
The Battle at Witmer's Farm (Bayly's Hill)

The red brick Witmer home is in the distance on the left side of the road atop the ridge. In the distance to your right front on the far side of the treeline is a rise known as Bayly's Hill. On the afternoon of June 26, French's 17th Virginia Cavalry formed on the hill to attack the Pennsylvania militia camped at the Witmer property across the road.

Continue about .1 miles and pull over on the right side of the road from the Witmer home (be careful of traffic).

Sixty-two-year-old Henry and sixty-year-old Catherine Witmer owned this well-kept farm. They had at least six children in 1863 (one account states they had seven daughters). During the Battle of Gettysburg several days later, the farm and surrounding properties were filled with the camps of Southern soldiers.

You may wish to step out of your vehicle to see the surrounding terrain.

You can see Bayly's Hill to your right rear (southwest) from this position. Most of the twelve companies of Jennings' militia camped and rested to your right front (southeast) across the road from the Witmer home. Some of Bell's cavalry were with them as well, and Jennings had approximately 600 men total. Behind and below you to the west, at a wooden bridge that crossed the small stream

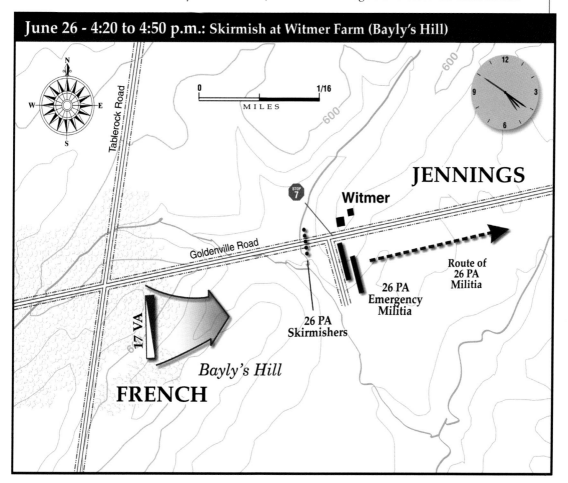

June 26 - 4:20 to 4:50 p.m.: Skirmish at Witmer Farm (Bayly's Hill)

there, Jennings placed a rear guard of about eighty men of Company B under Capt. Warner H. Carnahan.

Now look again at Bayly's Hill.

From north of Gettysburg, Col. William H. French's 17th Virginia Cavalry rode along Table Rock Road and arrived on Bayly's Hill, facing your position. The cavalrymen formed a battle line, sounded their bugles, and slowly advanced toward you and at the militia skirmish line and camp beyond. Just ahead of you along the road to the west, slightly below the top of the ridge, ran a sunken farm lane to your left (south) for several hundred yards. Seeing the Confederate advance, Jennings broke his men's respite and deployed them along the fence bordering the lane.

Jennings ordered his men to fire a volley, which unhorsed some of the Southern cavalry. French's horsemen fired a volley of their own and wounded and killed several of the militia. Jennings again decided that further resistance was futile and ordered his men to retreat east through the fields. Jennings tried to form another battle line beyond the hill southeast of Witmer's farmhouse (to the right front of the direction your vehicle is facing) but was relieved that French did not pursue. The Confederates were happy enough to round up Capt. Carnahan's rearguard and another 100 of the militia as prisoners, taking about 175 in all. French stripped his captives of their new guns and shoes, and held them here on the field under guard. The following morning, he marched them to the division's camp near Mummasburg. On the afternoon of June 28, Jennings arrived in Harrisburg with his fellow escapees to report to Governor Andrew Curtin that he had lost Gettysburg to the Confederates – an episode that paled in comparison to the fighting about to befall the town a few days later.

Continue ahead until you reach the intersection with Shrivers Corner Road.

Retreating militia that hadn't been captured used this road (taking it to the left) to escape toward Harrisburg.

To return to Gettysburg, turn right onto Shrivers Corner Road. After 1.1 miles, turn right onto the Old Harrisburg Road. After 3.4 miles turn left onto Carlisle Road, and after .4 miles you will return to the square.

Additional reading

For much more detail on Ewell's advance into Pennsylvania, and the June 26 skirmishing near Gettysburg, see Scott Mingus' scholarly book *Flames Beyond Gettysburg: The Gordon Expedition, June 1863* (Columbus, OH: Ironclad Publishing, 2009).

(Opposite page) The statue of Union General John Buford stands on McPherson Ridge watching for the approaching Confederates. (Stanley)

Tour of the First Day of the Battle of Gettysburg

"We're in a pretty hot pocket, my boy"

Although Gettysburg is often referred to as a "sleepy" little "unsuspecting" town upon which the momentous battle of the Civil War was thrust on July 1, 1863, that isn't quite true. Close to the Mason-Dixon line, the citizens of Gettysburg felt the brush of war during an 1862 raid when Jeb Stuart's Southern cavalry rode into Pennsylvania. Many of Gettysburg's young men had been fighting in Federal units since the beginning of the war. Like many other households across the country, a handful of local families were torn apart by the war. Gettysburg, too, had native sons fighting for the Confederacy.

Political tensions in the town were high. Democrats and Republicans squared off against one another over the prosecution of the war and a host of other issues. Rival newspapers waged an incessant war of opinions. In the few days leading up to the July 1863 battle, Confederate units actually advanced through Gettysburg while routing inexperienced local militia infantry and cavalry. Most of the Northern troops were captured and the rest ran for dear life toward Harrisburg. Gettysburg women filled their diary entries for the days of late June 1863 with anxious supplications that Providence would spare their town from the bloody battles that had ravaged similar hamlets in Virginia and Maryland.

It was not to be.

• • • • • • • • • • •

Tour Route of First Day of the Battle of Gettysburg

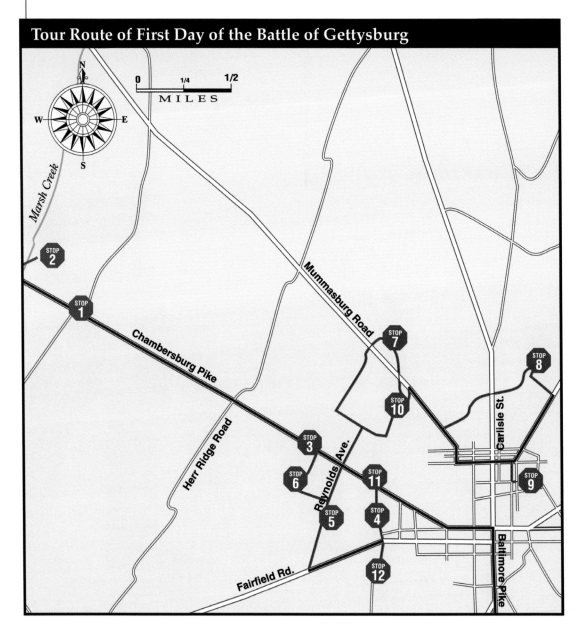

The best place to kick off a tour of Gettysburg is where many claim the "first shot" of the battle was fired on the morning of July 1, 1863. Ironically, the vast majority of visitors who come to Gettysburg each year never visit this site.

From the Gettysburg Visitor Center and Museum, exit the parking lot at the Taneytown Road entrance and turn right (north) toward town. Set your odometer to 0.0 as you turn.

After .6 miles, at the stoplight continue straight onto Washington Street. After another .7 miles, turn left (west) onto Chambersburg Street. After another .2 miles, at the stoplight bear right onto Buford Avenue (Rt. 30 West and historically the Chambersburg Pike) and reset your odometer to 0.0.

After 2.6 miles, turn left onto Knoxlyn Road, proceed about 100 feet and park in the graveled area on the left just beyond the small garage.

This area is private, but the owner permits brief parking for respectful visitors to the area. Walk back to Rt. 30, and directly ahead of you on the small rise on the other side of the road you will see a small granite monument next to the period brick home across the road. Look both ways and very carefully cross the road when traffic permits (you may wish to walk to your right a short distance in order to cross the road at that point).

Walk to the small monument and face to the west (toward the South Mountain range) looking down Rt. 30, which is also the old Chambersburg Pike.

Tour Stop 1
The First Shot of the Battle

Here at the location of the monument was Post No. 1 of Union Brig. Gen. John Buford's vedette or picket line, manned by troopers of the 8th Illinois Cavalry of Col. William Gamble's brigade. The two privates stationed here on the morning of July 1 were Thomas Benton Kelly and James O. Hale. They assumed their posts at 6:00 a.m., relieving the two troopers who had spent the previous three hours there. Sgt. Levi S. Shafer oversaw this post and several others on both sides of the Chambersburg Pike. The brick home here was owned and occupied at the time by Ephraim Wisler, a thirty-three-year-old blacksmith whose shop once stood just north of the home. A wooden rail fence enclosed the property, running along the ridge just west of the monument to the road, then along the road fronting the home with a gate allowing access to the front door. Note that in 1863, the surface of the Chambersburg Pike was level with the yard of this home where it rose over Knoxlyn Ridge (it was lowered in this area when the road was later improved and macadamized).

About 6:10 a.m., Hale looked at his watch and told Kelly the time. The troopers looked west down the pike and, according to Kelly, both men "saw a cloud of dust about three miles away. We watched it for a few minutes, and as it grew rapidly we realized something was up. At last we could make out a column of Confederate infantry with colors flying. I knew in an instant what kind of work was ahead of us." When Kelly could not locate Sgt. Shafer, he mounted his horse and galloped east to Herr's Tavern, where the reserve picket post was located. There, Kelly found his cousin, 1st Lt. Marcellus Ephraim Jones, the officer in charge of the post. "The Johnnies are coming!" yelled Kelly.

Because it was Jones' duty to send a courier farther east to the regimental and brigade camp at the Lutheran Seminary to report the news, he dispatched Sgt. Alexander Riddler. Jones then mounted his horse and, joined by Pvt. Morgan Hughes, galloped with Kelly back to the post at the Wisler home. The troopers kept their horses just beneath the ridge to the east (notice the swale on the far side of the home) so the Confederates would not see them and identify the soldiers as cavalry. Led by Jones, the troopers ran up to the fence (where you are now standing by the monument) and watched as a column of Confederate infantry approached from the west. The head of the column, led by an officer astride a light-colored horse, had almost reached the stone bridge spanning Marsh

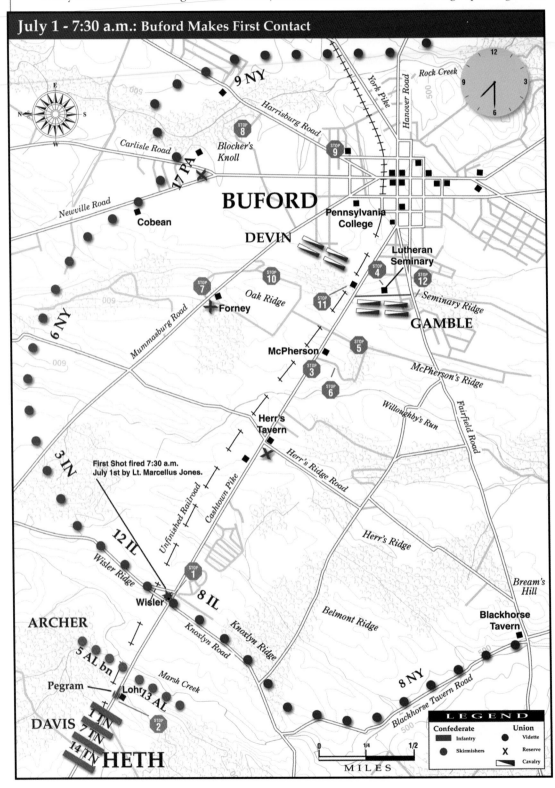

July 1 - 7:30 a.m.: Buford Makes First Contact

9 NY

Rock Creek

York Pike

Hanover Road

STOP 8

STOP 9

Carlisle Road

Blocher's Knoll

17 PA

Harrisburg Road

Newville Road

Cobean

BUFORD

DEVIN

Pennsylvania College

Lutheran Seminary

STOP 4

STOP 12

6 NY

STOP 7

STOP 10

Oak Ridge

Forney

STOP 11

Seminary Ridge

GAMBLE

Mummasburg Road

McPherson

STOP 5

STOP 3

STOP 6

McPherson's Ridge

3 IN

Herr's Tavern

Willoughby's Run

Fairfield Road

First Shot fired 7:30 a.m. July 1st by Lt. Marcellus Jones.

Herr's Ridge Road

Herr's Ridge

12 IL

Unfinished Railroad

Cashtown Pike

STOP 1

Bream's Hill

Wisler Ridge

Wisler

8 IL

Belmont Ridge

Blackhorse Tavern

ARCHER

Knoxlyn Road

Knoxlyn Ridge

5 AL bn

8 NY

Pegram

Lohr 13 AL

Marsh Creek

Blackhorse Tavern Road

STOP 2

1 TN

DAVIS

7 TN

14 TN **HETH**

LEGEND

Confederate		Union	
▬ Infantry		●	Vidette
● Skirmishers		X	Reserve
		⟋	Cavalry

0   1/4   1/2

MILES

Creek about one-half mile to the west. It was now about 7:30 a.m.

By this time Sgt. Shafer had also arrived at the post. Jones turned to him and asked to borrow his Sharps single-shot, breech-loading carbine. Jones rested the gun in a crotch of the fence, cocked the hammer, aimed down the pike at the column still tramping in the road, and squeezed the trigger. The bullet passed harmlessly above the heads of the gray infantry. However, it was the "first shot" fired that morning. The Battle of Gettysburg was now officially underway.

The sound of the shot triggered alarm in the Southern ranks. When the Confederates spotted Jones' detail atop the ridge ahead of them, they halted in the road. The men Jones fired at belonged to the brigade of Brig. Gen. James J. Archer, about 1,200 soldiers forming the vanguard of Maj. Gen. Henry Heth's Confederate division. With Archer was a battalion of artillery led by Maj. William "Willie" R. J. Pegram. Skirmishers from the 13th Alabama Infantry and 5th Alabama Battalion (and perhaps sharpshooters from the 7th Tennessee Infantry) were sent running north and south of the road along the west side of Marsh Creek (Heth did not have any cavalry with him). Pegram, meanwhile, unlimbered one of his guns, a 3-inch Ordnance Rifle, in the middle of the

The first shot monument located on Wisler Ridge, just three miles west of town. (Stanley)

road and swung it around to face Jones' position. In order to slow down Heth's advance, Federal cavalry from Jones' posts north and south along Knoxlyn Ridge began firing their single-shot carbines at the Southerners. Heth's skirmishers returned the favor, and a fitful exchange of small arms fire broke the stillness of the morning. Examine the bricks on the western side of the Wisler home and you can still see damage from Southern bullets.

Vedettes from the 12th Illinois Cavalry to Jones' right and the 8th New York Cavalry to his left began riding toward the Chambersburg Pike to join in the action. As Archer's skirmishers slowly and cautiously moved eastward toward the ridge, firing as they advanced, Pegram loaded his gun. His field piece was positioned directly across from the home of farmer Samuel Lohr, whose house and large barn sat south of the pike (we will visit this position next). Hearing the noise and seeing the cannon being loaded, Lohr stepped out of his house and shouted at the Southern artillerymen, "My God, you are not going to fire here, are you?" Getting no response, and seeing that the Confederates were not going to be stopped, Lohr ran back into his home.

Pegram's cannon was aimed and fired at the Federals atop the ridge where you are now standing, and since the shot was high, the projectile rained tree branches down on the troopers. Now it was the Federals' turn to be confronted by a local citizen. After Pegram's shot, a curious Ephraim Wisler crept out of his home and unwisely stood in the middle of the pike atop the ridge to watch the Confederates approaching from the west. Pegram fired another better-aimed round that hit the road near Wisler's feet, showering the shocked blacksmith with gravel and dirt. The terrified Wisler ran back into his home, apparently so mortified by the experience that he died of heart failure in his bed shortly after the battle.

More Federal cavalrymen from the reserve post at Herr's Ridge rode west to bolster the skirmish line at Knoxlyn Ridge as the Confederate skirmishers began pressing the troopers in earnest. Shortly after 8:00 a.m., as the Southern skirmish line approached within 100 yards, the Federal cavalrymen began withdrawing from the ridge, slipping slowly east toward town. When the initial firing got underway, the horses for the dismounted vedettes had been taken to the rear near the seminary, so the troopers fell back on foot. Their first withdrawal took them to Belmont Schoolhouse Ridge (in the distance behind you), where they set up another skirmish line. Thus far they had done exactly as they were trained and expected to do: make the enemy deploy and slow down their advance toward Gettysburg. They also kept Southern commanders wondering who and what was protecting the town. The Confederates had not yet identified Buford's troopers as veteran cavalry, and many of Heth's soldiers thought they had encountered only local militia that, characteristically, retreated when the bullets started flying. The Southern skirmish line pressed forward, pushing the Federals ahead of them while the balance of Heth's Division marched in column along the road.

"Tell [General] Lee to hold on just a little until I get my cow out of the pasture."

Gettysburg farmer to Alabama Confederates at the start of the battle, morning of July 1

At the time, only a few hundred of General Buford's troopers were on hand to slow down Heth's 7,500 infantry. Buford and his brigade and regimental commanders had by this time been notified of the Confederate advance, and buglers were sounding the alarm among the cavalry camps pitched along Seminary Ridge and Oak Ridge. The troopers prepared for battle while several hundred from Colonel Gamble's brigade galloped west to Herr's Ridge, the most prominent terrain feature the Confederates would encounter before reaching McPherson's Ridge. Their horses, too, were taken to the rear east of the seminary.

The Wisler home and property was in private hands for more than a century after the battle, but is now under National Park ownership. The small monument erected to mark Jones' opening round was put into place by Jones and several comrades in 1886. It is made of granite from Naperville, Illinois, and is sunk several feet into the ground to prevent it from being easily removed. In an interesting bit of historical trivia, Lt. James Mickler of Bell's Adams County Cavalry Company contested the advance of John B. Gordon's Confederate brigade toward Gettysburg just to the west of this area on June 26, 1863. Mickler purchased and occupied the Wisler home after the war ended.

Exit Knoxlyn Road and turn left (west) onto the Chambersburg Pike (Rt. 30). Proceed .5 miles and turn left into a gravel driveway (the first turn after you pass over the Marsh Creek bridge) where a large barn sits on the hill at the end of it. Turn your vehicle around to face the Chambersburg Pike. Note that this driveway is private property, so please be respectful.

Tour Stop 2
The Initial Advance of Heth's Division

The trace of the Chambersburg Pike in this area has changed slightly: note the old roadbed on the far side of the road to the north. That is the original trace of the road before it was straightened and raised in this area in the 20th Century. Just on the east side of this gravel driveway, fronting the road, was the home of farmer Samuel Lohr. The dilapidated remains of Lohr's springhouse can still be seen in the tangle of brush east of the house site. Willie Pegram unlimbered one of his 3-inch

Ordnance Rifles and fired it at the Federal cavalry vedettes atop Knoxlyn Ridge from the old roadbed directly in front of Lohr's home.

> *Exit the driveway and turn right (east) onto the Chambersburg Pike. You will once again cross Marsh Creek, which marks where the head of Heth's column (Archer's Brigade) was when Jones fired his "first shot."*

Along the eastern side of the creek here on both sides of the road is where Archer deployed his skirmish lines to push toward the ridge while the rest of Heth's Division marched on the road in column. The low areas surrounding the creek were quite swampy in 1863. The drive toward Knoxlyn Ridge provides a panoramic view of what faced the Confederates as they advanced (keep in mind that this area has more foliage today than it did in July 1863).

> *Drive east on the Chambersburg Pike and reset your odometer to 0.0 when you crest Knoxlyn Ridge. As you continue east, you will cross over a series of smaller ridges. The Federal cavalry used each of these ridges to make brief stands against Heth's advancing skirmishers. After .9 miles, you will see the prominent Herr's Ridge ahead of you. After about 1.0 mile, turn right at the stoplight onto Herr's Ridge Road. Pull off to the right side of the road after driving about 100 feet. Pay special attention to traffic conditions. Herr's Tavern sits atop the ridge in the southeast corner of the intersection.*

The tavern marks the location of the reserve picket post, commanded by Lt. Jones, for Buford's vedettes stationed on Knoxlyn Ridge. The thirty-three-year-old Jones (who had just eaten breakfast and fed oats to his horse) was "pacing back and forth under a tree" near the tavern smoking his pipe when his cousin Pvt. Kelly galloped up to inform him of the approach of the enemy.

The tavern, which has been considerably expanded from the original building, has an interesting history. Thomas Sweeney built it in 1815 to serve the heavily traveled route to western Pennsylvania and beyond. Shortly after it was built, some stories allege, the basement of the building was used for a counterfeiting operation. Frederick Herr purchased the tavern in 1828 and ran a successful food, beverage, and lodging house. Allegations of shady activities also surround Herr. He may have continued the counterfeiting business in the base-

Did You Know?

When the Confederates overran this area after pushing Buford's skirmishers eastward, the tavern remained behind Southern lines for the rest of the battle. The buildings served as one of the earliest Confederate field hospitals, and operating rooms were set up inside the tavern. Frederick Herr owned the tavern until his death in 1868. Herr's Ridge is also the ground from which Robert E. Lee first saw the battlefield upon his arrival from Chambersburg on the afternoon of July 1.

ment while operating a brothel on the upper floor. He did put the building to honorable use in one respect: prior to the Civil War, Herr's tavern was a safe stop on the Underground Railroad that assisted escaped slaves on their journey north to freedom.

When Heth's infantrymen pushed the Federal cavalry back to this point (about 9:00 a.m.), some 700 of Gamble's troopers formed a stubborn skirmish line along the crest of Herr's Ridge. The crest of the ridge for several hundred yards on both sides of the pike was much less wooded in 1863 than it is today. The cavalrymen were able to keep up a heavy rate of fire with their single-shot carbines compared with the infantry's muzzleloaders, but they knew their line could not hold indefinitely. Archer's Brigade formed a line of battle south of the pike just west of Herr's Ridge. Brig. Gen. Joseph Davis' large brigade, about 2,300 men, formed a battle line north of the pike but farther west (behind) Archer. Both commanders covered their fronts with skirmishers.

Willie Pegram brought his artillery forward and deployed guns on Belmont Schoolhouse Ridge to fire at the distant Federal line. The cavalry were only able to hold this position for about thirty minutes (about 9:30 a.m.) before being forced to run east to the two ridges that closely parallel one another. These ridges are collectively known as McPherson's Ridge. You can see this eminence in the distance to the east. By this time, Col. William Gamble's cavalry brigade had formed a battle line there south of the pike and north to a railroad cut, and the brigade of Col. Thomas Devin had continued the line, extending it all the way north to the Mummasburg Road. Confederate cannon was lined up all along the ridge and fired at the cavalry attempting to hold fast atop McPherson's Ridge.

Carefully turn around and drive back to the intersection with the Chambersburg Pike, reset your odometer to 0.0, and turn right toward town. As you descend into the valley between Herr's Ridge and McPherson's Ridge, you will cross a small creek called Willoughby's Run.

Some of the cavalry paused here to cool the heated barrels of their carbines as they made their way to Buford's lines on McPherson's Ridge and Oak Ridge. As you look up to McPherson's Ridge, you have a good view of what the Confederates saw when they later advanced against that position. On the right side of the road about 500 feet beyond the creek stood a tollgate house that collected money from traffic using the pike. The old tollgate house (made of stone) is incorporated into the home that now sits at this spot. The toll collector's home was on the other (north) side of the road.

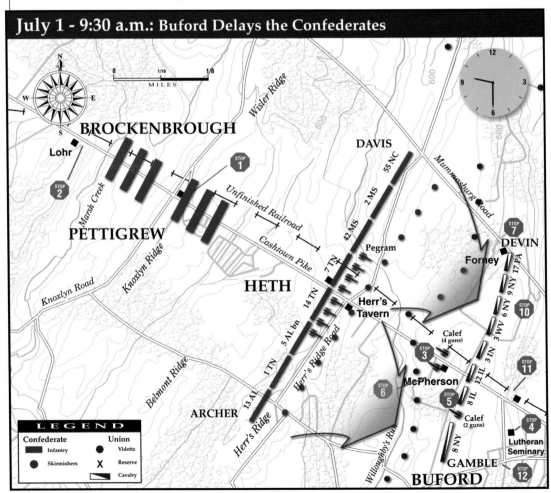

After .6 miles, you will crest the western arm of McPherson's Ridge. You will see a guide station on your right (the station is closed but comfort facilities are seasonally available). Pull into the station entrance on the far side of the parking lot and park your vehicle. Walk very carefully across the Chambersburg Pike when traffic permits to the statues and monuments. Along with the impressive equestrian statue of Federal Maj. Gen. John F. Reynolds is the standing portrait statue of General Buford.

Tour Stop 3
Buford's Line of Defense

Once his troopers were pushed off of Herr's Ridge, Buford deployed a heavy skirmish line facing west along the ridge on both sides of the road. He set up his main battle line behind you on the eastern arm of the ridge. Lt. John H. Calef and his Battery A of the 2nd U.S. Horse Artillery was attached to Buford's command. Calef set up two of his six 3-inch Ordnance Rifles north of the pike where Buford's monument is located. Two were unlimbered just south of the road, and the final section was located about 600 yards to the southeast to protect the left flank of Buford's main line. Buford's cavalry protected the artillery while they skirmished here.

Shortly before 10:00 a.m., Heth's main Confederate battle line, about 7,500 strong, appeared on the crest of Herr's Ridge to the west. As many as twenty cannon were unlimbered on that ridge. When he spotted this show of Southern arms, Lt. John Roder — in command of the two pieces of Calef's artillery stationed where the statue of Buford now sits — fired one of his guns without orders. It was the first Federal artillery shot of the battle. Heth ordered Pegram to open fire at the Federals, and the artillery of both sides raised the stakes of the developing action. Although Calef's six guns were heavily outnumbered, he held his ground.

The desperate nature of the situation prompted Buford to remark to Calef, "We're in a pretty hot pocket, my boy." The statue of Buford was sculpted by James Kelly and unveiled on July 1, 1895. It features four 3-inch Ordnance Rifle cannon barrels in its base.

A monument to the Maine Light, 2nd Battery (B) commanded by Capt. James A. Hall is also here, dedicated on October 3, 1899. The monument marks the battery's position after replacing Calef's battery when the Federal infantry of Reynolds' 1st Corps began to replace Buford's line about 10:15 a.m. The equestrian statue of Reynolds, the highest-ranking Federal officer killed in the battle, was dedicated on July 1, 1899. The statue is the work of Henry Kirke Bush-Brown, who also sculpted the Gettysburg equestrian statues of Generals Meade and Sedgwick. It was placed here, along the Chambersburg Pike, so more visitors would see it. (We will visit the area where Reynolds was mortally wounded later in the tour.)

Did You Know?

All four of the tubes in the Buford statue served in Calef's battery during the war. Calef tracked them down through the Ordnance Department for use in the statue, including tube No. 233 – the tube Roder used to fire the first Federal artillery shot of Gettysburg. A small oval plaque on that tube notes its significance (the tube is the one pointing toward the old guide station). During the dedication ceremony for the monument, Calef spiked the barrel (a battlefield tactic used if the gun is about to be captured, whereby a nail is driven into the fuse hole to render it useless) proclaiming, "I spike this gun that it may speak no more."

Exit the guide station parking lot, turn right onto the Chambersburg Pike, and reset your odometer to 0.0. After .5 miles, turn right onto Seminary Ridge Road. This road did not exist in 1863 (although there were fenced lanes here). The main entrance to the Seminary building was on the other (east) side. After a very short .1 miles, you will see the imposing brick structure of the Lutheran Theological Seminary, formerly known as Old Dorm and "The Edifice" during the war, on your left.

The cupola of the Old Dorm on the campus of the Lutheran Seminary was Buford's observation post during the fighting on the morning of July 1. (Stanley)

Tour Stop 4
The Lutheran Theological Seminary: Buford's Observation Post

Built in 1826, this was the first Lutheran Seminary established in the country. The building was known as Schmucker Hall, named for the president of the seminary, Samuel Schmucker. The hall served as a dormitory and administration building and was the only school building that stood on the campus during the battle (two brick homes were here on the campus, however). On June 30 and July 1, 1863, General Buford established an observation post in the cupola. The current cupola is not the original, which was destroyed in a lightning fire in August 1913. Buford's U.S. Signal Corps officer, Lt. Aaron B. Jerome, spent much of his time in the cupola with his spyglass trained west early on the morning of July 1. About the same time that Buford's vedettes discovered Heth's Division approaching Knoxlyn Ridge, Jerome also saw them and sent word to cavalry officers posted on the Seminary grounds.

Col. William Gamble, commander of Buford's 1st Brigade, had his headquarters and brigade encampment here on the grounds of the seminary. The building served as a field hospital shortly after the battle began until several weeks afterward, and was the last temporary hospital closed after the establishment of Camp Letterman Hospital. Many Confederate officers, including Maj. Gen. Isaac Trimble, who was wounded during Pickett's Charge, were treated here.

When he spotted the corps flag of Maj. Gen. John Reynolds' Federal 1st Corps as it marched north on the Emmitsburg Road, Jerome sent word of this to Buford. According to most credible accounts, Buford was in the cupola when Reynolds arrived on the grounds. Reynolds shouted up to Buford, "What's the matter, John?" Buford gave his famous reply, "The devil's to pay!" Descending, Buford met Reynolds and apprised him of the situation as the two and their staffs rode out toward the fighting along McPherson's Ridge.

A few minutes later, infantry from Reynolds' 1st Corps began streaming through this area from the Emmitsburg Road to relieve the dismounted cavalry fighting on McPherson's Ridge astride the Chambersburg Pike. Brig. Gen. Lysander Cutler's brigade arrived first, while the horses pulling the cannon of Capt. James Hall's 2nd Maine Battery galloped forward to relieve Calef's guns. When Reynolds was mortally wounded, he was carried back to the grounds of the seminary before being taken deeper into the rear.

Today's Seminary Ridge Road marks the approximate final battle line taken up by elements of the Federal 1st Corps (after they were pushed back from McPherson's Ridge later in the afternoon), and from which point the remnants of the corps were routed. Cutler's brigade was behind you on the other side of the Chambersburg Pike, Stone's brigade was to Cutler's left, Brig.

> ### Did You Know?
>
> Today, Schmucker Hall houses the Adams County Historical Society. The society's holdings include records, manuscripts, and diaries of the county from 1800 to the present. There are also 20,000 artifacts and thousands of historic battlefield photographs. Tours of the building, including the cupola, are available seasonally by appointment.

Gen. Solomon Meredith's "Iron Brigade" was posted here in front of the Seminary, and ahead of you was the brigade commanded by Col. Chapman Biddle. Once routed from this position, the Federals streamed east through and around Gettysburg before rallying atop Cemetery Hill. We will further discuss this action when we return to this area later in the tour.

> *Continue south along Seminary Road to the stop sign. On your immediate left was the home used by President Samuel S. Schmucker at the time of the battle. Schmucker was a well-known abolitionist, and one of the founders of the Lutheran Theological Seminary and Pennsylvania (later Gettysburg) College. During the battle, Confederates ransacked his house and he lost most of his library and personal possessions. The home was also used as a field hospital by both armies. Schmucker was never compensated for damages. Note the artillery projectile embedded in the south wall.*
>
> *Proceed straight until you reach the stop light at the intersection of Seminary Road and the Fairfield Road (Rt. 116). Through this area and to your right, Meredith's famed Iron Brigade marched at the double-quick behind Cutler's men to relieve the embattled cavalry on the ridge south of the Chambersburg Road. As they trotted toward the front, the infantry angled slightly to the northwest toward the McPherson farm and into the timber south of the farm known as "Herbst's Woods."*
>
> *Reset your odometer to 0.0 and turn right onto the Fairfield Road. After .5 miles turn right onto South Reynolds Avenue and reset your odometer to 0.0.*

Tour Stop 5
Line of Buford's Cavalry and the Federal 1st Corps on McPherson's Ridge

As you drive along South Reynolds Avenue, note that the low ground on your right was marshy in 1863, and the ridge here was dotted with fences enclosing crop fields.

> *After driving .3 miles you will see a War Department marker noting the location of Sgt. Charles Pergel's section of Lt. John Calef's horse artillery attached to Buford's cavalry division.*

Note that the thick trees on the left were not here at the time of the battle. Buford placed this third section of Calef's guns here on the left flank of the 8th New York Cavalry, while the other two sections were to the northwest along the Chambersburg Pike. This strategy — spreading the guns across a wide front — made it appear as if more artillery supported his cavalry (recall that Calef's cannon were outnumbered). From this position, Pergel's men fired at Confederate artillery posted atop Herr's Ridge.

After another .1 miles you will come upon the monument of Maj. Gen. Abner Doubleday on the right.

Dedicated on September 25, 1917, the statue commemorates this commander often (mistakenly) credited with inventing the game of baseball. Doubleday commanded the 3rd Division of Reynolds' 1st Corps before taking command of the corps when Reynolds was killed. Although Doubleday fought the corps valiantly here and along Seminary Ridge to the east later in the afternoon before the Federal line broke, army commander Maj. Gen. George G. Meade relieved him of corps command on July 2. Federal 11th Corps commander Maj. Gen. Oliver O. Howard accused Doubleday of permitting his corps to break before the 11th Corps on the right, thus causing the collapse of the Federal line along Seminary and Oak ridges. Doubleday held a grudge against the demotion for the rest of his life. Doubleday's portrait statue was unveiled on September 25, 1917, by his niece Alice Seymour Doubleday. It was designed by New York sculptor J. Massey Rhind.

This photo by an unknown photographer shows McPherson's Woods near the place where Union General John Reynolds was killed on the first day of the battle, and the sign which was erected in the mid 1880s. (LOC)

Just a short distance ahead is the monument of the 8th New York Cavalry, Colonel Gamble's brigade, Buford's cavalry division, marking the position of the regiment while it fought dismounted here. The monument was dedicated on June 9, 1889. After another .1 miles the wounding monument of Maj. Gen. John F. Reynolds is found on the left.

Park on the right to visit the monument and the informational waysides here.

The monument was dedicated on July 1, 1886, and closely approximates the location where Reynolds was shot about 10:40 a.m. while directing the 300 or so men of the 2nd Wisconsin Infantry of the Iron Brigade against Brig. Gen. James Archer's advancing Confederates. (Some scholars believe the actual location where Reynolds fell was closer to the present park road.)

Born in 1820, Reynolds was a native of nearby Lancaster, Pennsylvania, and an 1841 graduate of West Point. A shot struck him in the back of the head. Reynolds died almost instantly. It is often claimed that a Southern "sharpshooter" singled out Reynolds as a mark, but this is improbable. It is much more likely that he was killed by random fire from a soldier in the front rank of Archer's line. The shot may have come from a volley, because some of Reynolds' staff and horses nearby were also hit. The trees west (behind) the monument, known as Herbst's Woods (today often called McPherson's Woods or Reynolds' Woods) were much thinner in 1863 and served as a picnic area for locals in the decades preceding the battle. Cattle often grazed through the trees, so it was not difficult for soldiers to move through it.

You may wish to walk the path leading into the woods directly behind the monument. Your walk down the slope toward a small tributary of Willoughby's Run follows in the footsteps of the 2nd Wisconsin. When the 360 men of the 7th Wisconsin arrived in support, the 2nd Wisconsin continued forward into a heavy fight with the 7th Tennessee (about 250 soldiers) of Archer's Brigade. When you are finished examining the area, return to the park road and your vehicle.

After driving another .1 miles, on the right is the upright cannon barrel marking the headquarters of Gen. Doubleday.

You will find these markers scattered across the Gettysburg battlefield. Each upturned barrel denotes the headquarters of a general (both armies) commanding a corps, and one each for Robert E. Lee and George G. Meade. All the tubes were placed by June 1913 by the Federal government.

Just ahead on the right is the monument of the 8th Illinois Cavalry of Gamble's cavalry brigade. Note the name of Pvt. David Diffenbaugh, one of Gamble's orderlies, engraved on the bottom of the rear of this monument. Diffenbaugh was killed on July 1 and is buried in the Soldiers' National Cemetery (we visit his grave on a tour later in this book). This monument was dedicated on September 3, 1891.

At this point, you may wish to visit the McPherson farm area and the monuments south of the Chambersburg Pike. You may climb the fence surrounding the field and visit the barn, but please be respectful of this historic structure. The barn is believed to have been built as early as 1820, and was owned at the time of the battle by Edward McPherson (1830-1895). McPherson did not occupy the farm; John Slentz rented it and worked the land with his family. When the battle began, the Slentz family made its way toward town and stayed for a time at the Sweney home on Baltimore Street, a restaurant and bed and breakfast now known as the Farnsworth House. The barn is all that remains of the McPherson farm buildings that were here during the fighting. All of the structures were used as field hospitals.

Did You Know?

The statue of a soldier atop the monument of the 149th Pennsylvania Infantry along the Chambersburg Pike north of the McPherson Barn is looking toward the spot where the regiment's color bearers performed a feat of heroism on July 1. Early that afternoon, while the regiment lay in a ditch that ran in the area of the monument, the Pennsylvanians came under devastating artillery fire from more than thirty Confederate guns. To divert the projectiles, the regiment's flag bearers, under Color Sgt. Henry G. Brehm, took the colors about fifty yards northwest of the pike and took cover behind a pile of fence rails. The Confederate artillery then trained their muzzles on Brehm and his small group as the entire Federal line on McPherson's Ridge began to buckle. Seven men of the 42nd Mississippi Infantry stormed the color guard, killing and wounding several, while a few tried to get away with the flags. The valor of Brehm and his men saved the 149th Pennsylvania Infantry from even more casualties than they suffered that day.

At the southwestern corner of the intersection of Reynolds Avenue and the Chambersburg Pike is the interesting monument of the 143rd Pennsylvania Infantry, Col. Roy Stone's "Bucktail" brigade, Doubleday's division, 1st Corps. The heavy fighting in the morning along McPherson's Ridge stalled Heth's advance, and a lull settled over the battlefield about noon. The 143rd arrived with their brigade mates — the 149th and 150th Pennsylvania regiments — in this, their first battle. Initially posted on the western side of the McPherson buildings, the regiments were turned to face north along the Chambersburg Pike against newly-arrived Confederate infantry and artillery that appeared on Oak Hill. The Pennsylvanians stubbornly fought off assaults by a large brigade of North Carolinians led by Brig. Gen. Junius Daniel (Maj. Gen. Robert Rodes' Division, Richard Ewell's Corps) near the railroad cut you can see ahead to the north. However, when Heth's men renewed their advance from the west, the Pennsylvanians were caught in a devastating crossfire and fell back toward Seminary Ridge.

When the 143rd Pennsylvania broke under the pressure and retreated to the Lutheran Seminary area, the regiment's eighteen-year-old color bearer, Sgt. Benjamin Crippen, turned toward the pursuers and brazenly shook his fist at them. Crippen was shot dead for his act of defiance, which is depicted on the face of the monument. His death was regrettable not only to his comrades, but to many Southerners who watched his brave stubbornness with respect. This monument was dedicated on September 11, 1889.

At the stoplight ahead, turn left onto the Chambersburg Pike (Rt. 30) and reset your odometer to 0.0. After .1 miles, turn left onto Stone Avenue. After .2 miles, you will see the statue of John Lawrence Burns on your left.

Tour Stop 6
The Iron Brigade and John Burns, the "Hero of Gettysburg"

On the morning of July 1, 1863, shortly after the battle opened, Burns walked out of his home, crossed in front of the Lutheran Theological Seminary, and walked east toward the fighting. Eminel P. Halstead, one of Gen. Abner Doubleday's staffers, claimed to have met Burns at the time: "I met John Burns in the field east of the Seminary with an old [flintlock] musket on his shoulder . . . when near me he inquired, 'Which way are the rebels? Where are our troops?' I informed him they were just in front, that he would soon overtake them. He then said with much enthusiasm, 'I know how to fight, I have fit before!'"

Accounts vary, but after securing a new rifle, Burns encountered the 150th Pennsylvania Infantry near the McPherson farm. About an hour later, he joined the 7th Wisconsin Infantry of the Iron Brigade in the fighting at the eastern edge of Herbst's Woods, close to where Federal Maj. Gen. John F. Reynolds had been killed. (The 7th Wisconsin's monument will appear in the tour shortly.) Burns participated in the heavy fighting in this area, and later in the afternoon was wounded as many as three times (he claimed as many as seven) when the Federals began retreating. A shot to his leg brought the old man down, with the Confederates sweeping past him as he lay on the field. Burns remained on the field that night among the wounded and dead. The following morning he walked or crawled to the home of a friend, Alexander Riggs, on the Chambersburg Pike, and was taken home to recuperate.

This bronze sculpture of Burns was created by Albert G. Bureau, and was dedicated on the fortieth anniversary of the battle on July 1, 1903. The original location of the monument was farther east (likely closer to the site of his wounding) until Stone Avenue was built here and the monument relocated.

As you proceed on Stone Avenue, you will see the monument of the 7th Wisconsin Infantry, dedicated on June 30, 1888, on the right side of the road. This was the Iron Brigade regiment John Burns joined that morning. Confederate Maj. Gen. Henry Heth, who commanded the division that began the battle with Buford's cavalry, was wounded near here on the morning of July 1 while observing Archer's fight with the Iron Brigade.

The woods and low ground west of the 7th Wisconsin's monument is an area that intrepid battlefield walkers also like to explore. If you wish to visit that area along Willoughby's Run, park your vehicle on the right side of

This Matthew Brady photo shows the quarry just west of the McPherson barn and Herbst's woods in the background. (LOC)

the road near the monument. Behind the monument, look for a walking trail through the woods that follows the wooden fence. Carefully follow this trail until you reach the creek, and to your right, on the far side of the fencing, you will see the remains of a quarry. Stones excavated from this site were used for building structures before, during, and after the war. Confederates from Col. John M. Brockenbrough's Brigade (Heth's Division) had to circumnavigate this quarry during their advance, making them more vulnerable to the fire of

Archer's Brigade splashed across Willoughby's Run, from left to right. This view is taken 100 yards west of the 7th Wisconsin monument. (Stanley)

the 150th Pennsylvania Infantry of Col. Stone's "Bucktail Brigade" (Doubleday's division). If you walk along the creek in either direction, note how steep the banks are in some places. These natural barriers provided Confederates with some brief cover, but they were also very difficult to negotiate under fire.

As you proceed along the park road, it becomes Meredith Avenue when it curves sharply to the left.

In this area of the curve, as well as to your immediate right, many Federals and Confederates killed during the first day's fighting were buried in long trench graves. One of the few Confederate markers on the first day's battlefield is on your right. The marker for the 26th North Carolina of Johnston Pettigrew's Brigade was dedicated on October 5, 1985, to commemorate the regiment's intense fighting on this ground. Over the three days of the battle, the 26th lost more men than any other regiment at Gettysburg — 687 out of 840 present, a startling casualty rate of eighty-two percent.

Across the road is the monument of the Iron Brigade's 24th Michigan Infantry. Dedicated on June 12, 1889, the statue of the infantryman atop it features a regulation black dress hat instead of the typical kepi. Men of the brigade proudly wore this style of headgear as a badge of honor. When the Confederates saw who they faced on the morning of July 1, one was heard to say, "T'aint no militia. There's them black-hatted fellers again. That's the Army of the Potomac!"

Continue and pull up to the stop sign at the intersection with South Reynolds Avenue.

At this intersection (remember these roads did not exist at the time), many Federal and Confederate dead were buried in long trench graves. Federals were buried in the trenches dug through the area of the intersection, and Confederates were buried in trenches immediately behind you to the west.

Turn left and drive .2 miles. You will return to the stoplight at the intersection with the Chambersburg Pike (Rt. 30). Drive straight to continue onto North Reynolds Avenue. Park in the first space to the right, just before you reach the bridge over the railroad cut. There are several monuments here on the right and in the distance to the left.

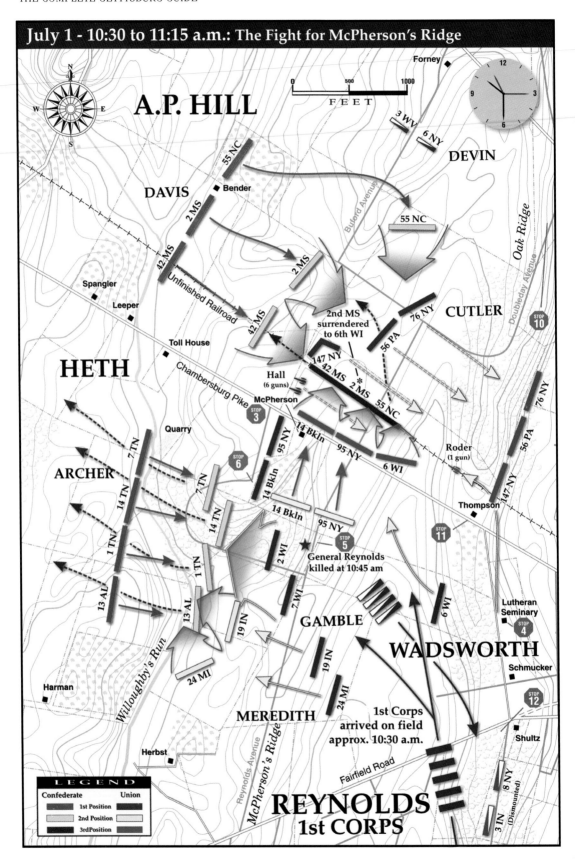

July 1 - 10:30 to 11:15 a.m.: The Fight for McPherson's Ridge

A.P. HILL

DEVIN

DAVIS

55 NC

Bender

2 MS

42 MS

Spangler

Leeper

Unfinished Railroad

42 MS

55 NC

2 MS

CUTLER

76 NY

2nd MS
surrendered
to 6th WI

56 PA

HETH

Toll House

Chambersburg Pike

147 NY

42 MS 2 MS

55 NC

76 NY

Hall
(6 guns)

McPherson

Quarry

14 Bkln

56 PA

7 TN

95 NY

95 NY

Roder
(1 gun)

ARCHER

14 TN

14 Bkln

6 WI

7 TN

1 TN

14 Bkln

95 NY

Thompson

147 NY

14 TN

1 TN

13 AL

General Reynolds
killed at 10:45 am

2 WI

19 IN

Lutheran
Seminary

13 AL

2 WI

GAMBLE

6 WI

Schmucker

24 MI

19 IN

WADSWORTH

Harman

24 MI

1st Corps
arrived on field
approx. 10:30 a.m.

Shultz

MEREDITH

Herbst

Fairfield Road

8 NY
(Dismounted)

REYNOLDS
1st CORPS

3 IN

LEGEND

Confederate	Union	
	1st Position	
	2nd Position	
	3rd Position	

The first on the right belongs to the 12th Illinois Cavalry of Gamble's cavalry brigade. During the opening fighting here, this regiment held Buford's line between the pike and the railroad cut ahead. At the time of the battle, the excavation for the railroad bed was nearly complete, but the tracks had not yet been laid. At the time of the battle, the railroad bed extended northwest only as far as Willoughby's Run. The cut, especially in its deepest section where it traversed the ridges here, served as both a natural breastwork and a death trap. The ridge to your right (east) is Oak Ridge. This bridge traverses what is known as the Middle (or Second) Cut.

Drive over the bridge and park on the right side of the road just on the other side.

Before Archer's Brigade engaged the Iron Brigade in the morning behind you to the south, Brig. Gen. Davis' Confederates fought Brig. Gen. Lysander Cutler's brigade (the first Federal infantry to arrive on the field) of the 1st Corps in the fields to your front left (northwest). The lead regiments in Cutler's marching column, about 630 men in the 76th New York and 56th Pennsylvania Infantries, crossed the Chambersburg Pike to the north and took up a position ahead of you along the ridge, facing west against Davis' men. The other three regiments of Cutler's brigade, the 84th, 95th, and 147th New York (nearly 900 soldiers in all) remained just south of the pike along the McPherson farm buildings. Pegram's Confederate gunners pounded away at their new Federal targets as Davis' 2,300 Mississippians and North Carolinians confidently marched behind their skirmishers toward the ridge.

Look in the distance to your left front (northwest). On Davis' left, the 640 men of the 55th North Carolina began angling their march toward you to envelop the Federals of the 76th New York arriving on Cutler's right flank. Seeing the flanking attempt, Col. William Hoffmann, commanding the 56th Pennsylvania to the New Yorkers' left, yelled for his men to angle to their right and fire a volley into the North Carolinians. These shots, the first documented shots fired by Federal infantry of the Battle of Gettysburg, struck down two members of the 55th North Carolina's color guard.

The 55th North Carolina and 2nd Mississippi answered with hot lead of their own, killing and wounding many. Maj. Andrew Grover, commander of the 76th New York, knew he was about to be flanked and ordered his right-most companies to face directly north at the North Carolinians. Seconds later, Grover fell with a mortal wound. In the meantime, the 147th New York of Cutler's brigade marched across the pike and the railroad cut to support Hall's Maine Battery, which had replaced Calef's two battery sections positioned near the Buford statue to your left rear (southwest). The men of the 42nd Mississippi of Davis' Brigade immediately fired volleys into the New Yorkers. Federal Division commander Brig. Gen. James Wadsworth recognized the position was untenable and ordered the Pennsylvanians and New Yorkers to the rear along Oak Ridge to your right (east). Hall likewise limbered his guns and rolled them down the pike to escape the onslaught. Cutler's men suffered horribly in their thirty minutes here. Only 79 of the 380 men of the 147th New York made it to safety. Overall, half the men of Cutler's three regiments north of the Chambersburg Pike were killed, wounded, or captured.

The Southerners successfully drove the Federals back, then many of Davis' men began running after them. While the other regiments of the Iron Brigade began battling Archer's Brigade to the south, the 6th Wisconsin and Cutler's 84th and 95th New York advanced to the pike from the McPherson farm and fired into Davis' exultant soldiers. The volley drew the Southerners' attention away from Cutler's three regiments taking cover in the woods along Oak Ridge. For protection, hundreds of Davis' men jumped into the railroad cut here and to your left (west), not realizing it was too deep to fire from and readily retreat out of if necessary. The Federals flooded the edge of the cut. Many Confederates were shot down and the rest could do little but surrender. On the left side of the road, note the monument of the 14th Brooklyn (84th New York Infantry). The soldier atop the monument was designed and placed to look down upon the men helplessly trapped in the railroad cut. It was placed here in October 1887.

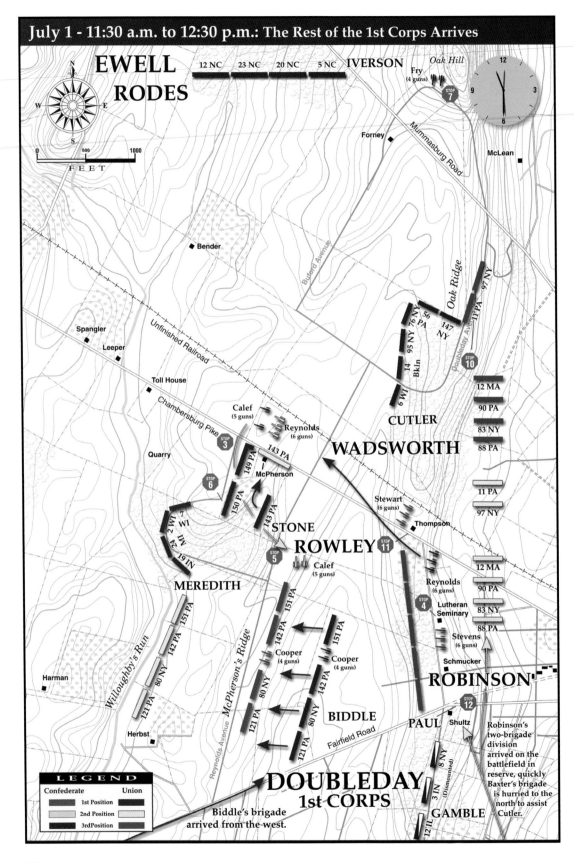

July 1 - 11:30 a.m. to 12:30 p.m.: The Rest of the 1st Corps Arrives

EWELL
RODES

IVERSON
12 NC 23 NC 20 NC 5 NC

Oak Hill
Fry (4 guns)
STOP 7

Forney

Mummasburg Road

McLean

Bender

Spangler

Leeper

Unfinished Railroad

Oak Ridge

Toll House

Chambersburg Pike

Calef (5 guns)

Reynolds (6 guns)

Quarry

143 PA

149 PA

McPherson

150 PA

STOP 3

STOP 6

7 WI

2 WI

24 IN

19 IN

MEREDITH

Willoughby's Run

151 PA

142 PA

80 NY

121 PA

Harman

Herbst

143 PA

STONE

ROWLEY

STOP 5

Calef (5 guns)

151 PA

151 PA

142 PA

Cooper (4 guns)

142 PA

Cooper (4 guns)

80 NY

121 PA

80 NY

121 PA

BIDDLE

McPherson's Ridge

Reynolds Avenue

Fairfield Road

DOUBLEDAY
1st CORPS

Biddle's brigade
arrived from the west.

6 WI

14 Bkln

95 NY

76 PA

56 NY

147 NY

11 PA

97 NY

CUTLER

WADSWORTH

Stewart (6 guns)

Thompson

STOP 10

Buford Avenue

Doubleday Avenue

97 NY

12 MA

90 PA

83 NY

88 PA

11 PA

97 NY

12 MA

90 PA

83 NY

88 PA

Reynolds (6 guns)

Lutheran Seminary

Stevens (6 guns)

Schmucker

ROBINSON

STOP 4

STOP 11

STOP 12

PAUL

Shultz

3 IN (Dismounted)

8 NY

GAMBLE

12 IL

Robinson's
two-brigade
division
arrived on the
battlefield in
reserve, quickly
Baxter's brigade
is hurried to the
north to assist
Cutler.

LEGEND

Confederate		Union
	1st Position	
	2nd Position	
	3rd Position	

0   500   1000
FEET

Lt. Col. Rufus Dawes, commander of the 6th Wisconsin, peered into the cut and saw "hundreds of Rebels" filling the chasm. Dawes' men spread out along the cut and yelled for Davis' men to surrender. Many of them did. Some of the braver Wisconsin soldiers jumped into the cut and fought hand-to-hand with members of the 2nd Mississippi, and soon a battle for the regiment's flag erupted. Cpl. Francis Waller of the 6th Wisconsin grabbed the flag with one hand, the flag bearer with the other, and escaped from the cut with his prize. Waller was later awarded the Medal of Honor. Maj. John Blair of the 2nd Mississippi was forced to surrender the men with him, and over 225 Confederates were captured here, most from the 2nd Mississippi. Cutler's men had exacted revenge on Davis' victory on the ridge to the north – but at a price; half of the 6th Wisconsin became casualties in the fight for the Bloody Railroad Cut.

Did You Know?

In 1996, in the railroad cut to your right, the bones of a soldier washed out of the southern bank during a hard rainstorm near the flank markers for the monuments of the 6th Wisconsin and 95th New York Infantry. His allegiance was not determined with any certainty, but there were several Confederates buried in the area. His remains were eventually interred in the Soldiers' National Cemetery.

The Oak Ridge Cut to your right is where the 16th Maine Infantry of Brig. Gen. Gabriel Paul's brigade (Brig. Gen. John Robinson's division, 1st Corps), was nearly surrounded as it tried to cover the rear of the broken corps later in the afternoon when the Federal line here west of town was broken. Before being captured, the men tore their flags from the staffs and ripped them to pieces. Each man stuffed shreds into their clothing so the Confederates could not make prizes of their beloved colors.

A few hundred yards to your left, in the ground just north of the railroad, gravediggers opened several long trenches to inter dozens of Confederates killed in the attacks over this ground. Just to their north were trenches in which Federal dead were buried.

"Spoke to Major [John] Hauser, got damned for going after the flag, and started for the rear ... Flag taking was pretty well knocked out of me."

Lt. William Pennington, 6th Wisconsin Infantry, shot twice during his attempt to capture the flag of the 2nd Mississippi Infantry near the railroad cut

On your right is the portrait statue of Federal Brig. Gen. James S. Wadsworth, commander of a division of the 1st Corps. Wadsworth's division, as previously noted, was the first Federal infantry division to enter the fight, and Cutler's brigade of the division was the first Federal infantry to fire shots in the battle. The statue depicts the general as he stood near this area, "with one arm directing the placing of his troops so as to withstand a charge of the Confederates." The statue was designed by R. Hinton Perry and dedicated on October 6, 1914.

At this point, you may wish to take a walk for a few minutes to see a marker and a portion of the battlefield seen by very few visitors. A very remote iron tablet marks the position taken by Capt. Abraham Hupp's 1st Virginia (Salem) Artillery, attached to Ewell's Corps, late on July 1. The remains of Confederate earthworks can also be seen at the location. To reach it, walk very carefully along the railroad tracks to the east for approximately 300 yards – keep in mind that this is an active railway, so please use caution. When you reach a gravel access road that crosses the tracks, carefully climb up the north (left) side of the red shale-covered embankment. At the top, you will find a footpath that follows the ridge to the east. Walk along this path about 100 yards, and you will reach the iron tablet for Hupp's Battery where the high ground overlooks a railroad maintenance yard.

Hupp placed a section of two smoothbore Napoleon guns at this position, facing the town, late on July 1 to participate in any attacks on the Federal position atop Cemetery Hill. Over the next two days, the battery fired in excess of 150 shells. Two representative cannon used to be here, but the Park Service, fearing vandalism at such a remote location, removed them years ago. Look just a few yards beyond the tablet, and the rare remains of Confederate earthworks at Gettysburg can be seen at the edge of the bluff. From here, you can also see the site of the very controversial destruction of the Oak Ridge railroad cut when the National Park Service traded land here in 1990 with Gettysburg College for a scenic easement over land owned by the school.

When you have finished examining the area, carefully return along the railroad to your vehicle. Drive less than .2 miles and turn left at the stop sign onto Buford Avenue. Reset your odometer to 0.0. After you turn, note the beautiful view of South Mountain to the west. In the distance to your right is Oak Hill.

Less than another .1 miles, the first monument on the right is that of the 3rd West Virginia Cavalry of Col. Devin's brigade (Buford's cavalry division), dedicated on September 28, 1898.

You are back on the western arm of McPherson's Ridge, and following the line from which Devin's brigade advanced when the fighting opened north of the Chambersburg Pike against Davis' Brigade.

The next monument is that of the 6th New York Cavalry of Devin's brigade on the right. This large monument, dedicated on July 11, 1889, was called the "Devin Monument" by the veterans due to the large plaque on the back that features a relief sculpture of Devin. Just beyond the monument is a wayside marker with information about Buford's cavalry fight here on July 1. You are also afforded an excellent view of the ground over which Davis' Brigade advanced from the west to attack Cutler's Federal brigade.

Just ahead is the monument of the 9th New York Cavalry, dedicated on July 1, 1888. The monument is called "Discovering the Enemy." Following the war, a heated dispute arose between veterans of the 8th Illinois Cavalry and regiments of Devin's brigade regarding who deserved credit for firing the "first shot" to open the battle. Cpl. Alpheus Hodges of the 9th New York Cavalry claimed that he had fired a shot at Confederates

The monument to the 17th Pennsylvania Cavalry on Buford Avenue still stands watch for the approaching Confederates. (Stanley)

north of this spot about daybreak on July 1, before Lt. Jones of the 8th Illinois Cavalry fired his shot at Heth's advance along the Chambersburg Pike. The dispute continued for several decades, but Jones is generally recognized to have fired the first shot that day.

The last monument before the stop sign is that of the 17th Pennsylvania Cavalry of Devin's brigade. This area was the farm of John S. Forney, whose home stood just behind the monument with his large barn to the right. All of the buildings were used as field hospitals during and after the battle, and were hit several times by artillery fire. When the buildings fell into disrepair in the early 1900s, they were removed. The trooper depicted on the monument is a postwar rendition of a member of the regiment, George W. Feree of Co. L. For the pose, Feree put on his wartime uniform and equipment for the sculptor, an unknown artist employed by the Smith Granite Company. The statue was dedicated on Pennsylvania Day at Gettysburg, September 11, 1889.

At the stop sign with the intersection of the Mummasburg Road, continue straight.

Tour Stop 7
Oak Hill and Rodes' Advance

Directly ahead of you is the Eternal Peace Light Memorial, dedicated on July 3, 1938 (the 75th Anniversary of the battle) by President Franklin D. Roosevelt. The monument celebrates the spirit of reconciliation between the soldiers. At the dedication, both a Federal and Confederate veteran unveiled the forty-seven foot high shaft. More than 1,800 veterans of the war were in attendance in the presence of some 250,000 spectators. The $60,000 cost of the monument was borne by Northern and Southern states. Even its construction is symbolic: the base is made of granite from Maine, and the shaft is constructed of Alabama limestone.

Paul Phillipe Crete designed the monument, while Lee Lawrie designed the base relief of the

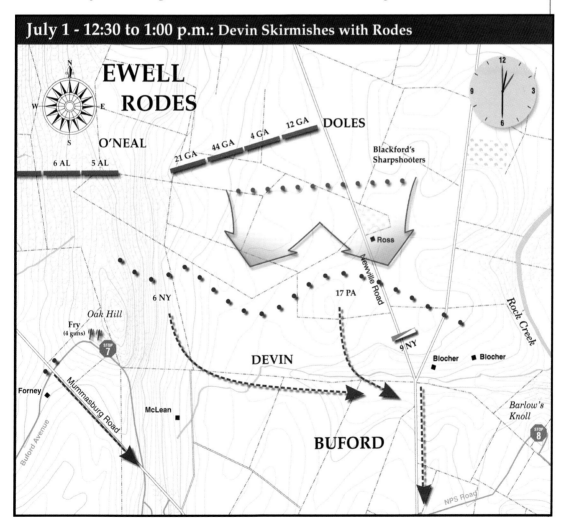

July 1 - 12:30 to 1:00 p.m.: Devin Skirmishes with Rodes

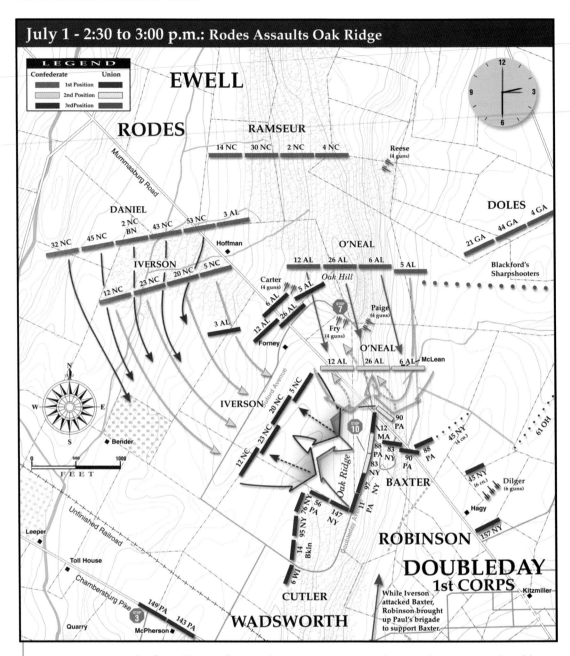

July 1 - 2:30 to 3:00 p.m.: Rodes Assaults Oak Ridge

two women on the front. The gas flame at the top was in use until 1979, when it was replaced by an electric light. In 1988, the gas flame was restored.

Park in one of the spaces provided in front of the memorial. As you stand on the steps of the memorial, there is a beautiful view of South Mountain to your right and front, the first day's field of battle, the town of Gettysburg, and the high ground beyond. The area is tranquil now, but on the afternoon of July 1, 1863 much of what you can see was filled with killing and dying.

Confederate Maj. Gen. Robert Rodes arrived here on Oak Hill from the north with his division, part of Richard Ewell's Second Corps, about noon on July 1. Rodes surveyed the unfolding situation and the Federal position along his front. Note that you can easily see the McPherson barn across the Chambersburg Pike. Before you are the fields (of wheat in July 1863) over which Davis' Confederates and Cutler's Federals fought during the morning. Rodes recognized that this hill afforded an advan-

July 1 - 3:00 to 3:30 p.m.: Daniel Continues the Assault

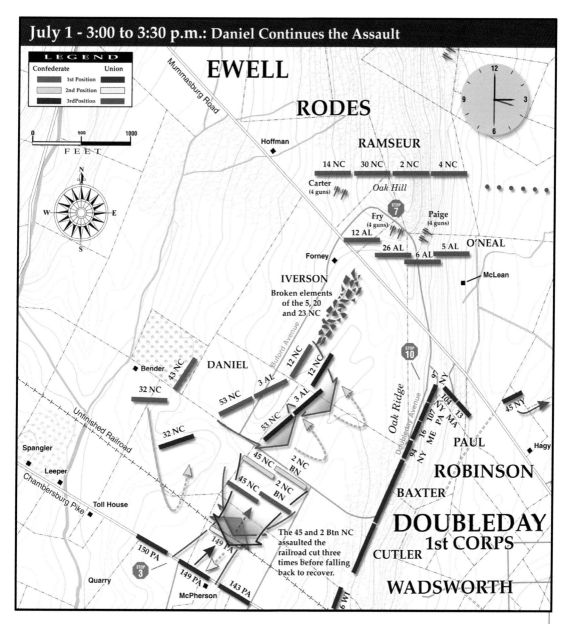

LEGEND

Confederate | Union
1st Position
2nd Position
3rdPosition

tageous position from which his artillery could sweep the field. He deployed his division in line of battle while his artillery dueled with Federal cannon for about an hour.

When all was ready, Rodes sent three brigades forward shortly after 1:00 p.m. Col. Edward O'Neal's brigade of nearly 1,700 men attacked toward the Federal right flank to your left front, Brig. Gen. Alfred Iverson's 1,400-man brigade advanced to Forney's field of clover directly in front of you, and Brig. Gen. Junius Daniel's large brigade of more than 2,100 moved off to your right in the direction of present-day Buford Avenue. This sweeping attack of more than 5,000 soldiers, however, was not well coordinated, and both O'Neal and Iverson were repulsed by the Federals with heavy loss. Waiting for the Confederates behind a stone wall along the line of trees and monuments to your left front were the Federal brigades of Brig. Gens. Henry Baxter and Gabriel Paul (Brig. Gen. John C. Robinson's division, 1st Corps). Paul's brigade of slightly more than 1,500 men successfully repulsed O'Neal's attack. Baxter's nearly 1,500 men stood up from behind the wall while Iverson's North Carolinians marched as if on parade. Without skirmishers, they had no idea such a large force of the enemy was directly in their front. The surprised Confederates were greeted by a sheet of lead that killed and wounded scores of men. Within a few short minutes, Iverson lost nearly two-thirds of his command in killed, wounded, and captured. The Federals were unable to hold their position in the face of Confederate reinforcements, however, and were ultimately forced back.

Continue on the park road.

As it begins to curve to the right, on your left is a good view of what is known as the "Gettysburg Plain." Note that this lightly undulating ground is where men of the Federal 11th Corps commanded by Maj. Gen. Oliver O. Howard fought after their arrival on the field early in the afternoon (we will examine these events shortly). Unlike the ground west of Gettysburg, the 11th Corps position had very few terrain features upon which to mount a sustained defensive effort.

Note how Oak Hill commands that low flat ground.

At the stop sign at the intersection with the Mummasburg Road, continue straight onto Doubleday Avenue and reset your odometer to 0.0. In less than .1 miles, follow the Auto Tour sign to the left onto Robinson Avenue for the "Barlow Knoll Loop." (We will return to Doubleday Avenue after visiting Barlow's Knoll.)

The portrait statue of Brig. Gen. John Cleveland Robinson, who commanded a division of the Federal 1st Corps, was sculpted by J. Massey Rhind. Rhind sculpted several of the portrait and equestrian statues on the field. It was dedicated on September 25, 1917 here on the ground his men defended on the first day of battle.

After another .1 miles, turn right onto the Mummasburg Road. After another .3 miles, turn left onto Howard Avenue and reset your odometer to 0.0. To your left is a view of the imposing Oak Hill from this flat, low ground. As you proceed to Barlow's Knoll you will pass a number of monuments of the Federal 11th Corps on the right side of the road.

Tour Stop 8
Barlow's Knoll

You are now roughly following the line taken up by Brig. Gen. Alexander Schimmelfennig's brigade of the 11th Corps. Many of the soldiers in the corps were German immigrants who could not speak English well or at all. Since these men had fled in panic during Lt. Gen. Thomas J. "Stonewall" Jackson's flank attack at Chancellorsville in early May, many Federals throughout the army derisively called them "The Flying Dutchmen."

The flat area you are driving through consisted of crops in 1863, enclosed by several fences that had to be negotiated by soldiers in this area. Only one farm lane traversed the ground, that of the Moses McLean farm to your left between your position and Oak Hill. The trees of McLean's large fruit orchard concealed the movements of O'Neal's Brigade as it advanced against the Federal 11th Corps units here on the plain.

After driving slightly more than .2 miles, note the monument of Battery I, 1st Ohio Light Artillery.

This battery of six 12-pounder Napoleons was commanded by Capt. Hubert Dilger, a former officer in the Army of Baden, Germany. Dilger's guns, posted on the slightly higher ground to your left, engaged in an artillery duel with cannon of Lt. Col. Thomas Carter's Artillery Battalion attached to Rodes' Confederate division and posted on Oak Hill. The experienced and talented Dilger, who

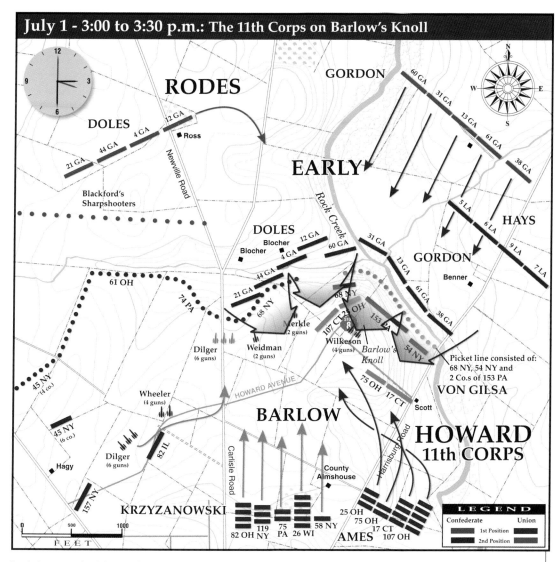

July 1 - 3:00 to 3:30 p.m.: The 11th Corps on Barlow's Knoll

RODES

DOLES

GORDON

EARLY

HAYS

GORDON

Blackford's Sharpshooters

DOLES

VON GILSA

Picket line consisted of: 68 NY, 54 NY and 2 Co.s of 153 PA

BARLOW

HOWARD
11th CORPS

KRZYZANOWSKI

AMES

LEGEND

had distinguished himself at the battles of Second Manassas and Chancellorsville, fought throughout the afternoon with the 13th New York Battery. His gunners were among the last Federal troops to leave this part of the field.

A popular story involving Dilger's performance holds that the artillery officer personally sighted on a gun in Carter's Battalion, and the resulting shot "spiked" the muzzle of the Confederate cannon. Dilger, however, did not claim such a feat in his official report, and the Southern artillerists claimed no such damage. Later stories of such a feat (including that of a Federal prisoner who claimed to have seen the plugged barrel) are likely apocryphal.

Part of the battery's monument here has a curious twist. Note the small left flank marker for the battery across the avenue. It was important to the veterans of the battery that visitors to the battlefield know that the gunners held an advanced position to the northwest during their fight against Confederates on Oak Hill. While inscribing the small marker, the veterans were unsure where it would be placed. The exact distance has never been filled in to this day, so the marker still reads "3__ YDS."

After .4 miles, you will reach a stop sign at the intersection with the Carlisle Road (Rt. 34). Continue straight on Howard Avenue and reset your odometer to 0.0. You will again pass

> *a number of 11th Corps monuments on the right side of the road. Like the area along the first part of Howard Avenue you just left, the terrain here during the battle consisted of crops surrounded by fences.*
>
> *After .2 miles you will see the old Almshouse Cemetery on your right, a burying ground provided for the indigent of the county (it is still in use today).*

The oldest burials date back to the early 1800s. The Adams County Almshouse stood approximately where the large brick building now stands in the distance to the south along the Harrisburg Road. The cemetery holds several rows of small simple stones. There is also one Civil War veteran buried there. During the fighting for the knoll ahead, some Federal artillery pieces unlimbered and fired from the cemetery.

Just ahead is the joint monument of the 25th and 75th Ohio Infantry regiments of Brig. Gen. Adelbert Ames' brigade, dedicated on September 14, 1887. The 25th Ohio suffered the second highest percentage of casualties – a staggering eighty-four percent – of all Federal regiments at the battle. Most were suffered here while the regiment fought alongside the brigade commanded by Col. Leopold von Gilsa.

> ### Continue to the summit of the knoll.

During the battle, this was known as "Blocher's Knoll," named for the Blocher family landowners whose farms were directly northwest along the Carlisle Road. Today it is commonly called "Barlow's Knoll," named for the Federal division commander who tried to hold the ground during the afternoon of July 1 in the face of overwhelming Confederate attacks from the north.

When 11th Corps leader General Howard assumed temporary command of all the Federal troops at Gettysburg on the afternoon of July 1, division commander Maj. Gen. Carl Schurz assumed control of the corps. After conferring with Howard near the high ground of Cemetery Hill south of Gettysburg, Schurz joined the two 11th Corps divisions that had advanced into the fields south of you and eventually lined up on the right flank of the Federal 1st Corps. When Brig. Gen. Francis C. Barlow, commander of the 1st Division, saw the high ground of Blocher's Knoll to his front, he ordered part of his division to advance and drive back Confederate skirmishers from Brig. Gen. George Doles' Brigade, part of Rodes' Division. Barlow's men were exposed to artillery fire from Oak Hill, and Maj. Gen. Jubal Early's Division of Ewell's Corps arrived from the Harrisburg Road and deployed in lines of battle in the fields to your north. (Note that the trees along Rock Creek were much thinner at the time of the battle.)

As you face the flagpole at the summit of the knoll, Doles' Brigade attacked Barlow's position from your left, while Brig. Gen. John B. Gordon's Brigade of Early's Division advanced against his front. Outnumbered and hit from both directions, Barlow's men were driven off the knoll, Barlow was seriously wounded, and he and many of his men were captured. The flagpole, installed in 1885 by survivors of the 17th Connecticut Infantry of General Ames' brigade of Barlow's division, marks the spot where the regiment's commander, Lt. Col. Douglas Fowler, was killed. An artillery shell severed Fowler's head shortly after he arrived on the knoll riding a white horse. Fowler's comrades were forced to leave his body behind when they retreated, and his body was never identified. Fowler's remains likely rest in one of the Unknown Dead sections of the Soldiers' National Cemetery.

Historians continue to debate whether Barlow's forward move to this knoll was wise, or if it needlessly exposed his men to being flanked and routed. Without continuity with the line of the rest of the 11th Corps, this position quickly became untenable. Brig. Gen. Wladimir Kryzanowski's Federal brigade, in reserve near the Carlisle Road, was ordered forward to assist Barlow's men, but the brigade could not beat back the Confederate assault. The Federals tried to rally to the south near the Almshouse, but were again routed when Early pressed his attack. The collapse of the Federal line

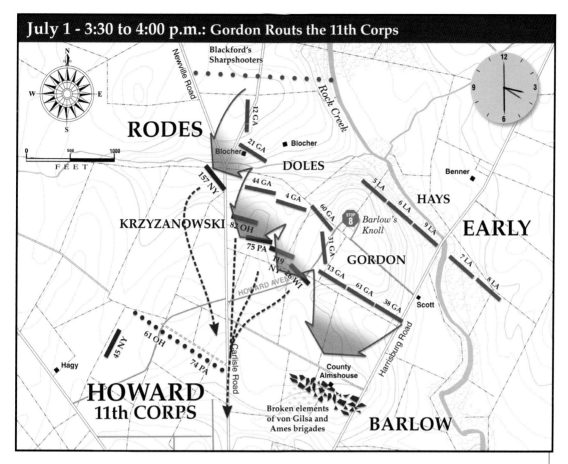

July 1 - 3:30 to 4:00 p.m.: Gordon Routs the 11th Corps

here precipitated the ultimate collapse of the entire 11th Corps.

The portrait statue of General Barlow, who was only twenty-eight-years-old at Gettysburg, was unveiled on June 6, 1922. Its creator was J. Massey Rhind. Due to the heavy fighting in this area, many soldiers were buried in the fields west and north of the knoll. Several trenches for both Confederate and Federal dead were dug between the knoll and Blocher's Run to the north. To the west on the other side of the Carlisle Road, several long trenches once held the bodies of Federals killed during the fighting north of town on the first day of the battle.

A marker seen by few visitors to this area is a stone that marks the advance skirmish line near Rock Creek of the 54th New York Infantry of von Gilsa's brigade. To slow down the attack by Confederates of Gordon's Brigade, von Gilsa ordered part of the regiment to advance northward toward the creek to engage them. To see the marker, walk down the north slope of the knoll while angling to the right toward a slight gap in the pine trees. Carefully walk a short distance through the pines until you reach a small open area. Walk to the utility pole here, then continue about twenty yards behind it, toward the creek, where you will locate the small advance marker.

Continue on the park road and descend the knoll. When you reach the stop sign at the intersection with the Harrisburg Road (Rt. 15), turn right and reset your odometer to 0.0. After .5 miles bear right onto Lincoln Avenue. Just a short distance ahead, turn left onto Stratton Street and reset your odometer to 0.0. After .1 miles, turn left onto Coster Avenue. Drive a short distance ahead to the dead end (you will see a line of monuments ahead of you). Carefully turn around and park on the right side of Coster Avenue.

Tour Stop 9
Coster Avenue and the Brickyard Fight

Tucked among the busy suburban streets of Gettysburg is Coster Avenue, a narrow strip of National Park land. This protected terrain features monuments to three Federal regiments that were nearly swallowed whole by attacking Confederates, as well as an impressive outdoor mural depicting their valiant stand as they attempted to come to Barlow's support on the afternoon of July 1.

In July of 1863, much of the terrain here consisted of open fields of corn, oats, and rye traversed by stout rail fences. To the south stood a small brickyard in the area of the present long commercial building to the right of the monuments. Running along the north wall of the present-day building was a tall rail fence that enclosed the brickyard.

When he received orders to advance from Cemetery Hill to support Howard's embattled 11th Corps Federals north of town, Col. Charles Coster took three regiments of his brigade — the 134th and 154th New York, and the 27th Pennsylvania — and marched them to the brickyard owned by John Kuhns that once stood here. From this vantage point, Coster could easily see Barlow's plight, for

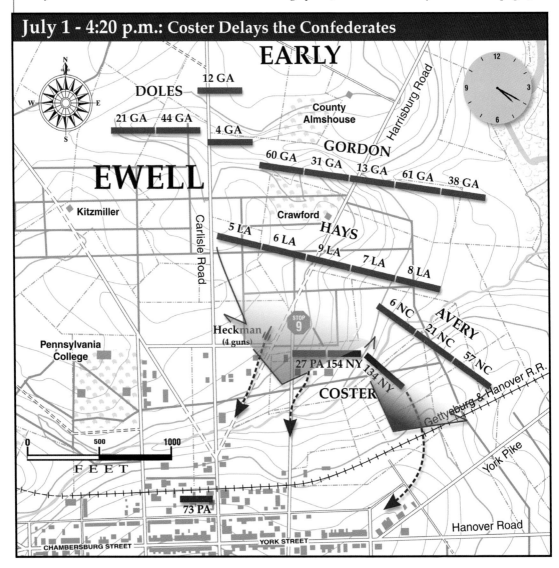

July 1 - 4:20 p.m.: Coster Delays the Confederates

his Federal line was already crumbling at Blocher's Knoll and the Almshouse. The retreating Federals raced back through town with Confederates hot on their heels and heading straight for Coster's 920 soldiers. The colonel decided to make a stand in an effort to cover the retreat of his comrades. He ordered his men to load their weapons and form a line along the fence.

The 2,500 Confederates approaching Coster's position were veteran infantry from the brigades of Brig. Gen. Harry Hays and Col. Isaac Avery. When the attackers climbed the slight knoll leading toward the brickyard, Coster's men opened fire, stunning the Southern advance for a few moments. While Coster's men were firing, Capt. Lewis Heckman's Battery K, 1st Ohio Light, rumbled into position and dropped trail on Coster's left. "I unlimbered and commenced firing as soon as possible, as the enemy were close to me and advancing," Heckman later recalled. His battery of four guns fired 113 rounds, most of which were canister. Although heavily outnumbered, Coster and Heckman offered a stubborn fight that slowed down the Confederate advance into the northern reaches of Gettysburg. The weight of numbers and length of frontage, however, ultimately prevailed. While Avery's line curled around

his right flank, Hays' Louisiana troops enveloped the left. As this was transpiring, the 6th North Carolina leaped the fence to attack the 154th New York, which held the center of Coster's line. The fate of the defenders of the brickyard was sealed. Only 359 of the 920 men who stood their ground escaped that afternoon to make their way southeast for Cemetery Hill.

A detail from the Coster Avenue Mural depicting the charge of Hays' Louisiana Tigers on Coster's troops defending the brickyard. (Stanley)

Realizing he had perhaps overstayed his welcome, Heckman ordered his gunners to limber and withdraw. The order did not come soon enough for two of the guns and their crews, however, which were captured. Coster's survivors and Heckman's gunners were caught in the throng of 11th Corps infantry, cavalry, and cannoneers making their way to safety south of town. The Federal 1st Corps was also breaking for the rear after their last stand west of town along Seminary Ridge. As one survivor put it, with probably as much of a ring of truth as sarcasm, "The few that did get away were the best runners."

The stunning mural on the north wall of the adjoining warehouse was painted by Mark Dunkelman and Johan Bjurman, and dedicated on July 1, 1988.

Reset your odometer to 0.0 and continue west on Coster Avenue. After slightly less than .3 miles, turn right onto Washington Street. After another .1 miles, turn left onto Lincoln Avenue. After another .1 miles, turn right onto College Avenue.

After another .6 miles, turn left onto Doubleday Avenue and reset your odometer to 0.0. You may wish to park in one of the spaces on the left side of the road in order to climb the tower for a view of this part of the battlefield. It is a magnificent vista and worth the effort.

Tour Stop 10
Rodes' Attacks – Federal Perspective

Note, again, how Oak Hill to the north commands the surrounding terrain. You are on a spot that would have been directly behind the V-shaped position of Brig. Gen. Henry Baxter's Federal brigade (Robinson's division, 1st Corps) as it formed to receive the afternoon attack of Col. Edward O'Neal's Alabamians from Oak Hill. On the right, with their right at the Mummasburg Road, the 90th Pennsylvania, 12th Massachusetts, 88th Pennsylvania, 83rd and 97th New York, and the 11th Pennsylvania waited behind the stone wall. To their left, farther along the stone wall, Cutler's Federal brigade (along with the 6th Wisconsin of the Iron Brigade) was arrayed. O'Neal attacked directly at you from Oak Hill, and Iverson's Brigade of North Carolinians attacked from the northwest, paralleling the Mummasburg Road.

One of the many interesting monuments here is that of the 90th Pennsylvania Infantry of Baxter's brigade, in the shape of a tree trunk. Note the bronze bird and nest near the top of the granite monument. According to a tale from this fight, a bird's nest was knocked out of a tree. Supposedly, amid a hail of bullets and shell a Pennsylvanian of the regiment picked up the nest, which contained terrified baby birds, and gently returned it to its tree.

As you drive along Doubleday Avenue, you have an excellent view to your right of John S. Forney's fields.

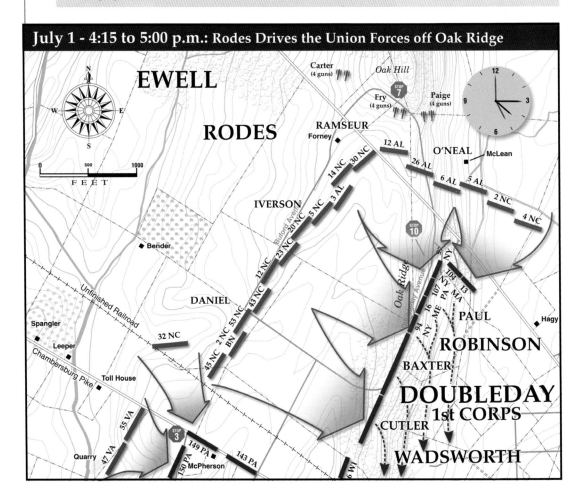

July 1 - 4:15 to 5:00 p.m.: Rodes Drives the Union Forces off Oak Ridge

Recall that this is where Iverson's Confederates were slaughtered by Baxter's men hiding along this stone wall. The small marker in the field, which you may wish to walk to and examine, denotes the point to which men of the 88th Pennsylvania Infantry counterattacked against the 20th and 23rd North Carolina regiments and captured large numbers of Confederates and two battle flags. This marker was dedicated on August 27, 1883, about six years before their regimental monument was placed here along the road.

After .5 miles along Doubleday Avenue, turn left at the stop sign onto North Reynolds Avenue. After another .2 miles, at the stoplight at the intersection with the Chambersburg Pike (Rt. 30) turn left and reset your odometer to 0.0. After .1 miles you will see a mounted cannon barrel on your right that marks the site of Robert E. Lee's headquarters during the battle. On your left is the Thompson stone house bearing the sign "Lee's Headquarters." Pull into the lot here.

Tour Stop 11
Robert E. Lee's Headquarters

Now a privately owned museum (active since 1921), this home was owned by Congressman Thaddeus Stevens in 1863 and rented to the widow Mary Thompson. Documentation shows that Lee's official headquarters were located where his tent and those of his staff were pitched in an orchard across the pike near where the headquarters cannon barrel marker now stands. Lee did, however, use the Thompson home occasionally for meetings and meals. Thompson remained in the home during the battle and prepared food, but later complained of the damage done to the home and the destruction of some of her property.

On the left side of the parking lot is a wayside marker near the Lincoln Highway Heritage Corridor marker, a non-Gettysburg battle bit of history that many visitors will enjoy reading about. To the right of the wayside is a War Department marker for Lt. James Stewart's Battery B of the 4th U.S. Artillery. On the morning of July 1, Stewart offered to assist General Wadsworth in the infantry fighting north of the Chambersburg Pike by placing three of his guns on the road, and the other three along the railroad cut here. Wadsworth agreed, the battery was brought forward, and the guns

Mrs. Thompson's house (as pictured in the late 1800s). Though credited as Robert E. Lee's headquarters, his headquarters tent was actually located in her orchard across the Chambersburg Pike. (LOC)

loaded with two loads each of canister. (Canister was a prepared projectile of iron balls, which turned the piece into a large shotgun. It was especially devastating as an anti-personnel charge.) The guns placed near here were partially concealed by a small grove of trees.

When the Confederates of General Joseph Davis' Brigade (Heth's Division) advanced from McPherson's Ridge to a point about 300 yards west of this position, Stewart's gunners let loose on them. "It was more than [the Confederates] could stand," Stewart later wrote. "They broke to the rear, where they halted, faced about, and advanced again, but meeting with such a storm of lead and iron, they broke and ran over the rising ground entirely out of sight." Stewart and his guns were forced

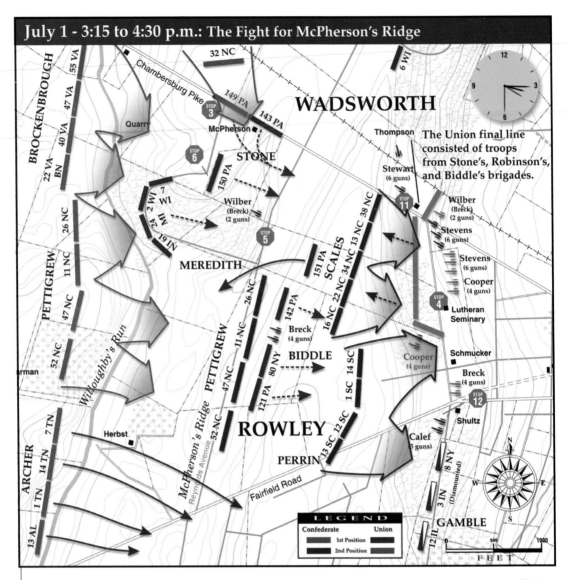

July 1 - 3:15 to 4:30 p.m.: The Fight for McPherson's Ridge

The Union final line consisted of troops from Stone's, Robinson's, and Biddle's brigades.

to fall back toward the town later in the afternoon when the Federal 1st Corps was pushed off these heights to Cemetery Hill south of Gettysburg.

> *Exit the parking lot, turn left onto the Chambersburg Pike (Rt. 30) and reset your odometer to 0.0. After .1 miles, turn right onto Hay Street. After another .2 miles, you will come to a stop sign at the intersection with Springs Avenue. Turn right onto Springs Avenue. (Note that this road was not here at the time of the battle.)*

Tour Stop 12

Col. William Gamble's Defense

Soldiers of the Federal 1st Corps advanced to the front on the morning of July 1 through fields that were here on both sides of this postwar road.

> *After another .1 miles, turn left onto Seminary Ridge Road. Drive to the stoplight at the intersection with the Fairfield Road (Rt. 116). Continue straight (the road becomes West*

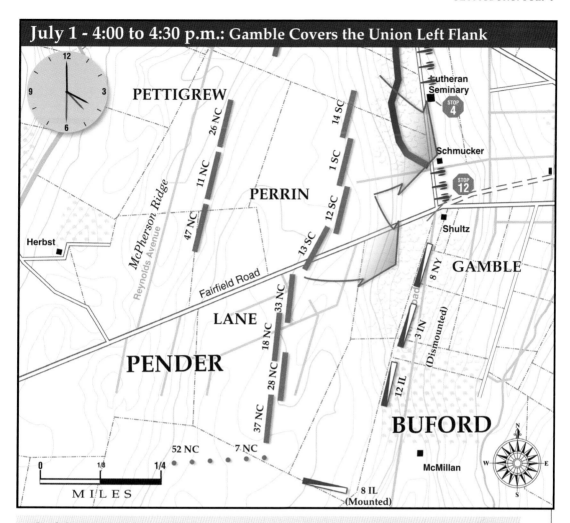

July 1 - 4:00 to 4:30 p.m.: Gamble Covers the Union Left Flank

Confederate Avenue) and after about thirty yards pull over to the right along the stone wall.

On the left is the ornate brick home of Elizabeth Shultz, the owner at the time of the battle. The house has been substantially enlarged since the war. Please note there was no road here at the time of the battle. A lane that ran along the seminary building ended at the Fairfield Road, and in this area there was a sparse grove of trees. A private lane from the Fairfield Road led to the Shultz home. In 1863, the stone wall on your right did not begin for another 200 yards. It continued a post-and-rail wooden fence that began on the far side of the Shultz home.

About 4:00 p.m. on July 1, General Abner Doubleday's line of the Federal 1st Corps just west of the seminary (approximately along present-day Seminary Ridge Road) stretched from just north of the railroad cut to the Fairfield Road. In order to protect the Federal left flank in this area, Col. William Gamble, commanding the brigade of Buford's cavalry that opened the fighting in the morning, moved his horsemen to this area. When the Confederate brigades of Brig. Gens. James Lane, J. Johnston Pettigrew, and Alfred Scales, together with those of Cols. Abner Perrin and John Brockenbrough (more than 7,000 men) advanced through the fields to the west against the position at the Seminary, Gamble deployed his men here to harass the Southern right flank.

Behind the stone wall running south of the Shultz home, Gamble dismounted and deployed three of his cavalry regiments: the 8th New York, 3rd Indiana, and 12th Illinois. The 8th Illinois Cavalry remained mounted and deployed south of the Fairfield Road. When the Confederates were only a few hundred yards away, the Federal line opened fire. Gamble's dismounted troopers behind the wall, firing into the Confederate right flank with their quick-loading single shot breechloading carbines, drew off most of Lane's Brigade to the south, effectively removing many of those 1,700 infantrymen away from the assault on the seminary line. Maj. Charles Lemmon of the 3rd Indiana Cavalry, who had told a comrade of his premonition of death earlier that morning, was mortally wounded while commanding his men behind the stone wall. The mounted troopers of the 8th Illinois Cavalry fired their carbines before drawing their sabers with a flourish as if they were about to charge into Lane's men.

Concerned about being charged by more than 400 horsemen, some in Lane's Brigade may have begun to form a "hollow square," an infantry tactic designed to receive such a charge and more commonly used during the Napoleonic era. The maneuver called for infantrymen to form into a large square formation, hollow in the center, which allows a mounted cavalry charge to be enveloped on all sides when it pierces the square. Debates continue whether this or any other square was formed on the afternoon of July 1, but evidence exists that one and possibly two "hollow squares" were formed by Confederates against Buford's cavalry (the second in response to another cavalry charge feint from the slope of Cemetery Hill later that evening as the Federals rallied upon the heights south of Gettysburg).

Gamble's defense of the Federal left flank bought some time for the stubborn resistance put up by General Doubleday along Seminary Ridge, but ultimately the superior enemy numbers drove the Federals east and south. The Federal 11th Corps was ultimately routed from its position to the north, and the two Federal corps fled through and around the town. Both Generals Howard and Winfield Scott Hancock — the latter had arrived late in the afternoon to take stock of the battlefield and take command at General Meade's order — rallied the Federal infantry and artillery at Cemetery Hill. Buford's cavalry took up a position south of Cemetery Hill along Cemetery Ridge to protect the developing left flank.

· · · · · · · · · · ·

The fighting on July 1 was a clear Southern victory. The day's fighting ended when Confederate General Ewell decided against attacking the Federals on the hills south and east of Gettysburg. The human cost of July 1, 1863, was enormous. The 11,500-man Federal 1st Corps inflicted about as many casualties on A. P. Hill's Corps as it had suffered — nearly 6,000 in all — in the fighting west of Gettysburg. Ewell's Corps suffered about 600 casualties north of town while inflicting about 3,400 on the Federal 11th Corps. By day's end, the Confederates commanded the western and northern heights, but the battered Federals were entrenching opposite them on Culp's Hill, Cemetery Hill, and Cemetery Ridge.

The dead of both sides lay in heaps on ground that only that morning was peaceful farm fields. The wounded sought medical treatment and some measure of comfort in homes, doorways, and on porches in and around town. Even as darkness fell and the day's fighting ended, men made their way to the battlefield. More Confederate soldiers and artillery poured onto the field, and five more corps of Federal infantry moved on roads leading to Gettysburg. Jeb Stuart, who received word of the Gettysburg battle shortly after midnight that evening, began moving three very exhausted brigades of Confederate cavalry from Carlisle and Dillsburg to Gettysburg. They would not reach the field until the afternoon of the following day.

To continue with the tour of the battlefield of July 2 and 3, reset your odometer to 0.0 and continue on West Confederate Avenue.

(Opposite page) The 111th New York Monument casts an early morning shadow on the Brien barn. (Stanley)

Tour of the Second and Third Day of the Battle of Gettysburg

"Men fired into each other's faces, there were bayonet thrusts, cutting with sabers, hand-to-hand contests, oaths, curses, yells and hurrahs ... but yet they did not waver."

During the evening of July 1 and the morning of July 2, additional units of both armies arrived on the field. On the Confederate side, the divisions of Maj. Gens. John Bell Hood and Lafayette McLaws of Longstreet's First Corps (more than 14,000 men) arrived and eventually took position on the southern end of the line. On the Federal side, the 5,200 men of the 12th Corps under Maj. Gen. Henry Slocum, who had arrived just south of the field late on the afternoon of July 1, were divided to guard the flanks of the Federal line: Brig. Gen. Alpheus Williams' division set up on the right flank on Culp's Hill a little more than a mile to your east, and Brig. Gen. John Geary's division marched to the south in the valley near Little Round Top.

Since the majority of both armies were now on the field, facing each other with only a mile of No Man's Land between them, the stage was set for the two more bloody days to come.

• • • • • • • • • • • • •

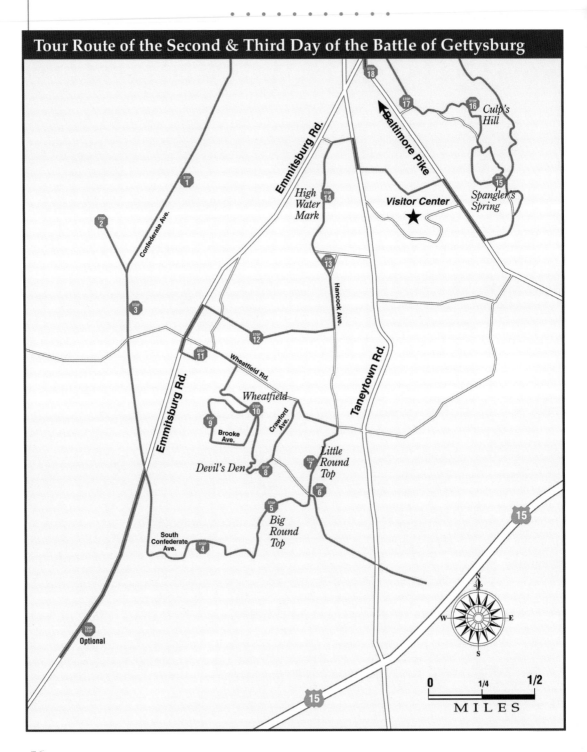

Tour Route of the Second & Third Day of the Battle of Gettysburg

We will now continue with the battlefield tour, which covers the events of both July 2 and 3. This is a continuation of the tour of July 1, the first day of the battle. If you are taking this part of the tour without having first toured the first day's field, simply turn onto West Confederate Avenue from the intersection with the Fairfield Road (Rt. 116) and follow the directions below.

Like the July 1 tour in this book, we will not exactly follow the National Park Service Auto Tour, because we will cover ground and visit many places and actions not seen by most tourists.

Continue along West Confederate Avenue. Please keep in mind that there was no road here at the time of the battle.

Tour Stop 1
The Virginia Memorial and the Confederate Line – Two Assaults on the Federal Center

After driving .1 miles you will see the home known as "Red Patch" on your left. It was built in 1900 by Gen. Charles H. T. Collis, the former colonel of the 114th Pennsylvania Infantry. Collis was not at Gettysburg with his regiment (known as "Collis' Zouaves") because he was recuperating from a wound suffered at Chancellorsville. After the war, however, Collis spent a lot of time on this battlefield (many of his men were killed here) and built this house as a summer home. He enjoyed the home only a short time; he died in 1902 and was buried at the head of the Pennsylvania Section in the Soldiers' National Cemetery.

The Confederate state memorials are sprinkled along West Confederate Avenue, and you will begin seeing them on your left after another .2 miles. The North Carolina State Memorial was sculpted by Gutzon Borglum, the creator of the portraits on Mount Rushmore. Dedicated on July 3, 1929, this memorial was the first placed on the battlefield after the Virginia State Memorial, which we will visit shortly.

Keep in mind as you drive that you are (generally speaking) following the southern half (center and right flank) of the Confederate line of battle. By July 3, the extended exterior line stretched from the ground near Big Round Top to the south along this line through the town all the way to ground northeast of Culp's Hill. If you look in the distance to the southeast, you can see both Little Round Top and Big Round Top.

The North Carolina State Monument appears frozen in time after a Pennsylvania ice storm. (Stanley)

During the evening of July 1 and the morning of July 2, additional units of both armies arrived on the field. On the Confederate side, the divisions of Maj. Gens. John Bell Hood and Lafayette

McLaws of Longstreet's First Corps (more than 14,000 men) arrived and eventually took position on the southern end of the line. On the Federal side, the 5,200 men of the 12th Corps under Maj. Gen. Henry Slocum, who had arrived just south of the field late on the afternoon of July 1, were divided to guard the flanks of the Federal line: Brig. Gen. Alpheus Williams' division set up on the right flank on Culp's Hill a little more than a mile to your east, and Brig. Gen. John Geary's division marched to the south in the valley near Little Round Top.

> *After a total of .6 miles along West Confederate Avenue, you will come to the Virginia Memorial. Stop here. We suggest you walk out in the field in front of the Virginia Memorial to gain a good view of the terrain and positions of both armies on this part of the field. A footpath extends east along the historic wood line and terminates at the spot known as the "Point of Woods" in the area where Lee was said to have met his men retreating from the unsuccessful July 3 assault. You will gain a wider perspective from that point, especially of the southern part of the field. Read the following brief overview of July 2 and 3 as you stand or sit at this site.*

· · · · · · · · · · ·

July 2 – Attack on the Center

The rising sun on July 2 illuminated an expanding battlefield. The dead and dying of both armies were strewn across the farmlands of the first day's field west and north of town. Many wounded had sought refuge in homes, barns, and outbuildings, and many more had been taken into homes in the town. If you were standing on this spot on the morning of July 2, you would have seen and heard a flurry of activity all around you. All along this line on Seminary Ridge, Robert E. Lee's infantrymen were taking position to your left and right. Southern artillery was bumping and rolling into line, and the guns unlimbered and turned their tubes toward the Federal position to the east. You would have seen staff officers and couriers galloping to and fro, taking orders to various unit commanders. Hunched skirmishers were cautiously advancing through the fields of ripe crops, taking shelter behind fences and buildings to examine the position of the enemy.

Across the valley ahead of you is the Federal position, across the front of which runs the Emmitsburg Road. Just as Lee's men were forming on the morning of July 2, Federal commander George Meade was likewise positioning units to take advantage of the terrain along his line. Geary's division was moved from Culp's Hill to the southern part of the line, where elements of the shattered 1st Corps were also stationed. The 11th Corps, also badly beaten on July 1, had taken up position late on the afternoon of July 1 on Cemetery Hill and were now well entrenched there. Maj. Gen. Daniel Sickles and his 3rd Corps, about 13,000 men, were moving to take up a position in the low marshy ground in front and just north of Little Round Top. The 13,500 infantrymen of Maj. Gen. Winfield Scott Hancock's 2nd Corps were spreading out in the center of the Federal line along Cemetery Ridge directly ahead of you. The 5th Corps, consisting of 13,200 men under Maj. Gen. George Sykes, was positioned in reserve near Powers' Hill well behind Hancock's position. By the early afternoon of July 2, all of Meade's army was on the field except for the roughly 15,000 men of Maj. Gen. John Sedgwick's 6th Corps, which arrived later that day.

Before dawn that morning, General Lee had attempted to find the left flank of the Federal army and so glean information about Meade's strength and dispositions. About 4:00 a.m., Lee sent Capt. Samuel Johnston of his staff to secretly make a reconnaissance of the Federal left. A civil engineer before the war, Johnston had joined the 6th Virginia Cavalry in 1861, but his talents brought him a commission in the engineers by August 1862. During the Fredericksburg and Chancellorsville campaigns,

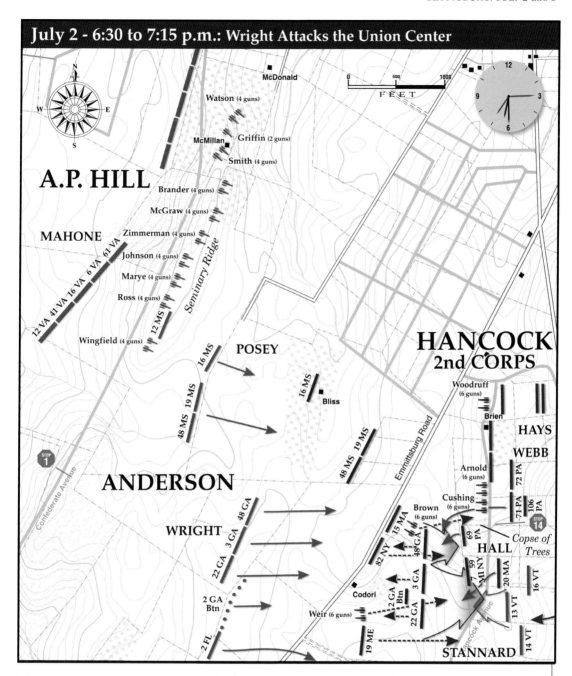

July 2 - 6:30 to 7:15 p.m.: Wright Attacks the Union Center

McDonald

Watson (4 guns)

FEET

0   500   1000

McMillan Griffin (2 guns)

Smith (4 guns)

A.P. HILL

Brander (4 guns)

McGraw (4 guns)

MAHONE Zimmerman (4 guns)

Johnson (4 guns)

Marye (4 guns)

Ross (4 guns)

12 VA 41 VA 16 VA 6 VA 61 VA

12 MS

Seminary Ridge

Wingfield (4 guns)

16 MS

POSEY

16 MS

Bliss

19 MS

48 MS

19 MS

48 MS

HANCOCK
2nd CORPS

Woodruff (6 guns)

Brien

HAYS

WEBB

Arnold (6 guns)

72 PA

ANDERSON

Cushing (6 guns)

Brown (6 guns)

71 PA 106 PA

STOP 14

Emmittsburg Road

48 GA

3 GA

WRIGHT

22 GA

15 MA

82 NY

48 GA

69 PA

HALL

Copse of Trees

7 MI NY

59

20 MA

16 VT

2 GA Btn

Codori

Weir (6 guns)

2 GA Btn

3 GA

22 GA

13 VT

2 FL

19 ME

14 VT

STANNARD

STOP 1

Confederate Avenue

Hancock Avenue

Johnston was praised by his superiors for discovering enemy positions and helping to place troops.

Johnston rode out with a small group in the dark and crossed the Emmitsburg Road. He seems not to have discovered the Federal left, but he did report that the imposing Round Tops were unoccupied. Debates ensue to this day about exactly where Johnston rode and how he got there. Federal troops were moving to the field via the Emmitsburg Road throughout the night, and vedettes from Buford's cavalry were stationed along Cemetery Ridge and stretched quite a distance south. Johnston did report seeing Federal troops in that area in the distance to your right front, but how he successfully rode through them and back again without being discovered remains a mystery.

Johnston reported his findings to Lee some time prior to 8:00 a.m. This information led Lee to believe that the hills south of the Federal position were unoccupied and that the enemy's line terminated somewhere north of them. Based on this information, he began formulating his plan of attack.

Early on the morning of July 2, just south of this spot at the next position, we will examine how a foray by United States Sharpshooters and elements of Buford's cavalry near the southern part of the Confederate line at Pitzer's Woods evolved into a sharp skirmish — the first fighting of the day. The Federals soon withdrew, but not before discovering that Southern troops were stationed at least

that far south — directly in front of the low ground General Sickles had been ordered to occupy with his Federal 3rd corps.

Lee finalized his plan to attack both Federal flanks. Longstreet's First Corps (minus the division of Maj. Gen. George E. Pickett, which was still at Chambersburg) held Lee's right flank. After taking a circuitous route that consumed several hours (a Federal signal station atop Little Round Top spotted the Southern movement) that is often called today "Longstreet's counter-march," the divisions of McLaws and Hood arrived and deployed along Warfield Ridge to the south

A winter glaze coats the trees and monuments near the Copse of trees. On July 2, Brig. Gen. Ambrose Wright's Brigade advanced as far as this area before retiring. (Stanley)

to attack what Lee thought was the vulnerable left flank of Meade's army. Meade's right flank on Culp's Hill to the northeast (where the Federals had spent the better part of the morning building defensive works) was to be attacked by General Ewell and his Second Corps.

Longstreet's attack got underway about 4:00 p.m. We will examine that part of the field when we reach it just ahead. Apparently, Lee hoped that Longstreet's troops would hammer the Federal left, and if not break through completely and roll up the line, at least cause Meade to move large numbers of troops there from other parts of his line. That, in turn, would leave weak spots somewhere that could be exploited by A. P. Hill's Third Corps, which would attack one brigade after another from south to north in an effort to find that weakness and crack through the Federal line. Longstreet's troops struck heavy blows on the southern end of the field in places that would be emblazoned on Gettysburg's historical roll — Devil's Den, the Bloody Wheatfield, and Little Round Top. Sometime just before 6:00 p.m., Hill's attack commenced. From your position and to your right, Hill's troops stepped off toward the distant Federal line.

Let's take a moment to consider the terrain you would see if you were standing here on July 2, 1863. Some historical fence lines have been rebuilt in the fields, but at the time of the battle many more traversed the ground, enclosing various crops, orchards, and cattle. Where Hill's men moved out, some of the fences had been torn down by Federal 1st Corps troops when they crossed these fields on their way to the July 1 fighting on McPherson's Ridge. The Emmitsburg Road, which you can see ahead in the distance at the base of Cemetery Ridge, was a mostly sunken road bordered by a stout rail fence. Beyond the road, you can make out what is today known as the "Copse of Trees," the so-called High Water Mark of the Confederacy where Pickett's Charge of July 3 climaxed. In July 1863, however, the copse consisted of little more than a small group of scrub trees that typically grow along fence lines and rock walls. Unlike today, the group of trees was all but indistinguishable among any other foliage growth along fences and borders.

Maj. Gen. Richard Anderson's Division of Hill's Third Corps began the attack on the Federal center directly ahead of you from the area of your position with the brigades of Col. David Lang and Brig. Gen. Cadmus Wilcox, nearly 2,500 men. These troops assisted some of Longstreet's troops by driving the Federal division of Brig. Gen. Andrew Humphreys of Sickles' 3rd Corps back from the road. However, Anderson's men were unable to get a foothold on Cemetery Ridge.

About 6:30 p.m., Brig. Gen. Ambrose R. Wright and his 1,400 Georgians (also part of Anderson's Division) stepped off toward the area south of the Copse of Trees. When they approached the Emmitsburg Road, they came under devastating artillery fire from Federal guns posted along Cemetery Ridge. The batteries of Lt. T. Fred Brown (located near the Nicholas Codori house you see ahead along the road), Lt. Alonzo Cushing, and Capt. William Arnold (near the Copse of Trees) pounded away and inflicted heavy casualties.

Just behind Wright marched the fragmented brigade of Brig. Gen. Carnot Posey, 1,300 Mississippians of Anderson's Division. The staggered advance captured the home and farm of William Bliss, which was located about halfway across the field to your left front (the farm was burned the following day). Some of the Mississippians continued a few hundred yards beyond the farm, where they opened fired on the Union artillerymen focused on Wright's advance.

As Wright's men hurried their pace to the fence along the Emmitsburg Road, they let out a fierce Rebel Yell. Federals of the 15th Massachusetts and 82nd New York Infantry of Brig. Gen. William Harrow's brigade of the 2nd Corps, about 600 men, answered with a volley of lead that dropped many of the Georgians. One Federal soldier called it "one of the most destructive volleys" he witnessed during the war. Wright's men continued, however, and broke the line of the New Yorkers and Massachusetts men holding the fence line, causing the Federals to literally run to the rear and the stone wall along Cemetery Ridge. Although Lieutenant Brown's gunners worked their tubes feverishly, blasting away at Wright with double canister, they were soon overrun. The Georgians attempted to turn the two captured Napoleons and fire upon the Federals, but Cushing's and Arnold's men pivoted their own guns and hammered the Southerners with canister.

Wright's men continued on, but with little support from Posey's Mississippians, most of whom did not cross the Emmitsburg Road. Virtually alone, Wright's survivors

An early morning fall view of the fields across which Confederates charged on both July 2 and 3. The Round Tops are visible in the distance. (Stanley)

were, as one wrote, "wild with enthusiasm and ardor, [and] on we pressed . . . the ground roared and rumbled like a great storm, and the shower of minie balls was pitiless and merciless." When they approached that part of the wall just south of the Copse of Trees (ahead to the right of the copse from your perspective) held by the 7th Michigan, 59th New York, and 69th Pennsylvania Infantry of Brig. Gen. John Gibbon's brigade of the 2nd Corps, they were met with volley after volley of musketry.

Brig. Gen. Alexander Webb of the Federal 2nd Corps rushed more troops forward from his brigade when the Georgians threatened to overlap the troops at the wall.

When even more Federals converged to the defense from right and left, the outnumbered and outgunned Georgians realized they could not take the position. The 48th Georgia Infantry, which had lost fifty-seven percent of its men and a battle flag, began the long retreat to Seminary Ridge. The 3rd and 22nd Georgia withdrew when the men of the 13th Vermont Infantry of Brig. Gen. George Stannard's brigade of the 1st Corps rushed at them with bayonets fixed.

Wright's Brigade, which had reached this "High Water Mark" before the assault known as Pickett's Charge would try it the following day, suffered shocking casualties. About one-half of his 1,400 men were killed, wounded, or captured. All but one of his regimental commanders had been killed. The 15th Massachusetts and 82nd New York Infantry, which had tried to defend the fence along the Emmitsburg Road, suffered fifty-five percent casualties. Wright later bitterly complained that Posey's Brigade offered no support, and that his men could have held their position and the captured artillery if the Mississippians had done their job.

The assault fizzled out (for reasons difficult to determine) in A.P. Hill's northern sector. The critical wounding of Maj. Gen. Dorsey Pender almost certainly played a role in this. Ewell's men later attacked East Cemetery Hill (and captured it temporarily) and made lodgments on Culp's Hill, but could not drive away the Federal defenders. We will examine these actions in detail later in the tour.

. . . .

July 3 – Pickett's Charge, the Confederate Perspective

An equestrian statue of Robert E. Lee sits majestically atop the Virginia State Memorial after a winter snowstorm. (Stanley)

The view from this point also offers the best Southern perspective of the most famous aspect of the Battle of Gettysburg: Pickett's Charge, or more correctly "The Pickett-Pettigrew-Trimble Charge." (For the sake of brevity, we will use the term Pickett's Charge throughout the text). The Virginia Memorial, designed by Frederick Sievers and dedicated on June 8, 1917, features a lifelike equestrian statue of Robert E. Lee at the top. The memorial also honors the bravery and sacrifice of the typical Virginia soldier. At the base on the front are seven figures that represent the various backgrounds of the men of the Army of Northern Virginia. The soldier on the left, depicted tearing a cartridge to load, was a professional before the war. Next to him, a mechanic holds his rifle with bayonet fixed. A former artist fires his pistol, while a pre-war man of business swings his musket in hand-to-hand combat. The bugler, like the cavalryman, is young — typical of the many teenagers who enlisted to fight for the Confederacy. The farmer represents the most typical avocation of the Southern soldier. Among the feet of

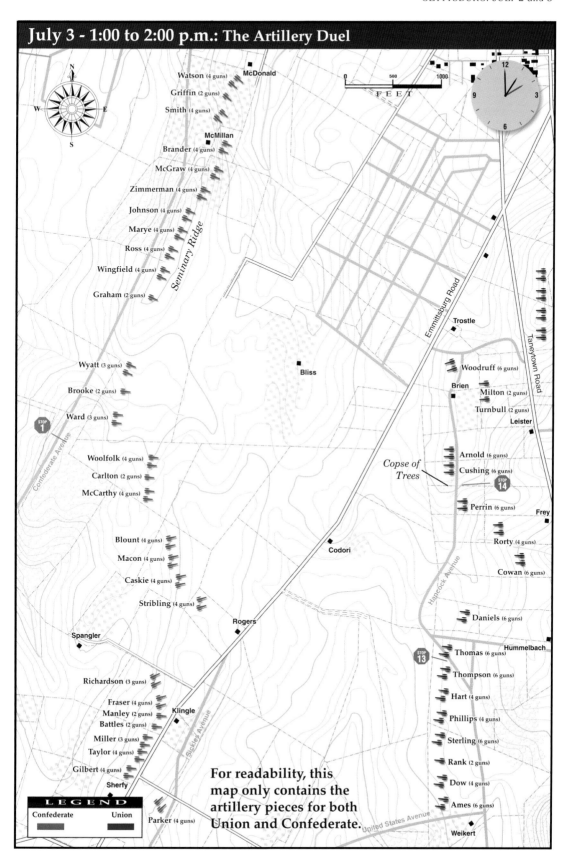

July 3 - 1:00 to 2:00 p.m.: The Artillery Duel

Watson (4 guns) McDonald

Griffin (2 guns)

Smith (4 guns)

McMillan

Brander (4 guns)

McGraw (4 guns)

Zimmerman (4 guns)

Johnson (4 guns)

Marye (4 guns)

Ross (4 guns)

Wingfield (4 guns)

Seminary Ridge

Graham (2 guns)

Wyatt (3 guns)

Brooke (2 guns)

Ward (3 guns)

STOP 1

Confederate Avenue

Woolfolk (4 guns)

Carlton (2 guns)

McCarthy (4 guns)

Blount (4 guns)

Macon (4 guns)

Caskie (4 guns)

Stribling (4 guns)

Rogers

Spangler

Richardson (3 guns)

Fraser (4 guns)

Manley (2 guns) Klingle

Battles (2 guns)

Miller (3 guns)

Sickles Avenue

Taylor (4 guns)

Gilbert (4 guns)

Sherfy

Parker (4 guns)

Bliss

Emmittsburg Road

Trostle

Taneytown Road

Woodruff (6 guns)

Brien

Milton (2 guns)

Turnbull (2 guns)

Leister

Arnold (6 guns)

Copse of Trees

Cushing (6 guns)

STOP 14

Perrin (6 guns)

Frey

Codori

Rorty (4 guns)

Cowan (6 guns)

Hancock Avenue

Daniels (6 guns)

Hummelbach

STOP 13

Thomas (6 guns)

Thompson (6 guns)

Hart (4 guns)

Phillips (4 guns)

Sterling (6 guns)

Rank (2 guns)

Dow (4 guns)

Ames (6 guns)

United States Avenue

Weikert

For readability, this map only contains the artillery pieces for both Union and Confederate.

LEGEND
Confederate	Union

0   500   1000

F E E T

the group can be seen all manner of the debris of battle. Note that Lee's face is turned not only across the ground that witnessed so much carnage and loss of his men, but directly across the field at his counterpart, as represented by Maj. Gen. George Meade's equestrian statue (erected in 1896). If you haven't yet done so, you may wish to walk the footpath that extends east to the "Point of Woods" for a much wider and useful perspective of the field.

Pickett's Charge advanced over this ground, which arguably is the most famous soil associated with the American Civil War. General Longstreet, Lee's "Old War Horse," was put in charge of planning the assault. Three brigades from Maj. Gen. George E. Pickett's recently arrived division under Brig. Gens. James Kemper, Lewis Armistead, and Richard Garnett, just more than 5,000 men, formed in the woods directly to your right. These men were fresh and rested. To the rear of your position, two brigades from Dorsey Pender's Division (now commanded by Maj. Gen. Isaac Trimble because of Pender's mortal wound) formed for action. These brigades under Col. William Lowrance (Brig. Gen. Alfred Scales' Brigade) and Brig. Gen. James Lane, slightly more than 2,000 men, lined up west of where the park road behind you is now. In front of them and to their left, four brigades under Brig. Gen. Johnston Pettigrew (commanding for the wounded Maj. Gen. Henry Heth) lined up inside the tree line: Col. John Brockenbrough's Virginians; Brig. Gen. Joe Davis' Mississippians and North Carolinians; Tennessee and Alabama soldiers under Col. Birkett Fry (commanding for the captured Brig. Gen. James Archer); and Pettigrew's own brigade of North Carolinians under Col. James Marshall. These four brigades fielded about 6,000 men. In all, perhaps as many as 12,000 - 13,000 Southerners were poised to attack. From one end to the other, the line of battle stretched about one mile. Fronting the infantry in a nearly continuous line, Southern artillery along the entire eastern crest of Seminary Ridge trained its muzzles on the Federal line. As many as 150 cannon were ready to fire on Cemetery Ridge before the infantry advanced.

Look across the field to the Federal position atop the crest of Cemetery Ridge. Parts of the 1st and 2nd Corps under Maj. Gens. John Newton and Winfield Scott Hancock, respectively, manned the stone wall. The Southern attack would fall against those troops.

Intermittent skirmish fire broke out between the lines, with a more sustained and determined fight erupting on the grounds of the Bliss farm which stood in the field to your left. Harassing fire by Confederate sharpshooters posted in the buildings caused Federal infantry to advance and put the farm to the torch.

July 1913. A sea of tents, temporary residences of both Union and Confederate veterans, dots the Gettysburg landscape at the 50th Anniversary of the battle. Note the Round tops on the right and the (now gone) Ziegler's Grove tower at rear left. (LOC)

July 3 - 2:00 to 2:30 p.m.: The Assault Begins

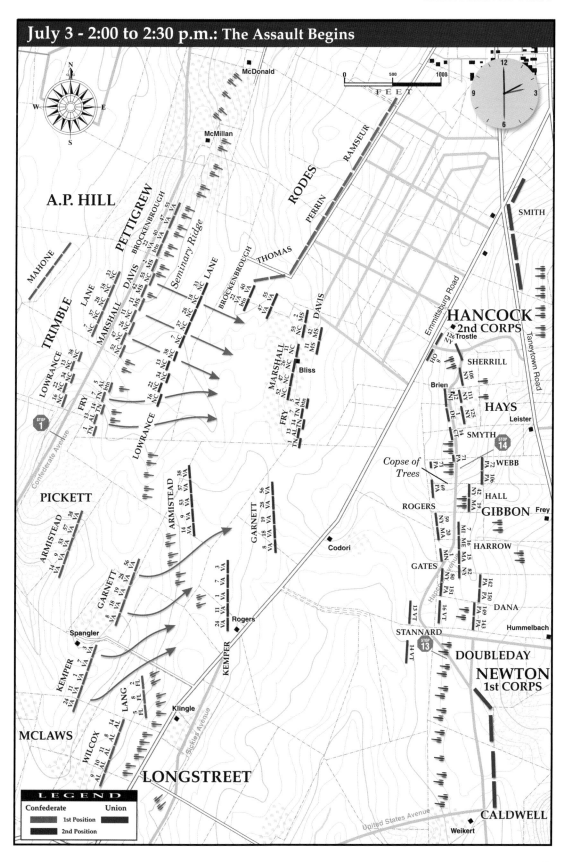

It was about 1:00 p.m. (watches were not synchronized or even on the same time, and estimates vary widely) when a pre-arranged signal cannon opened the Southern artillery barrage. Lee believed that a massive cannonade of the Federal line along the ridge south of the town's cemetery would soften resistance to the coming infantry assault. Once his roughly 150 guns opened up along the line here, and were answered by 115 Federal cannon arrayed on Cemetery Ridge, the noise was nearly overwhelming. Infantry on both sides hugged the ground to avoid the shells and shrapnel. Much of the inferior Confederate ammunition exploded too early, too late, or not at all. Much of it carried long, endangering supplies and even Meade's headquarters to the rear. Northern shells killed and wounded scores of Southerners before they had a chance to rise and begin their march to destiny.

"We waited patiently and wished, though dreaded, for the signal to commence the action, and probably for the order that would seal our fate."

Capt. John T. James, 11th Virginia Infantry during the July 3 artillery duel

About this time, skirmishing began between the cavalry forces of Maj. Gen. Jeb Stuart's Southern riders and Federals of Brig. Gen. David Gregg's cavalry division about four miles east of where you are standing. Gregg's troopers protected the rear of the Federal right flank beyond Culp's Hill. Stuart had moved his cavalry division east and then south in an effort to draw Gregg out. About seven miles to the southwest near the little town of Fairfield (behind Lee's lines), troopers in Maj. Samuel Starr's undersized 6th U.S. Cavalry regiment rode along the Carroll Valley to intercept Confederate wagons believed to be easy targets. Unbeknownst to them, they were riding straight into a fight with Virginia cavalry that would all but destroy their regiment.

Back at Gettysburg, Brig. Gen. Henry Hunt, Meade's Chief of Artillery, rode along the lines of his gunners unlimbered along Cemetery Ridge to help direct their fire. After nearly an hour of dueling (the length of the barrage is hotly debated; participants estimated it as short as fifteen minutes to as long as two hours), Hunt ordered his gunners to stop firing and save their rounds for the enemy infantry sure to follow. The slowing rate of enemy fire convinced Southern artilleryman Col. E. Porter Alexander, to whom General Longstreet tried to shift the responsibility of judging when the infantry should advance, to notify General Pickett that if he was going to attack, he had better do so quickly.

Pickett rode to Longstreet, who had been watching the field from a fence line to your right (south). "General, shall I advance?" Longstreet was not in favor of an attack against the center of the Federal position. In his memoirs, he wrote that he told General Lee that he believed the charge was doomed to failure. When Pickett implored him for the signal to begin, Longstreet was unable to give the command. Instead, he offered a slight nod of his head.

While some Confederate artillery continued shelling the Federal line, Southern commanders ordered their men to prepare to advance. Musicians pounded a beat, and color bearers moved to the front on which to dress the lines. Sergeants and corporals made sure that companies were lined up where they needed to be. Everyone knew the task before them could only be a desperate and bloody one, but many of the men were confident of success — perhaps none more so than Robert E. Lee himself, who had watched his men beat less favorable odds many times before.

On the extreme right, General Kemper dressed his line on Garnett's right flank. Behind Garnett, General Armistead positioned his brigade. Pickett rode along the lines of his men just as they were about to step off. He encouraged them in a loud voice, "Up men, and to your posts! Don't forget today that you are from old Virginia!"

On the Confederate left, Pettigrew's men had a straight line to their target. However, his lines were not entirely organized and the front two brigades advanced ahead of the others, leaving the balance to rush to catch up. Trimble's pair of brigades in the center advanced behind the right side of Pettigrew's men.

As the massive human wave advanced toward Cemetery Ridge, Federal artillery opened up once again. Batteries atop Little Round Top, which you can see in the right-distance, also fired upon the advancing Confederates. When Kemper's Brigade (on the far right) reached the Emmitsburg Road, its commander turned northward to realign his advance in the general direction of the present-day Copse of Trees. This exposed his right flank to a deadly Federal artillery fire. Federal skirmishers posted along and near the Emmitsburg Road also opened on the Southerners. Before long, gaps opened up and down the advancing line. Heads, legs, and arms flew into the air and shells ignited grass and crop fires. The afternoon of July 3 was hazy and humid, with temperatures in the high 80's and hardly a breeze, so the powder smoke hung over the battlefield like a dark cloud. We will continue with the examination of Pickett's Charge when we reach the opposite end of this field.

> *Reset your odometer to 0.0. Continue driving south and after .5 miles turn right onto Berdan Avenue. Continue the short distance to the monuments in a small clearing.*

Tour Stop 2

July 2 - Morning Foray by U.S. Sharpshooters and Buford's Cavalry

Near here in these woods owned by Samuel Pitzer, troopers of Col. Thomas Devin's brigade of Buford's cavalry, with companies of the 1st U.S. Sharpshooters, skirmished with Confederates from A. P. Hill's Third Corps on the morning of July 2. At the close of the fighting the previous day, Buford's two cavalry brigades were posted south of Cemetery Hill to protect the Federal left. When the sun

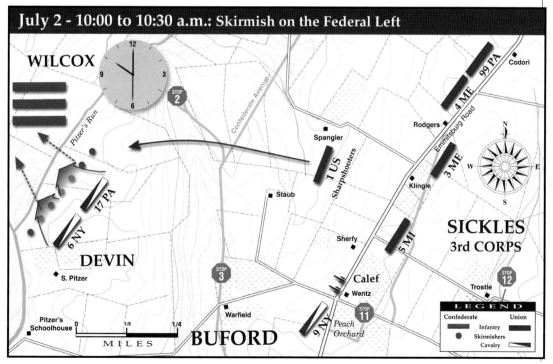

rose shortly after 5:00 a.m. on July 2, Capt. Benjamin Coffin led a company of the 9th New York Cavalry forward into these woods (a narrow strip at the time with open land behind it all the way to Willoughby's Run) and captured a black man, apparently a servant of one of Longstreet's staff officers. The talkative prisoner gave the Federals the first indication that Longstreet's Corps was on the field.

A second patrol of the 9th New York Cavalry, advancing farther south later that morning, saw a large body of Brig. Gen. Cadmus Wilcox's Confederate brigade advancing into position. The New Yorkers skirmished briefly with the Southerners. Col. Hiram Berdan's 1st U.S. Sharpshooters, supported by the 3rd Maine Infantry, advanced into these woods to reconnoiter them on the orders of Brig. Gen. Henry Hunt and Maj. Gen. Daniel Sickles. Devin ordered men of his 6th New York Cavalry to advance and support them. Devin's 17th Pennsylvania cavalrymen were also ordered into the woods and charged Southerners on horseback several times, but were repulsed by superior numbers.

The firefight in this strip of woods revealed that the Southern line extended at least this far south. The news concerned Sickles, who was already worried about his assigned position in the low ground well east of the Emmitsburg Road. Any study of Sickles' later unauthorized and much-debated move forward to the Joseph Sherfy Peach Orchard and along the Emmitsburg Road (discussed later in the tour) must begin at this spot.

On July 3, the right of Pickett's line formed in these woods in preparation for Pickett's Charge.

The monument of the New York companies A, B, D, and H of Berdan's 1st U.S. Sharpshooters was dedicated on July 2, 1889, and that of the Vermont company F on July 15 of the same year. The marker here showing the participation of the 3rd Maine Infantry in this initial fighting of the second day was installed the following October.

> *Return to West Confederate Avenue, turn right, and reset your odometer to 0.0.*
> *After .1 miles, turn right to visit the Longstreet Monument.*

Tour Stop 3
July 2 - Longstreet's Assault

The monument of Lt. Gen. James Longstreet was sculpted by Gary Casteel and dedicated on July 3, 1998. Unlike the other equestrian monuments on the field, this one is at ground level rather than atop a tall pedestal.

> *Return to West Confederate Avenue, turn right, and reset your odometer to 0.0.*

Devin's cavalry and the U.S. Sharpshooters advanced through this area to your right on the morning of July 2, and came in contact with Wilcox's Confederate brigade.

> *After another .1 miles, you will see the state memorials of Louisiana and Mississippi.*

Both are popular examples of interpretive sculpture. The Louisiana State Memorial was dedicated on June 11, 1971, and that of Mississippi on October 19, 1973. The figure atop the Louisiana monument represents the "Spirit of the Confederacy" who soars in triumph over her fallen soldiers. In her right hand is a flaming cannonball, which represents the artillery branch. Many visitors miss completely the Dove of Peace in the reed stalks below her. Reclining on the base of the monument is a figure that represents a fallen gunner of the Washington Artillery of New Orleans, clutching the flag to his heart.

The Mississippi monument is on the spot where the Confederate brigade of Brig. Gen. William Barksdale, Longstreet's Corps, stepped off to begin its July 2 charge. The statues depict

July 2 - Longstreet Attacks the Union Left

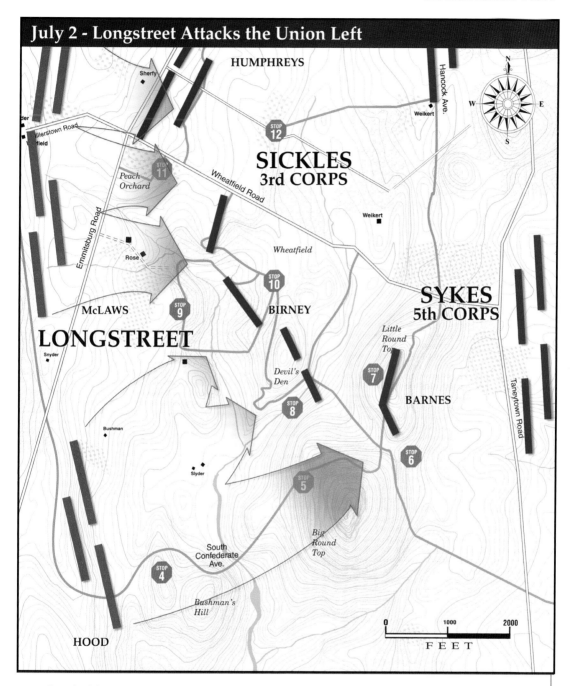

HUMPHREYS

Sherfy

Weikert

STOP 12

SICKLES
3rd CORPS

Peach Orchard

STOP 11

Wheatfield Road

Emmitsburg Road

Rose

Weikert

Wheatfield

STOP 10

SYKES
5th CORPS

McLAWS

STOP 9

BIRNEY

LONGSTREET

Snyder

Little Round Top

STOP 7

Devil's Den

BARNES

STOP 8

Bushman

STOP 6

Slyder

STOP 5

Big Round Top

South Confederate Ave.

STOP 4

Bushman's Hill

Taneytown Road

Hancock Ave.

0   1000   2000

FEET

HOOD

---

two of Barksdale's soldiers during their advance across the farms of Joseph Sherfy and Abraham Trostle, which you can see directly ahead of you across the Emmitsburg Road. The color bearer has fallen, and his comrade is swinging his musket at the enemy to protect the flag.

A wayside here describes the July 2 charge of Barksdale's 1,600-man Mississippi brigade. Barksdale's men were part of Gen. Lafayette McLaws' Division that deployed here to your left and right along the southern tip of Seminary Ridge and onto Warfield Ridge about 3:30 p.m. If you walk up to the wayside, you will have an excellent view of Sherfy's Peach Orchard on the knoll directly ahead of you on the far side of the Emmitsburg Road where Barksdale's men attacked (we will discuss that part of the assault when we visit the Peach Orchard later in the tour). To prepare for Longstreet's assault on the Federal left, McLaws' and Hood's divisions had marched about eighteen miles since sunrise that morning, so they were already exhausted by the time they arrived.

To your right and on the other side of the Millerstown Road ahead, were 2,100 men from Brig. Gen. Joseph Kershaw's Brigade. Behind them were two supporting brigades, Brig. Gen. Paul Semmes' 1,300 men and 1,600 more under Brig. Gen. William Wofford. These last three brigades attacked in the general direction of the George Rose farm on Barksdale's right. Confederate artillery deployed on the ridge in front of the infantry.

The nearly 7,000 men of Maj. Gen. John Bell Hood's Division deployed farther south along Warfield Ridge on Kershaw's right. (We will examine these attacks as we proceed along the tour.) An excellent view of the ground over which Longstreet's assault unfolded can be had from the observation tower you will see ahead.

The "Spirit of the Confederacy" soars over her fallen soldier atop the Louisiana State Memorial. (Stanley)

Continue to the stop sign ahead at the intersection with the Millerstown Road. Go straight, and in .1 miles you will see the upright cannon for Longstreet's headquarters (which some sources put at or near Pitzer's Schoolhouse some 900 yards to the west).

This marker was placed during the winter of 1920-21. The identification of Longstreet's headquarters at the schoolhouse, however, is almost certainly incorrect. No evidence of a fixed headquarters exist for the First Corps commander, and the designation of the school building likely arose from early commercialization rather than documented history. Other than a tent that may have been pitched for the general behind his corps' line, Longstreet's "headquarters" were probably "in the saddle."

On your left is the Warfield Ridge Tower (or the "Longstreet Tower"), which affords an excellent view of the battlefield of July 2. To the east you can easily see, in addition to much of the July 2nd and 3rd days' fields, the Round Tops, the Peach Orchard, Culp's Hill, and the southern half of the Federal line. The farm to the southwest owned by President Dwight D. Eisenhower can also be seen from the tower. Eisenhower purchased the farm in 1951, and today it is a National Historic Site administered by the National Park Service.

As you continue on West Confederate Avenue, in another .2 miles you will have an excellent view of both Big Round Top and Little Round Top on your left.

Continue to the stop sign at the intersection with the Emmitsburg Road (Rt. 15). If you wish to visit South Cavalry Field to examine fighting that took place on the Confederate right flank before and during Pickett's Charge, turn right and reset your odometer to 0.0 (If you wish to continue with the main tour, continue straight on West Confederate Avenue and skip ahead to where we resume the main tour.)

After .7 miles, note the monument of the 6th Pennsylvania Cavalry (known as "Rush's Lancers") along the road to your left. Continue another .4 miles and you will see a small elevated open area with markers to your left. Continue ahead, carefully turn around where safe to do so, and return to the grassy area and carefully park on the right side of the road. (Parking is limited and not easily available here along this busy road, so please exercise extreme caution.)

Walk up to the clearing, and you are now on the part of the field called "South Cavalry Field."

Optional Tour Stop
July 3 - Merritt's Fight on South Cavalry Field

On July 3 the surrounding area (all of which is in private hands except for this clearing and a small strip of land we will visit shortly) witnessed a great deal of skirmishing between Federal cavalry and Confederate infantry before, during, and after Pickett's Charge. The Federal cavalry available here and to the east just off the Federal left flank was considerable — two brigades totaling nearly 3,000 horsemen. In fact, the opportunity to use these cavalry following the repulse of Pickett's Charge has led some modern historians to postulate that a coordinated assault by the troopers and fresh Federal infantry may have been able to exploit a weakness in the Confederate right flank to the northwest.

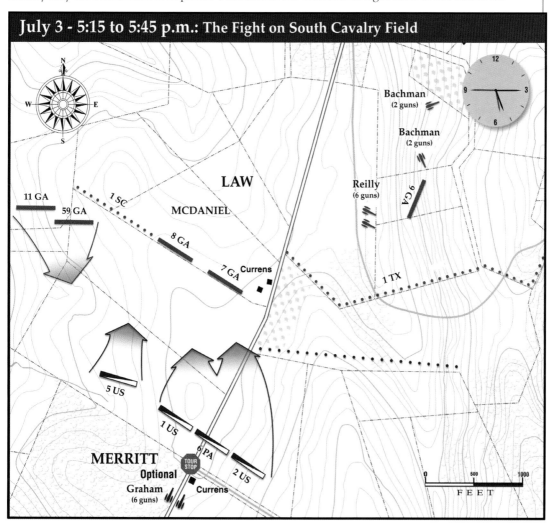

July 3 - 5:15 to 5:45 p.m.: The Fight on South Cavalry Field

One of the brigades, commanded by Brig. Gen. Elon J. Farnsworth of Brig. Gen. Judson Kilpatrick's division, fought over ground farther along West Confederate Avenue (as it becomes South Confederate Avenue) that we will visit later in the tour. (Kilpatrick's other brigade, commanded by Brig. Gen. George A. Custer, fought that afternoon at East Cavalry Field about four miles to the northeast on July 3.)

The other brigade was a veteran group of U.S. Cavalry Regulars in Buford's division commanded by newly promoted Brig. Gen. Wesley Merritt. Merritt, twenty-seven-years-old and an 1860 graduate of West Point, had been elevated to brigadier only a few days before the battle. He was one of three young officers jumped from junior grades to brigadier general — the others being Custer and Farnsworth — nicknamed the "Boy Generals." Merritt's brigade consisted of the 1st, 2nd, 5th, and 6th U.S. Cavalry regiments, plus the 6th Pennsylvania Cavalry, altogether about 1,300 troopers. The 400 cavalrymen of the 6th U.S. Cavalry, however, had been sent to Fairfield eight miles to the southwest on the morning of July 3, so that regiment was not here with the rest of Merritt's brigade.

Merritt's troopers had been performing picket and guard duty in Maryland since June 29, and were in Emmitsburg eight miles to the south on July 2. On the morning of July 3, Cavalry Corps commander Maj. Gen. Alfred Pleasonton ordered Merritt to the Gettysburg battlefield. Face north toward the main battlefield. When Merritt arrived with his four regiments, many of his men dismounted and began advancing through the woods nearly a mile to your left (west) on the other side of the Emmitsburg Road.

Col. John L. Black, commanding a small detail of 100 troopers of the 1st South Carolina Cavalry on the Southern right flank near the Emmitsburg Road, spotted the advancing 6th Pennsylvania Cavalry of about 240 troopers (two companies of the regiment had been detailed to army headquarters). The cannonading preceding Pickett's Charge had not yet begun. Black reported the enemy troopers to Brig. Gen. Evander Law, a brigade commander in Longstreet's First Corps, and formed a dismounted line of battle to confront Merritt's advance. Black's force was augmented with both Confederate artillery and infantry. Two guns from Capt. James Hart's horse battery from South Carolina unlimbered in the Emmitsburg Road about .3 miles north of where you passed the 6th Pennsylvania Cavalry monument. The 340 men of the 9th Georgia Infantry of Brig. Gen. George "Tige" Anderson's Brigade of Hood's Division advanced along the Emmitsburg Road from their position west of Big Round Top and also began skirmishing with Merritt's troopers.

In the early to mid-1900s, South Cavalry Field was easily accessible to the public. (GNMP)

The 6th Pennsylvania Cavalry had difficulty advancing through the fields to your north, but once Capt. William M. Graham's battery of horse artillery began throwing shells at the Confederate skirmishers, the Pennsylvanians were able to move forward. Merritt's other regiments came into the line and began pushing Anderson's infantrymen back toward the Confederate guns. By this time, the cannonading preceding Pickett's Charge to the north had gotten underway.

Hearing that the Federal cavalry advance in this area was heavier than expected, General Law ordered more Georgians of Anderson's Brigade to bolster the line of the 9th Georgia, and sent a section of Capt. James Reilly's battery to unlimber on this side of the Emmitsburg Road to Hart's left rear. Once exposed to converging Southern artillery fire, Merritt's advance slowed, but the Federals were still able to overlap the 9th Georgia's line. That tactical success convinced the Southerners to fall back. The arrival of the 7th and 8th Georgia Infantry, probably fewer than 500 soldiers, forced Merritt to extend his line farther, and the arrival of several hundred more infantry from the 11th and 59th Georgia evened up the opposing lines. The fighting lasted for more than two hours and perhaps nearly as long as three hours; by this time, the Southern infantry attacking in Pickett's Charge on the main battlefield was being beaten back.

Before continuing back along the Emmitsburg Road to the north to a stop seldom seen by battlefield visitors, you may wish to take a moment to examine the markers here.

Note that one of the markers lists the 6th U.S. Cavalry of Merritt's brigade; as previously mentioned, that regiment was not present here on the afternoon of July 3 but was at Fairfield instead. Just prior to 1900, when the War Department was mapping the possible locations of park roads, a route to be called "Cavalry Avenue" was proposed to begin here at the Emmitsburg Road, proceed generally northeast, and terminate at South Confederate Avenue just northeast of Bushman's Hill. The road would have allowed visitors to ride the area of the positions of

In the 1880s William Tipton photographed many of the monuments and markers throughout the battlefield, including this image of the Second U.S. Cavalry marker on South Cavalry Field. (GNMP)

Merritt's and Kilpatrick's cavalry on July 3. It never came to fruition, but in this small clearing you may be able to distinguish the trace of the old lane that passed in that direction.

Reset your odometer to 0.0 and continue north on the Emmitsburg Road.
After a little more than .1 miles you will see a narrow grassy lane on the left side of the road that continues west. Carefully park on the right side of the road. Be mindful of traffic and exercise extreme caution.

This lane is on ground through which Merritt's cavalry advanced and skirmished with Anderson's Brigade and Black's South Carolina cavalry. Walk the short distance back to the markers for the 1st and 2nd U.S. Cavalry and the 6th Pennsylvania Cavalry. With his sizable infantry force, General Law counterattacked over the ground to the north on this side of the Emmitsburg Road, threatening to overlap Merritt's left flank (held by the 5th U.S. Cavalry) near the far end of this lane. Law claimed to have doubled Merritt's line back upon itself to the road, but the cavalrymen had already begun to retreat. Law halted his advance and Merritt reorganized his troops in this area. "Everyone fought like a tiger," claimed a member of the 1st U.S. Cavalry, but each side recognized that little was to be gained by pressing an attack. Both Law and Merritt held their ground until after dark.

Depending on the amount of foliage, you may be able to see the Eisenhower Farm and the open ground directly to the north, ground that would have been directly behind Lee's right flank and center on the afternoon of July 3. General Farnsworth's brigade, which fought against the Confederate line next to Merritt northeast of this position, was not coordinated in its efforts with any other

Federal unit, Merritt's brigade in particular. Following the repulse of Pickett's Charge, Federal army commander Maj. Gen. George Meade could have sent a force of fresh regiments from Maj. Gen. John Sedgwick's 6th Corps and these 3,000 cavalrymen on a foray behind Lee's right flank to capitalize on the large-scale infantry repulse. "Kilpatrick's mistake was in not putting Farnsworth in on Merritt's left," Confederate General Longstreet wrote in his memoirs, "where he would have had an open ride, and made more trouble than was ever made by a cavalry brigade. Had the ride been followed by prompt advance of the enemy's infantry in our line beyond our right and pushed with vigor, they could have reached our line of retreat."

Whether such a counterattack could have significantly damaged Lee's line or interfered with the Confederate army's successful retreat will never be known.

To resume the main tour, continue north on the Emmitsburg Road, return to the intersection with West Confederate Avenue, turn right, and reset your odometer to 0.0.

The Michael Bushman farm, with fall colors in full glory on Big Round Top in the distance. (Stanley)

On your left as you proceed is an excellent view of the Michael Bushman farm as well as the John Slyder farm just beyond it. Further to the north is George Rose's farm (which we will visit later in the tour). Slyder's property, which was being farmed by a tenant in July 1863, will be visited shortly.

After .3 miles the Alabama State Memorial is on your right. This monument stands at approximately the center of the formation of Brig. Gen. Evander Law's Brigade prior to Longstreet's assault of July 2. To your left is an open view of the Slyder farm.

The central figure on the Alabama State Memorial, dedicated on November 12, 1933 and sculpted by Joseph W. Urner, represents the spirit of the state. She comforts the figure on the left, which represents "Spirit," and has been wounded in battle. At the same time, she urges on "Determination," the figure on the right. Note the ammunition box that is being passed from one to the other, a metaphor demonstrating that the fight must continue.

After another .1 miles there is a wayside on the left describing Longstreet's Assault of July 2. Here the park road becomes South Confederate Avenue. Reset your odometer to 0.0 at this point and continue.
After .3 miles, note the large boulder on the right side of the road and the path beside it that leads up the slope of this hill southwest of Big Round Top, called Bushman's Hill.

Tour Stop 4
July 3 - Farnsworth's Charge

From near the top of this hill, Brig. Gen. Judson Kilpatrick, commander of the Federal 3rd Cavalry Division of 3,300 troopers, launched an attack with one of his brigades against the Confederate right following the repulse of Pickett's Charge.

To walk the path that leads to monuments and markers of Kilpatrick's division and the point where Farnsworth's Charge originated, park your vehicle on the right side of the park road here. About 120 feet along the path is a War Department marker for Kilpatrick's division on the left side. Behind this marker is a path that will lead you to the monument of the 18th Pennsylvania Cavalry about 200 feet farther up the slope.

On Pennsylvania Day, September 11, 1889, veterans of the 18th Pennsylvania Cavalry of Farnsworth's brigade dedicated this monument to mark the ground through which they advanced against Confederate skirmishers. Keep this location in mind, then return to the Kilpatrick divisional marker and continue back along the main path.

The walk to the summit of Bushman's Hill will take about ten minutes. As you walk, take note of the large boulders scattered to your left and right, and keep in mind that this hill was not nearly as densely wooded in 1863 as it is now. Follow the main path until you reach the top of the hill, where you will see the monument of the 5th New York Cavalry on a large boulder. Nearby is the War Department marker for Lt. Samuel S. Elder's Battery E, 4th U.S. Artillery, which was attached to Kilpatrick's division.

Kilpatrick's division consisted of the brigades of Brig. Gens. George A. Custer and Elon J. Farnsworth. Following the fight at Hunterstown about four miles northeast of Gettysburg on the evening of July 2, against the Confederate cavalry brigade of Brig. Gen. Wade Hampton, Kilpatrick's brigades camped near Two Taverns a few miles south of Gettysburg. Like Merritt, Kilpatrick was ordered to the battlefield on the morning of July 3. Farnsworth's brigade departed first and passed behind much of the Federal line to march toward the left flank.

When Custer's brigade reached the area behind the right flank to follow Farnsworth, Brig. Gen. David Gregg, commanding the Federal 2nd Cavalry Division, asked Custer and his men to stay there. Gregg had spotted Jeb Stuart's Confederate cavalry advancing upon that flank and needed Custer's support to protect the vulnerable area. (Custer and his troopers won fame that afternoon in the fight at East Cavalry Field.) As a consequence, Kilpatrick was without Custer's brigade here on the Federal left flank.

As Pickett's Charge reached its height opposite the Federal center, Kilpatrick concluded that an assault from his position atop Bushman's Hill against the Confederate right flank in his front could successfully roll up the Southern line upon its center. Skirmishers of the 1st Texas and 47th Alabama Infantry were posted in an east-west line that generally follows a portion of today's South Confederate Avenue. Beyond them, Kilpatrick saw what appeared to be vulnerable Confederate artillery posted just south of the Michael Bushman farm.

From his line here that faced north, Kilpatrick ordered the 390 troopers of the 1st West Virginia Cavalry, commanded by Col. Nathaniel Richmond, to assault the 1st Texas skirmish line in the valley below. The West Virginians began at a trot and increased their pace as they negotiated the large boulders on the slope. When they reached the bottom, a stout rail fence in front of much of the Confederate skirmish line brought the horsemen to a stop. While the Texans fired on them, some cavalrymen

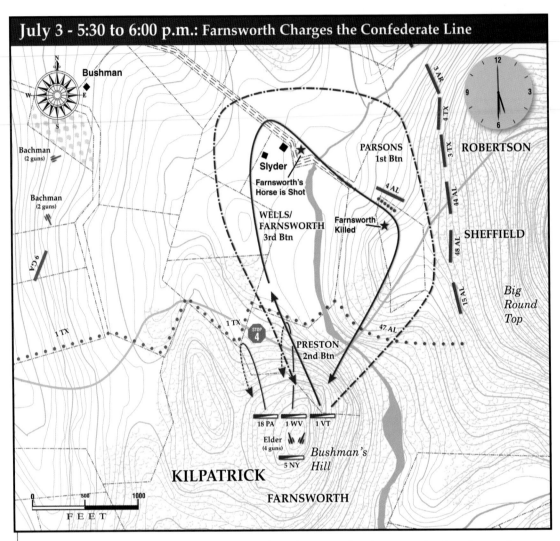

July 3 - 5:30 to 6:00 p.m.: Farnsworth Charges the Confederate Line

slashed at the rails with their sabers while others dismounted and attempted to knock over the posts. Once enough holes were made in the fence, the West Virginians galloped toward the Confederates. One of the Southerners remembered that "the ground trembled as they came, they rode down our skirmishers and charged us, and in a few seconds were [up]on us."

The Texas skirmishers fired into the cavalrymen while guns from Reilly's Confederate artillery posted near Warfield Ridge to the west opened on them. The cavalrymen then hit the line of Texans posted behind a large stone wall. With no time to reload, many Texans swung their muskets like clubs and knocked several cavalrymen out of their saddles, triggering a hand-to-hand combat with the troopers using their pistols and sabers. One Southerner thought the West Virginians to be in "a state of intoxication." Soldiers of the 9th Georgia Infantry, posted near the Emmitsburg Road, also fired into the Federals. Realizing that he had ridden into a maelstrom and nearly surrounded by the enemy, Col. Richmond ordered his men to retreat toward Bushman's Hill.

The 18th Pennsylvania Cavalry on the left of Kilpatrick's line had not yet moved out. "Why in hell and damnation don't you move those troops out?" Kilpatrick barked at their commander, Lt. Col. William Penn Brinton. At Brinton's order, his more than 400 Pennsylvanians trotted down the slope, flanked by squadrons of Maj. John Hammond's 5th New York Cavalry on either side (the balance of the 5th New York supported the Federal artillery battery of Lt. Samuel S. Elder posted here on the summit). The Pennsylvanians, however, suffered the same fate as their West Virginia comrades and fell back in confusion.

Brig. Gen. Evander Law, who had been shifting troops to deal with Merritt's threats along the Emmitsburg Road to the west, grew increasingly worried about the aggressiveness of the Federal cavalry in this area. The 300 men of the 4th Alabama Infantry were marched from their position at the western base of Big Round Top toward the Slyder Farm to face south. The balance of his brigade — the 44th, 48th, and 47th Alabama (facing east to Big Round Top) — was turned around and moved slightly forward to face west across the Plum Run Valley. With the 1st Texas Infantry and Capt. William Bachmann's guns (plus perhaps a section of Reilly's) facing east on the other side of the valley, any of Kilpatrick's forces that advanced would find themselves nearly surrounded.

Kilpatrick probably wished that the 600 men of the 1st Vermont Cavalry had attacked sooner, but now the young commander, known to many of his men as "Kill-Cavalry" due to his penchant for costly mounted charges, ordered the Green Mountain troopers to advance. According to many accounts, Farnsworth and several other subordinates initially protested, citing the rugged terrain and the double repulse of the West Virginians and Pennsylvanians. (Recall how the ground looked as you walked up the slope, and examine the boulders and uneven ground that surrounds you.) Ultimately, Farnsworth decided to personally lead the mounted charge of the 1st Vermont Cavalry.

To examine the ground over which the 1st Vermont collided with the Confederates, walk back down the path to return to your vehicle.

Reset your odometer to 0.0 and continue on South Confederate Avenue. After .2 miles you will see waysides describing Farnsworth's Charge on the left side of the road.

At the 1st Vermont Cavalry's position atop Bushman's Hill behind you, the regiment divided into three battalions for the charge. Four companies were in each battalion. Lt. Col. Addison Preston, commanding the regiment, led one battalion with Maj. William Wells and Capt. Henry Parsons leading the other two. Preston's battalion was dismounted, however, and supported the charge of the other two by deploying behind a stone wall at the base of Bushman's Hill.

On the right of the attacking column (about .2 miles farther down South Confederate Avenue), Parsons' charging battalion aimed for the Slyder farm, which you can see in the distance beyond the waysides. They quickly came under fire from the recently arrived 4th Alabama Infantry. Wells' battalion charged through the area where you are standing and came under not only infantry fire but shells flying from Bachmann's artillery posted near Warfield Ridge to your left front (as you face the waysides).

> *"General, if you order the charge I will lead it, but you must take the awful responsibility."*
>
> **Brig. Gen. Elon Farnsworth to cavalry commander Brig. Gen. Judson Kilpatrick, objecting to the order to make the charge**

A wounded Parsons went down, and the rest of his battalion began to break formation under the heavy Alabama fire. The troopers turned west but, seeing the heavy Confederate forces near Devil's Den to the north, continued turning west and then south. Soon, they too were running the gauntlet of Confederate artillery. General Law, standing and watching from near Bachmann's guns, later stated that the Federals rode "in gallant style."

Farnsworth's horse was shot, but he was given a replacement and continued riding with Wells' battalion. Due to the rocky ground, fences, and Confederate infantry and artillery fire, Wells' bat-

A bas-relief depicting Farnsworth's charge (Farnsworth is shown falling backward) on the face of the Brig. Gen. William Wells monument. (Stanley)

talion lost cohesion. Soon small groups of mounted cavalrymen, like Parsons' men to the east, tried to gallop and cut their way out back to Bushman Hill.

Continue on South Confederate Avenue. About 300 feet ahead is the statue monument of Brig. Gen. William Wells of the 1st Vt. Cavalry on the right.

Through this area, Wells' battalion charged northwest toward the Slyder farm. A major at the time of the battle, Wells would rise to brigadier general by war's end. For his bravery during Farnsworth's Charge, Wells was awarded the Medal of Honor in 1891. J. Otto Schweizer sculpted the statue, dedicated on July 3, 1913, the fiftieth anniversary of the battle. Note the bas relief in the boulder on the front depicting Wells' battalion during the charge. Many of the figures, including General Farnsworth in the lead, were modeled after actual members.

After another .2 miles the "D-shaped" field of the Slyder Farm, which contains the monument of the 1st Vermont Cavalry, is visible on the left. To visit the monument of the 1st Vermont Cavalry at the high point of the field, park your vehicle on the right side of the road.

Farnsworth and his small mounted group burst over the stone wall behind the monument. From the opposite end of this field, infantrymen of the 15th Alabama commanded by Col. William Oates fired on them. Both Farnsworth and his horse were shot. By the time the twenty-five-year-old brigadier crashed to the ground in the vicinity of the monument, he had been struck by five bullets. He refused to surrender but died soon after.

Farnsworth's troops charged across the Slyder farm on July 3. This photo of the Slyder house was taken in 1935. (LOC)

Besides losing their brigade commander, the 1st Vermont Cavalry suffered heavily among its ranks. By the time the remnants of the regiment made it back to safety, sixteen had been killed or mortally wounded, more than a dozen otherwise wounded, and thirty-five were missing. General Kilpatrick's attempt at glory on the Federal left proved a bloody failure. On October 9, 1889, surviving members of the 1st Vermont came to this spot to dedicate their monument near where Farnsworth went down. The mention of his death on the monument is the only memorial on the battlefield to the sole Federal brigadier general killed behind Confederate lines while making a charge.

From the 1st Vermont Cavalry monument, you may also easily walk the short distance to the buildings of the Slyder farm. A path leading to the farm begins on the west side of the monument. As you stand near the stone home, you have a good view of the very rocky and undulating terrain over which Kilpatrick's cavalry charged.

> *Return to your vehicle and reset your odometer to 0.0.*
>   *After .2 miles you will come to the parking area on the left side of the road for the Big Round Top self-guided walking tour.*

Tour Stop 5
Big Round Top

> *Walking the path that leads to the summit of this large hill is only for those in good physical condition. The summit is 246 feet above the valley below.*

During Longstreet's assault of July 2, two Alabama regiments from General Law's brigade under the command of Col. William Oates briefly occupied Big Round Top. It was from that point that the initial attacks against the left flank of the Federal 5th Corps line on Little Round Top were launched. That evening, the Alabamians were forced down into the valley to the west by elements of the Federal 5th and 6th Corps who took position on the hill.

Keep in mind that no road existed through this area in 1863, but several rough trails used by the property owners to move timber traversed the area. The hill was thickly wooded at the time of the battle, similar to the condition today. Any attempts to post artillery on the hill by either side would have been a nearly impossible task and its effectiveness would have been very limited.

Should you walk the trail, you will find several monuments at the top. Notable among them is a monument of the 20th Maine Infantry, showing the regiment's position on the evening of July 2 and throughout July 3 following its famous fight on the southern spur of Little Round Top. The monument was dedicated on October 3, 1889, about three years after the regiment's more well-known Little Round Top monument was placed. As you walk the trail and approach the summit, take note of the stone walls built by the Federals for defense on July 2 and 3.

A tall iron observation tower erected by the War Department stood on the summit of Big Round Top, affording visitors an impressive view of the battlefield and miles of the surrounding land. Following World War II, the tower was dismantled for safety reasons.

> *After another .2 miles, take the first right onto Wright Avenue and park immediately to the left in the parking area.*

Tour Stop 6
July 2 - Fight of the 20th Maine Infantry on Vincent's Spur of Little Round Top

The most popular Little Round Top spot to visit, second only to the western summit of the hill itself, is this southern spur where Col. Joshua Chamberlain's 20th Maine Infantry fought off several attacks by the 15th and 47th Alabama Infantry of General Evander Law's brigade.

During Longstreet's assault of July 2, Col. William Oates, commanding the 15th Alabama, was attracted by the heights of Big Round Top to your rear. General Law's orders to the contrary, Oates scaled the hill with his regiment, and the 47th Alabama followed. Just a short time before, men of the 2nd U.S. Sharpshooters, who had conducted a delaying action by firing and falling back as Longstreet's assault pushed northeastward, had also scaled the hill, divided into two parties, and took up position on the southern and eastern slopes. The sharpshooters, attached to Brig. Gen. Hobart Ward's brigade of Sickles' 3rd Corps, were initially on the skirmish line west of Devil's Den.

In his final charge against Joshua Chamberlain's men, Confederate Col. William Oates claimed he made it as far as the boulder (lower left), which was behind the 20th Maine's position. (Stanley)

The small monument ahead of you on the slope is that of the 20th Maine Infantry, Col. Strong Vincent's brigade, Federal 5th Corps. Face north toward the monument. Over the ground to your left, men from the 4th and 5th Texas and 4th Alabama Infantry, nearly 1,200 soldiers from Maj. Gen. John Bell Hood's Division, Longstreet's Corps, assaulted the western face of Little Round Top. Defending the hill were Federal 5th Corps regiments of Col. Strong Vincent's brigade, about 950 men of the 16th Michigan, 44th New York, and 83rd Pennsylvania Infantry. Ahead of you, on this southern outcropping now called "Vincent's Spur," about 360 men of the 20th Maine Infantry held the extreme right of the line. The opposing sides during this attack were nearly evenly matched, but the Federals had the advantage of the high ground and fighting on the defensive.

The large boulders leading up the slope of the hill in all directions (many were destroyed to build the park roads in this area) quickly ruined the formations of the Southern regiments. "The huge rocks forming defiles through which not more than 3 or 4 men could pass abreast . . . [broke] up our alignment," admitted Lt. Col. King Bryan of the 5th Texas Infantry. It was tough going for the Texans and Alabamians, who made several unsuccessful attempts to dislodge the Federals.

The 15th Alabama and part of the 47th Alabama Infantry, perhaps as many as 600 men combined, attacked down the slope of Big Round Top behind you and through your position in an effort to reach the 20th Maine's line. A volley from Col. Chamberlain's men blunted the assault. Recognizing the vulnerability of his left flank, Chamberlain extended his line, then "refused" two of his companies by pulling them back in an open "V" formation. The monument of the 20th Maine marks the position where the regimental colors were planted, and the point of the "V" from which the left of the line was refused. Earlier, Chamberlain had sent the men of Company B of his regiment to the left behind a stone wall in the saddle between the two Round Tops. Unknown to Oates' men, those Federals had joined with the U.S. Sharpshooters (who had snuck to the stone wall as they

> ## *"When the signal was given, we ran like a herd of wild cattle."*
>
> **Col. William C. Oats, 15th Alabama recounting how his regiment withdrew from Little Round Top**

shadowed Oates' advance down the slope of Big Round Top) and were hidden directly on the right flank of the Alabamians.

Chamberlain's men fought desperately while holding off the attacks by superior numbers. Repulsed in his fourth attempt, Colonel Oates began a steady withdrawal of his men. Chamberlain ordered his men to place their bayonets on their rifles, and before he could order a charge his men were rushing down the slope directly toward your position. The men of Company B and the Sharpshooters began firing into the retreating Alabamians, who were now assaulted from two directions. Dozens of Oates' men were captured, while the rest retreated back up Big Round Top and through the valley to the west. The southern slope of Little Round Top was secure.

The monument of the 20th Maine was dedicated in June 1886. Look at the ground east of the monument (to the right as you face it). The dirt road that heads north was not here at the time of the battle — the spur continued its gentle slope in that direction. The roadbed is all that remains of Chamberlain Avenue, which has greatly altered the terrain of Vincent's spur. Along what was higher ground before the road was graded here, Chamberlain refused the companies on his left to meet the Southern assault over this ground. About sixty yards along the avenue, a portrait statue of Chamberlain was to have been erected on a large boulder on the right side (the boulder can still be seen today); Chamberlain, however, refused the honor.

The left flank marker of the 20th Maine denotes the end of the Union line on July 2, shown here surrounded by the beauty of a fall day in Gettysburg. (Stanley)

To the east, a short walk along a footpath leads to a small stone marker signifying the position behind a stone wall taken up by the men of Company B, 20th Maine, along with some of the 2nd U.S. Sharpshooters. It was from this point that these Federals fired into the right-rear of Oates' men as they retreated. Law's Brigade suffered about 500 total casualties during the battle, a loss of more than twenty-five percent.

If you wish to examine seldom-visited monuments of Maj. Gen. John Sedgwick's Federal 6th Corps, exit the parking area, reset your odometer to 0.0, and continue east on Wright Avenue; otherwise continue with the main tour. After .3 miles you will see a War Department marker for Col. Lewis A. Grant's 2nd Brigade, 2nd Division, 6th Corps.

Continue to the stop sign at the intersection with the Taneytown Road. Continue straight ahead to remain on Wright Avenue.

There is a row of 6th Corps monuments on the left side of the road. Much of Sedgwick's Corps was kept in reserve during the battle.

To return to the tour after visiting the final monument, carefully turn your vehicle around and proceed back to the Taneytown Road intersection. Continue straight ahead until you reach the stop sign, and you have returned to the area of Vincent's Spur. Turn right onto Sykes Avenue and reset your odometer to 0.0.

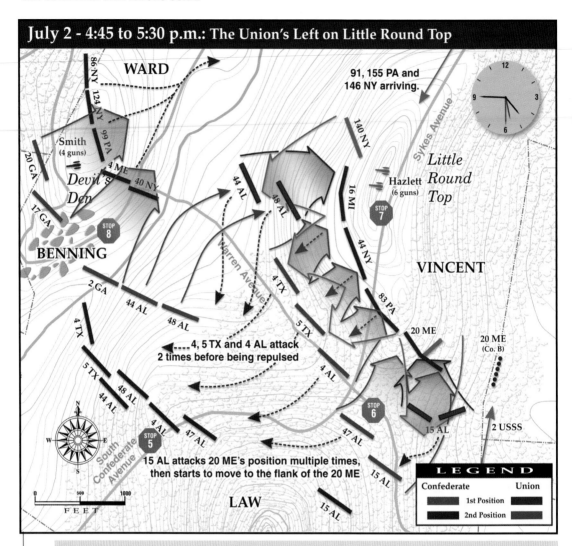

July 2 - 4:45 to 5:30 p.m.: The Union's Left on Little Round Top

To continue with the main tour, proceed to the stop sign. Turn right onto Sykes Avenue and reset your odometer to 0.0.

On your left you will soon see the monument of the 83rd Pennsylvania Infantry, Vincent's brigade, Federal 5th Corps. Dedicated on September 12, 1889, the monument features a statue of Vincent on the top. Although memorials to individual commanders were not permitted on Pennsylvania unit monuments at the time, the veterans of the regiment skirted the restriction by not specifically identifying the statue as that of Vincent. The statue may mark the general location where the mortally wounded Vincent was carried by his men before being taken farther to the rear. Note that a small stone marker just beyond the monument, placed in 1878 (the current marker is an exact replica of the broken original placed in 1978) was intended to mark the site of his wounding, but is more likely the spot to which Vincent had been carried by his men after being wounded further up the slope to the north.

After .2 miles you will reach the summit of Little Round Top.

Tour Stop 7

July 2 - Desperate Battle for the Heights of Little Round Top

Remember that no road was here at the time of the battle. There are several walkways that you may use to walk up to the summit, which affords one of the most famous and popular views of all Civil War battlefields. At the time of the battle, Ephraim Hanaway owned about thirty acres of the western face, while Jacob Weikert owned the land along the eastern slope.

From the summit you can see many landmarks of the battlefield. Beginning to the south (left), Big Round Top looms over its smaller sister hill. Next in the distance are the huge boulders of Devil's Den at the southern part of Houck's Ridge (named after local landowner John Houck). To the right front, landmarks in the center of the battlefield can be seen, such as the Codori farm near the center of the field over which Confederate infantry during Pickett's Charge advanced. To the right, the Federal line along Cemetery Ridge and many of its monuments are visible, such as the large Pennsylvania State Memorial. Look west toward the horizon. If the day is clear, you should easily be able to see the South Mountain range about ten to twelve miles distant (on average). In the valley just below you is the meandering Plum Run creek, which may be visible depending upon the growth of ground cover.

> "A handful of men can't drive those Yankees from that place ..."
>
> **Lt. Robert Coles, 4th Alabama Infantry describing the Federal position atop Little Round Top**

Walk to the area of the large monument of the 91st Pennsylvania Infantry where you have a clear view of the ground ahead and below.

In July 1863, this western face of the hill was mostly clear of timber, much of it having been removed sometime prior to the battle. Just as it is today, most of the area behind you was densely wooded in 1863.

Late on the afternoon of July 2, Longstreet's assault rolled in this direction from Warfield Ridge in the distance to your left and passed through the farmlands between. Contrary to orders, Maj. Gen. Daniel Sickles shrugged off the low ground he was assigned and advanced his Federal 3rd Corps toward the Emmitsburg

This 1863 photograph shows the obstacles over which the Confederates of Law's Brigade struggled in order to attack the Federal position. (LOC)

Road, leaving Little Round Top undefended except for a Federal Signal Corps station manned by only a small party. Just to the west of the John Slyder farm that you visited earlier, the 2nd U.S. Sharpshooters tenaciously slowed the Confederate advance toward Devil's Den and Little Round Top. Five Confederate regiments, nearly 2,000 men, advanced toward your position while Southerners were attacking Federal infantry and artillery at Devil's Den and Houck's Ridge. Maj. Gen. Gouverneur K. Warren, the talented Chief Engineer of the Army of the Potomac, recognized the importance of this hill to the rest of the Union line. Warren sent for help from Maj. Gen. George Sykes' 5th Corps. Col. Strong Vincent voluntarily led his brigade from its position northwest of Little Round Top up the slope, using an old logging road on the north side to do so.

The Gouverneur Warren statue surveys the morning mist hanging low in Plum Run valley below the summit of Little Round Top. (Stanley)

Vincent deployed his regiments here, with the 20th Maine on the left at the spur you visited earlier. On its right was the 83rd Pennsylvania and the 16th Michigan, with the 44th New York holding the right flank. The Confederates made several attacks up the rocky slope directly in front of you. During an attack that threatened to pierce his line near the right, Vincent jumped atop a large boulder (possibly one just north of the monument of the 44th New York Infantry to your left which resembles a castle) and yelled to his men, "Don't give an inch, boys, don't give an inch!" A Confederate bullet slammed into his groin, inflicting a mortal wound.

To bolster Vincent's line, General Warren rushed more troops onto the hill. Finding Col. Patrick O'Rorke with his 140th New York Infantry to the north, Warren hollered, "Paddy, give me a regiment!" Warren took responsibility for the movement, and O'Rorke rushed his 450 men, dressed in colorful

Zouave uniforms, to the top. Two companies deployed on the right flank near your position and immediately engaged the 48th Alabama and 4th Texas Infantry advancing up the slope just a handful of yards away. The rest of the 140th New York joined their comrades while the rest of their brigade, commanded by Brig. Gen. Stephen Weed, hustled up the slope to join in the fight. Like Vincent, O'Rorke mounted a boulder near the regiment's colors and was also felled by a Confederate bullet.

While Vincent's and Weed's brigades fought to hold the hill, Lt. Charles Hazlett and his gunners of Battery D, 5th U.S. Artillery, manhandled their guns up the slope from the northeast. The terrain was too rocky for the battery's horses to maneuver, so the men (with assistance from Weed's infantrymen) grabbed the guns and pushed and pulled them to the top, bringing them into position behind Weed's line. The muzzles could not be depressed enough to fire directly on the Confederates near the summit,

> *"I would rather die on this spot than see those rascals gain one inch of ground."*
>
> **Brig. Gen. Stephen Weed's final words after his wounding on Little Round Top**

but Hazlett was able to send shells into the Southerners farther back in the valley. The psychological effect on both sides was not lost on the desperate Federals. "No military music ever sounded sweeter," mused a member of the 44th New York Infantry.

While Colonel Chamberlain's 20th Maine Infantry fought on the left, the Federals here on the western slope held off the strong assaults delivered by the Alabamians and Texans. Attacks by the 4th Texas Infantry lost momentum when their commander, Lt. Col. Benjamin F. Carter, was badly wounded. A bullet likewise brought down General Weed near Hazlett's cannon, severing his spine. When Lieutenant Hazlett leaned over Weed to comfort him, a bullet slammed into Hazlett's head, killing him instantly.

Unable to break the Federal resistance, the Confederates ended their direct attacks on Little Round Top and withdrew toward Big Round Top, Devil's Den, and the valley beyond. Confederate riflemen posted among the boulders of Devil's Den continued to fire at Federal troops here through-

This 1909 panoramic view of the Gettysburg battlefield from the summit of Little Round Top offers a perspective of the terrain that until recently could not be seen. (LOC)

out the evening and much of the following day.

There are many monuments, markers, and waysides to visit on Little Round Top. The most famous monument is the bronze statue of Maj. Gen. Gouverneur K. Warren — who is often referred to as "The Savior of Little Round Top" — on a large boulder to your right. Dedicated on August 8, 1888, the Warren statue is the only major monument at Gettysburg that was completely funded by private contributions. Following Warren's death in 1882, veterans of his first command early in the war, the 5th New York Infantry, spearheaded a successful private appeal for $5,000 to erect the statue. Karl Gerhardt sculpted the nine-foot likeness depicting Warren staring intently over the field with binoculars in hand.

Along the walking path to your left is the monument of the 140th New York Infantry, which features a bronze bas relief bust of Col. Patrick O'Rorke near the spot he was killed. Some visitors rub Paddy's nose for good luck (but we encourage you to resist, since this is damaging to the monument).

Farther to the left is the large monument of the 44th and 12th New York Infantry in the shape of a castle. Designed by Maj. Gen. Daniel Butterfield (Meade's Chief of Staff), it was dedicated on July 3, 1893. The tower is forty-four feet high, and the inner chamber measures twelve feet square. Along the slope in front of the monument can be seen remains of the stone wall put up by Colonel Vincent's men during the evening of July 2, and more of the stone wall erected by Federal soldiers can be seen proceeding north just below the front slope — called the "military crest" — along the length of Little Round Top.

> *Drive to the stop sign and turn left onto the Wheatfield Road. Reset your odometer to 0.0.*

As you turn you will see a small hill to your right called Munshower Knoll. This is part of the ground (along with the lower ground to the north) that General Sickles was ordered to occupy with his Federal 3rd Corps on July 2. At the time of the battle, the road you are now driving on was an Adams County road that connected the Taneytown Road with the Emmitsburg Road. This area was crisscrossed with rail fences and stone walls. As you drive along the Wheatfield Road, study the higher ground to your front and left. Unhappy with his lower, marshy position, Sickles decided it was better to advance his corps toward the Emmitsburg Road and occupy that higher terrain. Traffic allowing, if you look back to your left rear and note the imposing height of Little Round Top, it is difficult to understand how the general did not recognize the importance of the hill. His decision would significantly affect the combat later that afternoon, though whether for good or for ill is still a hot topic of debate.

> *After .2 miles take the first left onto Crawford Avenue. You are now driving along the Plum Run Valley known as "The Valley of Death" between the Round Tops and the heights of Houck's Ridge.*

Tour Stop 8
July 2 - The Valley of Death and Devil's Den

The fighting of July 2 left nearly 900 dead of both sides strewn throughout this picturesque valley. On your left is the portrait statue of Brig. Gen. Samuel Crawford, a native of nearby Fayetteville, sculpted by Ron Tunison and dedicated in 1988. The 2,800 men of Crawford's Pennsylvania Reserves division, part of George Sykes' 5th Corps, attacked from your left on July 2 into Confederates advancing from your right. The Southern troops had just shattered the Federal lines in and near George Rose's "Bloody Wheatfield." The Federal effort stopped their penetration after intense fighting.

Markers for the Regular units can be seen on Houck's Ridge to your right, an area nicknamed "Regulars Ridge."

After another .2 miles you will come to a stop sign at the intersection with Warren Avenue. Continue straight to stay on Crawford Avenue and proceed a short distance to the parking spaces on the left for Devil's Den.

Directly ahead of the parking spaces is the boulder-strewn low area known as the "Slaughter Pen." Confederates from Gen. Law's Brigade, Longstreet's Corps, attempted to advance through this difficult area and sought cover behind the boulders. Photographs of the dead taken here within days of the battle attest to the heavy fighting in this area. Note that there was no road here at the time of the battle. In order to construct the park road, many large boulders in this area were removed and later used as material for park road foundations as well as to aid in the construction of monuments.

Behind you are the enormous boulders of Devil's Den, on land owned at the time of the battle by John Houck. The rocks were a mixed blessing: a

A tranquil moment in the Devil's Den, a far cry from the chaos and death on July 2 and 3. (Stanley)

hindrance for soldiers to advance through, and cover for soldiers to hide behind. Look at Little Round Top to your northeast. During and after the failed attack against the rocky heights on the late afternoon and early evening of July 2, Confederates hid among the boulders and fired on Federal infantry and artillery posted on the summit. The shooting continued on July 3. Confederates here probably fired upon cavalrymen participating in Farnsworth's Charge farther south.

The igneous rocks of Devil's Den are said to be 180 million years old. The rocks continue to erode, and a close examination reveals where chucks of boulders have broken off over the ensuing years. Human history in the Devil's Den area is also quite old. Several hundred years ago, Indians hunted across this land. Local tradition holds that in a field of several acres just to the south, a rather large fight called "The Battle of the Crows" occurred between warring Indian tribes. Before and after the battle of Gettysburg, local residents routinely found arrowheads and other Native American artifacts in the area of Devil's Den and the Round Tops.

Following the battle (and even for years afterward) soldier remains were found among the boulders. In some cases, mortally wounded men fell between the rocks and died there. In other instances, Federal burial parties simply threw corpses into the crevices rather than go to the extra effort of dragging them elsewhere and digging a grave in the rocky soil.

Proceed on the park road as it curves sharply to the right around the boulders of Devil's Den. When you reach the top of the hill, parking will be available on the right side of the road.

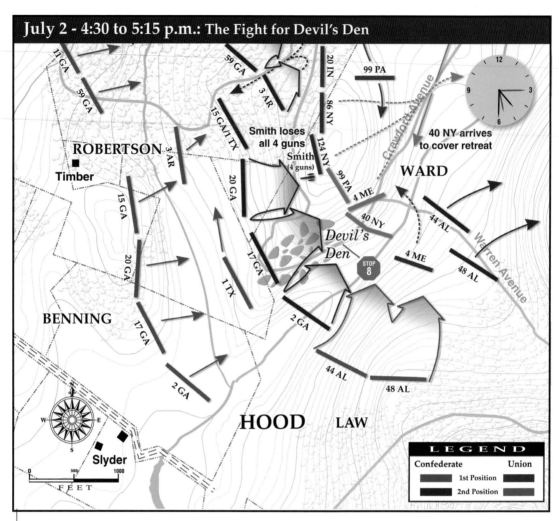

July 2 - 4:30 to 5:15 p.m.: The Fight for Devil's Den

Stand here on the left side of the park road where you have a clear view to the south. You will see an excellent view of the terrain across which thousands of Longstreet's men assaulted on July 2. Just below you is what is popularly called the "Triangular Field" of George W. Weikert (whose home is to the west of the field). You can also see the farms of John Slyder and George Rose, and in the distance both the Emmitsburg Road and farther away, Warfield Ridge.

As mentioned earlier, Maj. Gen. Daniel E. Sickles was dissatisfied with his assigned position along the low ground north of Little Round Top (to your rear) and marched his entire Federal 3rd Corps forward (west) to higher ground along the Emmitsburg Road. Most of the brigade of Brig. Gen. Hobart Ward, nearly 2,000 soldiers, was posted here atop Houck's Ridge. At this time they constituted the left flank of the Army of the Potomac. Both flanks of Hobart's line were "in the air," a term that means they were unsupported and could be easily turned by enemy troops (similar to Brig. Gen. Francis Barlow's situation at Blocher's Knoll on July 1). Hobart's left flank was here among the boulders, and his right flank ended several hundred yards north along Houck's Ridge near a wheatfield owned by George Rose — soon to be known forever as "The Bloody Wheatfield." The 4th Maine and 124th New York Infantry held the left of the line here atop Devil's Den, with the 86th New York, 20th Indiana, and 99th Pennsylvania extending Hobart's line to the right (north). Capt. James Smith's 4th New York Battery unlimbered four of its six cannon on Hobart's left, and the other two guns were posted off his right flank. The 2nd U.S. Sharpshooters, which was attached to the brigade, fanned out to the west and formed a skirmish line. (This is the same sharpshooter unit that conducted a delaying action back to Big Round Top in front of General Law's advancing Confederate brigade, and eventually ended up on the left flank of Col. Joshua Chamberlain's 20th Maine on the south slope of Little Round Top.)

To help secure his vulnerable left flank, General Ward ordered the 4th Maine down into the valley to your left rear (southeast), where Col. Elijah Walker formed a line across Plum Run.

Now turn slightly right and face west toward the Emmitsburg Road.

As Longstreet's assault got underway and the rest of Sickles' 3rd Corps was being attacked near the road to your west, Southern infantry from Brig. Gen. Jerome Robertson's Brigade advanced toward Ward's line from directly in your front. When Law's attack on Little Round Top began to your left (south), Captain Smith's guns opened an intense close-range artillery barrage against the infantry, and a long-range counter-battery fire against the Southern guns on Warfield Ridge (where the Confederates began their assault). As you face the Triangular Field, the 900 men of the 1st Texas Infantry and the 3rd Arkansas attacked directly toward where you are standing (Robertson's 4th and 5th Texas Infantry attacked Little Round Top behind you). Smith trained his muzzles against the Texans and Arkansans as they climbed the slope directly ahead of you. "Give them solid shot! Damn them, give them anything!" Smith yelled as the Confederates stepped within 300 yards.

Look north along the length of Houck's Ridge.

The 3rd Arkansas walked into a volley of fire from Ward's blazing line, after which the 99th Pennsylvania, 20th Indiana, and 86th New York rushed part way down the slope and pushed back the outnumbered Arkansans approximately 75 yards. The 1st Texas advanced to the stone wall bordering the bottom (southwest) side of the Triangular Field. Capt. Smith could not lower the muzzles of his artillery low enough to hit the Southerners there. While the Texans fired on Smith's gunners, silencing the battery for a time, the 600 men of the 44th and 48th Alabama Infantry of Law's Brigade approached — unseen by Ward's men

This 1880s photo of Devil's Den offers a rare view of this famous outcropping of rocks before Crawford Avenue was added, which altered the area greatly. (GNMP)

— from the south along the Plum Run Valley at the base of Big Round Top.

The 3rd Arkansas tried to break the right side of Ward's line on Houck's Ridge, but was unsuccessful. The arrival of 350 men of the 17th Maine of Col. Regis de Trobriand's 3rd Corps brigade on their left flank (on the southern edge of Rose's wheatfield), made it nearly impossible for the Arkansans to even hold their position. The men of the 1st Texas, perhaps seeing support approaching in the form of the Alabamians on their right, climbed over the stone wall at the base of the Triangular Field and headed for Smith's guns at your position. Fire from the 124th New York stopped them. Col. A. Van Horne Ellis, commander of the 124th New York (recruited in Orange County, New York and known as the "Orange Blossoms"), steadied his men by calmly folding his arms over his chest as he stood and watched the fighting. From his vantage point Ellis soon realized that a thrust from Houck's Ridge/Devil's Den down into the Triangular Field was what was needed to shove back the Texans.

Did You Know?

One of the most famous photographs taken in Devil's Den was staged. A short walk down the road from the top of Devil's Den will take you to the "Sharpshooter Nest." This spot is where Alexander Gardner took a photograph a few days after the battle that supposedly depicted a dead Confederate sharpshooter among the rocks. This photograph — perhaps the most famous view of the battlefield — is reproduced on a wayside marker at the entrance to the spot where the body was found. Scholarship by noted photographic researcher William Frassanito debunks Gardner's caption. It appears certain that Gardner photographed the corpse in a nearby location before moving the body north about seventy yards up the slope to Devil's Den. There, Gardner created the dramatic image of a dead "sharpshooter" in his "nest" that generations of viewers have come to instantly recognize. Note the clear view of Little Round Top's crest afforded to Southern riflemen from this position.

Ellis called for his mount, but one of his officers cautioned him that he would make too tempting a target on horseback. "The men must see us to-day," he replied, climbing into the saddle. The charge of the "Orange Blossoms" slammed into the 1st Texas and sent the exhausted Southerners reeling. Although successful, the New York attack cost the regiment dearly: a Confederate bullet knocked Ellis from his horse and killed him. Some of his men picked up their colonel, carried him to the rear, and lay his body on a rock. Note the monument here of the 124th New York Infantry, which features a sculpture of Ellis standing resolute and calm, arms folded, just as he had while watching Robertson's men attack his position. The monument is the only one on the battlefield that contains a full-length representation of a regimental commander. Tradition holds that the monument stands on the rock on which his body was laid. The bronze sword and sash are replacements of the original granite, which was vandalized and destroyed years ago.

Desperate for support, General Ward sent to his division commander, Maj. Gen. David B. Birney, for reinforcements. Guided by the sound of Smith's guns, the 40th New York and the small 6th New Jersey, about 600 men all told, marched from the northern end of the Plum Run Valley to Ward's embattled position.

The 44th and 48th Alabama were intent on taking Smith's four pieces, which were now more vulnerable because the 124th New York was no longer fighting on Houck's Ridge next to them. As that fight raged, the 4th and 5th Texas and the 4th Alabama began their attack against Col. Strong Vincent's brigade on Little Round Top to your left rear (southeast). As if matters were not bad enough already for Ward's men, a Confederate brigade of 1,400 Georgians under Brig. Gen. Henry Benning was advancing in a northeasterly direction toward the Triangular Field — heading straight for Houck's Ridge. Squeezed by heavy fire from both the 48th Alabama and half of Benning's Brigade, the 4th Maine in the valley to your left began retreating toward Ward's main line here on the ridge. The incessant fire of the 1st Texas Infantry drove Smith's gunners from their pieces. The left flank of the Army of the Potomac was near a breaking point.

Face the Triangular Field to the southwest again.

Law's attack on Little Round Top (in your left-rear), was reaching its high water mark. Directly in front of you, Robertson's and Benning's superior numbers seemed more than Ward's men could bear. To your right, Brig. Gen. George "Tige" Anderson's Brigade of more than 1,800 Georgians was bearing down on de Trobriand's brigade in Rose's woods and the southern end of his wheatfield.

As Captain Smith begged for help to rescue his guns, some of Ward's men desperately charged down the slope in one, final show of resistance. Smith's three guns on the ridge were overrun (one had been hit earlier in the fighting by a Confederate shell fired from Warfield Ridge and had been withdrawn) and Ward's entire line began retreating along the ridge to your rear, covered by fire from the 40th New York and 6th New Jersey. Three of Smith's guns were now in Confederate hands, as was Devil's Den. The victorious Southerners held it for the rest of the battle.

Continue on the park road, and after about .1 miles take the first left onto Cross Avenue. Pause here momentarily.

Tour Stop 9
July 2 - Prelude to the Bloody Wheatfield

Cross Avenue is named after Col. Edward E. Cross, commander of a brigade in Maj. Gen. Winfield S. Hancock's Federal 2nd Corps. The brigade included Cross' own 5th New Hampshire. Behind you on Ayers Avenue (which you may wish to visit at a later time) is the monument to the 5th New Hampshire, which stands on the spot where Cross was mortally wounded leading his brigade near Rose's field of wheat on July 2. Anderson's brigade of Georgians advanced through this area (almost directly at you) toward the wheatfield. Cross' brigade, along with those of Brig. Gen. Samuel Zook and Col. Patrick Kelly, advanced through the wheatfield under fire from Anderson's soldiers and part of Brig. Gen. Joseph Kershaw's Brigade. As he was about to advance his brigade against Anderson, Cross was shot in the stomach while standing behind the line of his old 5th New Hampshire. A Confederate rifleman hiding behind a large rock only forty yards away (across the park road) brought the colonel down; just moments later a sergeant of the 5th New Hampshire killed the Confederate. Cross lingered at a field hospital behind Culp's Hill and died shortly after midnight. His final words were

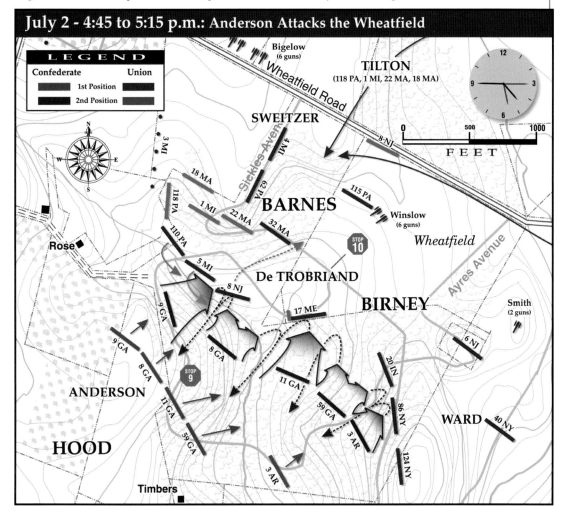

July 2 - 4:45 to 5:15 p.m.: Anderson Attacks the Wheatfield

recorded as these: "I wish that I would live to see the rebellion suppressed and peace restored. . . . I think the boys will miss me."

> *Continue, and Cross Avenue curves sharply to the right and becomes Brooke Avenue. Pause here.*

Brooke Avenue is named for Col. John R. Brooke, the twenty-four-year-old commander of a brigade in the Federal 2nd Corps.

> *At this point, before discussing the battlefield action further, you may wish to see an obscure feature of the battlefield: the ruins of a home Anderson's Confederates passed by during their advance. Many battlefield trampers seek the location of this home. Safely park your vehicle where the park road curves sharply to the right. In the woods to your left, you should be able to discern a walking path. Walk the path toward the higher ground in front of you for about 150 yards. At the top of the rise and across a stone wall (about fifty yards below the pasture uphill to your right) is the stone foundation of the George W. Weikert house.*

Weikert lived here with his wife and two daughters in July 1863. During the battle, however, Weikert was serving in Co. C of the 1st Potomac Home Brigade Cavalry, a Federal unit raised in Maryland and known as "Cole's Cavalry." Following the war, Weikert served as Gettysburg's chief of police for a number of years. This location is commonly referred to as the "Timbers House" because an African-American named John Timbers lived here after Weikert moved to a home outside town following the war. It is commonly believed that the depressed Timbers later hanged himself here, but some scholars believe he may have been lynched.

> *If you visit the Timbers house site, return to Brooke Avenue when you have finished examining the area. Continue on the park road.*

As you drive along Brooke Avenue you will begin to see monuments along the right side of the road. This signifies that you are entering the area through which Brooke's brigade of 850 men, which rushed to the relief of Cross' brigade at the orders of division commander Brig. Gen. John Caldwell, launched a counterattack against Anderson's Confederates. During the bat-

The Rose Farm barn withstood the Peach Orchard and Wheatfield fights on July 2, but could not weather a wind storm in 1934. (GNMP)

tle, this area was wooded like it is now, and this first part of Brooke Avenue generally parallels a farm lane that was here at the time. It extended from George Rose's farm to the northwest to your right along Rose's Run, then to his wheatfield to your northeast.

> *Pause at the point where you see the War Department marker for Kershaw's Brigade on the left side of the road.*

After entering Rose's wheatfield about 800 yards to your right front (northeast), Brooke ordered his men to fire at will against Anderson's Georgians. After a few minutes Brooke ordered his men to fix bayonets, grabbed the flag of his 53rd Pennsylvania Infantry, and led his men straight toward the enemy. Brooke pushed the Confederates into the woods here just south of the Rose farmhouse (of which you will have a good view shortly) in the area of the road on which you are driving. Brooke's men advanced as far as 75 yards to the right of this road.

From there, however, they were able to see the fresh brigade of Brig. Gen. Paul Semmes, McLaw's Division, lined up in Rose's field to your left. Semmes' Brigade consisted of the 10th, 50th, 51st, and 53rd Georgia Infantry and numbered more than 1,300 men. The 50th Georgia was the farthest to your right just south of the Rose house, and was supporting Kershaw's fight against Brig. Gen. Samuel Zook's brigade (an action we will examine shortly).

Semmes' Georgians advanced to the wood line on your left and exchanged volleys with Brooke's men. Caught out in the open, the Georgians soon fell back. Brooke advanced to a position about fifty yards on your right, with his line bent in the shape of a crescent, its middle bulging toward Semmes' men. Brooke had advanced farther south than either Kelly or Zook (ahead of you to your right front), and by doing so found himself nearly trapped by a surging enemy: Semmes in his front and Anderson on his left. In addition, his men had an average of but five bullets left.

As both Confederate brigades poured their fire into Brooke's line, Brooke climbed onto a boulder so his men could see him and so he could better direct his men. (Remarkably, Brooke survived and later marked this boulder, which is visited on the Rock Carvings Tour in this book.) From his vantage point, Brooke easily saw that he was nearly surrounded and could no longer hold his position. After fifteen minutes of intense close-distance small arms combat, he ordered his survivors to with-

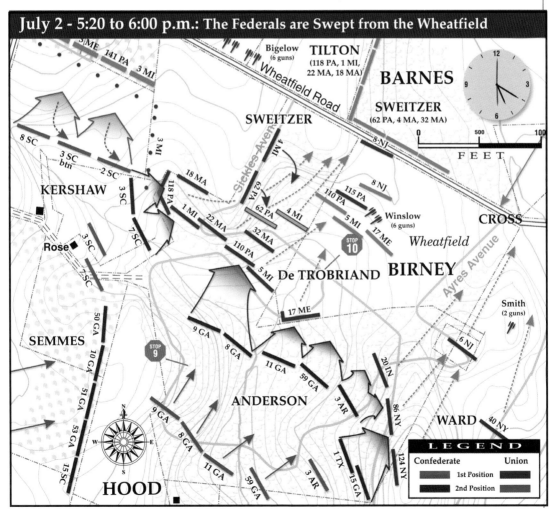

draw north toward Rose's wheatfield. To the northwest, Zook and Kelly were similarly pummeled by heavy numbers of Southern infantry and forced into a chaotic retreat. (Zook was mortally wounded as he led his men into the Wheatfield; we will visit that spot later in the tour.)

Evidence of the extremely heavy (and very confused) fighting in this area and to the west on the George Rose farm was found after the battle in the form of hundreds of dead Federals and Confederates. The latter were laid to rest in trench graves dug throughout this area on both your left and your right.

Continue nearly .2 miles and you will see the stone home of George Rose on your left. Brooke Avenue curves sharply to the right and becomes de Trobriand Avenue. Pause here just as the road turns right.

As Brooke's brigade advanced into its fight with Anderson's and Semmes' men behind you, the brigades of Cols. William Tilton and Jacob Sweitzer (Brig. Gen. James Barnes' division, Maj. Gen. George Sykes' 5th Corps) fought part of Kershaw's South Carolina brigade over this ground. Kershaw's 2,100 men split into two wings as they advanced east from Warfield Ridge. The three left-most regiments — the 2nd South Carolina, 3rd South Carolina Battalion, and 8th South Carolina — passed north of the Rose home and marched straight for Federal infantry and artillery posted in the Sherfy peach orchard. The 3rd and 7th South Carolina comprised Kershaw's right wing (the 15th South Carolina advanced from the south behind Anderson's men) and advanced directly toward you from your left (west). The knoll ahead of you is called "Stony Hill." Tilton's brigade of 650 Federals formed there while Sweitzer's 420 men advanced behind them and faced west toward Sherfy's peach orchard.

Tilton's men heard Kershaw's South Carolinians coming before they could see them. All around your position, according to one of the Federals, "the musketry rolled in continuous roar . . . the ground trembled, the trees shook and limbs quivered." When the Southerners appeared on the slope behind you, Tilton's men unleashed a volley. This was Tilton's first fight as a brigade commander, but he quickly recognized that he would not be able to hold the knoll against superior numbers that overlapped his exposed position. He sent word back to Barnes for reinforcements, but the latter ordered him and Sweitzer to withdraw to the northeast.

With the Stony Hill uncovered, Kershaw's right wing (the 3rd and 7th South Carolina) advanced and took it. Just as the Federal line here northwest and west of Rose's wheatfield was breaking apart, Cross' and then Brooke's brigades arrived from Cemetery Ridge to your northeast and engaged Anderson behind you, as previously described. Zook's and Kelly's brigades, also of Caldwell's division, advanced toward your position. Zook's nearly 1,000 men and Kelly's Irish Brigade of more than 500 men outnumbered the 800 Confederates of Kershaw's right wing. Kershaw asked for help from Semmes' Brigade, which was behind him. While the rest of Semmes' men battled Brooke to your south, the 300 men of the 50th Georgia Infantry moved to Kershaw's assistance. Kershaw's own 2nd South Carolina, about 375 strong, joined the line after suffering a withering fire from Federal artillery stationed in the Peach Orchard.

Rose's buildings and 236 acres of land, caught squarely in the middle of Longstreet's massive assault of July 2, served as a temporary Confederate field hospital — particularly Rose's large barn, of which only the ruins of the stone foundation remain today. Between 500 and 1,000 Confederates were buried on the grounds of the Rose farm, in addition to a number of Federal dead. Approximately eighty identified graves appear on an 1866 list for the farm, including that of Lt. Col. Francis Kearse, commander of the 50th Georgia Infantry of Brig. Gen. Paul Semmes' Brigade. The twenty-five-year-old Kearse was killed early in the assault by Federal artillery fire that hammered the brigade during its advance. He was eventually buried in an orchard near Rose's springhouse. Exhumed in 1871 along with others on this farm, Kearse was reburied in the Gettysburg Section of Laurel Grove Cemetery in Savannah, Georgia.

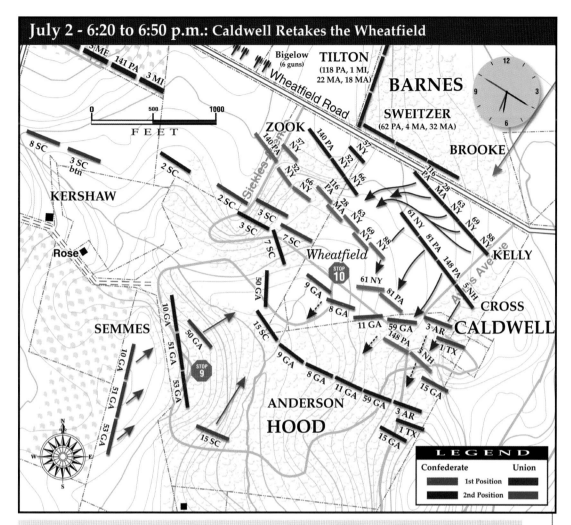

July 2 - 6:20 to 6:50 p.m.: Caldwell Retakes the Wheatfield

Drive a short distance ahead until you see the monument of the 110th Pennsylvania Infantry of de Trobriand's brigade (Federal 3rd Corps) on your right.

Kelly's Irish Brigade attacked toward the Stony Hill directly where you are now. Lined up parallel to the park road on your left was Zook's brigade. Squeezed on both sides, Kershaw's three South Carolina regiments broke under pressure and retreated in the direction of the Rose house. The Federals, however, would not be able to hold this advanced position for long.

Continue on the park road and pause just before you reach the stop sign at the intersection with Sickles Avenue.

Please note this section of the present-day park road was part of Rose's wheatfield, which extended about 150 yards behind you until coming to a point on the far side of de Trobriand Avenue.

On your right is the monument of the 4th Michigan Infantry of Sweitzer's brigade (Barnes' division, 5th Corps). On the front of the monument is a relief of a soldier holding a flag. During the Wheatfield fighting we will discuss next, the Michigan regiment covered the Federal rear as General Caldwell's brigades were driven through the Wheatfield. The Michiganders lost more men captured (seventy-six of its 342 men) than any other regiment in this fighting. When the Georgians of Brig.

Gen. William Wofford's Brigade attacked from the west, several Confederates grabbed the colors of the 4th Michigan. The regiment's commander, Col. Harrison H. Jeffords, drew his sword and struck down the Confederate holding aloft his prize. Jeffords was quickly surrounded, bayoneted several times, and killed. The Federal flag was recaptured. The monument, dedicated on June 12, 1889, depicts Jeffords defiantly holding the beloved colors for which he gave his life.

> *To examine the Wheatfield, turn left onto Sickles Avenue and park on the right side of the road near the wayside that describes the fighting.*

Tour Stop 10
July 2 - Whirlpool in the Bloody Wheatfield

George Rose's wheatfield, immortalized during the July 2 fighting as "The Bloody Wheatfield" or simply "The Wheatfield," marks almost exactly the geographic center of the heaviest fighting during Longstreet's assault. The twenty-six-acre patch of ripe summer wheat became a killing field as units from both sides were fed into it from several different directions. It is also one of the more confusing aspects of the battle for most visitors. The recent clearing of trees surrounding the Wheatfield (they were not here during the battle) has opened up vistas that will assist you to better understand this piece of terrain and the fighting that occurred here, as well as the Wheatfield's context with the rest of the battlefield.

Surrounded on three sides by Wofford's Georgians to the northwest, Kershaw's South Carolinians to the west, Semmes' Georgians southwest, and Anderson's Georgians to the south, Federal Brig. Gen. John Caldwell knew his 2nd Corps division was in a dangerous spot in the Wheatfield. Stand and face to the southwest, back toward the 4th Michigan Infantry's monument and the intersection you just drove through. Caldwell moved Sweitzer's brigade of 1,000 men to cover the southern corner along the stone wall that bordered the field as the rest of his brigades streamed through the Wheatfield behind you.

Perched on the crest of a fog-shrouded Wheatfield, Winslow's 1st New York Light Battery monument stands ready, as if to stop a Confederate onslaught. (Stanley)

After Col. Jeffords of the 4th Michigan was killed, and the Federal line here began to break and stream northeast through the Wheatfield, two brigades of U.S. Regular Infantry to the southeast (your left) moved forward toward your position to engage the heavy Southern line. In front was Col. Sidney Burbank's 950-man brigade (Ayers' division, Sykes' 5th Corps) consisting of the 2nd, 7th, 10th, 11th, and 17th U.S. Infantry. Behind Burbank were 1,500 soldiers from Col. Hannibal Day's brigade consisting of the 3rd, 4th, 6th, 12th, and 14th Regulars.

Burbank advanced and wheeled his brigade to his left, directly through your position, to make a stand against Semmes' and Anderson's Confederates fighting directly in front of you. Because the Georgians were in the woods, Burbank couldn't see them. The colonel ordered his men to fire a volley into the trees. When no response was forthcoming, Burbank waited. A short time later, the Rebel Yell broke out in the timber and the Georgians burst into the clearing. Another volley from the Regulars staggered the advancing Southern line. In a move of extraordinary luck, Wofford's Georgians arrived from the northwest (your right) at this time in three heavy lines of battle. Colonel Day's brigade of Regulars was advancing behind Burbank, but the position here where you are standing was now utterly untenable in the face of more than 6,500 Confederates enveloping Rose's wheatfield. Noise, smoke, death, and rampant confusion enveloped the area around where you are standing. Federal orders to retreat were yelled out. "The roar of musketry was so extensive that a great portion of our command did not hear the order to fall back until some minutes after it was given," recalled Capt. William Clinton of Burbank's 10th U.S. Infantry. "The enemy at this time was in front and on both our flanks."

Realizing his Regulars were about to be swallowed whole by the Confederates, Gen. Romeyn Ayers ordered Burbank and Day to retreat and surrender the Wheatfield. Anderson's and Semmes' winded Confederates, who had fought tooth and nail for each yard of ground between this point and the George Rose farm, advanced directly toward you as they fired into the backs of the retreating

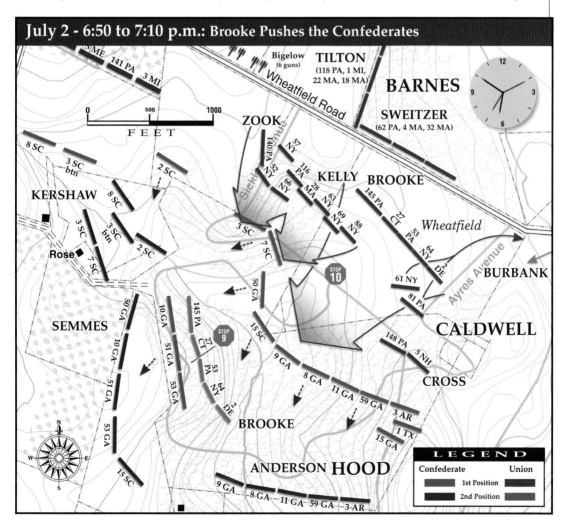

July 2 - 6:50 to 7:10 p.m.: Brooke Pushes the Confederates

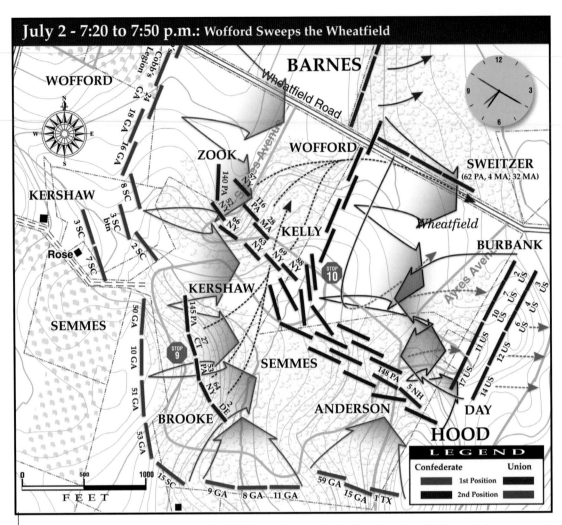

July 2 - 7:20 to 7:50 p.m.: Wofford Sweeps the Wheatfield

Federals. Many Regulars fell in the field behind you. The hell in the Wheatfield was "almost a semi-circle of fire," remembered an officer in Burbank's 11th U.S. Infantry. "[T]he slaughter was fearful."

As the victorious Confederates attempted to push farther into the valley between Devil's Den and the Round Tops to your left-rear, Brig. Gen. Samuel Crawford countercharged with his Pennsylvania Reserves Division (as previously described when we visited Crawford's statue in the Valley of Death) and stopped them from capturing ground beyond Devil's Den and Houck's Ridge.

Three of Burbank's regiments — the 7th, 10th, and 17th Infantries — lost in excess of fifty percent casualties in their few minutes here. The total loss for the brigade was forty-seven percent. Sweitzer's brigade also suffered heavily, leaving nearly fifty percent of its members on the field. The 4th Michigan Infantry, its Colonel Jeffords lying dead in the Wheatfield, lost almost half of its soldiers during its rear guard action near where you are standing. Even Day's brigade of Regulars, which was supporting Burbank and so not directly engaged, suffered twenty-five percent casualties during its skedaddle from the Wheatfield. The Federals lucky enough to survive the "Bloody Wheatfield" ran for safety near Little Round Top and the line north.

After some of the hardest, bloodiest, and most confusing combat of the Civil War, the Southerners finally took control of George Rose's wheatfield. That night the acreage became a No Man's Land between the two lines. Had you been standing on this spot during the late afternoon and early evening hours of July 2, 1863, you would have been hard-pressed to move more than a step or two in any direction without tripping on the dead and the dying. The Rose farm yard, the woods to your front, and the wheatfield were covered with men from both sides. Many Federals unlucky enough to have been seriously wounded here remained where they fell until the Confederates retreated on July 4.

Walk into the Wheatfield.

Just north of the center of the field is the monument of Capt. George B. Winslow's 1st New York Light Battery B. Winslow's guns were the only artillery, North or South, fighting in the Wheatfield on July 2. As the Federals retreated through the field early in the fighting, Winslow's gunners supported them by firing shell and case shot into Rose's woods at the pursuing Georgians and South Carolinians.

The monument location provides a good vista to view the general movements in the Wheatfield. Face south with the monument at your back (face in the direction the guns are pointing). You are looking at the advancing Confederate line. Rose's woods are in front of you, and you can see the stone wall that lines the far edge of the Wheatfield. During the early fighting, Anderson's Georgians attacked Federals posted at the stone wall and at the base of Stony Hill on your right-front. Kershaw's South Carolinians attacked from the field you see on the far side of Stony Hill. Following localized Federal counterattacks, Anderson's soldiers dislodged de Trobriand's infantry from the wall directly in front of you. As the Federal retreat rushed past where you are standing, Winslow knew he had to limber his guns or risk having them captured.

Due to the recent battlefield reclamation efforts of the National Park Service, the Wheatfield now looks much as it did during the battle, as shown here in this colorized 1880s photograph of the Zook Monument. (GNMP)

Once Winslow withdrew, Caldwell's Federal division moved into the field from your rear and drove the Southerners back into the woods. On your right, Wofford's Georgians pushed the Federals off Stony Hill and Caldwell's Federals broke in the face of superior numbers from Kershaw's, Semmes', and Anderson's brigades. Along the ridge to your left, Burbank's and Day's U.S. Regulars were swept away by Semmes' and Anderson's victorious Southerners. In the Plum Run Valley (or "Valley of Death") farther to your left, Crawford's Pennsylvania Reserves countercharged and held the Southerners from advancing deeper in that direction.

Directly to your north near the Wheatfield Road that borders the northern edge of the field, you will find the sixteen-foot tall shaft monument that marks the approximate location where Federal Brig. Gen. Samuel K. Zook was mortally wounded while leading his brigade into the Wheatfield. Zook, who filled the air with profanity when excited and was loved by his men, was mortally wounded when a Confederate bullet entered his stomach and lodged in his spine. He died in a Federal hospital while Pickett's Charge raged the following afternoon. The monument was placed by the Gen. Zook

The Irish Brigade Monument, one of the most photographed on the Gettysburg battlefield, resting among the colorful leaves of a crisp fall day. (Stanley)

Grand Army of the Republic Post of Norristown, Pennsylvania, and dedicated on July 25, 1882.

Continue on Sickles Avenue, and a short distance ahead you will see the Irish Brigade Monument on your left.

This monument was designed by John H. Duncan and sculpted by William Randolph O'Donovan, and memorializes three of the five regiments of Col. Patrick Kelly's Irish Brigade (Caldwell's division, Hancock's 2nd Corps) – the 63rd, 69th, and 88th New York regiments. The other two regiments – the 28th Massachusetts and 116th Pennsylvania – have monuments of their own just ahead on top of the Stony Hill. This statue is one of the most popular on the battlefield. Dedicated on July 2, 1888, it features a polished granite Celtic cross with bronze inset. Note the trefoil — the symbol of the 2nd Corps — at the top, and the five medallions below that show the numbers of all five regiments of the brigade, the seal of the state of New York, and the seal of Ireland.

The most notable and recognizable feature of the monument, however, is the bronze sculpture of an Irish wolf hound at the base. In a reclined pose, the sculpture represents faith and devotion. Visitors often leave dog biscuits and treats by the front paws of the sculpture.

Easily missed is the bronze plaque on the right side of the base of the monument. Showing an artillery battery in action, it commemorates Capt. James Rorty's 14th New York Independent Battery. Rorty's battery had been attached to the Irish Brigade for a time beginning in 1861. On July 2 it served just to the north of this spot, where it suffered heavily trying to hold its ground against attacks by the Confederate brigades of Brig. Gens. Cadmus Wilcox and William Barksdale.

Continue on Sickles Avenue. When it begins to curve sharply to the right you are in the area commonly referred to as "The Loop."

The Loop traverses the ridge along the knoll known to many veterans as Stony Hill. On your left and right are several Federal monuments of regiments that defended the hill during Longstreet's July 2 assault. Notable, on your left as you climb the hill, is the monument of the 2nd Company Andrews Sharpshooters of Massachusetts. It is the granite monument of a soldier standing behind a rock (atop a boulder where a member of the unit was posted that day) facing southwest toward the Confederate attack against Stony Hill. This small detachment, attached to the 22nd Massachusetts Infantry (Tilton's brigade, Barnes' division, Sykes' 5th Corps) fought against Wofford's Georgia brigade advancing across the ground in front of the monument. Note that the barrel of the soldier's rifle is missing; it was not broken, but instead was never finished. The sculptor, who worked for the Boston Marble & Granite Co., did not have a large enough block of granite to finish the weapon. The monument was designed by M. H. Murphy of Worchester and dedicated on October 8, 1885.

Continue as the road curves to the right.

When you reach the summit you will see on your left the monument of the 116th Pennsylvania Infantry, one of the most poignant on the field. It depicts a dead soldier lying along a damaged stone wall. The 116th Pennsylvania, one of the five regiments of the Irish Brigade, was posted here just before the Confederates renewed their attack on Stony Hill during Longstreet's July 2 assault. During a momentary lull prior to the attack, the regimental commander, Maj. St. Clair A. Mulholland, walked a short distance forward and saw a dead young Pennsylvanian who had been shot through the head. The sight of a slight smile on the boy's face never left Mulholland's memory. The episode was the inspiration for this monument, which was dedicated on September 11, 1889, and sculpted by James H. Kelly. If you look at it closely, you will see that the soldier still clutches his broken musket, apparently swung as a club before receiving his fatal wound. The depiction of the brutal reality of war makes this monument unique among most, and demonstrates that death is the only victor of any battlefield.

About 1900, the "Loop" near the Rose Farm looked much different than today. (GNMP)

Continue on Sickles Avenue to the stop sign at the intersection with the Wheatfield Road. Turn left, and after .3 miles you will see the Peach Orchard of farmer Joseph Sherfy on your left. Turn left onto Birney Avenue and park on the right side of the road.

Tour Stop 11
July 2 - Sickles' Line Cracks at the Peach Orchard

Stand on the slight rise of the Peach Orchard and look west for a magnificent view of much of the ground traversed by Longstreet's infantry on July 2.

As previously mentioned, Maj. Gen. Daniel E. Sickles moved his Federal 3rd Corps on the afternoon of July 2 from its assigned position north of Little Round Top to the west onto this higher ground. Earlier that morning, the foray by units of the U.S. Sharpshooters and elements of General Buford's cavalry had uncovered the presence of Confederate infantry in the woods along Seminary Ridge to the west. Buford's cavalry brigades held the position here on the night of July 1 and the morning of July 2, but were sent off the battlefield by Cavalry Corps commander Pleasonton. Except for about 100 troopers of the 9th New York Cavalry left behind with Sickles, the last of Buford's men left the field for Taneytown, Maryland, by 1:00 p.m. to rest and guard wagons. Federal army commander Maj. Gen. George Meade was angry that Pleasonton had ordered Buford away, since no Federal cavalry remained on the field except for small headquarters guards. Sickles' corps — the left flank of the Federal line — had just lost its cavalry screen in this important sector.

Sickles asked General Meade to examine his assigned position, but the army commander was

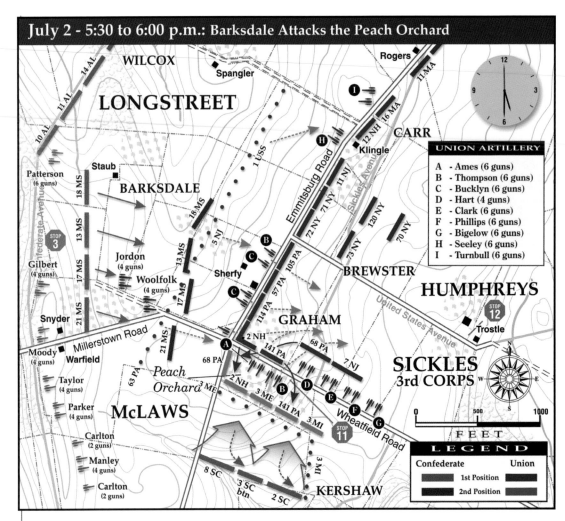

July 2 - 5:30 to 6:00 p.m.: Barksdale Attacks the Peach Orchard

busily attending to other pressing tasks. Sickles' move forward carried most of his 10,000-man corps (consisting of two large divisions instead of the customary three smaller divisions) here along the Emmitsburg Road. He deployed his corps in a wide V-shape, with the point of the V (pointing west) near the Peach Orchard. The right arm of the 3rd Corps stretched north along the Emmitsburg Road while the left arm angled back toward Devil's Den. In this position the 3rd Corps was far ahead of the rest of the Federal army along the Cemetery Ridge line. Like General Barlow's advanced position at Blocher's Knoll north of town on July 1, Sickles' line created a vulnerable salient. Longstreet's assault stepped off Warfield Ridge just minutes after Sickles took up his position here.

Face the Emmitsburg Road immediately to the west.

On your left, running from the orchard southeast to Devil's Den, Sickles placed the 5,100-man division of Maj. Gen. David Birney. (Several of Birney's units later fought along the Wheatfield line, as previously discussed.) The 1,500 Pennsylvanians of Brig. Gen. Charles Graham's brigade deployed here at the orchard with the line stretching from the Wheatfield Road along the Emmitsburg Road for nearly 400 yards to a lane leading to the farm of Abraham Trostle. The very point of the "V" where the Wheatfield Road meets the Emmitsburg Road was held by 350 men of the 2nd New Hampshire of Col. George Burling's brigade. This was the weakest part of Sickles' line. Several batteries of artillery were placed along the Wheatfield Road pointed southwest.

Farther to your right, 1,800 soldiers from Col. William Brewster's "Excelsior" brigade, part of Brig. Gen. Andrew A. Humphrey's division (4,900 men total) took up their position along the Emmitsburg Road on Graham's right, with Humphrey's two remaining brigades posted immediately to the rear and ready to move wherever they were needed. Brewster's New Yorkers covered a front spanning several hundred yards from the Trostle lane to Daniel Klingle's farm. Klingle's red frame home and barn, which can be seen along the Emmitsburg Road to your north, housed his farming and shoemaking operations. When Federal officers told Klingle to take his family and leave, the farmer responded, "If I must die, I will die at home." He was finally convinced to vacate the premises when it was made perfectly clear what was about to unfold on his property. Federal artillery was posted near Klingle's home to protect Brewster's right flank.

A full moon rises over the monument dedicated to two artillery batteries, Battery F Pennsylvania Light Artillery and Hampton's Battery, stationed in the Peach Orchard on July 2. (Stanley)

As you stand at or near the Peach Orchard, turn and look to your left (south) along the Emmitsburg Road.

Longstreet's July 2 assault was designed to attack en echelon, beginning with Longstreet's rightmost brigade under Law. Once that brigade became engaged, the one on its left would advance to attack, and so forth until the entire line extending to your right front was engaged. Lee's strategy was designed to "roll up" the Federal left flank and/or draw in additional troops from other parts of Meade's line. Reinforcements would leave a weak point somewhere that Lee hoped his troops could exploit. As previously noted, General Ewell's Second Corps troops on Lee's far left (miles away to your northeast) were to attack the Federal right at Culp's Hill when they heard the sound of Longstreet's artillery.

Unfortunately for the Confederates, Longstreet's attack suffered tactical and personnel problems that prevented it from achieving all its goals. Elements of Law's Brigade were drawn farther south toward the Round Tops (as previously discussed), division commander John B. Hood was seriously wounded very early in the action, and Longstreet's soldiers met stiff advanced resistance at George Rose's farm, his wheatfield, and at Devil's Den. The Federals were in substantial numbers, and their advanced position absorbed much of the immediate blow delivered by Longstreet.

When skirmishers from both sides began their shooting to your front before the assault got underway, Sickles was at General Meade's army headquarters along the Taneytown Road seeking permission for a move he had already made. When sixty Confederate guns opened fire against Sickles' line, Meade and Sickles galloped close to this spot. Sickles offered to return his corps to the rear, but Meade informed him it was too late. "You must fight it out where you are; I'll move troops at once to support you," he informed his 3rd Corps leader.

After the intense hour-long artillery barrage and the commitment of Hood's Division to the attack, Longstreet bided his time before sending in the 1,600 Confederates of Brig. Gen. William Barksdale's Brigade (McLaws' Division). When he released them, they marched directly toward the Peach Orchard from the west. The 57th and 114th Pennsylvania regiments (the latter known as Collis' Zouaves) of Brig. Gen. Charles Graham's brigade (posted along the road to your immediate right) ran forward and engaged Barksdale's men at Sherfy's house across the road to your right

front. Outnumbered, the Federal regiments to your right suffered heavy losses; the 141st Pennsylvania, for example, lost 149 of its 200 men. As Barksdale surged forward directly toward where you are standing, and the Alabamans of Brig. Gen. Cadmus Wilcox's Brigade (1,700 men, Anderson's Division, Hill's Third Corps) plus 700 Floridians of Col. David Lang's Brigade bore down on the Federal line farther north near the Peter Rogers house, Sickles' line began to break apart.

Though they had not snatched Little Round Top from the Federals, the Confederates did pierce Meade's left in three places — Devil's Den, Rose's wheatfield, and the Sherfy peach orchard salient. As his men began to fall back, Sickles' right leg was struck by a Confederate shell (we will visit the location shortly), and his limb was later amputated. The wound ended his military career.

Lang's, Wilcox's, and Barksdale's victorious brigades pushed toward Cemetery Ridge after the Federals. One of Barksdale's regiments, the 21st Mississippi Infantry, diverted southeast along the lane leading to the Abraham Trostle farm. The regiment's new direction sent it straight for Capt. John Bigelow's Federal artillery battery, which was making a desperate stand against the Southern attacks in an action we will examine shortly.

Fading sunlight glistens off the 73rd New York Monument situated in the middle of Excelsior Field near the Peach Orchard, with the Sherfy Barn in the distance. (Stanley)

As you can well imagine, the desperate fighting of July 2 on this portion of the field left many hundreds of corpses that needed to be buried as quickly after the battle as possible. Several trench graves were filled with bodies on the property of John Wentz to the north, and many Confederates were buried in and around the Peach Orchard itself. Detailed exhumation records were kept for the vast majority of remains removed from the field after the war. Very few were removed from among the fruit trees. Some historians speculate that as many as several dozen Confederates remain buried here. Indeed, many hundreds of Confederate dead buried on the battlefield (approximately 1,500 according to the calculations of several historians) have never been found.

The area where you are standing is well ornamented with monuments placed by Federal veterans proud of the stubborn stand they made here on July 2. On the high ground of the orchard along the Wheatfield Road, note the impressive monument of Hampton's Battery F, Independent Pennsylvania Light Artillery, which features a bronze statue of an artilleryman clutching a rammer. The cup at the bottom end of the rammer was used to send a charge down the barrel, and the sponge at the top was used to swab the barrel after the shot to extinguish any sparks. Due to high casualties suf-

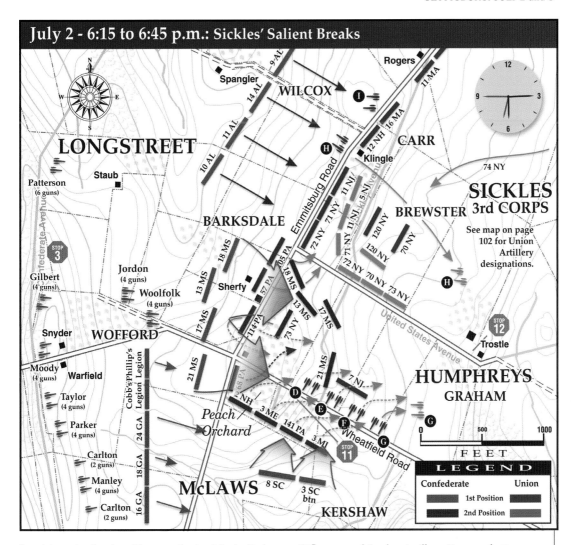

July 2 - 6:15 to 6:45 p.m.: Sickles' Salient Breaks

fered in prior battles, Hampton's six 3-inch Ordnance Rifles served in the Artillery Reserve battery under Capt. James Thompson. Of the 105 cannoneers present on July 2, twenty-eight were later listed as casualties. Survivors of the battery, recruited mostly in Pittsburgh, Pennsylvania, and surrounding Allegheny County, dedicated this monument in November 1890. The life-like six-foot high statue was created by C. F. Hamilton.

North of the Wheatfield Road on either side of Sickles Avenue, two monuments deserve special examination. On the west side of Sickles Avenue rests the monument of the Excelsior Brigade. On its top is a spread-winged eagle. Even though the five regiments of the brigade in Sickles' Corps — the 70th, 71st, 72nd, 73rd, and 74th New York Infantry — were entitled to erect separate monuments, they decided to create this one memorial to their comradeship. Each of the five sides of the pentagonal base contains plaques to each regiment, which are also symbolized by the five highly polished columns. Note the empty pedestal inside. It was to have held a bronze bust of Sickles (who organized the brigade and served as its first colonel), but it was never completed. The money appropriated for the sculpture was rumored to have been stolen by Sickles himself. That general and 5th Corps leader Maj. Gen. George Sykes are the only Federal infantry corps commanders unrepresented by a statue on the field. The Excelsior Brigade monument was created by Theodore Bauer and dedicated on July 2, 1893, the thirtieth anniversary of the fight at the Peach Orchard.

To the east on the other side of Sickles Avenue is the unique monument of the 7th New Jersey Infantry shaped like a minie bullet. The most common rifle projectile during the war, the bullet was perfected by French army officer Claude-Etienne Minie. This monument rests on the spot where the regiment's colonel, Louis R. Francine, was mortally wounded as his men supported Graham's brigade during the defense of the Peach Orchard. Francine died on July 16. Of the regiment's 331 men, fifteen were killed, eighty-six were wounded, and thirteen went missing. The monument was dedicated on June 30, 1888.

> *Follow Birney Avenue around the Peach Orchard until it intersects with Emmitsburg Road (Rt. 15), keep a careful eye on traffic, and turn right. Just over the rise on your left you will soon see the Joseph Sherfy farm house, fronted by the monuments of the 57th and 114th Pennsylvania regiments. These Keystone State troops charged into Barksdale's advancing brigade here. Just after the Sherfy house turn right onto United States Avenue and reset your odometer to 0.0.*

Tour Stop 12
July 2 - Bigelow's Heroic Stand at the Trostle Farm

This avenue approximates the historic lane that during the battle led to the Abraham Trostle farm. As you pass through the intersection with Sickles Avenue, to your left and right were several trench graves filled with the remains of Union and Confederate soldiers killed in this area.

Not long after the battle was over, Timothy O'Sullivan shot this famous view of the Trostle house. Dead horses from Bigelow's battery are visible throughout the Trostle yard. (LOC)

> *After slightly less than .4 miles, the Abraham Trostle farm is on your left. Stop when you reach the large barn and exit your vehicle to examine the surrounding terrain.*

The Trostle farm (more than 134 acres owned by Peter Trostle and leased to his son Abraham and his wife Catharine) was General Sickles' headquarters during the battle. More specifically, his headquarters was established under the large Swamp White Oak tree on the right side of the road opposite the barn and just west of the upright cannon marker denoting his headquarters. The "Sickles Tree" is one of the most well known of the several "witness" trees on the battlefield.

Look toward the top of the south wall of the Trostle barn facing you. In the bricks just below the diamond-shaped vent on the right side you will see a large hole made by a Confederate artillery projectile on July 2. If you wish, walk the short distance along the path west of the barn, which leads to the north and to a small monument. The small monument, placed in 1901, marks the spot where Sickles was hit in the right leg by a Confederate artillery shell while atop his horse and watching the action to the west. With his limb hanging by shreds, he was placed on a stretcher and carried to the rear in full view of his men. Ever the showman, Sickles chomped on a cigar and waved at his troops to give them confidence. One of his division commanders, General Birney, took command of the 3rd Corps.

Proceed slightly ahead to the Trostle house.

Just west of the home is the small monument of the 9th Battery, Massachusetts Light Artillery commanded by Capt. John Bigelow. The small monument (one of three to the battery on the field) stands in sharp contrast to the enormous work performed here by Bigelow and his gunners on July 2. The monument is carved in the shape of an artillery ammunition chest and marks the approximate spot of the battery's second position that day; their first position was along the Wheatfield Road southeast of the Peach Orchard when Longstreet's assault opened upon the 3rd Corps line. How the battery, which consisted of six 12-pounder smoothbores, got from that position to where you are now standing on the Trostle property is one of the many amazing episodes of the battle.

Many of the guns, limbers, and caissons of several Federal batteries had to be dragged by hand from the area of the Peach Orchard when the Confederates rushed over it because so many artillery horses had been killed. The last battery to leave was Bigelow's, which continued to rain canister into Kershaw's South Carolinians and Barksdale's Mississippians. When he was finally ordered to leave,

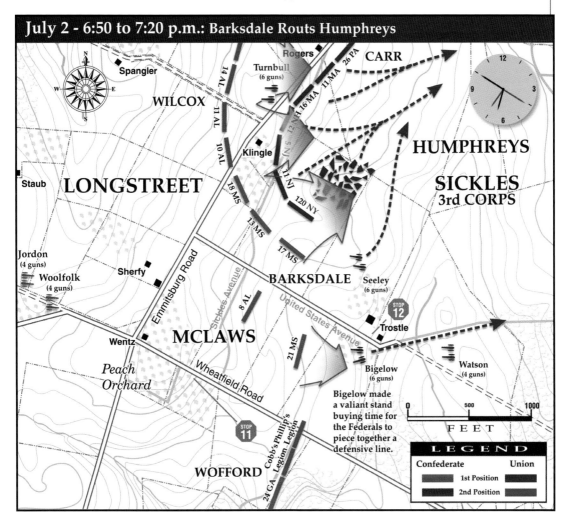

July 2 - 6:50 to 7:20 p.m.: Barksdale Routs Humphreys

Bigelow's surviving horses and men dragged the guns northeast toward the Trostle farm, with his cannoneers firing along the way "by prolonge." This risky and dangerous tactic required that ropes be tied to each gun's trail ring, and the rope tied to the limber. Horses then pulled the limber and gun rearward, but this permitted the gun to still be fired. When the gun was fired, the kick from the shot shoved the gun backward while the crews ran alongside to load, aim, and fire again, repeating the process over and over. Bigelow's battery executed this maneuver for several hundred yards until they reached the Trostle property. They prepared to limber up and retreat to the Federal line on Cemetery Ridge, but they soon discovered their work on the left side of the line was far from over.

The monument to the 9th Battery, Massachusetts Light Artillery, sits just behind "CORA," (her name is on the back of the tube) a 12-lb Napoleon named by the artillery crew that manned her. The Trostle Barn is in the background. (Stanley)

Lt. Col. Freeman McGilvery, in command of the 1st Volunteer Brigade of the Federal Reserve Artillery, rode up and found Bigelow as his men were preparing to pull out. Just as he stopped, McGilvery's horse was shot by four Confederate bullets. Turning to Bigelow, McGilvery shouted, "Captain Bigelow, there is not an infantryman back of you along the whole line which Sickles moved out; you must remain where you are and hold your position at all hazards, if need be, until at least I can find some batteries to put in position and cover you!" Both officers knew the order intended to sacrifice Bigelow's guns and men until a new line behind them could be shored up.

Trapped here among fences and stone walls, Bigelow ordered his men to fire solid shot near the ground at the enemy only fifty yards distant. Look directly to the south and you will see a slight knoll where the Confederate skirmishers hid. Bigelow ordered his crews to bounce the shells over the knoll and into the 21st Mississippi Infantry on the right, and some of Kershaw's men to the left. While his men loaded and fired, the enemy continued to advance. A volley from Mississippi infantry tore into Bigelow's cannoneers, and "men and horses were falling like hail," remembered one eyewitness. Before too long, Bigelow was nearly surrounded.

> ## *"Bullets were coming into our midst …and a Confederate battery added to our difficulties."*
>
> ### Capt. John Bigelow, 9th Massachusetts Light Artillery, of his battery's stand at the Trostle Farm

With no visible support in any direction, and about to be overwhelmed, Bigelow decided to retreat. As his men dragged the first gun through a hole in the stone wall, it overturned and blocked it. While the crew worked to right it, other crews knocked down as many stones as they could and then smacked the few remaining horses, sending the guns flying over the wall. Six of Kershaw's men on the left fired at Bigelow, who was on his horse near the wall. Two of the bullets slammed into Bigelow and two hit his horse.

When he fell off near the wall, a pair of his gunners rushed to his side while others tried to defend their overrun pieces with rammers, rocks, and anything else they could swing or throw. Bigelow mustered enough energy to yell at his men to try to retreat.

Bigelow's bugler Charles W. Reed, together with one of his aides, lifted the wounded commander on a horse and slowly led him to the rear. When some Confederates tried to capture them, Reed beat them off with his sword. Others leveled their muskets at the trio and a Confederate officer ordered them "not to murder us in cold blood," Reed later recalled. Amidst whizzing minie balls and shrieking shells from enemy guns firing from the Peach Orchard and the Emmitsburg Road, Reed's little party somehow made it to safety. All the way, remembered Bigelow, "Bugler Reed did not flinch; but steadily supported me." In their wake, the survivors left four of the six guns, eighty-eight dead horses (nearly all of the battery's mounts), and twenty-eight men — one-fourth of the battery killed, wounded, or captured.

Captain Bigelow recovered from his wounds and returned to the battery later that fall. He commanded it for another year before being discharged because of illness. The little granite monument at the Trostle farm, silent witness to the larger-than-life action of his men and battery here, was dedicated in 1885.

The Trostle buildings were employed as a field hospital by the Federal 3rd Corps, and the property suffered a great deal of damage. Catharine Trostle later testified that in addition to the crops and many personal items taken or destroyed, there were fifteen dead horses near the house and about 100 on the rest of the property — many of them from Bigelow's battery. The Trostles were never compensated for their damages. The horses were burned and buried on the property surrounding the house and barn, and many more were disposed of on the other side of the park road. Numerous trench graves filled with the dead of both armies were buried on the property north of the barn running from the Emmitsburg Road to Plum Run. In January 1899, the farm was sold to the U.S. Government.

Continue to the small white outbuilding beyond the house.

Look closely just below the peak of the roof in the wall of this building facing the road. You will see an artillery shell cemented into place there. This shell did not hit this building, nor is it the one that struck the barn (some years ago Trostle family descendants donated the latter projectile to the park). This shell may be another that the family found on the battlefield and cemented into the building for posterity.

Continue to the stop sign at the intersection with Sedgwick Avenue (which comes in from your right) and Hancock Avenue (which proceeds to your left). Pause here.

On your immediate right is the stone home of George and Ann Weikert. The farm consisted of seventy eight acres and featured a very large barn. One of the family's sons, eighteen-year-old Andrew Valentine Weikert, was a private in Co. C of the 1st Potomac Home Brigade Cavalry (a Federal unit mustered in Maryland known as Cole's Cavalry). Shortly after Longstreet's assault began flooding toward this area on July 2, the family fled the home and it was soon taken over for use as a field hospital. Near the home that afternoon, Col. Strong Vincent's 5th Corps brigade awaited orders. Recognizing the importance of defending Little Round Top to the south, Vincent took responsibility and marched his brigade from this Weikert farm to the rocky hill, where he would soon be mortally wounded.

Turn left onto Hancock Avenue and reset your odometer to 0.0.

Tour Stop 13

July 2 - Longstreet's Assault at Cemetery Ridge

After less than .1 miles, the portrait statue of Fr. William Corby, chaplain of the 88th New York Infantry of the famed "Irish Brigade," will be seen on your right.

Although Corby is depicted here, the statue can be said to memorialize the service of the hundreds of chaplains who served various units of both armies at Gettysburg.

The New York State Auxiliary Monument, just north of the Corby Monument, shown being dedicated in 1925, honors services rendered by those corps, division, and brigade commanders not elsewhere honored on the field. (LOC).

Late on the afternoon of July 2, as the Irish Brigade was forming to march toward George Rose's wheatfield and into action against Longstreet's assault, twenty-nine-year-old Corby addressed the men of the brigade gathered here. As shell and shot flew all around the area, Corby climbed onto a rock that some say is the very rock upon which the statue rests. (Some scholars, however, believe it may have been one now destroyed to make way for the Pennsylvania State Memorial farther along the avenue). Corby prayed over the men and gave them absolution. According to a survivor, some of General Hancock's Federal 2nd Corps in the vicinity fell silent as they watched the service. Corby admonished all of them, Catholic and non-Catholic alike, that the Church would deny Christian burial to any man who did not do his duty this day. With his purple stole around his neck, Corby blessed the men and released them into battle. When the day was over, 198 of the men of the brigade would be dead or mortally wounded.

Following the war, Corby served two terms as president of the University of Notre Dame, rebuilding the college after it had been nearly destroyed by fire in 1879. In 1888, Corby was invited to a reunion of the Irish Brigade for the twenty-fifth anniversary of the battle, and veterans applied to have the priest awarded the Medal of Honor. The request was denied.

Corby died of pneumonia on December 28, 1897. Instead of having fellow priests bear his casket, as was customary, aging Civil War veterans draped the coffin in the old flag of the 88th New York and carried him to his grave. A rifle volley was fired as he was lowered into the ground at Notre Dame.

St. Clair A. Mulholland, former major in the 116th Pennsylvania Infantry of the Irish Brigade on July 2, led the Catholic Alumni Association to honor Corby with a statue at Gettysburg. On October 29, 1910, this statue by Samuel Murray of Philadelphia depicting Corby delivering absolution was dedicated here, the first portrait statue of a non-general erected on the battlefield. An identical copy of the statue was placed outside Corby Hall on the campus of Notre Dame the following year. Due to the Notre Dame football connection and Corby's pose here, Gettysburg enthusiasts have taken to affectionately calling the statue "Fair Catch Corby."

On your left you will pass a number of artillery and infantry monuments and markers that show the positions of these units on July 2, when the Federal line was firmly established here as Longstreet's assault reached its end.

After another .2 miles you will see the large Pennsylvania State Memorial ahead. Bear left as you approach the memorial, and on your left you will see the tall monument of the 1st Minnesota Infantry. Park on the right side of the road here and walk over to the monument to examine the vista afforded to the west and the ground of Longstreet's assault of July 2 from this perspective.

(See maps on pages 59 and 107 as a reference for this section.)

In the distance beyond the monument to your left front, along this side of the Emmitsburg Road, is Sherfy's peach orchard (the location of the "V" advanced line assumed by Maj. Gen. Daniel Sickles' Federal 3rd Corps as discussed earlier). Sometime after 6:00 p.m., while Sickles' corps was being decimated and scattered, Federal 2nd Corps commander Maj. Gen. Winfield Scott Hancock knew he had to buy time to reinforce the line here along Cemetery Ridge. When he realized just how sparsely defended

A setting sun paints the fields "blood red" in front of the Pennsylvania and Minnesota monuments. These fields were defended by Willard's brigade against Floridians and Mississippians of Longstreet's and A. P. Hill's commands on July 2. (Stanley)

the ridge was, and while Sickles' men were running to the rear, Hancock exclaimed, "My God! Are these all the men we have here?" The enemy line, and particularly the men of the 8th and 11th Alabama Infantry (Wilcox's Brigade, Anderson's Division, Hill's Third Corps) were closing in from just 300 yards away. Hancock turned to Col. William Colvill, commander of the 1st Minnesota, and pointed southwest. "Advance, Colonel, and take those colors."

Eight companies, 262 of the regiment's 330 men, were available. Colvill turned and ordered them to "Forward, double-quick march" into the low ground of Plum Run in the distance in front of the monument. Though vastly outnumbered, the Minnesotans heroically charged into Wilcox's nearly 1,700 Alabamians. Southern bullets "were coming like hailstones and whittling our boys like grain before the sickle," recalled one Minnesotan.

Colvill's sudden attack, however, was delivered with such force that it knocked Wilcox's men back for a moment and allowed the Federals to take cover along Plum Run. The Minnesotans, according to Wilcox, charged twice more, a brazen show of determination. While the Alabama troops maintained a heavy fire against Colvill's men, General Barksdale's Brigade advanced eastward on Wilcox's right flank (to your left front).

Turn your gaze to your right front.

In the distance, some 700 Floridians of Col. David Lang's Brigade, Anderson's Division, had already crossed the Emmitsburg Road and were advancing on Wilcox's left flank. Despite Hancock's efforts, it appeared as though lower Cemetery Ridge was about to crack wide open. Help, however, arrived just in time in the form of the 111th, 125th, and 126th New York of Col. George Willard's brigade (Brig. Gen. Alexander Hays' division, Hancock's 2nd Corps). Hancock had summoned the regiments from their posting north of the Copse of Trees. Willard's men engaged Barksdale as Federal artillery arrayed along the line here threw shells into the advancing Confederates.

Barksdale's advance had reached its zenith. The Mississippians held their position for a few minutes before falling back westward. Willard's New Yorkers pursued them, but Confederate artillery firing from the captured Peach Orchard hammered them still. A piece of Southern shell struck the unfortunate Willard in the head, sheared off most of his face, and killed him instantly. The 439 men of the 19th Maine Infantry, part of Brig. Gen. William Harrow's brigade (Brig. Gen. John Gibbon's division, Hancock's 2nd Corps) managed to hold the line and beat back Lang's Floridians.

The fiery white-haired William Barksdale fell about the time Willard was killed. As his men were fighting to hold back the advancing New Yorkers, Barksdale was hit by small arms and artillery fire near Plum Run. When his Mississippians retreated in the face of a Federal countercharge, they were unable to remove their general from the field. Later that evening, a detail from the 14th Vermont Infantry found Barksdale bleeding and lying against his dead horse. At a Federal hospital at the Jacob Hummelbaugh farm, a doctor pronounced his wounds mortal and Barksdale died sometime during the night.

Confederate brigade commander Brig. Gen. William Barksdale, mortally wounded on July 2. (LOC)

Longstreet's assault had shot its bolt, and A. P. Hill's men on lower Cemetery Hill were falling back after meeting stiff resistance that saved the Federal line there from complete collapse. The Minnesotans paid a heavy price for their heroics. More than two-thirds of their men and officers, 215 Minnesotans, lay dead or wounded — a casualty rate of eighty-two percent. Hancock later praised the charge, saying "There is no more gallant deed recorded in history." The next day, July 3, the few Minnesotans left fought against Pickett's Charge; seventeen more fell.

In 1867, veterans of the 1st Minnesota erected a marble urn among the graves of their fallen in the Soldiers' National Cemetery, the first regimental monument on the Gettysburg battlefield. The monument here (sculpted by Jacob H. Fielde) shows a soldier of the regiment going into the battle against Wilcox's Brigade at the double-quick. It was erected in 1893 and dedicated on July 2, 1897. Examine the bronze plaque on the base of the monument, which depicts the regiment's daring charge on July 2. A smaller marker, south of the Copse of Trees and also placed in 1893, marks where the remnants of the regiment fought during Pickett's Charge.

Continue to the Pennsylvania State Memorial.

The largest monument on the battlefield, the nearly seventy-foot high Pennsylvania Memorial features bronze plaques around its base containing the names of all Pennsylvania soldiers who fought in the battle. Upon examination, you will note that there have been a number of corrections on these plaques over the years.

In 1907, as the fiftieth anniversary of the battle approached, Pennsylvania appropriated $150,000 for a memorial to honor all of its soldiers who participated here. Various artists submitted more than eighty designs. In 1909, construction began on this massive memorial designed by architect W. Liance Cottrell.

The Pennsylvania Memorial, the largest on the battlefield, is dedicated to the Pennsylvanians who defended their hearth and home. Here it is silhouetted against a summer sunset. (Stanley)

Atop the dome is a twenty-one foot statue of the "Goddess of Victory and Peace" similar to the one atop the Soldiers' National Monument in the National Cemetery. Sculpted by Samuel Murray, it was fashioned from the bronze of melted Civil War cannon. In her right hand, the statue holds the sword of war aloft, while her left holds a palm leaf of peace.

A walkway surrounds the base of the dome, which is accessible to the public by a stairwell inside where a panoramic view of the battlefield is available. Four archways and Ionic columns support the dome. Granite monoliths adorn the top of each archway and memorialize the four branches of military service. Murray also sculpted these. A scene of the Pennsylvania Bucktail Brigade's fight of July 1 on the McPherson farm honors the infantry. Using a photograph of horses in action, Murray sculpted the scene of cavalry; and the other two scenes depict artillery and the Signal Corps. The names of thirty-four Pennsylvania general officers who commanded troops during the battle appear on the pediment beneath the dome.

Eight portrait statues, each eight feet high, stand in the space between each column. At the time of the 1910 dedication, however, they had not yet been completed due to a lack of funds. Pennsylvania appropriated an additional $40,000 the following year to complete them, and they were ready by the time of the 1913 battle anniversary. President Abraham Lincoln is the only non-Pennsylvanian represented on the monument. The others are the state's war governor, Andrew Gregg Curtin, army commander George Gordon Meade, 1st Corps commander John Fulton Reynolds, 2nd Corps commander Winfield Scott Hancock, 3rd Corps commander (following Sickles' wounding on July 2) David Bell Birney, and cavalry division leader David McMurtrie Gregg. The last — identified as "Pleasonton" — has often confused visitors. Many assume it is the statue of Federal Cavalry Corps commander Alfred Pleasonton, but the cavalryman was not from Pennsylvania nor had he ever resided in the state. (His permanent residence had always been Washington D.C.) His older brother Augustus James Pleasonton, however, lived in Philadelphia and commanded militia troops there as a brigadier general, so the statue — which is a fair likeness — almost certainly represents Augustus. J. Otto Schweizer sculpted Lincoln, Pleasonton, and Gregg, and Lee Lawrie created those of Meade, Reynolds, and Birney. W. Clark Noble sculpted the statue of Curtin, and Cyrus Dallin sculpted Hancock's statue.

When you finish examining this and other monuments in the area, continue straight on Hancock Avenue.

Tour Stop 14

July 3 - The High Water Mark of Pickett's Charge

Since you are approaching the "High Water Mark" and the area of the zenith of Pickett's Charge of July 3, many Federal units that served along this line placed their monuments here. When the road curves sharply to the right, note the small stone monument on your left denoting the area where Maj. Gen. Winfield S. Hancock, commander of the Federal 2nd Corps, was wounded during the attack. Hancock was sitting on his horse when a bullet passed through the pommel of his saddle and entered his inner right thigh up near the groin. He was helped off his mount by nearby soldiers from the 13th Vermont Infantry and a tourniquet was applied to staunch the bleeding. When he withdrew a bent nail from the wound (which almost certainly came from the pommel), Hancock mistakenly thought the Southerners were low on ammunition and shooting anything they could get their hands on — including nails. His recovery was slow, and only several months later was the actual bullet discovered and removed. The wound, however, plagued him for the rest of his life.

A beautiful Gettysburg sunrise silhouettes the 72nd Pennsylvania Monument at the High Water Mark. (Stanley)

Ahead on the left about .2 miles is the High Water Mark and Copse of Trees. Parking is available on the right side of the road.

This area, and the many monuments that decorate the landscape here, can only be fully appreciated by walking it. An excellent view of the field of Pickett's Charge (as well as the attack on the Federal center on July 2) is afforded anywhere along the stone wall to your left (west).

Before discussing Pickett's Charge, let's take a moment to revisit Confederate Brig. Gen. Ambrose Wright's July 2 attack in this area with his brigade of Georgians. Walk down near the stone wall on the other side (west) of the Copse of Trees. From this vantage point you can clearly see the Nicholas Codori house and postwar barn to your left front along the Emmitsburg Road. As Longstreet's en echelon attack (followed by A. P. Hill's men) rolled northward from your far left (south) to this position, Wright's brigade (part of Hill's Third Corps) attacked across the fields and over the Emmitsburg Road running in front of your position. His right flank extended beyond the Codori buildings. After pushing back Federal skirmishers along the road, Wright's men overran Lt. Fred Brown's Federal artillery battery posted between the stone wall and the Emmitsburg Road. The Georgians reached the stone wall immediately south of the Copse of Trees before being repulsed by Federals from Brig. Gen. John Gibbon's division, Hancock's 2nd Corps,

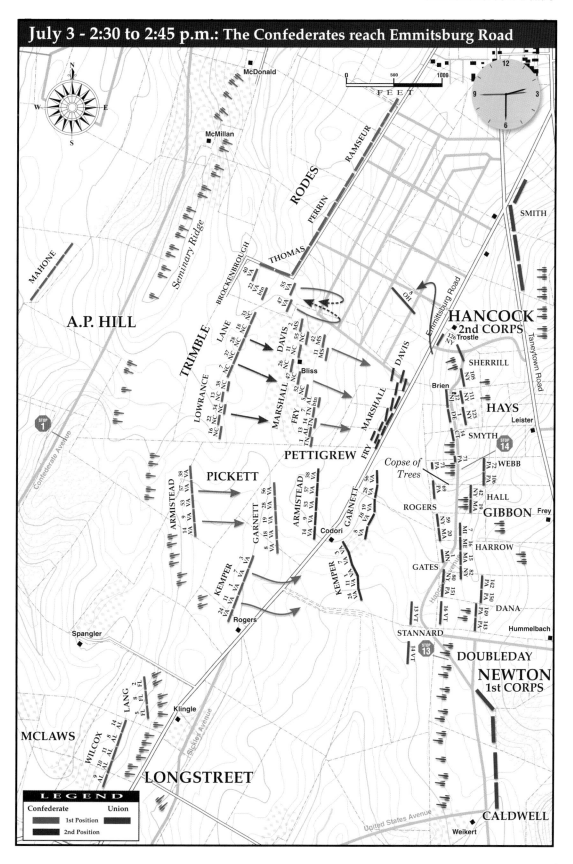

July 3 - 2:30 to 2:45 p.m.: The Confederates reach Emmitsburg Road

as well as the 13th Vermont from Brig. Gen. George Stannard's brigade (Reynolds' 1st Corps) and Federal artillery.

If you were standing here between 2:00 and 3:00 p.m. on the afternoon of July 3, 1863, you would have been an eyewitness (from the Federal perspective) to the grand assault itself. Keep in mind that earlier that morning, Confederate attempts to take Culp's Hill (a little less than a mile behind your right rear) failed. As Lee's Southerners were stepping off for the assault that afternoon, Maj. Gen. Jeb Stuart and his cavalry were beginning their assault (not specifically coordinated with Pickett's Charge) against Federal cavalry three miles to the east of your position.

Look to your far left front, beyond Codori's farm, to the tree line of Spangler's Woods several hundred yards south of the Virginia Memorial (which you can clearly see in the distance straight ahead of where you are standing). There, the brigades of Generals James Kemper and Richard Garnett, with General Armistead's just behind, began advancing. All were Virginians of George Pickett's Division (Longstreet's First Corps). To your right front, along the tree line north of the Virginia Memorial, the brigades of Generals John Archer (commanded by Col. Birkett Fry), James Pettigrew (commanded by Col. James Marshall), Joseph Davis, and John Brockenbrough were arrayed to march straight forward against the Federal line. These troops, under Pettigrew, had the shortest distance to traverse to reach the stone wall. At the center of the attacking line (around the area of the Virginia Memorial), North Carolina brigades under Generals Alfred Scales (commanded by Col. William Lowrance) and James Lane, both of Pender's Division (Hill's Third Corps) advanced behind the right side of Pettigrew's wing of the attack. These troops were commanded by sixty-one-year-old Maj. Gen. Isaac Trimble.

Walk to your right to the famous "Angle" in the stone wall where it jogs to the west just north of the Copse of Trees.

Here, the men of the 71st Pennsylvania Infantry of Webb's famed Philadelphia Brigade watched as the nearly mile-long line of Southerners, flags snapping in the humid summer breezes, steadily

advanced toward thcm. Note their monument here, dedicated on June 30, 1887. At its top you will see "California Regiment," the regiment's unusual nickname. When the war began, California wanted to be represented by a regiment in the Eastern army. Recruits in Philadelphia and New York City were formed into the 1st California Infantry, but by 1862 Pennsylvania claimed the unit and renumbered it. The nickname, however, stuck through to the end of the war and is proudly inscribed on the monument.

Federal artillery aligned all along Cemetery Ridge behind you to your left and your right (including the guns as far away as the summit of Little Round Top) blew great holes in the Confederate lines as they advanced. The remnants of Lt. Alonzo Cushing's battery fired from behind the wall to your left. On the other side of the battery was the 69th Pennsylvania Infantry of Webb's brigade. Note the stone posts along the wall connected by a chain. Each section of this "fence" represents a company of the 69th Pennsylvania posted here that afternoon, and was dedicated July 3, 1887.

To the 69th Pennsylvania's left and rear, the rest of Webb's brigade, as well as the brigades of Col. Norman Hall, Brig. Gen. William Harrow, and Col. George Stannard, anxiously waited along the stone wall as far as the area where Hancock's wounding monument stands. Farther along the wall to your right were the men of Brig. Gen. Alexander Hays' division of the 2nd Corps, who would receive the Southern attack as far north as Emanuel Zeigler's grove. Emanuel and Sarah Ann (Culp) Zeigler's home sat along the Emmitsburg Road to your north, on the east side of the road across from the location of the present-day McDonalds restaurant.

As the entire Confederate line reached the Emmitsburg Road in front of you, Federal artillerymen began switching their charges to canister — tin cans full of iron balls (picture enormous shotgun charges). "The havoc produced upon their ranks was truly surprising," remembered one Federal eyewitness. The anti-personnel rounds blew men down in groups of eight and ten at a time. Pettigrew's infantry on the Southern left (your right) reached the Emmitsburg Road first and exposed themselves to a terrible fire as they climbed over the fences lining the thoroughfare. The sunken road gave them

Old friends Union Maj. Gen. Winfield S. Hancock (circled on left of painting) and Confederate Brig. Gen. Lewis Armistead (circled on right) faced one another during Pickett's Charge. Both fell with wounds, but only Hancock would survive. This scene is from the restored 1883 Cyclorama of the "Battle of Gettysburg" by French artist Paul Philippoteaux. (GNMP)

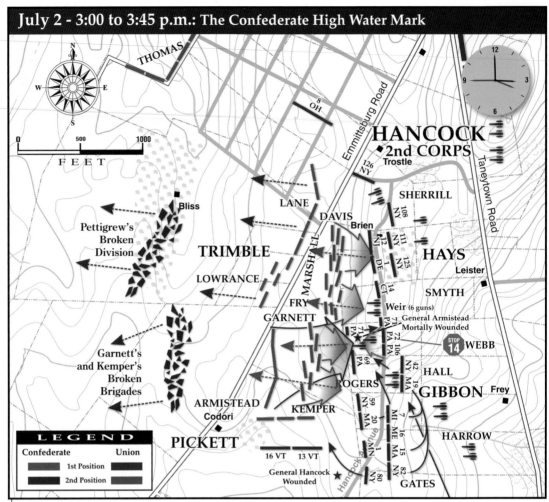

July 2 - 3:00 to 3:45 p.m.: The Confederate High Water Mark

a few moments' shelter before they again became sitting targets as they climbed over the last remaining fence on the far side. To the amazement of many Federals, the Confederates took a minute or so to dress their ranks under fire, which by this time was so intense that only some 1,000 of Pettigrew's approximately 4,000 men were able to continue beyond the road.

Pickett's roughly 4,500 men (advancing on your left front) negotiated fences along the road as well and began angling left past the Codori Farm in your direction. Lowrance's and Lane's men under Trimble, meanwhile, were also approaching the Emmitsburg Road. By this time, Federal fire had reduced the entire attacking force so effectively that only 5,000 or so soldiers (this is a good estimate, as we will never know with any exactitude) were still able to advance on your side of the Emmitsburg Road. In other words, more than one-half of the original Confederate column had been whittled away by death, injury, fear, or exhaustion. Visible everywhere were Southern troops — singly, in small knots, and in larger groups, wounded and unwounded — making their way back to Seminary Ridge. Aligned along this front to receive those brave enough to continue were some 7,000 Federal infantry and artillery. The odds of a Confederate victory had diminished considerably.

Look now to your far left, in the area near the Hancock wounding monument where Colonel Stannard's Vermonters were posted. When Kemper's men (on the far Confederate right) angled toward you around the Codori farm, Stannard saw an opportunity to fire into Kemper's exposed right flank. Stannard ordered his 13th Vermont to advance, and Southerners from the 11th and 24th Virginia fired into them. The 16th Vermont joined their comrades and poured a volley into the Virginians. Col.

Wheelock Veazy of the 16th Vermont watched "great masses of men . . . disappear in a moment" as they mowed down the Virginians. Many threw down their arms and surrendered. Seeing the danger on his flank, Kemper moved quickly to his exposed right and fell within 100 yards of the stone wall with a bullet near his groin.

The Federal batteries continued to hammer the Confederates surging up the slope. So much powder smoke filled the air with its acrid smell that it was becoming difficult for one side to see the other. Some of Kemper's men gave the Rebel Yell and ran to the wall. Garnett's men closed in on the men at the wall just south of the Copse of Trees to your left. Just a few yards away to your left rear, the badly wounded Lt. Alonzo Cushing continued working his remaining two guns of Battery A, 4th U.S. Artillery. Twenty-two-year-old Cushing had been wounded in the shoulder and groin, but refused to leave his guns. He had double loads of canister loaded into his tubes, each blowing wide swaths in the mass of Virginians. By this time any semblance of lines and organization was gone; the attackers lurched forward as a thick gray-brown mob. As Pickett's survivors closed in, Cushing yelled, "I will give them one more shot!" Moments later a bullet struck him in the mouth and instantly killed him. Cushing was later buried with full honors in the cemetery at West Point. Near the spot where he died are the representative guns of his battery and a marker placed in his memory in 1887 by family members, former comrades, and close friends.

Closer to the wall to your left you will see a small granite monument with its top carved in the shape of a scroll. Stand near it and face west. You are now in the general area where Brig. General Lewis Armistead and a few dozen of his men temporarily pushed soldiers from the Philadelphia Brigade away from the wall and briefly "captured" Cushing's guns, which by this time were silent and its commander dead. Armistead had led his men the last difficult yards with his hat held aloft on his sword. Here, inside the wall, he placed a hand on one of the cannons near this monument and was immediately shot down. The Virginians' limited success proved short-lived. Armistead, one of General Hancock's close pre-war friends, was comforted by one of Hancock's officers and lamented the news that his friend, too, had been wounded. Half of the men with Armistead were killed and many others

This 1918 view looks south from the Zeigler's Grove observation tower (now gone). It offers an excellent perspective of both the Union line of defense and the fields over which Confederates charged. Meade Avenue (lower left) has been removed, as has the semi-circular avenue that ran north of the Copse of Trees. (LOC)

wounded and taken prisoner. Although Armistead's wounds were not thought to be mortal, he died July 5 at a Federal field hospital.

While Webb's brigade was beating back the Confederates here near the Copse of Trees, Federal reinforcements rushed in from several directions. Even some of Sickles' men to the rear near the park road, unable to shoot at the enemy, hurled rocks over their comrades into the enemy masses. Corpses representing General Lane's dead North Carolinians were found after the battle in the southern part of Zeigler's Grove near the small Abram Brien farm house. These men can be considered to have penetrated the Union defenses the farthest, but were unable to withdraw. The Brien house and barn are visible along the road to your right rear.

A short distance east of the High Water Mark, Union commander Maj. Gen. George G. Meade had his headquarters in the Lydia Leister home, seen here in this July 1863 Timothy O'Sullivan photograph. (LOC)

Survivors of the assault fortunate enough to avoid death, capture, or maiming streamed back westward. As many discovered, getting back across the nearly one mile of open ground was nearly as hard as crossing it in the first place. Scores refused to make the dangerous effort and surrendered. Confederate losses were about fifty percent, and some of the Southern regiments lost as many as eight out of every ten men. The 14th Tennessee Infantry of Archer's (Fry's) Brigade began July 1 with 365 men. By July 3, only sixty remained to participate in Pickett's Charge. When it was over, only three soldiers out of the entire regiment were left to answer roll call. Federal casualties for the attack were about twenty-five percent.

As the few thousand Southern infantry filtered their way back onto Seminary Ridge, General Lee rode out among them in front of where the Virginia Memorial now stands and accepted blame for the failure. "Your men did all men could do," he told the despondent General Pickett. "The fault is entirely my own." Lee expected General Meade to counterattack, and advised Pickett to prepare his division for it. "General Lee," Pickett lamented, "I have no division now." To his dying day, Pickett maintained some level of bitterness toward Lee for what transpired at Gettysburg.

Once Confederate prisoners had been secured, and the wounded attended to, some semblance of order was regained amidst the scene of carnage. A few moments passed during which the Federals took stock of what they had just accomplished. A few men began to cheer. The trickle spread through the ranks like an ocean wave that grows stronger as it approaches the shore. Within a short time, thousands of Meade's men were cheering their throats hoarse. After suffering defeat after humiliating defeat at the hands of Lee's army, they suddenly realized what they had done — repulsed Lee's grandest infantry charge of the war. The cheering rippled through Hancock's men, rolled to the south, and even spread to the Federals perched atop Little Round Top. The cheering was so loud that Lee's men across the field surely heard it.

Skirmishers went back to their deadly duty while the opposing armies watched one another. No one defending their lines had any idea that the battle had reached its end until the Confederates began retreating from the field late on July 4 and the morning of July 5.

The vast number of dead bodies and animal carcasses scattered all around Gettysburg turned the once-picturesque quiet community into a mass graveyard. Within a few days, many hundreds of Federal dead were buried in trenches on the east side of present-day Hancock Avenue. The ground between the Codori farm south to the intersection of the park road with the Emmitsburg Road was riddled with grave trenches filled with unidentified Confederates. The field of Pickett's Charge west of the Emmitsburg Road had so many graves that one could hardly walk it without stepping on one. Although most of the Southern remains were removed in the 1870s and shipped south to Hollywood Cemetery in Richmond and elsewhere, for years farmers tilling their fields routinely turned over bones to the surface. All over the field, and particularly west of the Copse of Trees and east of Hancock Avenue, the remains of scores of dead horses (especially artillery horses) were burned and buried.

As mentioned previously, the growth hailed today as the Copse of Trees and the "High Water Mark of the Rebellion" was in 1863 a nearly indistinguishable pocket of scrub trees. What drew the attention of the Confederates to this spot was the concentration of Federal artillery arrayed here, and the infantry along the stone wall and the Angle. The title "High Water Mark," however, was bestowed on the group of trees by battlefield historian John B. Bachelder after he toured the area with one of Pickett's veterans after the war. As a result of Bachelder's influence, the High Water Mark of the Rebellion monument was prominently placed here and ceremoniously dedicated on June 2, 1892. The bronze book on the monument lists the units of both armies that participated in the grand assault of July 3. There are many monuments sprinkled about the Cemetery Ridge line, and if you have the time each is worth a visit. Be sure to examine the equestrian statue of Federal army commander Maj. Gen. George Meade, sculpted by Henry K. Bush-Brown and dedicated on June 5, 1896. It directly faces the statue of General Lee atop the Virginia Memorial on Seminary Ridge.

Once you are finished examining the area, we will head for Culp's Hill. Return to your car and drive straight ahead until you reach the stop sign. Turn right and continue straight. Drive past the parking lot for the Soldiers' National Cemetery until you reach the intersection with Taneytown Road. Turn right onto the Taneytown Road and reset your odometer to 0.0.

After .1 miles, turn left onto Hunt Avenue. Drive another .5 miles, turn right onto the Baltimore Pike, and reset your odometer to 0.0. Continue straight for .3 miles and turn left onto Carman Avenue. After .3 miles, bear right onto Colgrove Avenue and reset your odometer to 0.0. Culp's Hill is actually two hills. You are now on the lower hill, separated from the higher summit ahead by a wide saddle.

After .1 miles, you will see the monument of the 2nd Massachusetts Infantry resting on a boulder on the left side of the road.

Tour Stop 15
Spangler's Spring and Lower Culp's Hill

Except for the urn dedicated to the 1st Minnesota Infantry in the Soldiers' National Cemetery, this is the first regimental monument erected on the battlefield. The regiment's veterans association purchased this piece of land to erect the monument, which was put in place in 1879. The regiment was part of Col. Silas Colgrove's brigade, Maj. Gen. Henry Slocum's Federal 12th Corps. The Massachusetts outfit was under the command of Harvard graduate Lt. Col. Charles R. Mudge, who launched an ill-advised charge against Confederate breastworks at the base of Culp's Hill. These works had been occupied by Slocum's troops the previous day, but were abandoned when troops were pulled out of the line to move to other parts of the threatened Federal line. Confederates from Brig. Gen. George "Maryland" Steuart's Brigade (Maj. Gen. Edward Johnson's Division, Ewell's Second Corps) promptly took up a position there.

The attack began from the slightly higher ground south (behind you) on the morning of July 3. When he received the order to make the assault, Colonel Mudge exclaimed, "Boys, it is murder. But these are our orders!" The regiment marched toward the trees and boulders surrounding Spangler's Spring and made it as far as the boulders farther along the road to your right front before being driven back. The survivors reformed along a stone wall west of the monument. The 27th Indiana Infantry on Mudge's right advanced to Spangler's Meadow on the right side of the road and was also repulsed. Mudge was right: the attack was murder, and he was one of its victims. The popular commander was shot in the throat during the assault and killed.

Spangler's Spring has been a popular attraction for visitors since just after the battle. Here, visitors in 1903 enjoy a summer sojourn at this historic site. (LOC)

Continue straight and you will see Spangler's Spring on your left. Park in one of the spaces available straight ahead.

This natural spring is one of the most popular landmarks of the battlefield. Contrary to popular battle lore, soldiers of both sides did not congregate together here to drink water. Soldiers of the Federal 12th Corps gratefully drank the waters of the spring on July 2 while constructing log and dirt earthworks on the hill to the north, and Steuart's Confederates used it when they occupied the works that night. The position on July 3 of the 2nd Massachusetts and 27th Indiana, only yards away, put the spring in No Man's Land until later that morning when the Confederates abandoned the works and the Federals controlled it once more.

The spring's popularity after the war caused a great deal of damage to it, so in 1895 the War Department constructed the present stone and concrete cover over it; a metal door permitted access to the water. Some time later, the spring dried up, so park officials ran a city water pipe to the spring to feed it. This same pipe fed water to the nearby comfort station as well. The pipe subsequently broke, however, so the comfort station was closed and the spring is no longer supplied with water.

Exit the parking lot via the road on the left side of the parking spaces and bear right onto Slocum Avenue. Reset your odometer to 0.0.

Tour Stop 16
July 2 and 3 - Battles for Culp's Hill

As you ascend Culp's Hill, keep in mind that much of this high ground was less wooded during the battle, which allowed a much clearer view through the trees. You will pass many monuments and markers on both sides of the park road, each worth examining. Most of them were dedicated during

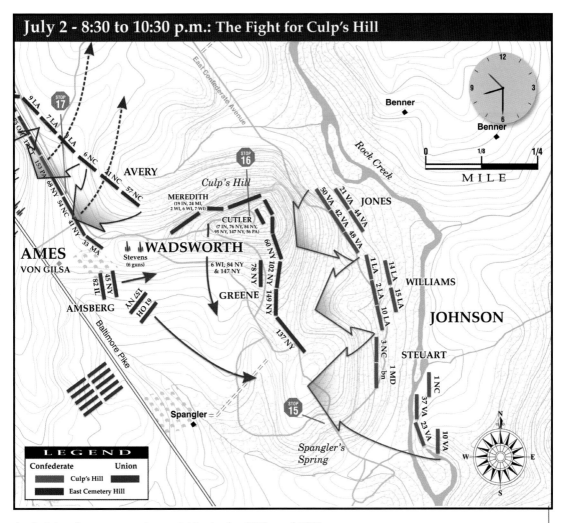

July 2 - 8:30 to 10:30 p.m.: The Fight for Culp's Hill

the height of monumentation activities in the 1880s and 1890s.

The road approximates the positions taken by regiments of General Slocum's Federal 12th Corps. Slocum's corps arrived on the battlefield late on the afternoon of July 1 and occupied this hill the following morning. To help you orient yourself on Culp's Hill in relation to the rest of the battlefield and the rest of the Federal lines, examine the accompanying map and keep in mind that Confederate attacks were delivered from your right (east) on this lower part of the hill from the direction of Rock Creek, and from your right front ahead of you (northeast) at the summit. From the summit of the hill ahead, the Federal line extended from your left front to the Baltimore Pike to Cemetery Hill, then south along Cemetery Ridge to the Round Tops. Thus, you are driving on the curved "barb" of the so-called "fish hook" line assumed by the Federal army, with the pointed hook end snagged in the area of Spangler's Spring behind you.

Brig. Gen. John Geary's division took up a position that ran just north of Spangler's Spring all the way to the summit along the line you are following. Brig. Gen. Thomas Kane's brigade of 700 men formed on Geary's right, along the line as you begin ascending the hill. Farther ahead and to the summit, the 1,400-man brigade of sixty-two-year-old Brig. Gen. George Sears "Pap" Greene's New Yorkers formed. Pap Greene was a civil engineer with a keen mind for building defensive works. His stout defense of the Federal right on Culp's Hill would be his greatest contribution during the war.

Behind Greene, the nearly 1,800 men of Col. Charles Candy's brigade (commanded by Col.

George Cobham) dug in. Behind Kane, Col. Archibald McDougall's brigade of Brig. Gen. Thomas Ruger's division, 1,800 strong, formed along a stone wall. From the very summit, the men of Greene's leftmost regiments could see elements of the Federal 1st Corps extending the line west toward the Baltimore Pike. Most of the morning of July 2 was spent building breastworks; this work was completed by noon. Traces of the breastworks can still be detected; if you stop along the road before reaching the top and examine areas of the ground a few yards to the right (east) of the road, you may be able to distinguish them.

Monuments to the Union regiments involved in the Culp's Hill fighting dot the entire length of Slocum Avenue. These two monuments are to the 82nd Pennsylvania and 65th New York regiments. (Stanley)

After driving about .7 miles you will reach the summit of Culp's Hill. After parking, walk over to the portrait statue of General Greene on the southeast part of the summit.

The 6,000 Confederates of Maj. Gen. Edward Johnson's Division (Ewell's Second Corps) heard and watched as the Federals constructed works on Culp's Hill. Johnson's men were poised to attack Culp's Hill when Longstreet's artillery opened on the Federal left flank late on the afternoon of July 2, but no orders to assault had yet arrived.

About 6:00 p.m., most of the 12th Corps received orders to pull out of their Culp's Hill positions and rush south to Cemetery Ridge to assist in defending against Longstreet's assault. Lee's plan to roll en echelon from right to left was working, and gaps were opening elsewhere in the Federal line. Ruger's division left first and the rest soon followed, leaving only Greene's New Yorkers to defend the hill. About three-quarters of the defenders of Culp's Hill had been stripped away. To provide early warning against an attack, Greene ordered the 200 men in his smallest regiment, the 78th New York, to move down the slope to the east and southeast to act as skirmishers. He also stretched his line farther to the right to cover a wider front, but even after he did so half the distance to Spangler's Spring was nothing but empty undefended space.

Just before 7:00 p.m., orders finally arrived for Johnson to attack. Unfortunately for him, he was short an entire brigade because the 1,300 men of Brig. Gen. James Walker's "Stonewall Brigade" were entangled with Federal infantry and cavalry along the Hanover Road to the east. Darkness was gathering as Johnson's men worked their way west across Rock Creek and up the rocky wooded slope of the hill, driving back Greene's skirmishers. The skirmishers of the 78th New York passed through their comrades and formed behind the line. Greene ordered his men to "hold the works under all circumstances" as Johnson's men advanced screaming the Rebel Yell. Both of Meade's flanks were now in danger of collapsing.

Help for Pap Greene was on the way. Maj. Gen. Oliver O. Howard ordered Col. George von Amsberg's 11th Corps brigade to Culp's Hill from Cemetery Hill, and two 1st Corps regiments hustled south to Greene's right. Johnson's Confederates assailed Greene's works at least four times in the darkness, but were thrown back each time. On Greene's right, however, the defensive line held by

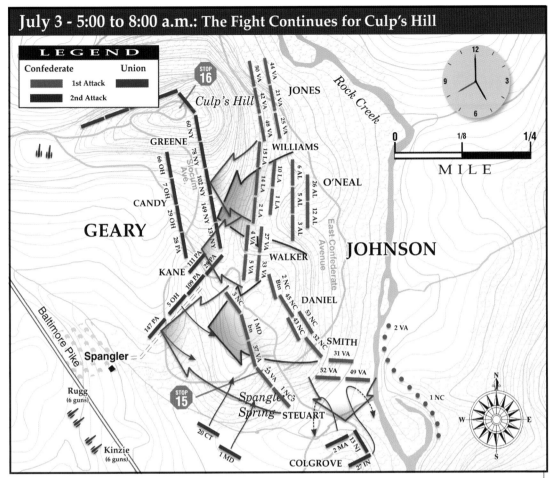

July 3 - 5:00 to 8:00 a.m.: The Fight Continues for Culp's Hill

the newly arrived 61st Ohio, 157th New York, and 71st Pennsylvania regiments was stretched to the breaking point. Steuart's Virginians successfully drove the Federals from their breastworks. Greene's flank was on the verge of being rolled up.

For a second time, help for the embattled Greene arrived. Two more regiments of von Amsberg's brigade — the 45th New York and 82nd Illinois — and three regiments of Brig. Gen. Lysander Cutler's brigade of the 1st Corps (6th Wisconsin, 84th New York, and 147th New York) worked their way in the blackness to the right of Greene's line as Steuart's Virginians attacked up the slope. This heavy force of Federals forced the Southerners back into their captured breastworks. By 11:00 p.m., the night fighting for Culp's Hill had ended, but additional Federal troops continued arriving during the night. The rest of General Slocum's 12th Corps returned from the southern part of the field (where it was not seriously engaged). They would be sorely needed the next day because Southern reinforcements arrived throughout the early morning hours of July 3.

Prior to 5:00 a.m. on July 3, Federal artillery and small arms fire opened on the Confederates, preempting their planned attack. The fighting for the hill would continue until late in the morning. Brig. Gen. John Jones' Virginians east of the summit opened fire on Greene's New Yorkers. To the south, on the lower hill east of Spangler's Spring, the 700 men of the 1st Maryland Potomac Home Guard engaged the 2nd Virginia of General Walker's Brigade, but after suffering more than ten percent casualties the Marylanders marched north behind Greene's line here atop the hill. The 20th Connecticut of Colonel McDougall's brigade went into line near where the Marylanders had fought and began what would be a five-hour firefight with the 10th Virginia of Steuart's Brigade. By the time the sun broke over the horizon, the Federal 12th Corps and its supports were in a full-scale fight for defense of the hill with six veteran Confederate brigades.

As Greene masterfully swapped tired regiments low on ammunition with fresh ones, the Southerners attempted to ascend the slope from the east in the face of a galling fire. "The hill in front of this position was, in my opinion, so strong that it could not have been carried by any force," admitted Brig. Gen. Junius Daniel of General Rodes' Division (Ewell's Second Corps).

General Steuart prepared his Confederates for one final assault southward. As his men advanced across an open field (today called Pardee's Field, which we will visit shortly) the fire from the Ohioans and Pennsylvanians of Kane's brigade ripped through their ranks and brought them to a halt. The North Carolinians of Daniels' Brigade attempted to advance on Steuart's right, but their several charges were likewise repulsed and Daniels finally ordered his men to fall back. General Walker's Stonewall Brigade also failed to dislodge Greene's steadfast men. The seven-hour slugfest for possession of Culp's Hill was over.

The right side of General Meade's line had held — just barely — thanks in no small part to Pap Greene's impressive engineering of breastworks and shifting of troops to meet threats over a wide front. His portrait statue is here upon the summit of the hill that witnessed his finest hour. The securing of Culp's Hill secured the vital Federal supply line along the Baltimore Pike, which ran directly behind the eminence.

When Greene died in 1899, his last wish had been that a large rock from the summit of the hill be laid over his grave. A two-ton boulder was dutifully removed and relocated over his final resting place in Warwick, Rhode Island. On September 26, 1907, this statue by R. Hinton Perry was dedicated by Pap Greene's admiring soldiers and comrades. Greene's likeness looks southeast down the slope where the momentary Confederate breakthrough took place on the evening of July 2.

The observation tower here on the summit provides a spectacular view of the battlefield and the rest of the Federal line, as well as the terrain east and south over which the Confederates attacked this stronghold.

As you begin descending from the summit, reset your odometer to 0.0. After .2 miles you will see a wayside on your right that describes the July 2 night attack on the Federal position atop East Cemetery Hill.

You can easily see the slope rising to East Cemetery Hill directly ahead of you from this position.

Tour Stop 17
July 2 - Night Attack on East Cemetery Hill

When Longstreet's July 2 assault began, the Confederate artillery attached to Maj. Gen. Richard Ewell's Second Corps opened fire on Cemetery Hill and Culp's Hill. Rodes' Division and men from Early's division (both of Ewell's Second Corps) were ordered to assault Cemetery Hill. The order seems to have given both commanders pause. Army of the Potomac artillery commander Brig. Gen. Henry Hunt's massed artillery on Cemetery Hill and Ridge hammered Ewell's guns with so much destruction that it was after 7:00 p.m. before Ewell's attack against East Cemetery hill got underway — about the same time Johnson's move on Culp's Hill began.

Drive another .1 miles and continue straight onto Wainwright Avenue. After another .1 miles you will begin driving along the base of East Cemetery Hill. Pause here.

Two brigades of Early's Division, Brig. Gen. Harry Hays' Louisiana Tigers and Col. Isaac Avery's North Carolinians (approximately 2,200 men total) marched from their position southeast of town to the area to your right (north) to form for the attack on Cemetery Hill. The high ground was defended by General Howard's 11th Corps, which had been sorely battered on July 1, and nearly two dozen cannon. Hays would strike the hill directly from the north while Avery's men (on Hays' left) advanced from the northeast. Rodes' Division was ordered to swing out of town and approach the hill from the west and northwest, hopefully squeezing the Federal defenders from three sides.

Darkness was falling when Avery's men appeared in a meadow east of the hill (to your right). Federal batteries pounded them with shot and shell. The Confederates continued the advance showing tremendous determination in the face of what looked to be overwhelming odds. Hays' Southerners followed suit, moving quickly forward on Avery's right. Within a few minutes Hays' men were no longer being pounded by artillery fire because the steep slope made it impossible for the Federal cannon tubes to be lowered enough to hit them.

Stubborn Federal resistance was discovered when the Louisianans reached the low stone wall ringing the base of the hill. Only by swinging their muskets like clubs could the 7th and 9th Louisiana regiments push back the men of the 25th and 75th Ohio. Jumping over the north wall, the Tigers quickly pushed into the rear of the 25th and 107th Ohio regiments. It was so dark, however, that the Ohioans only knew where their attackers were by their Rebel Yells and discharging rifles. The enemy "came on us about dark yelling like demons with fixed bayonets," recalled a member of the 75th Ohio.

Avery's men farther south hit the Germans of the 54th and 68th New York and easily pushed them back up the slope. The New Yorkers' retreat was "cowardly and disgraceful in the extreme," complained Capt. Bruce Ricketts, a Federal battery commander posted atop the hill. The New Yorkers were so panic stricken as they ran to safety that several blundered directly into Rickett's firing guns and were killed by canister.

Rodes' attack from the northwest was not yet underway when Hays and Avery were busy pushing the advanced Federal line up the slope. Many of Hays' Tigers made it to the top of the hill and the fighting around the Federal battery of Capt. Michael Wiedrich became a maelstrom of gun butts and bayonets. While Federal infantry battled the Louisianans, Wiedrich's gunners tried to beat

In the early darkness of July 2, Confederates under the command of Brig. Gen. Harry Hays and Col. Isaac Avery charged across this field in their quest to take East Cemetery Hill. The attack faltered when supporting troops failed to arrive. (Stanley)

the enemy back with their ramrods. Rocks were picked up and used by both sides. The fight soon resembled something akin to a crazy mob rather than two organized opponents. One of Hays' men stood at the muzzle of one of Wiedrich's guns and claimed it as his own. An artillerist yanked the lanyard and blew the Tiger into more bits than could be found for burial. At least one Federal gun was captured and another spiked to silence it. The Confederates had done the seemingly impossible: they had captured East Cemetery Hill.

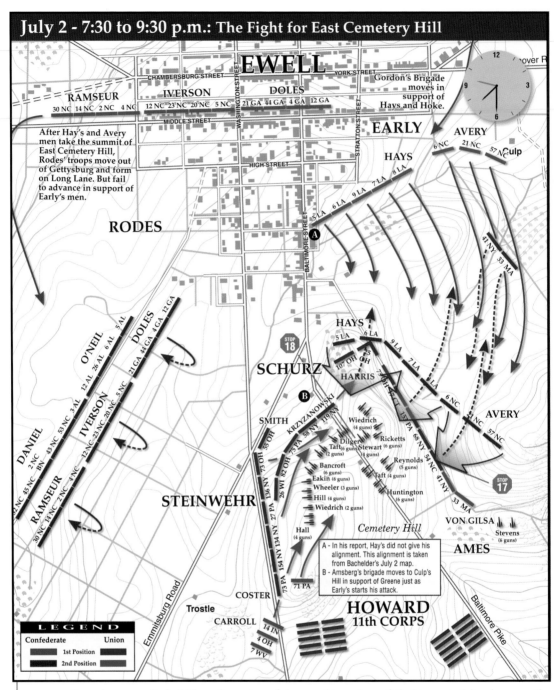

July 2 - 7:30 to 9:30 p.m.: The Fight for East Cemetery Hill

But where was Rodes? The other wing of the attacking pincer failed to materialize because the commander was late getting his men organized. When all was ready and the brigades were aligned outside the town, the division advanced in tepid fashion to the base of the heights. Rodes, who may have been ill that evening, had effectively turned over command to a brigadier. After examining the defenses and consulting with other officers, they determined the attack was too late to support Early's troops. What could have been would never be.

Without reinforcements, the Confederates on top of the hill were doomed to be swept off it. The few hundred Louisiana Tigers and North Carolinians around Wiedrich's and Ricketts' guns waited and listened as Federal troops marched toward them from the southwest. Additional 11th Corps troops and three regiments from General Hancock's 2nd Corps also made their way to the fighting. Hays held his fire because he was unsure if the approaching infantry was friend or foe. When several massed volleys tore into his men, Hays returned it, but knew the battle was lost. He reluctantly ordered his command to fall back down the hill.

A Federal countercharge into Avery's men by soldiers of Col. Samuel Carroll's brigade of the 2nd Corps drove them back as well. Cemetery Hill, the linchpin of the Federal line, had been saved. The slope leading up to it from the north and west, however, was strewn with the dead and dying of both sides. One of them was the mortally wounded Col. Isaac Avery, who had been shot in the neck. The summit of East Cemetery Hill was filled not only with wounded and dead, but the wreckage of the fierce battle for the Federal guns. Mass graves were dug over the ensuing days to inter those whose attack on East Cemetery Hill had been their last.

Continue straight to the stop sign, bear right onto Lefever Street, and reset your odometer to 0.0. After .3 miles, make a hard right at the stop sign onto East Confederate Avenue and reset your odometer to 0.0.

Immediately on your left is the red brick Henry Culp farmhouse, owned by the National Park Service. Since it is close to Culp's Hill, the property served as a large field hospital for Ewell's Second Corps, primarily for Early's Division.

After .2 miles, pull over at the old-fashioned wayside that describes the July 2 and 3 Confederate attacks on Culp's Hill.

Culp's Hill is directly in front of you, and you are looking at it from the northwest. Note that the hill was much less wooded in 1863. Rock Creek, through which Ewell's soldiers marched to attack the hill, meanders through the woods to your left. Drive about .7 miles along the avenue. You are in the

A view of East Cemetery Hill looking south to the Hancock equestrian statue. (Stanley)

heart of the Confederate advances up the hill to your right. Along the way on your left you will see a number of iron markers for the brigades and regiments that participated in the attacks.

Continue straight ahead until you reach the stop sign. Turn right and you have returned to the Spangler's Spring area. Bear right onto Slocum Avenue, reset your odometer to 0.0, and bear immediately left onto Geary Avenue.

After .3 miles you will see Pardee Field on your right.

The field is named after Col. Ario Pardee, Jr., commander of the 147th Pennsylvania Infantry (Kane's brigade of the 12th Corps). This field south of Culp's Hill was defended by Col. Kane's regiments on the morning of July 3, when the Federals attempted to win back soil taken by Confederates the previous evening.

After another .1 miles, turn left at the stop sign onto Slocum Avenue. After driving another 300 feet bear left onto Williams Avenue. Exercise caution since this is a very narrow park road. Drive another .3 miles and turn left to return to the Baltimore Pike. After .1 miles turn right at the stop sign onto the Baltimore Pike. After another .1 miles you will see East Cemetery Hill on your right and Cemetery Hill proper on your left.

To visit the area, parking is available in the lots on the right side of the road just past the hill.

Tour Stop 18
Cemetery Hill – Linchpin of the Federal Line

The top of East Cemetery Hill gives a good view to the west of the ground over which Hays' and Averys' Confederates attacked on the night of July 2, although much of the terrain to the northeast has been destroyed by development. Here at the summit stands the equestrian statue of Maj. Gen. Winfield Scott Hancock, commander of the Federal 2nd Corps. Sculpted by F. Edwin Elwell and dedicated on June 5, 1896, the statue depicts Hancock with hand outstretched to steady the panicked Federals who fled here on July 1 after being routed west and north of town.

Although perhaps better known for his contribution in the defense against Pickett's Charge on July 3 along Cemetery Ridge to the south, it is fitting that Hancock's imposing figure dominates the battlefield area here. The securing of Cemetery Hill and the surrounding heights for the Federals created a solid line of battle that General Lee was unable to break over the ensuing two days. Amidst thoughts of the carnage Americans waged upon one another at Gettysburg in July 1863, Hancock's steadying hand speaks to the result of the war — a unified nation — as loudly as it did for routed soldiers simply trying to find a place to make a stand — and someone to help lead them to victory.

. . . .

You have now completed the tour of the main battlefield. You may now wish to visit Cemetery Hill, crowned by the town's historic Evergreen Cemetery and the Soldiers' National Cemetery. You are also encouraged to visit avenues that run through areas of the field not covered by this tour, such as Ayers Avenue, parts of Sedgwick and Sickles Avenues, and Pleasonton Avenue. In addition, there are many monuments along the Emmitsburg and Taneytown roads, and the Wheatfield Road bordering the northern boundary of the Bloody Wheatfield. If you are able to do so, we suggest you walk rather than drive as much of the field as possible so you can fully appreciate the terrain and immense scope of this battlefield. Select a particular action or a particular day and follow the maps in the book — walk in the footsteps of the soldiers. (If you wish to take even more maps with you to study in the field, we suggest you purchase a paperback edition of Bradley M. Gottfried's outstanding *The Maps of Gettysburg: An Atlas of the Gettysburg Campaign, June 3 - July 13, 1863*. You can pick one up in the Gettysburg Visitor Center and Museum Bookstore or at a local bookstore in town. Personal explorations on foot or by bicycle will give you an appreciation for the battle and battlefield of Gettysburg that can't be savored from an asphalt road. Hopefully, *The Complete Gettysburg Guide* will spark interest for you in a particular action, unit, or commander, and you will often be able to find a book or books dedicated to that particular interest.

Remember that this ground — hallowed by those who sacrificed sweat and blood over it — is ornamented with monuments and memorials, making it the largest sculpture garden in the entire world. Those veterans, whichever color uniform they wore, ornamented the field not just for themselves and their comrades, but for you. They wanted you to see it all. They wanted you to learn from it.

(Opposite page) The Michigan Cavalry Brigade monument honors those who fought at East Cavalry Field. (Stanley)

Tour of the Fight at Brinkerhoff's Ridge, July 2 and the Battle at East Cavalry Field, July 3

"It was the moment for which cavalry wait all their lives"

Although overshadowed by Pickett's Charge, which occurred at roughly the same time on July 3, 1863, the cavalry fight on East Cavalry Field near Gettysburg was a significant mounted clash, and the most well known of the several fights that took place between the mounted arms of both armies during the battle. The East Cavalry Field fight was also the largest. It is also largely misunderstood by many students of the war and casual visitors to the battlefield.

The East Cavalry Field battle is often hailed as

the fight of "Custer vs. Stuart," a title that regrettably ignores the salient role of the Federal commander on the field, Brig. Gen. David McMurtrie Gregg. It was General Gregg who determined to remain in the area of the Hanover and Low Dutch roads behind the right flank of the Federal Army. Had it not been for that decision and Gregg's direction of the fighting, Stuart and his troopers may have created enormous mischief and damage on July 3.

A brief discussion of Stuart's motivation for advancing to what became East Cavalry Field is in order. Popular history characterizes the July 3 cavalry fight as one sparked by Robert E. Lee's "orders" for Stuart to coordinate his movement with Pickett's Charge (the large afternoon infantry assault against the center-right of the Federal line on Cemetery Ridge). As the story goes, Stuart rode toward the right-rear of the Federal Army to act as one major assault force in a two-pronged attack, with the other prong being Pickett's Charge. However, there is no evidence that Lee specifically planned this concert of action; in fact, there is available evidence to refute that interpretation.

Confederate cavalry commander Maj. Gen. J.E.B. Stuart. (LOC)

First, no coordinated movement is ever mentioned or even outlined in Lee's, Stuart's, or any other officer's official report. There is not a single contemporary letter, diary, or other document contending the two movements were coordinated in any way. Second, Stuart's troopers began moving out of their camps about 6:00 a.m. on July 3 — long before the infantry attack that day was even formulated. There is no record anywhere that anyone, at any time, later gave Stuart specific instructions about his movements or any information that had to do with the planned infantry assault. Finally, Stuart had one of his artillery pieces fire several shots when he arrived atop Cress Ridge (which became his position for the upcoming fight), and it is often claimed that these shots were to "notify" Lee of his arrival at the planned jump-off point for the assault. However, because the massive cannonading preceding Pickett's Charge may have already begun (and there at least were several artillery duels taking place on other parts of the field), no one on the main Confederate line on Seminary Ridge would have been able to distinguish those particular shots as any type of a signal from Stuart. Additionally, it would have made no sense for Stuart to announce his presence in that manner to Federals near the Hanover Road (particularly Gregg and his troopers) unless he wanted to reveal his position (which would have been counter-productive). To put it simply, why make all that noise and let the enemy know your location, if the idea is to sneak behind him?

A recently re-discovered and published recollection from one of the artillerymen in Custer's brigade may yield a clue to this issue of coordination. In William B. Styple's (editor) *Generals in Bronze: Interviewing the Commanders of the Civil War* (Kearny, N.J.: Belle Grove Publishing, 2005), artillery commander Lt. Alexander C. M. Pennington related a postwar conversation with one of Stuart's staffers named Maj. Henry B. McClellan. According to Pennington, McClellan told him that when he arrived at his position, "Stuart looked in every direction but could find no sign of our [Federal] troops, so he ordered a gun out and ordered it to be fired in different directions in hopes of getting an echo or a reply from one of our guns, and then through his glass locate the smoke." According to McClellan, they received a reply from one of Pennington's guns following the third shot. Evidently, then, the cannon fire was merely an instrument to locate Federal troops in the area of the Hanover Road, and not any type of signal to General Lee. The myth about Stuart's movement being coordinated with

Pickett's Charge is simply a postwar embellishment designed to further romanticize the Confederate effort on the final day of the Gettysburg battle. It is apparent that Stuart had no specific knowledge about exactly what was planned for the Confederate infantry on July 3 as he rode to Cress Ridge. His goal was to engage the cavalry force on the Federal flank with the hope of exploiting it to his advantage.

Few students of the battle recognize the importance the large skirmish at Brinkerhoff's Ridge along the Hanover Road on July 2 had on Gregg's recognition that the area was a critical road junction and must be held in order to protect the rear of the army — and thus its supply line and possible mode of retreat. Gregg and his Federal 2nd Cavalry Division reached the intersection at the Hanover and Low Dutch roads (about three miles southeast of Gettysburg) just to the rear of the Federal right flank shortly after noon on July 2. The troopers spent nine hours in the saddle to reach the battlefield. Gregg's division consisted of three brigades, but he had only two with him on July 2 and 3, plus artillery (the 2nd Brigade, commanded by Col. Pennock Huey, was guarding the army's wagon trains in Westminster, Maryland). Col. John B. McIntosh commanded the 1st Brigade, which consisted of the 1st New Jersey Cavalry, the 1st Maryland Cavalry, and the 3rd Pennsylvania Cavalry. Capt. Alanson M. Randol's Horse Artillery Batteries E and G of the 1st U.S. Artillery were attached, as well as Capt. William Rank's Battery H of the 3rd Pennsyl-

vania Heavy Artillery. Maryland cavalry called the Purnell Troop were also attached. The brigade was short by two regiments, however. The 1st Pennsylvania Cavalry was on the field but had been detailed to Federal Army commander Maj. Gen. George G. Meade's headquarters as well as the Cavalry Corps wagon guard; and the 1st Massachusetts Cavalry had been detached to the Reserve Artillery.

The 3rd Brigade, led by General Gregg's cousin Col. J. Irvin Gregg, consisted of the 4th Pennsylvania Cavalry, the 16th Pennsylvania Cavalry, and the 10th New York Cavalry. The New Yorkers were already familiar with this area of Gettysburg, for the regiment had spent more than two months there in 1861 camping and drilling on the very fields upon which they now briefly rested. During their brief respite after the hard ride, everyone heard — and some could see — the late afternoon fighting on July 2 that was beginning to break out across the fields south and east of town. The 4th Pennsylvania Cavalry of John Gregg's brigade was ordered to ride to and guard the Federal left flank (and would not

Union cavalry commander Brig. Gen. David M. Gregg. (LOC)

return until late evening), so the division was very low on manpower.

During the mid-afternoon of July 2, skirmishers of Maj. Gen. Henry W. Slocum's Federal 12th Corps infantry began engaging Confederate infantry holding Brinkerhoff's Ridge, a prominent rise across the Hanover Road about one-quarter mile west of General Gregg's position. To provide relief to the foot soldiers, Gregg ordered forward a squadron (approximately two companies) of his 10th New York Cavalry and a section of the 3rd Pennsylvania Heavy Artillery. The artillery unlimbered near the Abraham Reever house to give them a clear field of fire all the way to the ridge, while the New York troopers deployed on the right (north) of the Hanover Road, directly facing the Confederate troops holding a stone wall along the crest of the ridge.

The Southern troops were the infantrymen of the vaunted "Stonewall Brigade," about 1,400 men

Tour Route of Brinkerhoff's Ridge and East Cavalry Field

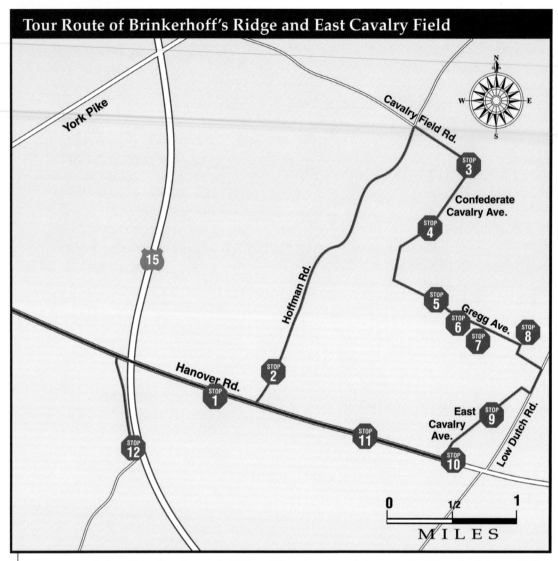

commanded by Brig. Gen. James A. Walker. When he spotted the arrival of Gregg's division, Walker (without orders) pulled his troops out of line facing the Federals atop Culp's Hill and faced them east on the Hanover Road to protect that vulnerable flank. The skirmish that resulted at Brinkerhoff's Ridge, therefore, effectively removed an entire Confederate brigade from the assault on Culp's Hill. Given the narrow Federal victory there, it is fair to assume the presence of another 1,400 men may well have turned the tide on that rocky wooded slope.

One prominent Confederate commander who watched much of the fighting along the Hanover Road was Jeb Stuart. The cavalier had recently arrived on the battlefield with just over one half of his cavalry force after a grueling eight-day ride through Virginia, Maryland, and Pennsylvania. The cavalry chief carefully studied Gregg's deployments and realized that the terrain behind the Federal right flank was conducive to a movement by his troopers. About 7:00 p.m., Stuart left the scene to examine the condition of his own command.

Both sides fought stubbornly for the Brinkerhoff's Ridge position until about 8:00 p.m., when the Confederates drew off. Gregg also withdrew back to the Hanover and Low Dutch Road intersection a couple hours later, and then marched his command to the Baltimore Pike behind Culp's Hill. The clash between the two forces on the flank unwittingly set into motion a major collision the next day between the cavalry forces of Stuart and Gregg, the depleted command of the latter to be augmented by George Custer's brigade.

Early the following morning, Federal Cavalry Corps commander Maj. Gen. Alfred Pleasonton ordered Gregg to move his division closer to Cemetery Hill. Gregg knew, however, that his position at the critical road junctions near Hanover Road could not be abandoned without gravely harming the security of the Federal right flank. Ultimately, Pleasonton permitted Gregg to detach one of the brigades in Brig. Gen. Judson Kilpatrick's 3rd Cavalry Division, bivouacked at Two Taverns, to cover the area. Gregg sent a message to Kilpatrick's camp and began moving toward Cemetery Hill. By the time Gregg's courier arrived at Two Taverns, Brig. Gen. Elon J. Farnsworth's brigade in Kilpatrick's division had already departed for the Federal left flank near Big Round Top, but Custer's brigade remained.

Custer's brigade, made up of the 1st, 5th, 6th, and 7th Michigan Cavalry regiments, was known as the "Wolverine Brigade." Attached to the brigade was Battery M of the 2nd U.S. Horse Artillery under Lt. Alexander C. M. Pennington. When he heard Gregg's request, Custer abandoned his route behind Farnsworth and turned his column to the Hanover and Low Dutch Road intersection.

Even with Custer on the way, Gregg was still worried about what might happen if the position was left uncovered — even for a short time. Contradicting Pleasonton's orders, Gregg retraced his steps and marched both his brigades back to the Hanover Road, then set up a picket line from the infantry's right on Wolf's Hill to the western rise of Cress Ridge. When he had arrived, Custer deployed at the road intersection and faced his regiments toward Cress Ridge and the Rummel farm. Gregg's decision covered every inroad leading to the rear on the Federal right flank. The protection was in place none too soon.

Shortly after noon, Gregg received a note from Pleasonton that a large column of Confederate cavalry had been seen riding eastward along the York Pike straight for the right flank. The body of men was Jeb Stuart and his nearly 5,000 troopers and artillery. (It is often claimed that Stuart had more than 6,000 men on the field, but regimental returns show that of the 6,700 men in the units, fewer than 5,000 were present for duty on July 3). Surprisingly (given what he knew), Pleasonton also ordered Gregg to relieve Custer's regiments and return them to Kilpatrick at the army's left flank.

Shortly after the massive artillery barrage that preceded Pickett's Charge began, other Confederate cannon opened fire from atop Cress Ridge opposite Gregg's and Custer's position. Pennington unlimbered his artillery along the Hanover Road and returned the fire. Dismounted Confederate cavalry were spotted advancing from the ridge. Gregg rode up to Custer and asked him to stay. "Say you never got the message [to leave]," Gregg implored. "I need you here."

"I will only be too glad to stay, if you will give the order," Custer replied. That short exchange sealed the composition of the force Jeb Stuart would face that afternoon. What followed were several hours of mounted and dismounted cavalry fighting — complete with hand-to-hand saber duels, pistol engagements, and spectacular mounted charges. Many troopers on both sides thought the day's battle was the hardest and most deadly of the war. Through much of the action, opposing horse artillery waged devastating counter-battery duels. The end result was decisive: Gregg denied Stuart an inroad to the Federal flank.

As the sun fell on the final day of battle at Gettysburg, Stuart's and Gregg's men fell back to their original positions at the Rummel Farm. Pickett's Charge had also ended in failure, bringing the fighting on the field of Gettysburg to a close.

We will first visit the battlefield at Brinkerhoff's Ridge, and then proceed to East Cavalry Field.

Brinkerhoff's Ridge

To reach Brinkerhoff's Ridge, begin at the town square in Gettysburg and turn onto Rt. 30 East (York Road). After .2 miles, bear right at the Y to drive on Rt. 116 East which turns into the Hanover Road. After about .3 miles, you will cross Rock Creek. In 1863, there was a covered wooden bridge here.

After another .3 miles, you will crest Benner's Hill (77° 12' 46"W, 39° 49' 45"N). On your right is a park road, Latimer Avenue, that leads to Confederate battery positions. Benner's Hill was an important artillery platform during the attacks on Culp's Hill on July 2 and 3 and anchored the Confederate left flank.

The farm of Daniel Benner was on the right side of the Hanover Road just past Latimer Avenue, and Christian Benner's farm is beyond the hill closer to Rock Creek. Note that there are also markers on the left side of the road. To stay with the tour, do not turn here. If you wish to visit Benner's Hill, return to Hanover Road when you have finished.

As you pass the park road leading to Benner's Hill, you are driving roughly parallel to the initial

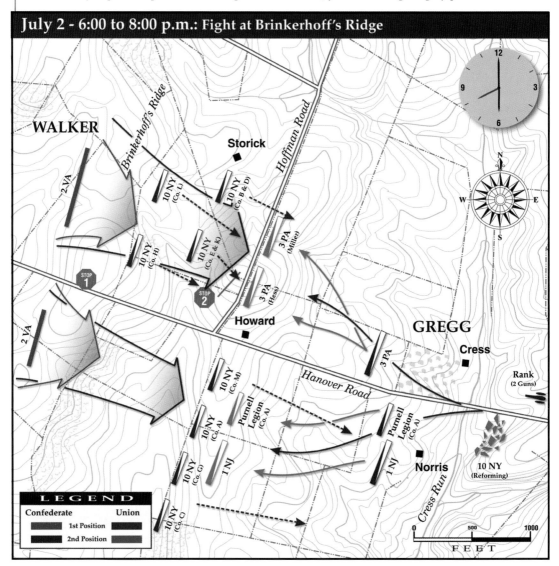

July 2 - 6:00 to 8:00 p.m.: Fight at Brinkerhoff's Ridge

skirmish line of the Stonewall Brigade, which was to your left and set back about 400 yards from the road. Its skirmish line stretched about one mile from the base of Benner's Hill to the western base of Brinkerhoff's Ridge, which is slightly more than one mile to your front. The Stonewall Brigade was the command that attacked Gregg's Federals at Brinkerhoff's Ridge, so keep this location in mind as you proceed.

Approximately .3 miles past Benner's Hill is the beautifully restored Daniel Lady stone farmhouse on your left (77° 12' 25"W, 39° 49' 38"W).

Built about 1835, the wartime home and barn were used as hospitals during and after the main battle; several burials were made in the yard and garden. Lady's fruit orchard stood to the left of the barn in 1863. Soldiers made several carvings in the interior of the German-style barn, and the house and barn were damaged by Union artillery fire from Powers' Hill, all of which can be seen today. Today, the 140 acres are the home of the Gettysburg Battle-field Preservation Association. Founded in 1959, the GBPA has played an important role in saving much of the battlefield from development.

After another 1.1 miles, you will see on your left the monument of the 10th New York Cavalry of Col. John Irvin Gregg's brigade, Brig. Gen. David McMurtrie Gregg's division (77° 11' 25"W, 39° 49' 20"N).

Tour Stop 1
Monument of the 10th New York Cavalry on Brinkerhoff's Ridge

This monument was dedicated on October 9, 1888. It rests in the front yard of a home here on the southern slope of Brinkerhoff's Ridge, named after farm owner Henry Brinkerhoff. In the fields behind the modern home, Companies H and L of the 10th New York Cavalry were pushed back to Brinkerhoff's Ridge ahead of you by the advancing 2nd Virginia Infantry of Walker's Stonewall Brigade just as the fight got underway. The Virginians advanced to the high ground of the ridge.

The monument to the 10th New York commemorating its role in the fight for Brinkerhoff's Ridge late on afternoon of July 2. (Stanley)

Continue another .2 miles and turn left onto Hoffman Road (77° 11' 12"W, 39° 49' 17" N). On your immediate left you will see a War Department marker that briefly describes the July 2 fighting along the ridge. Continue slightly less than .1 mile and turn left into an entrance for a utility plant. You may park your vehicle here, but because this is private property, please take care not to block the entrance or access to the gate. In 1863, this was an unnamed dirt road.

Tour Stop 2
The Fight for Brinkerhoff's Ridge

Exit your vehicle and walk to Hoffman Road. The original stone wall that lined the other (eastern) side of this road in 1863 stood until it was removed by the property owner during the fall of 2008. Decades ago, this wall was still several feet high, just like it was in 1863. Note that because this area was dotted with working farms in 1863, the vegetation — particularly in the areas behind you — was not as thick as it is today. If you had stood here on July 2, 1863, you would be in the thick of the fighting.

When he spotted the arrival of Gregg's cavalry, Brig. Gen. James A. Walker moved his Stonewall Brigade (the 2nd, 4th, 5th, 27th, and 33rd Virginia Infantry regiments, about 1,400 men) out of the line facing Culp's Hill northeast past the Daniel Lady Farm to Brinkerhoff's Ridge. From that position behind you, the Virginians could see Federals forming a skirmish line in the lower farm fields in front of you.

Late in the afternoon Walker dispatched 300 men of the 2nd Virginia Infantry, commanded by thirty-nine-year-old Col. John Quincy Adams Nadenbousch, atop the ridge. As they arrived, Jeb Stuart and his staff pulled up rein near their left flank (on your side of the Hanover Road) to watch the developing action. Nadenbousch and his men quickly realized that the skirmishers forming to their front were cavalry, and not the Federal 12th Corps infantry they were expecting to meet.

Walk toward the Hanover Road. Skirmishers of the 10th New York Cavalry of Col. J. Irvin Gregg's brigade advanced in the fields to your left, and the two sides kept up an incessant picket fire. Capt. William D. Rank's Battery H of the 3rd Pennsylvania Heavy Artillery, attached to Gregg's division and serving as horse artillery, unlimbered their section of two 3-inch Ordnance Rifles on either side of the Hanover Road just behind Cress Run, which you can see in the bottom of the valley.

From the Hanover Road, you can get a view of Brinkerhoff's Ridge in the distance to your right. (Be mindful of traffic along this busy road.) As you face the Hanover Road, off to your left you can see Cress Ridge, and in the valley meanders Cress Run. The home on your side of the stream, near the road, is the John Cress farmhouse.

As the opposing skirmishers fired at each other, each side witnessed an episode that momentarily diverted some of their attention. A mounted rider burst onto the scene, galloping over the crest of Brinkerhoff's Ridge (from your right to your left) hotly pursued by a small group of Confederate horsemen. The rider was Dr. Theodore Tate, surgeon of the 3rd Pennsylvania Cavalry of Col. John B. McIntosh's brigade (Gregg's division). A resident of Gettysburg, Tate had attempted to visit his family shortly after the division's arrival but was blocked by Southern cavalry. Rather than be taken prisoner, he decided to make a break for it. Col. J. Irvin Gregg ordered Capt. Rank to fire a couple shells at the Southern horsemen. The iron missiles halted the pursuit, allowing Tate to make his escape. As the fighting continued, some of Gregg's dismounted men got so close to Stuart and his party about 7:00 p.m., the Confederate cavalry commander hopped into his saddle and galloped west to slip out of danger and rejoin his command. Nadenbousch sent skirmishers from his 2nd Virginia Infantry forward (toward you from your right), to press back the New Yorkers.

To support his thin skirmish line, Gregg sent his troopers on foot up the ascent toward your position, and a foot race broke out between the Federals and the Virginians for possession of the stone wall. "The wall was the key of the position," affirmed Lt. William Brooke-Rawle of the 3rd Pennsylvania Cavalry, "as both the enemy and ourselves at once perceived." The 3rd Pennsylvania Cavalry, slightly more than 300 men commanded by Lt. Col. Edward S. Jones, advanced toward the stone wall bordering Hoffman Road. Company A of the Purnell Legion, sixty-six troopers who were mostly Marylanders commanded by Capt. Robert E. Duvall, advanced on the far side of the Hanover Road directly across from you, and the nearly 200 troopers of the 1st New Jersey Cavalry under Maj. Myron H. Beaumont advanced on the Marylanders' left flank.

By this time the fighting was quite intense. One of Gregg's troopers later recalled, "[I]t fairly rained lead. I was never in such a shower of bullets before nor since. . . . We found our clothes riddled with bullets." The Pennsylvanians reached the wall before the Virginians, and some of the Federals knocked out some of the rocks to better rest their carbines inside the powerful breastwork. Rank's gunners continued pounding the Southerners with his two cannon. Darkness was falling quickly, so Nadenbousch made one final effort by shifting his Virginians to the left to try and out-flank the 3rd Pennsylvania troopers holding the wall. The Virginians ran down the slope, screaming the Rebel Yell all the way. When they hit the Federals, they momentarily routed the company on the flank, but a countercharge sent the Confederates tumbling back up the slope. No more assaults were made, and Gregg held his line. The rebuffed Nadenbousch marched his men back to rejoin the Stonewall Brigade. Shortly before 10:00 p.m., Gregg pulled his men back to the intersection of the Hanover and Low Dutch roads. Stuart, however, now knew that the Federal Cavalry was on the flank, and in some force.

The fight for Brinkerhoff's Ridge had implications for the Army of Northern Virginia far beyond a contest for a largely forgotten ridge. The engagement had pulled the Stonewall Brigade out of the fight for Culp's Hill on the evening of July 2, depriving the Confederates of 1,400 battle-hardened men. Whether or not they may have tipped the scale in the favor of Maj. Gen. Richard Ewell's attack with his Confederate Second Corps is debatable. Of perhaps more importance is the fact that General Gregg obtained a good long look at the relatively flat and open ground on the Federal right flank between Cress Ridge and the road intersection. The flank was secured on good high ground at Culp's Hill. But where there is high ground there must be low ground — and Gregg knew that any attack the next day must come from the latter.

. . . .

East Cavalry Field

To visit East Cavalry Field, turn left back onto Hoffman Road and reset your odometer to 0.0. As you drive along this road, which was a narrow dirt lane in 1863, note how it winds its way along the original road trace. Exercise caution here, as the road is narrow in places and some curves are sharp. You will pass several wartime structures. (Two are of special note. First, the beautiful wartime stone home of George Trostle on your left after .8 miles. After another .3 miles is the Jacob and Rebecca Rinehart farm on the left. The barn is thought to date to the war, but the house does not. A cavalry hospital was established in the original home, and at least one of Custer's troopers wounded on July 3 was initially cared for there.)

After a total of 1.4 miles, turn onto Cavalry Field Road on your right (77° 10' 20"W, 39° 50' 28"N). Drive less than .1 miles and you will see the Isaac Miller farm and tannery on your left. Miller's farm was used as a hospital for the wounded in Stuart's cavalry division (as well as for wounded and captured Federals) after the East Cavalry Field fighting of July 3. A postwar addition was built onto the house, but the original home and barn were constructed in the early 1800s.

Shortly after passing the Miller farm, the road begins to narrow. The Park property of East Cavalry Field begins at this point, and the road appears much as it would have in 1863. At that time, the road was sunken in places and lined with a wooden fence. Exercise caution while driving.

The William A. Sweetland fence post burial marker near the East Cavalry Field. (Stanley)

Once you leave the York Pike you are on the route Jeb Stuart and his cavalry took to reach Cress Ridge with the hope of mounting a successful attack on the Federal right flank. Stuart had with him nearly 5,000 troopers plus several batteries of artillery.

About 100 yards past the Miller farm, slow down (be careful of traffic) when you see an unusual home on the right that has only its roof showing above ground. Just beyond is a thick stand of woods known in 1863 as Cress Woods.

Pause at the wood line. Along this line of timber you will see a lone fencepost near a large tree about thirty yards in from the road. According to original accounts, a badly wounded Confederate of Stuart's cavalry who died at the Miller farm on July 3 was buried along the tree line two posts in from the road. This spot has been memorialized by generations of local farmers with that lone-standing fencepost. Recent research by Gettysburg Licensed Battlefield Guide Gary Kross suggests the deceased may have been Lt. William A. Sweetland of Co. K, 16th Virginia Cavalry, part of Brig. Gen. Albert Jenkins' Brigade (commanded on July 3 by Lt. Col. Vincent Witcher). It has not been definitely determined if the soldier's body was ever removed to a different resting place, so he may still repose at this spot.

Slowly drive ahead and in slightly fewer than 100 yards you will see a thin break in the woods on the right side. If you look carefully, you will see the remains of an old road trace. This the wartime trace of the John Rummel farm lane where it joined the road here. It offered access to the farm prior to the building of the park road.

After another .1 miles, the road curves sharply to the right and becomes Confederate Cavalry Avenue (77° 10'01"W, 39° 50'18"N).

Tour Stop 3
Jeb Stuart's Position on Cress Ridge

At this curve, note that the old road trace of this farm lane can be seen ahead of you as it continues into the woods. Wade Hampton's Brigade, just shy of 2,000 men strong, was ordered by Stuart to use this old farm lane (which was lined with a fence on both sides and hidden by the woods) to enter the field under cover. Jeb Stuart, the horse artillery, and the brigades of Brig. Gens. William Henry Fitzhugh "Rooney" Lee and Albert Jenkins rode to the right along the ridge that the park road follows ahead and deployed while Hampton was getting into position.

You are now on Stuart's position atop Cress Ridge, the highest point in the area for a considerable distance. However, the view is not unlimited. Note that you cannot see the very bottom of the ridge from this position. As you walk along the park road (which was not here at the time of the battle, although a fence line enclosing farm fields approximated its trace) you will see markers for Jones' Battalion of Capt. Charles A. Green's Louisiana Guard Artillery, which

This view on Confederate Avenue on East Cavalry Field looks from Stuart's position toward the Rummel Farm in the distance. (Stanley)

had been detached from Ewell's infantry corps since the cavalry fight at Hunterstown the evening before. The battalion consisted of two 10-pounder Parrotts and two 3-inch Ordnance Rifles. The woods behind these markers were known as Cress' Woods. In and along these trees (which were much thinner in 1863 than today) the cavalrymen formed.

Return to your vehicle and reset your odometer to 0.0. After .1 miles, you will reach the position taken by Capt. James Breathed's Battery of the 1st Stuart Horse Artillery, with a marker on the left. The battery consisted of four 3-inch Ordnance Rifles.

After another .1 miles, you will reach the position taken by Capt. William M. McGregor's Battery (Beckham's Battalion) of the 2nd Stuart Horse Artillery, again with the marker on the left. The battery consisted of two Napoleons and two 3-inch Ordnance Rifles.

Continue for another .1 miles and you will reach the John Rummel farm, which you can see in the distance on your left (77° 10' 14"W, 39° 50' 03"N). On your left is a marker denoting the position of Capt. Thomas E. Jackson's Charlottesville Battery. Stop here.

Tour Stop 4
The Rummel Farm and the First Confederate Artillery Shots

Just behind you on the right side of the road is a stone marker for Wade Hampton's Brigade. It was near that spot that the wartime trace of the Rummel farm lane emerged from the woods.

When his men and artillery were formed in line along the ridge, Stuart ordered Capt. William H. Griffin to bring forward one of the four 10-pound Parrott Rifles of his 2nd Baltimore Light Artillery. He then ordered Griffin to fire a shot from near here to try and get an answer from the Federals and thus determine their position (again note that it was not any sort of signal to Robert E. Lee). After the third shot, an answer from one of Lt. Pennington's guns arrived. According to Stuart's staffer Maj. Henry B. McClellan, the shot flew right into the muzzle of Griffin's gun, broke both wheels, dismounted the barrel, and rendered it useless. Pennington did not know of his miraculous shot until McClellan informed him of it in a postwar conversation.

In his postwar memoirs, McClellan wrote that Stuart ordered four shots fired in each direction of the compass, contradicting his conversation with Pennington. McClellan's statement seems unlikely.

It would have been illogical for Stuart to fire behind his position, for he had just ridden up from that direction. Firing directly along the left or right of his line would have been extremely dangerous to his own men. In all probability, Stuart fired only three shots, each aimed differently to strike in a broad stroke across his front in the direction of the Hanover Road, where he expected Gregg's force to be. This is in keeping with McClellan's conversation with Pennington, and makes the most sense.

The large barn of John Rummel you see to your left was here at the time of the battle. The house, however, is a postwar home. The original Rummel house (a log structure) stood slightly to the left and in front of the present home as you see it from this vantage point (the foundation of the old

In 1905, William Tipton took this photo of the Rummel farm. The only structure that survives from the battle today is the Rummel barn. (ACHS)

springhouse still can be seen on the property behind the original home). The Rummel buildings consisted of the log home, the large barn, a blacksmith shop, and the springhouse, all sitting on 165 acres of rolling farmland and woodlots. The barn still shows damage done by artillery shells. Even though the farm is protected under National Park boundaries, it is still private land, so please do not trespass.

From the position to your right front, shortly before 1:00 p.m., Confederate troopers advanced on foot to take possession of the area surrounding the Rummel farm buildings. The men were from two brigades: Jenkins' (led on July 3 by Lt. Col. Vincent A. Witcher in place of the wounded Jenkins), and Rooney Lee's (commanded by Col. John Chambliss in place of the wounded Lee, who fell at Brandy Station on June 9). When a detachment of the 6th Michigan Cavalry of Custer's brigade spotted the advancing troopers, Custer ordered Pennington to fire on them from his guns near the Hanover Road. The Federal tubes got the best of Griffin, however, and about one-half of his horses were killed and four men were wounded. Griffin withdrew his battery of four 10-pounder Parrott Rifles, and Capt. Thomas Jackson's Charlottesville Battery came forward to a position behind you to engage Pennington. Green's artillery battalion, as well as the batteries of Breathed and McGregor, also came into line.

Custer began to form his brigade in line of battle, and Col. John B. McIntosh, commander of the 1st Brigade of Gregg's division, ordered the troopers of his 1st New Jersey cavalry alongside them near the Lott Farm on either side of the Low Dutch Road. At this point Gregg arrived back on the field, assumed command, and asked Custer and his brigade to remain with him (as previously discussed). Custer agreed.

Note that it was from this position near the marker for Jackson's Battery that Stuart watched most of the battle.

After another .1 miles, Confederate Cavalry Avenue curves to the left. At this point, pause and look behind you to get an idea of Stuart's commanding position atop Cress Ridge.

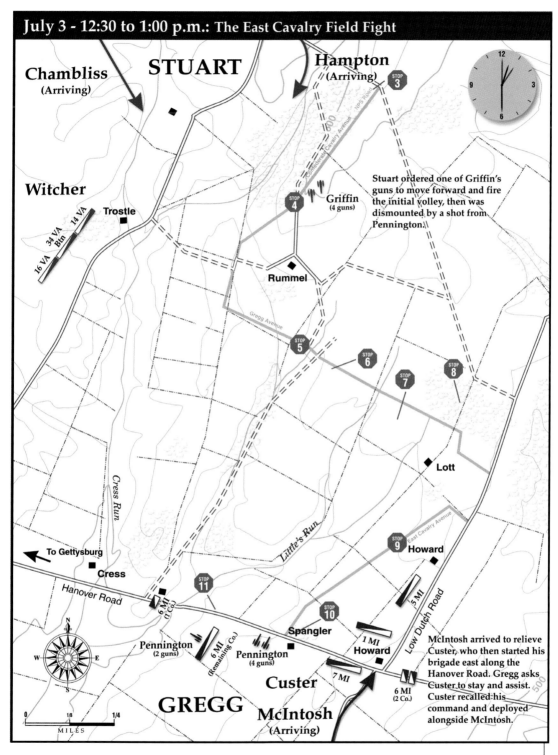

July 3 - 12:30 to 1:00 p.m.: The East Cavalry Field Fight

Chambliss
(Arriving)

STUART

Hampton
(Arriving)

STOP 3

Witcher

Trostle

34 VA Btn   14 VA

16 VA

Stuart ordered one of Griffin's
guns to move forward and fire
the initial volley, then was
dismounted by a shot from
Pennington.

STOP 4

Griffin
(4 guns)

Rummel

Gregg Avenue

STOP 5

STOP 6

STOP 7

STOP 8

Lott

Cress Run

Little's Run

East Cavalry Avenue

STOP 9   Howard

To Gettysburg

Cress

Hanover Road

STOP 11

6 MI
(1 Co.)

Low Dutch Road

.5 MI

STOP 10

Spangler

1 MI
Howard

McIntosh arrived to relieve
Custer, who then started his
brigade east along the
Hanover Road. Gregg asks
Custer to stay and assist.
Custer recalled his
command and deployed
alongside McIntosh.

Pennington
(2 guns)

6 MI
(Remaining Co.)

Pennington
(4 guns)

7 MI

6 MI
(2 Co.)

Custer

GREGG   McIntosh
(Arriving)

N
W   E
S

0   1/8   1/4
MILES

From his vantage point, Stuart could see McIntosh's and Custer's troopers deploying west toward the Rummel buildings. Stuart readied his hidden troopers — the brigades of Hampton and Fitz Lee — to hit the Federals in their flank once Gregg and Custer were exposed.

After advancing over the low ground to your right, 172 men from Witcher's 34th Battalion of Virginia Cavalry occupied Rummel's barn and a fence line to your left about halfway to the tree line.

Witcher's men took John Rummel prisoner, but his wife Sarah was allowed to leave. Witcher's men found themselves at a disadvantage when skirmishing with the Federals because each man had only ten rounds of ammunition for their Enfield rifles. Keep in mind that because of the terrain, Gregg and Custer could only see the Confederates surrounding the Rummel property; they could not see Stuart's main line of battle atop Cress Ridge.

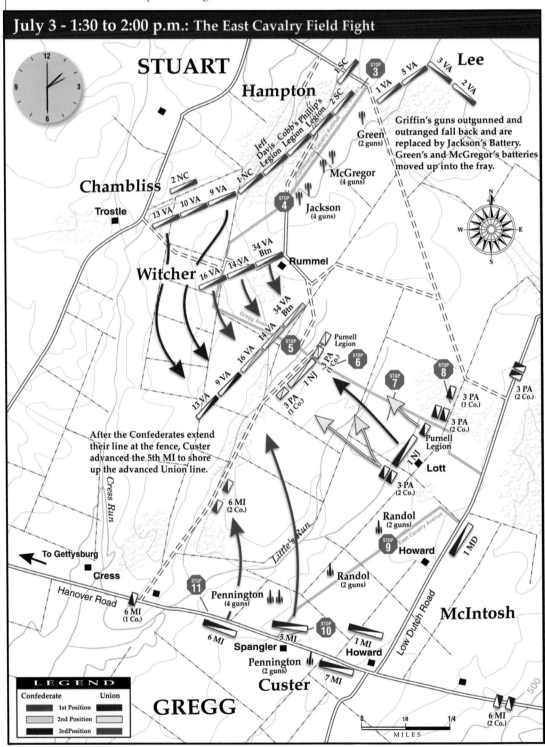

July 3 - 1:30 to 2:00 p.m.: The East Cavalry Field Fight

To support his skirmish line, McIntosh ordered up the men of the 3rd Pennsylvania Cavalry, and brought in the balance of his brigade when the fighting became heavy. We will now continue along the park road (which becomes Gregg Avenue as it curves again to the left) to get a better perspective of the fighting. Note as you drive that you have an excellent view of the Rummel Farm on your left.

> *After another .3 miles, you will see the 1st New Jersey Cavalry monument on your left (77° 10' 12"W, 39° 49' 43" N). There is also a wayside marker here that is slightly misleading because it states that Stuart's "objective was to exploit the anticipated success of the Confederate infantry assault on Cemetery Ridge." It is still worth examining for its description of the fighting.*

Tour Stop 5

Monument of the 1st New Jersey Cavalry and the Charge of the 5th Michigan Cavalry

The high number of casualties listed on the front of the 1st New Jersey's monument is a testament to the hard fighting performed by the regiment during the war.

Look to the right of the monument, and you will see the trace of Rummel's farm lane, which today is little more than a footpath. As you look to the Rummel Farm, you are facing directly north.

Stuart had not planned for such a large dismounted fight in the fields surrounding the Rummel buildings ahead of you. His hope had been to send a large mounted force toward the Hanover and Low Dutch Road intersection he had observed the evening before. The cannonading that preceded Pickett's Charge was still ongoing, and all of the troopers here plainly heard it.

Custer deployed the men of his 5th Michigan Cavalry dismounted toward Chambliss' troopers to the west side of Rummel's barn (to the left side from your perspective). All of the 5th Michigan Cavalry was armed with the new seven-shot Spencer repeating rifles (not the carbine model, which would be issued a few months later). The devastating fire from these guns pushed the Southerners back. Running low on ammunition, however, the Michiganders also began falling back. Maj. Noah H. Ferry of the 5th Michigan cheered his men on, and then fired a few rounds from the Spencer rifle of a wounded comrade. Turning to his men, Ferry shouted, "Rally, boys! Rally for the fence!" At that moment, a Confederate bullet struck his skull and killed him instantly. Unable to recover his body in the face of Witcher's advancing men, Ferry lay on the field until the following morning, when he was recovered by a detachment of his 5th Michigan comrades.

Gregg's and Custer's artillery continued pounding the Confederates on the Rummel Farm, and Witcher's and Chambliss' men began to fall back to the line atop Cress Ridge. The Federals stayed on their heels and took possession of the Rummel buildings, clearing them of the enemy. A brief lull in the fighting ensued when the Federals at the Rummel Farm got a glimpse of Stuart's line and artillery atop Cress Ridge.

Stuart, however, still intended to stick with his original plan. He ordered the 300 men of the 1st Virginia Cavalry, led by Col. James H. Drake, to charge the Federal line in your direction. As they trotted across the fields, Gregg rode to Col. William D. Mann, commander of the 7th Michigan of Custer's brigade, and ordered his regiment of nearly 400 troopers to countercharge. Not to be left behind, Custer trotted to the head of the regiment, drew his blade with a flourish, and pointed it straight at the Virginians. They, too, went off at a gallop.

The Pennsylvanians on the right fired into the Southerners as they spurred their horses on. When the two sides collided, one Federal officer who watched the stunning spectacle described it as "the waves of the sea upon a rocky shore, until all were mixed in one confused and tangled mass." The color bearer of the 7th Michigan was shot off his horse, and the flag was lost to the Virginians. Chambliss sent a staffer to Hampton for assistance, who in turn sent his Jeff Davis Legion and the 1st North Carolina, more than 600 men combined. With the weight of numbers against them, the Michiganders were pushed back toward the Hanover Road. The 1st New Jersey, 3rd Pennsylvania, and the 5th and 6th Michigan fired volleys into the Confederates, and several counterattacks by the 7th Michigan Cavalry sent the Confederates back toward the Rummel Farm. However, Stuart recognized that an assault by only part of his force had nearly hammered the Federals back to the Hanover Road (the point he wished to reach). He concluded that a much larger mounted strike had a chance to wipe the enemy off the field.

> *Reset your odometer to 0.0. About forty yards distant is Cress Run, which you will cross. After .1 miles, you will see the William Brooke-Rawle Flagpole monument on your right (77° 10' 05"W, 39° 49' 40"N).*

William Brooke-Rawle (right) stands next to the flagpole that bears his name in this early 1900s Tipton photo. (GNMP)

Tour Stop 6

The Brooke-Rawle Flagpole Monument

A flag rarely flies today from this pole, a battlefield monument erected in 1909 in honor of Lt. William Brooke-Rawle of the 3rd Pennsylvania Cavalry (1843-1915). Brooke-Rawle wrote extensively about the fighting at East Cavalry Field, and ended the war as a brevet lieutenant colonel. At this spot, the 9th and 13th Virginia Cavalry regiments broke through the line of the 5th Michigan Cavalry and temporarily rode into the rear of the Wolverines.

> *Slightly less than .2 miles beyond the flagpole is a parking area on your right (77° 09' 53"W, 39° 49' 36"N). The large monument to your right is the Michigan Cavalry Brigade monument, and the grassy lane leading to it is Custer Avenue. There is also a wayside marker here.*

Tour Stop 7

The Michigan Brigade Monument and Stuart's Mounted Assault

Exit your vehicle and look toward the Rummel Farm. Note that because of the terrain, you cannot see the crest of Cress Ridge from this position. The same is true from the opposite side of the field: someone standing at Stuart's position would not be able to see you. In the distance to your right rear are the buildings of the Jacob Lott Farm.

Stuart decided upon a large mounted charge to sweep away the horsemen of Gregg's division and Custer's brigade. On the left side of the line were nearly 400 men of the 2nd Virginia Cavalry, commanded by Col. Thomas T. Munford in Fitz Lee's Brigade, who advanced dismounted. The 1st and 5th Virginia regiments, another 450 troopers, lined up mounted (the 3rd Virginia Cavalry remained in reserve). On their left was Wade Hampton's 1,200-man brigade consisting of the 1st and 2nd South Carolina, the 1st North Carolina, Jeff Davis Legion, and Phillips' Legion (Hampton's Cobb's Legion remained in reserve). When the bugle sounded, the long line first moved at a walk directly toward your position, and after a short interval increased its speed to a trot. "It was the moment for which cavalry wait all their lives," one of Stuart's troopers reminisced. "If the Federal cavalry were to be swept from their place on the right, the road to the rear of their center gained, now was the time."

The beautifully dressed lines, with guidons snapping in the breeze and sabers held upright at the ready, impressed the waiting Federals. Capt. William E. Miller of the 3rd Pennsylvania Cavalry, who would be awarded the Medal of Honor for his part in repulsing the approaching charge, admired the precision of the Southern ranks. "A grander spectacle than their advance has rarely been beheld. They marched with well-aligned fronts and steady reins. . . . All eyes turned upon them." Stuart's troopers maintained their lines well even though they had to navigate several ditches and at least two fences that had to be torn down to allow them to proceed.

When the Confederates were about half way across the field, Pennington's and Randol's gunners fired canister at them from their positions behind you. The fire blew holes in the Confederate line, but they continued trotting toward the Federal line. Gregg ordered his only reserve regiment, Custer's 1st Michigan Cavalry, to charge into the left flank of the massive wave of Southern cavalry. Col. Charles H. Town, who commanded these 400 troopers, was dying of tuberculosis. Although weak and barely able to speak, he refused to leave the service and his beloved regiment. Town ordered his men forward,

The Michigan Brigade Monument is dedicated to the Wolverines who fought at East Cavalry Field. (Stanley)

although barely able to manage more than a whisper. As he had previously with the 7th Michigan, Custer spurred up to Town, drew his saber, and rode alongside him.

As both sides picked up their pace toward what promised to be a massive collision of men, steel, and horse flesh, dismounted Federals on the flanks fired into the Confederates and Pennington and Randol kept up their artillery fire in an attempt to soften the assault. Stuart's artillerymen likewise maintained their fire on Gregg's line. For a better view of the action, Stuart and his staff rode along Cress Ridge in the distance to your left front. When a Federal shell dropped close to Stuart, Major McClellan implored his leader to move to safer ground. Stuart would have none of it, standing fast on his horse with his eyes glued on his men.

Near the Jacob Spangler home along the Hanover Road behind you, some Michiganders in the front began to show their anxiety. Custer waved his saber, turned to the 7th Michigan, and shouted, "Come on, you Wolverines!" and spurred his horse. (We will soon visit the site where this took place.) The 1st Michigan hit the left flank of Wade Hampton's columns so hard that Captain Miller likened it to "the falling of timber, so sudden and violent that many of the horses were turned end over end and crushed their riders beneath them."

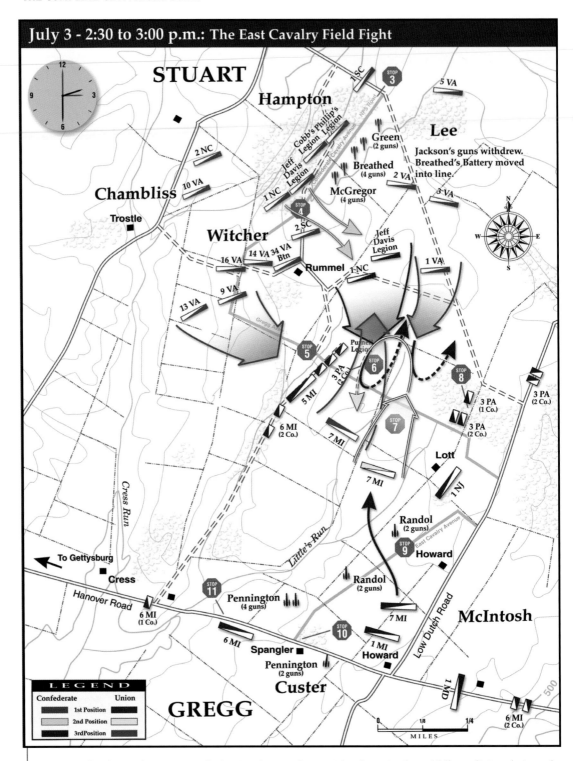

July 3 - 2:30 to 3:00 p.m.: The East Cavalry Field Fight

The 400 Wolverines struck the Southern column right about in the middle, splitting their ranks and shoving troopers one upon another. A Confederate bullet hit Custer's horse Roanoke in the foreleg, throwing the young general to the ground. Custer leapt to his feet and jumped on the first riderless horse he spotted to continue fighting with his blade. With the Confederate assault momentarily in disarray, Federal commanders realized an opportunity for a counterassault.

Col. Russell A. Alger ordered the 600 men of his 5th Michigan Cavalry to mount up and charge. The regiment ran to their horses and jumped in the saddle. Although their charge was rather disorganized, it had its intended effect when the Wolverines crashed into the right flank of Fitz Lee's advancing column. Likewise, Colonel McIntosh gathered his staff and as many men as he could find — including his headquarters escort — and charged the small group into the right front of Fitz Lee's men.

Capt. Miller of the 3rd Pennsylvania Cavalry of McIntosh's brigade held his position, as ordered, in the woods north of the Jacob Lott farm to your immediate right. (We will visit this location shortly.) As the fighting raged to his front, Miller could not stand by idly any longer. His companies were hidden in a slight depression in the woods and were not seen by the Confederates. The captain turned to Lt. William Brooke-Rawle and said, "I have been ordered to hold this

> *"Since the war, while going over the field in company with Mr. Rummel, he told me that he had dragged thirty dead horses out of [his] lane."*
>
> **Capt. William E. Miller,**
> **3rd Pennsylvania Cavalry**

position, but if you will back me up in case I am court-martialed for disobedience, I will order a charge." Brooke-Rawle agreed, so Miller ordered his men to fire a volley, draw their sabers, and move out. The squadron rode out of the woods and over the slight rise in front, and they crashed directly into the Confederate column. Miller's impetuous charge cut off nearly a third of the Confederates, which they then drove back toward Cress Ridge. Miller's saber was broken near Rummel's barn and he was shot in his left arm. The Pennsylvanians advanced to within 100 yards of Breathed's Battery before turning around and cutting their way back toward the Lott farm.

Moments later, men of the 1st New Jersey Cavalry, in reserve along the Low Dutch Road, spotted Confederates near the Lott buildings. The Jerseymen spurred their mounts and smashed into Fitz Lee's left flank just south of where Miller's charge had struck. As they drove forward, several soldiers in the 1st New Jersey saw an officer fighting his way through the action. The Southerner turned out to be Wade Hampton. Hampton's position was near a fence (which is marked by the diagonal line of trees you see ahead of you in the field). The New Jersey men drove for Hampton and surrounded him, slashing at him with their sabers. Hemmed in by the fence, the big South Carolinian fought for his life with his blade, a heavy four-foot straight sword. He managed to slash one Federal out of his saddle and shoot two others with his pistol. The odds were heavy, however, and one Federal brought down his sword on Hampton's head, slicing through his scalp; another shot him in the side from behind. "You dastardly coward — shoot a man from the rear!" Hampton yelled. With blood running down his head and his torso on fire from the bullet wound, Hampton was struck once more on the head. He turned to face the offender, raised his heavy sword over his head, and brought it down on the Federal's skull, cleaving his head in two down to his chin.

Hampton continued turning this way and that, cutting and parrying in an effort to stay alive. Finally, some of his men spotted their embattled commander and rode to his rescue. The severely injured Hampton somehow managed to leap his horse, a large bay named Butler, over the fence and galloped toward Cress Ridge. His wounds were painful and serious, but not mortal. He was taken to the rear in an ambulance.

The brave Federal attacks sucked the momentum from Stuart's mounted charge, and it was now obvious it would not be successful. The Confederates pulled back north of the Rummel Farm, leaving a skirmish line to protect the rear. When Federal pursuers approached too close, Stuart person-

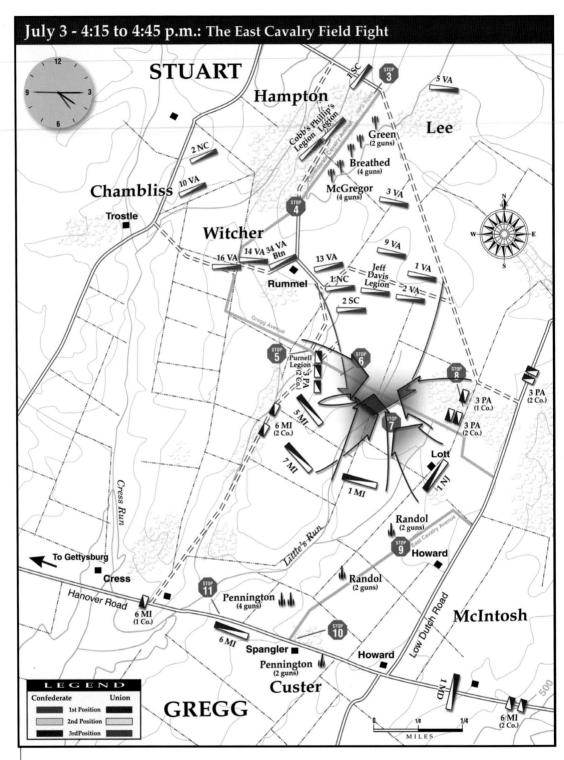

July 3 - 4:15 to 4:45 p.m.: The East Cavalry Field Fight

ally rallied the 1st Virginia Cavalry to countercharge, ending the pursuit. Pickett's Charge, just a few miles to the west, was ending about the same time the three hours of intense cavalry fighting drew to a close. Both sides kept up a skirmish fire until dark. The fields to your front were covered with hundreds of dead and wounded, along with hundreds of dead horses. Many of the men died locked in mortal combat with their opponent. In at least one instance, farmer Rummel found the corpses of a Northerner and a Southerner that had to be literally pried apart, rigor mortis having set in.

The casualties were heavy on both sides. Custer's Michigan brigade suffered 219 casualties, most of them in the 1st and 7th Michigan during their mounted charges. McIntosh's brigade took nearly forty casualties. On the Confederate side, Lt. Col. Witcher's 34th Battalion Virginia Cavalry suffered very heavy casualties, perhaps as high as seventy percent of the battalion's original number. The rest of Stuart's men suffered about 250 casualties from all causes.

Capt. James H. Kidd of Custer's brigade believed that Gregg's prescience had saved the Federal right flank from Stuart's foray. "If Custer's presence on the field was, as often has been said, 'providential,' it is General D. M. Gregg to whom, under Providence, the credit for bringing him there was due," Kidd later wrote. "We can see that the engagement which he fought on the right at Gettysburg, on July 3, 1863, was from first to last a well planned battle . . . in which every detail was the fruit of the brain of one man, who from the time he turned Custer to the northward, until he sent the First Michigan thundering against the brigades of Hampton and Fitzhugh Lee, made not a single false move. . . . That man was General David McMurtrie Gregg."

As a sign of the unity among the four regiments in the Michigan cavalry brigade, and representative of their cohesive fighting on this field, the brigade chose to erect the single massive Michigan Brigade Monument here instead of four individual monuments scattered about the field. Dedicated in 1889, it features a typical Wolverine trooper at the top, with a medallion of Custer below it. Note that the statue directly faces the trace of the perpendicular fence line, which was the scene of so much heavy fighting. On the front of the monument is a bronze frieze of the charge of the 1st Michigan Cavalry.

The monument stands in what would have been the middle of the 1st and 7th Michigan's mounted charge that day. If you face the Rummel farm with the monument at your back, the charge originated at the Hanover and Low Dutch roads to your rear. The Michiganders thundered along both sides of you and crashed into Wade Hampton's troopers in the field ahead.

After dark, Custer's brigade rejoined Kilpatrick's command on the left flank of the Federal line several miles to the southwest.

You may wish to walk about forty yards farther along the road to visit the monument of Co. A of the Purnell Legion of Maryland cavalry of McIntosh's brigade. This monument was placed here on October 23, 1890.

> *Drive another .1 miles and you will see the Gregg Cavalry Shaft on your left (77° 09' 47"W, 39° 49' 33" N). Pull over to the right in the parking area.*

Tour Stop 8
The Gregg Cavalry Shaft and the Monument of the 3rd Pennsylvania Cavalry

A grassy lane allows access to the monument and that of the 3rd Pennsylvania Cavalry beyond it, which marks the area where Capt. Miller made his desperate charge. Dedicated on October 15, 1884, the Gregg Cavalry Shaft commemorates the bravery of both the Federal and Confederate cavalry that fought here, and is one of only a handful of Civil War battlefield monuments to honor both sides.

About 150 feet behind the Gregg Cavalry Shaft is the 3rd Pennsylvania Cavalry's monument, dedicated on September 5, 1890. A squadron of the regiment commanded by Capt. William E. Miller was ordered to hold its position in the woods to the right (east) of this monument. If you walk to these woods, you will notice that the ground drops off slightly inside the tree line. The depression hid Miller's squadron from the sight of the charging Confederates. Miller was awarded the Medal of Honor in July 1897 for launching (against orders) his heroic mounted charge. In 1877, Miller returned to the battlefield and discovered his broken saber among the relics collected by farm owner John Rummel. After the war, Miller lived in Carlisle and served as a state senator. He died in 1919 and was buried in the Soldiers' National Cemetery at Gettysburg (one of only two awardees of the Medal of Honor buried there). His grave is visited in the cemetery tour included in this book.

Reset your odometer to 0.0. Gregg Avenue will curve to the right and then back to the left. When it curves left, you will see the monument of the 1st Maryland Cavalry of McIntosh's brigade on your right.

This monument was placed on October 25, 1888. If this veteran unit had remained in this position during the fighting, it may have materially aided the 7th Michigan during its attack. However, Colonel McIntosh moved the troopers into the woods to your left front to guard the Low Dutch Road intersection.

After a total of .2 miles, you will come to the Low Dutch Road (77° 9' 38"W, 39° 49' 26"N). Turn right, drive another .1 miles, and turn right onto East Cavalry Avenue.

The two-story frame house and farm buildings directly in front of you belonged to Jacob Lott. Note that the old Lott farm lane continues ahead (this is private property) but the park road curves to the left.

After slightly less than .2 miles you will see the War Department marker of Capt. Alanson M. Randol's battery of the 1st U.S. Artillery (four 12-pounders) on your left.

Tour Stop 9
Position of Sections of Randol's Battery

These markers were placed in 1907-08. Note, however, that the actual positions of the guns (and those marked ahead) were about 100 yards to your right on the slight rise in the field. If you exit your vehicle along the road here and look directly to the north (in the direction of the Michigan Brigade Monument, which you can easily see), you can take in the excellent view

The Gregg Cavalry Shaft honors both Union and Confederate soldiers who fought here on East Cavalry Field. (Stanley)

This early 1900s Tipton photo shows Randol's position. The modern park road follows this two-wheeled path. (GNMP)

and field of fire that Randol's gunners enjoyed from that position as the Confederate troopers galloped toward where you are standing. Just ahead on the left is a War Department placard describing the movements of the batteries in the 2nd Brigade of the Horse Artillery.

After another .1 miles you will come to the marker for Lt. James Chester's section of Randol's battery. Slightly less than .1 mile beyond is the marker of Lt. Alexander C. M. Pennington's battery.

From his position on the plateau about 100 yards to your right rear, Pennington fired the first return shot at Griffin's Battery atop Cress Ridge, which struck the muzzle of the Southern gun and dismounted it.

Along the Hanover Road just ahead to your left, is the monument of the 1st Maine Cavalry.

Tour Stop 10
Monument of the 1st Maine Cavalry

The 1st Maine, commanded by Lt. Col. Charles H. Smith, was kept in reserve by General Gregg. During most of the battle the regiment supported Gregg's artillery and did not actively participate in the fighting. The Maine survivors erected this monument on October 3, 1889.

Proceed to the Hanover Road, which is Rt. 116 (77° 10' 10"W, 39° 49' 04"N).

Tour Stop 11
Monument of Rank's Battery, 3rd Pennsylvania Heavy Artillery

The two-story red brick home on the other side of the road ahead of you was the Joseph Spangler farm. Owned today by the Park Service, it served as Custer's headquarters during the battle as well as a cavalry field hospital once the fighting ended. In the field to the right of the large Spangler barn, Custer formed the 7th Michigan for the charge. It was here he yelled his famous line, "Come on, you Wolverines!" before galloping in the direction of the Michigan Brigade monument to your right rear. To the left of the home is where the 1st Michigan formed for the charge.

Turn right (west) and reset your odometer to 0.0. After .1 miles, on your right you will see the monument of Capt. William D. Rank's Battery H of the 3rd Pennsylvania Heavy Artillery (77° 10' 21"W, 39° 49' 07"N).

Rank's gunners were set up on this position during the July 2 fight at Brinkerhoff's Ridge (they were not present on July 3). This monument was placed on September 17, 1891.

Continue on the Hanover Road for another .1 miles and note the wartime brick home of Abraham Reever on the right. Drive another .2 miles and you will cross Cress Run. On the right is the wartime home of John Cress, which is set back slightly from the road (on the west bank of the run).

After another 1.2 miles you will reach the Rt. 15 overpass, and immediately on the far side of the overpass take the second left turn onto Highland Avenue (77° 11' 58"W, 39° 49' 29"N). Reset your odometer to 0.0.

After .4 miles along Highland Avenue, you will see the monument of the 16th

Pennsylvania Cavalry on your left. Allowing for traffic conditions, park carefully here and examine this monument.

Tour Stop 12
Monument of the 16th Pennsylvania Cavalry

Very few people visit this remote location. Placed here on October 15, 1884, on what was the wartime Ephraim Deardorff farm, the monument marks the position of the left flank of Gregg's picket line. The line connected with the infantry pickets of Brig. Gen. Thomas H. Neill's 6th Corps posted on Wolf's Hill to the south. This remote position demonstrates how effectively Gregg covered the right flank and rear of the Federal Army against attack on July 3 and why – despite Cavalry Corps commander Alfred Pleasonton's orders to the contrary – this ground and road network near the Low Dutch Road and Wolf's Hill could not be abandoned.

Turn your vehicle safely around and return .4 miles to the Hanover Road. To return to Gettysburg, reset your odometer to 0.0, turn left onto the Hanover Road, and you will reach Gettysburg in 1.5 miles. You will reach the town square after a total drive of 1.8 miles.

Additional reading

The best modern work devoted to the fighting at Brinkerhoff's Ridge and East Cavalry Field is Eric J. Wittenberg's *Protecting the Flank: The Battles for Brinkerhoff's Ridge and East Cavalry Field, Battle of Gettysburg July 2-3, 1863* (Celina, OH: Ironclad Publishing, 2002), which was heavily consulted for this tour. Wittenberg was the first modern historian to demonstrate, and emphasize, the critical role that the July 2 fighting at Brinkerhoff's Ridge had on the next day's large-scale cavalry battle at the Rummel Farm. Also of value are the accounts of the East Cavalry Field fighting in Jeffry Wert's *Gettysburg: Day Three* (New York: Simon & Schuster, 2001) and Edward G. Longacre's *The Cavalry at Gettysburg: A Tactical Study of Mounted Operations during the Civil War's Pivotal Campaign, 9 June-14 July 1863* (Rutherford, N.J.: Fairleigh Dickinson University Press, 1986).

(Opposite page) This William Tipton image is looking east into the town of Hunterstown, with the town square being in the mid ground, on the right is the Tate Farm and Blacksmith Shop. (GNMP)

Tour of the Battle of Hunterstown, July 2

"I'll lead you this time boys, Come on!"

The cavalry battle at the small cross-roads hamlet of Hunterstown four miles northeast of Gettysburg took place on the late afternoon and evening of July 2, 1863. The fight garnered little attention until 2006 when development seriously threatened to obliterate the battlefield. Efforts by legislators, the Adams County Land Conservancy, the Hunterstown Historical Society, and concerned citizens and historians, however, have helped to protect this nearly pristine little battlefield.

On the afternoon of July 2, as the second day of the battle at Gettysburg got underway, Confederate cavalry commander Maj. Gen. James Ewell Brown "Jeb" Stuart and three brigades of his horsemen (about half of his total force) arrived in the Gettysburg area after an eight-day long ride through Virginia, Maryland, and Pennsylvania. Stuart and Army of Northern Virginia commander Gen. Robert E. Lee had been unable to communicate with each other while their respective commands marched separately into the Keystone State. While searching for his army and after delays due to several battles and skirmishes along the way, Stuart finally received word while in Carlisle, Pennsylvania on the night of July 1 to hurry to Gettysburg since a major battle had begun there. An all-night march brought Stuart and his cavalrymen through Hunterstown, with the brigade of Brig. Gen. Wade Hampton, about 2,000 strong, bringing up the rear. Hampton passed through Hunterstown and proceeded south to join Stuart near Gettysburg, but his small rear guard, still near the Hunterstown square, clashed with the advance squadron of Federal Brig. Gen. Judson Kilpatrick's cavalry division. Kilpatrick's force totaled about 3,500 men. A running fight through the town between the two small groups ensued, and soon most of the opposing forces were drawn into a battle on the road and farm fields south of town. The fighting, which ended in a tactical stalemate, lasted until after dark.

Confederate cavalry officer Brig. Gen. Wade Hampton. (LOC)

The Battle of Hunterstown, besides having been a hotly contested fight on the far left flank of Lee's Army of Northern Virginia, was significant in that it was the scene of the very first mounted charge by newly promoted Brig. Gen. George Armstrong Custer, the commander of one of Kilpatrick's brigades. It also witnessed one of the many episodes in which Custer came within a whisker of being captured or killed during the war. Had his life not been saved at the last moment at Hunterstown by one of his orderlies, the debacle at the Little Big Horn thirteen years later would have no significance in Custer lore.

Kilpatrick's other brigade was commanded by the likewise newly promoted Brig. Gen. Elon John Farnsworth. Farnsworth's men were not much engaged at Hunterstown, but the following day, July 3, Farnsworth led a mounted assault of his own on the Gettysburg battlefield, a charge that bears his name and also claimed his life.

Hampton had no artillery with him, but Kilpatrick had two horse artillery batteries, eleven cannon total, commanded by Lts. Alexander C. M. Pennington and Samuel Elder.

The small, quaint town of Hunterstown today harkens back to its atmosphere of 1863. Several wartime homes and buildings are still extant, many of them used as hospitals after the battle. The main battlefield itself remains relatively untouched, except for a large utility plant that occupies and obscures the southeastern section. The battlefield student, fortunately, can still easily see and interpret most of the fighting.

Hunterstown was founded in 1741 by Irish settler David Hunter along an old Indian trail. When Adams County was formed from York County, Hunterstown vied with neighboring Gettysburg to be the seat of the new county. After Gettysburg was chosen, Hunterstown remained a "sleepy little town" of wagon-makers, gunsmiths, cigar makers, and farmers. There were also several successful chair makers in the village; in fact, Hunterstown was long nicknamed "The Rocking Chair Capital of the World." Initially known as "Woodstock" and then "Straban Center," Hunterstown was called "the hot-bed of rebellion" during the American Revolution, and Hunter distinguished himself as an officer in the Continental Army. President George Washington stopped in the village in 1794 for a short rest while returning from the events of the Whiskey Rebellion to the west.

> To visit Hunterstown and the battlefield, begin in Gettysburg at the square and turn onto Rt. 30 East, the York Road and set your odometer to 0.0. In 5.4 miles, you will see Coleman Road on your left. (Please note that after .9 miles, you will see a road and sign pointing to Hunterstown on your left - do not take this road. After the tour, you will return to Gettysburg via this road.) Turn left onto Coleman Road, and reset your odometer to 0.0.
>
> After 1.6 miles, you will come to a stop sign. Bear left here onto Shrivers Corner Road. You are now following the advance of Kilpatrick's division to Hunterstown.
>
> After .4 miles, you will come to a slight rise in the road and you have reached the area where the opening skirmish of the Battle of Hunterstown took place.

· · · · · · · · · · ·

Tour Route of the Battle of Hunterstown

Tour Stop 1
The Opening Skirmish

Co. A. of the 18th Pennsylvania Cavalry, Kilpatrick's advance led by Capt. Llewellyn Estes of Kilpatrick's staff, formed a skirmish line and charged from this rise. They clashed in the road ahead with Hampton's rear guard composed of about forty troopers of Cobb's Legion Cavalry's Co. C, commanded by Col. Pierce Young. In 1863, this was a dirt road. Note the yellow vinyl-sided home on

William Tipton captured this view of Hunterstown in the early 1900s. The camera angle looks west along Shrivers Corner Road. (GNMP)

your right. This was the wartime home of Jesse McCreary and his wife Jane Ann. The running fight that began in front of McCreary's house eventually burst into the town square ahead. Forty-seven-years-old at the time, McCreary was the village tailor and had three daughters, one of whom had a son named Eddie – later known as "Gettysburg Eddie" Plank – the famous baseball player inducted into the Hall of Fame in 1946.

The McCreary house was originally a log home, and still retains the original logs on three sides beneath the siding that appears today.

McCreary's neighbor, a local Hunterstown teenager named Jacob Taughenbaugh, who lived in an old stone house just to the south, watched the thrilling action from in front of his home: "In a minute, somebody fired a shot [and] then, the [Federal] officer called out, 'Draw…SABERS!'

There was a rattling, then, 'CHARGE!' Down the street they came, hard as they could go, waving their sabers and yelling."

Drive another .2 miles and watch for Red Bridge Road on your right. Turn onto Red Bridge Road and pull over where safe to do so, keeping mindful of private property.

Tour Stop 2
The Town Square

Once Young's men reached the square, they reformed their scattered ranks. The small grassy area to your left, which contains a War Department marker, was the dirt-surfaced town square in 1863. On the north side of the square is an 18th-century log home that was owned by William Grass, while George Grass owned a home to the right. On the south side of the square (on the other side of Shrivers Corner Road) you can see the beautifully restored brick Grass Hotel, owned then by Jacob Grass, which became Kilpatrick's headquarters as the battle developed. It also served as a large hospital after the battle for the wounded of both sides, as did many of the homes and buildings in and around the town.

Young reformed his men here in the square as many terrified citizens looked on. Young ordered his men to countercharge against Estes and his Pennsylvanians, and the two groups galloped straight at each other. When they collided, each side slashed at each other with their sabers, but the slightly outnumbered Georgians were forced back through the square, where they turned left at the John Tate Blacksmith Shop to rejoin Hampton's brigade south of Hunterstown (that part of the road they took to exit the square no longer exists, but we will visit its location shortly).

While here (or after completing the tour of the battle), you may wish to visit the nearby Great Conewago Presbyterian Church Cemetery. The founding of the church dates back to Hunterstown's earliest history, with a log church built in the 1740s near the site of the present church. There are many interesting graves there, including that of Robert Bell, discussed in the tour of the June 26 skir-

mish west of Gettysburg. Capt. Bell commanded the Adams County Cavalry Company that, along with the 26th Pennsylvania Emergency Militia, clashed with the advance that day upon Gettysburg by the Confederate brigade of Brig. Gen. John B. Gordon.

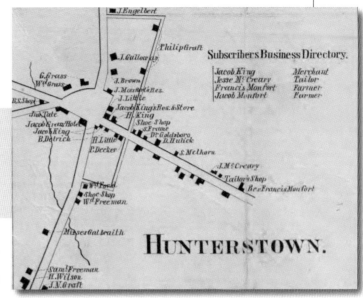

To visit the cemetery, proceed on Red Bridge Road for .3 miles, and the entrance is on the left. Park your vehicle near the upper (furthest) entrance to the cemetery (77° 09' 39"W, 39° 53' 13"N).

Robert Bell's grave is located to the right just inside the entrance. He is buried here with his wife Abigail King as well as several other family members. To the left of the entrance is a flagpole, as well as a monument, dedicated to Civil War dead buried here. There are quite a number of old and

This 1858 map of Hunterstown shows how the town looked during the July 1863 fight just outside of town. (LOC)

interesting gravesites in the cemetery. If you visit the cemetery, return to the tour by driving back along Red Bridge Road to Shrivers Corner Road.

Turn your vehicle around (if you have not visited the cemetery) and return to Shrivers Corner Road. Reset your odometer to 0.0 and turn right.

Proceed slowly if traffic allows, and after about 100 yards you will see the Tate home on your left, which is a yellow house with wood clapboard siding. Note the larger shed about thirty yards further along the road on the same side – this post-war building rests slightly east of the original location of the Tate Blacksmith Shop, which was a log structure. Originally, the road south from the town square ran between the Tate home and the shop, and traces of the original roadbed can still be seen today. This now non-existent road was the one used

The barn of the 1700s John Tate farm has seen its share of history, from George Washington's visit to the Battle of Hunterstown. (Stanley)

by Young's men to escape the Federal troopers (we will re-join this road after the next turn).

The John Tate home and Blacksmith Shop have an interesting history that predates the Civil War. In October 1794, President George Washington stopped here to re-shoe one of his horses during his return from quelling the Whiskey Rebellion. To return to Philadelphia from Bedford, Pennsylvania, Washington and his aides used this main east-west road, known then as the Great Road or Black's Gap Road. Traveling through Fort Loudon, Chambersburg, Hilltown, and Mummasburg, Washington and his party reached the Joshua Russell Tavern on the Biglerville Road on the night of October 24. The beautifully restored tavern, four miles north of Gettysburg (on Rt. 34) can still be seen today. The following morning, Washington reached Hunterstown and stopped here at Tate's shop to have a horse re-shod, while he and his men rested by the nearby Beaver Dam Creek, which runs along the west side of the shop location and which can still be seen today. Note the culvert where the creek passes underneath the road. Washington's group then traveled on to New Oxford, Wrightsville, and then to Philadelphia.

The old blacksmith shop building was removed in the late 1970's, and its boards were reused to build a shed on private property in nearby Wenksville.

After .1 miles from Red Bridge Road, turn left onto Hunterstown Road (77° 09' 46"W, 39° 52' 58"N). Immediately on your left at this intersection is a small monument, dedicated on July 2, 2008, to commemorate the Battle of Hunterstown. You may pull over to park where safe to examine the monument, the only one that commemorates the battle.

Continue another .1 miles, and on your left is the approximate location where the now non-existent road came from the square. The part of this road behind you was constructed in the early 1900s to straighten out the road when the old road that ran between the Tate buildings was closed.

Continue another fifty yards, and you arrive at the Tate/Felty Ridge, which was the Federal position during the battle.

The Hunterstown battlefield viewed from Union position looking toward the Confederate position in the distance. The Felty farm is in the middle ground. (Stanley)

Tour Stop 3
The Tate/Felty Ridge

Kilpatrick's cavalrymen took position here as they followed the escape of Young's troopers. As several troopers conducted reconnaissance on several roads in the area, the 1st and 7th Michigan of Custer's brigade deployed on the ridge to your left, and the 5th and 6th Michigan deployed to your right. Pennington's battery marched behind them to take position on the right.

Continue down the ridge and pause at the bottom, traffic allowing (exercise extreme caution).

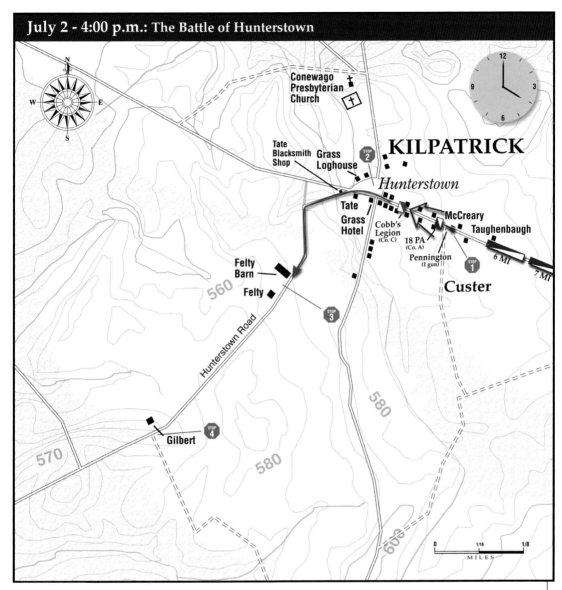

July 2 - 4:00 p.m.: The Battle of Hunterstown

    Just ahead of you, to your right, is the wartime brick home of John Felty. Felty's large wooden barn, torn down in 2007, was located just north of the home. You may be able to still see its stone foundation.

Continue to the Felty Farm.

    You may pull briefly into the driveway to examine the property, but keep in mind that the land is private. Please be courteous and do not block access to the property, and permission from the property owner should be sought if you plan to spend more than a few moments here. From his position on the ridge behind you, Custer saw Young's defiant small group of troopers ahead in the road where it curves to the right. Custer ordered Co. A of the 6th Michigan Cavalry, commanded by Capt. Henry E. Thompson, to charge down the road into Young's position. Before Thompson could give the order, however, Custer drew his saber and yelled, "I'll lead you this time, boys. Come on!" Custer galloped down the road and the approximately fifty troopers of Thompson's company followed him. Note that in 1863, this road was lined with stout fences that forced the cavalry to stay in the road.

By this time, however, Hampton had turned most of his Confederate cavalry around and began deploying skirmish lines on both sides of the road ahead, just out of the view of the Federals on the Tate/Felty Ridge. Reset your odometer to 0.0 and continue on the Hunterstown Road. You are now following Custer's charge against Young's cavalrymen.

After .2 miles the road will begin to curve to the right.

Tour Stop 4
Custer's Horse is Shot

On the right side of the road is the wartime home of J. G. Gilbert, and the ridge ahead of you was called Gilbert's Ridge, the Confederate position during the battle. On the left side of the road is an entrance to a utility plant that has unfortunately changed much of the southeastern part of the battlefield. You may pull into the entrance to park and examine the field, but be careful to be courteous and not block access to the gate.

At this curve in the road, Custer's men collided with Young's squadron. After several moments of brutal hand-to-hand fighting, Custer's horse was shot dead and as it fell in the road here, it trapped Custer underneath. Custer's men soon were outnumbered as dismounted Confederate skirmishers from the Phillips Legion came forward on the right side of the road, and skirmishers from the 2nd South Carolina Cavalry advanced on the left side of the road. Custer tried to struggle free as the Southern skirmishers poured a galling fire into his troopers. Four more companies of the Cobb's Legion galloped down the slope of Gilbert's Ridge to your left, and the Federals were outnumbered and nearly completely surrounded. During what must have seemed like mob fighting, over a dozen Federals were dropped from their saddles, and as many Confederates were wounded or killed. Pennington's battery atop the Tate/Felty's Ridge to your right, after drawing a bead on Hampton's lines beyond the Gilbert house, began firing shells at them.

Lt. Col. William Delony, the commander of the Cobb's Legion, galloped into the fray with his men. Like Custer, Delony's horse was shot and fell on him, trapping him temporarily. Some of Custer's Wolverines tried to cut him with their sabers, but Delony's bugler intervened and saved his commander's life. Custer's situation, however, was more desperate. While Confederates swung their sabers and shot at the boy general as he struggled to his feet, Custer's orderly, twenty-three-year-old Pvt. Norvell Churchill, galloped to Custer's side. As a Confederate was about to saber Custer, Churchill shot the assailant, reached down to his commander, and Custer swung himself into the saddle behind Churchill. The private turned his horse and beat a hasty retreat back up the road to the safety of the Federal lines at the Felty farm. Over half of the 6th Michigan's Co. A was killed or wounded, and the rest spurred their mounts and followed Custer as fast as they could.

Young's Georgians and dozens more of Hampton's cavalrymen countercharged and galloped toward Kilpatrick's line, using both the road and the fields on either side. Dismounted skirmishers of the 6th and 7th Michigan had deployed near

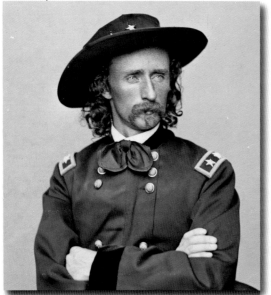

Union cavalry officer Brig. Gen. George Armstrong Custer. (LOC)

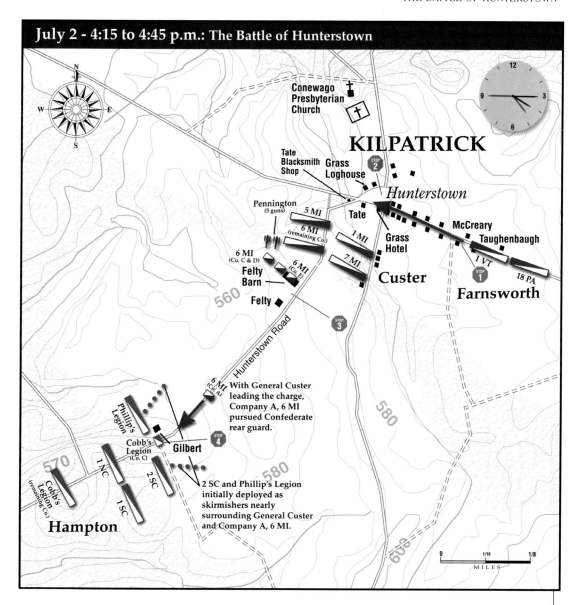

July 2 - 4:15 to 4:45 p.m.: The Battle of Hunterstown

the Felty house and below Tate's side of the ridge, and were ready to receive the Southerners. Some of the Wolverines had also taken position in Felty's large barn, and began shooting at the Confederates from their cover. Upon reaching the Federal line, the countercharge began to break down, and Pennington trained his muzzles on the disorganized Southerners. One of the shells dropped into the barn, and the Federals there scrambled from the building.

Hampton slowly advanced a battle line along both sides of the road, and Farnsworth's brigade trotted into line on Custer's right flank while some of the men helped to manhandle Elder's guns into position on the ridge behind Felty's barn. The weight of the Federals' artillery and stout position convinced the Southerners that it was suicidal to stay, so the survivors of the Confederate countercharge quickly withdrew, and Hampton sent back word to Stuart for artillery support.

As desultory skirmishing continued in the fields, and Kilpatrick's cannon blazed away at the Confederates, Capt. C. A. Green's Louisiana Guard Artillery (attached to Maj. Gen. Richard Ewell's Corps) arrived just before sunset to support Hampton. Green deployed his section of 10-pounder Parrott guns atop Gilbert's Ridge. An artillery duel ensued, with Pennington getting the better of Green – one of the Parrott guns was hit in the axle and dismounted, four of his draft horses were killed, one crewmember was killed, and fifteen others were wounded.

The artillery duel lasted well after dark, with some accounts placing the cessation as late as 11:00 p.m. Outnumbered and outgunned, Hampton methodically withdrew part of his brigade toward Gettysburg to Stuart's headquarters at the William Stallsmith farm, while leaving the bulk of his men to hold their position on Gilbert's Ridge throughout the night to protect the Army of Northern Virginia's left flank. Hampton had lost nine men killed, five wounded, and seven missing. Kilpatrick lost thirty-three killed, wounded, and missing, with most of the losses in the 6th Michigan's Co. A, which had made the initial charge on Young and the Cobb's Legion squadron.

Kilpatrick received orders to march to Two Taverns along the Baltimore Road and withdrew his division after the artillery duel ended. The road and adjoining fields were sprinkled with the dead

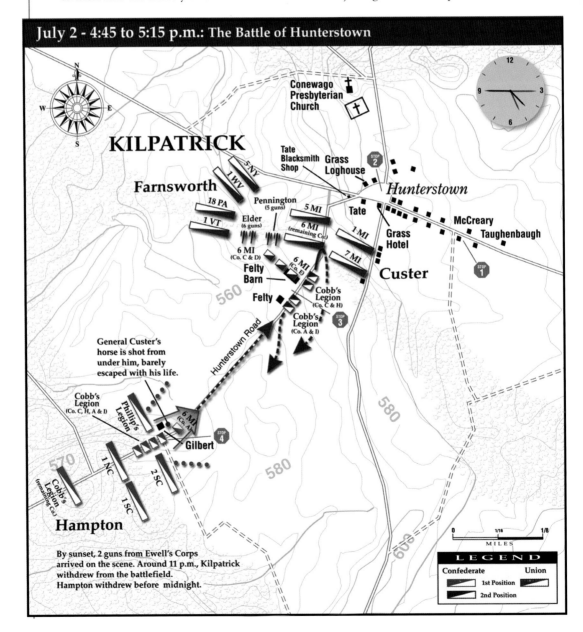

July 2 - 4:45 to 5:15 p.m.: The Battle of Hunterstown

and wounded of both sides, and several buildings in and around Hunterstown, including the Grass Hotel, served as makeshift hospitals. Dozens of dead horses dotted the landscape. Although the fight at Hunterstown was relatively small compared to the butchery taking place at Gettysburg, many of both Hampton's and Kilpatrick's units remembered it as some of the most brutal fighting of the war. None of them would get any rest soon – the next day, July 3, Farnsworth's brigade of Kilpatrick's division went into the fight on the Federal left and suffered heavy losses, while Hampton's and Custer's brigades (the latter fighting alongside the Federal cavalry division of Brig. Gen. David Gregg) slugged it out at the Rummel Farm east of Gettysburg.

To return to Gettysburg, reset your odometer to 0.0 and turn left on the Hunterstown Road from the utility plant entrance. Upon ascending Gilbert's Ridge after .1 miles (77° 10' 24"W, 39° 52' 21"N), you may wish to examine Hampton's Confederate position.

After 2.0 miles from the utility plant, note the old wooden farmhouse on the right of the road. This was the Henry Picking farm, which served as a Confederate hospital during the Gettysburg battle. Henry Kyd Douglas, formerly on Maj. Gen. Thomas J. "Stonewall" Jackson's staff, was taken here to recuperate from a wound in the shoulder suffered on July 3. Many Gettysburg wounded were treated in Picking's home and barn.

After another 1.6 miles from the Picking home, you will reach Rt. 30. Turn right at the stop sign here to drive west, and you will reach the Gettysburg square after 1.2 miles.

Additional reading

The most modern scholarship and interpretation of the Battle of Hunterstown is included in a chapter in *Plenty of Blame To Go Around: Jeb Stuart's Controversial Ride to Gettysburg* by Eric J. Wittenberg and J. David Petruzzi (Savas Beatie, 2006). See also an excellent article in the July 1989 issue of *Gettysburg Magazine* by Gettysburg National Military Park Ranger Paul M. Shevchuk titled "The Battle of Hunterstown, Pennsylvania, July 2, 1863."

(Opposite page) View of Fairfield battlefield looking toward the Confederate position on July 3. (Stanley)

Tour of the Battle of Fairfield, July 3

"Shall one damn regiment of Yankees whip my whole brigade?"

On a road and in farm fields just outside the town of Fairfield, behind the lines of Robert E. Lee's Army of Northern Virginia, a cavalry battle erupted on the afternoon of July 3 about the time "Pickett's Charge" was taking place at Gettysburg. The action receives little attention in the history books, only two small plaques commemorate the action, and very few people visit the site. Most students are surprised when they learn a Federal cavalry regiment was all but decimated there, and two Medals of Honor were issued for bravery.

"The Sixth U.S. Regular Cavalry numbers among the things that were," reflected Confederate Brig. Gen. William E. "Grumble" Jones a few weeks after the close of the Gettysburg Campaign in his official report. Given the unflattering nickname that succinctly described his wet-hen personality, Jones intended to leave no doubt that near Fairfield, Pennsylvania, on July 3 – just seven miles southwest of the Gettysburg battlefield – the troopers of his proud "Laurel Brigade" nearly wiped out the 6th U.S. Cavalry in a fight behind Southern lines.

Confederate cavalry commander Brig. Gen. "Grumble" Jones. (LOC)

In early 1863, the 6th U.S. Cavalry, the only Regular cavalry regiment raised after the start of the Civil War, was assigned to the Reserve Brigade of Brig. Gen. John Buford's 1st Cavalry Division. This brigade of Regulars consisted of the 1st, 2nd, 5th, and 6th U.S. regiments, plus the 6th Pennsylvania Cavalry (known as "Rush's Lancers"). Just a few days before the battle of Gettysburg, young Capt. Wesley Merritt, an 1860 graduate of West Point and most recently a member of Federal Cavalry Corps commander Maj. Gen. Alfred Pleasonton's staff, was himself promoted to brigadier general and the command of the Reserve Brigade. Fifty-two-year-old Maj. Samuel "Old Paddy" Starr temporarily commanded the brigade until Merritt's promotion. A thirty-year veteran of the service, Starr, like Grumble Jones, was an ill-tempered strict disciplinarian whom former Federal Army commander Joseph Hooker once described as "a tough old bird."

When Merritt took command, Starr returned to his former command at the head of the 6th U.S. Cavalry. Few of the troopers, however, wanted the crusty old Celt in any capacity. His harsh disciplinary tactics had become legendary. One of his favorites was to place an offender astride a wooden fence, tie his feet below and his hands behind his back, with a horse's nosebag strapped over the hapless trooper's head. For this embarrassing and novel type of punishment, Starr earned the moniker "Old Nose Bag."

While the rest of Buford's division fronted the left of the Army of the Potomac's advance into Pennsylvania in late June 1863, Merritt's brigade was sent by Pleasonton to Mechanicstown (present-day Thurmont), Maryland, to guard wagon trains and picket the roads and mountain passes. In the early morning hours of July 2, as the armies at Gettysburg formed their battle lines for a second day of fighting, Merritt's Regulars set off for Emmitsburg, where they made camp and picketed to the south and west to watch for elements of Lee's army.

The following morning, July 3, an "old farmer" who claimed to live near Fairfield rode into Merritt's camp and reported that a large train bulging with booty confiscated from Keystone State farms was parked in one of his fields. And it was ripe for the taking. The stranger assured Merritt that the train, behind Lee's lines, had only a few guards of mounted infantry, adding that it was "a right smart chance for you'uns to capture it, [since] the soldiers are all over at the big fight." The carrot thus dangled, Merritt made arrangements for the train's capture.

When an order arrived for Merritt to bring his brigade up to Gettysburg, the young brigadier dispatched Starr and his 6th U.S. Cavalry to Fairfield to capture the Rebel train and hold the town, in order to block a likely line for Lee's possible retreat. Merritt was confident that the regiment could accomplish the mission, but Starr's command was undersized. One squadron had been detached to Cavalry Corps headquarters as an escort, leaving Starr with only about 400 horsemen. Many troopers expressed doubt about the suspicious-looking stranger's story, wondering whether he was in fact a Confederate spy and if they were about to ride into a trap.

Starr moved his column toward Fairfield with the "farmer" at his side to act as a guide. Despite the pall of skepticism over the mission, the troopers relished the adventure of riding behind enemy lines in pursuit of stolen booty. Lt. Tattnall Paulding later wrote that "all was excitement . . . when you imagine capturing a hundred wagons laden with spoils." The ride to Fairfield was about eight miles, and the grizzled Starr remained quiet for much of the way. When he reached the valley south of the hamlet about noon, the guide urged Starr to halt the column.

To cover his left flank, Starr detached a squadron under Capt. George Cram to march along a railroad bed that skirted the valley's edge. He led the rest of the troopers into the town. Once in the streets, some troopers interrogated citizens while others fanned out in search of the wagon train. Informed by a local that some Confederates and wagons had indeed passed out of town on the road to Ortanna only minutes before Starr's arrival, one detachment under Lt. Christian Balder (a Prussian immigrant with six years' service in the army) galloped off in pursuit. When he spotted the prize in the road ahead, Balder formed a line of battle and charged the lumbering wagons. The initial skirmish touched off a fight that would eventually draw in most of Jones' 1,500-man Confederate cavalry

Tour Route of the Battle of Fairfield

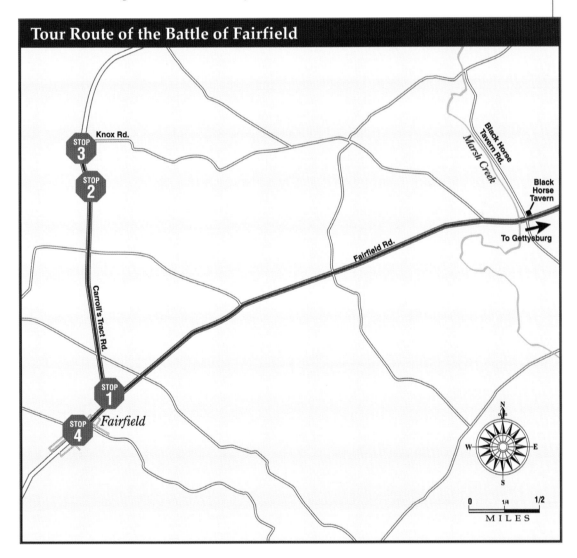

brigade and artillery against Starr's small command. By the time the fighting ended, nearly all of the Regulars, including Starr himself, were captured, wounded, or killed. The mysterious "stranger" (who has never been identified) disappeared about the time the shooting began, leaving history to wonder whether he had set up the Federals for a hard fall.

. . . .

To visit the Fairfield battlefield from the Gettysburg town square, turn onto Rt. 30 West (Chambersburg Street) and set your odometer to 0.0.
After .2 miles you will pass through a stoplight. Continue straight onto Springs Avenue (do not bear right here to continue on Rt. 30).
After another .4 miles, turn left onto Seminary Ridge Road. Drive another .1 miles and at the stoplight turn right onto Middle Street. Reset your odometer to 0.0. This road becomes the Fairfield Road (Rt. 116 West). You will travel a total of 6.8 miles to reach Fairfield.

There are some sights to see along the way, and they will be seen at the following points:

At 1.8 miles you will see Bream's Hill Road as it bears off to your right (it connects back onto Rt. 116 after about 1/3 of a mile).

This road is the original Fairfield Road trace as it wound its way over Bream's Hill. In 1946, the modern road here was straightened out to its present trace, with this part of the hill cut out. The Fairfield Road, one of the Army of Northern Virginia's routes of retreat along with the Chambersburg Pike, followed what is now Bream's Hill Road. Robert E. Lee, according to several accounts, stood along the road at the top of Bream's Hill on July 5 to watch the procession of his army column. If you wish, drive along Bream's Hill Road to get a sense of the original trace of this route. It will bring you back onto the present road.

This photo of the Black Horse Tavern is an excellent portrayal of the tavern in the early 1900s. (LOC)

At 2.1 miles you will see Francis Bream's Black Horse Tavern on your right.

Built in 1813 by William McClellan (or McClelland), the property of more than 400 acres featured a well-known tavern in the fieldstone building. Maj. Gen. Lafayette McLaws' Confederate division camped here on the evening of July 1, and the house, barn, stables, and all outbuildings were used as hospital facilities for nearly 300 wounded. Some seventy members of McLaws' and Brig. Gen. John B. Hood's divisions were buried on the farm. According to an Austrian officer accompanying the Confederate army, during the battle the tavern "seemed a regular rendezvous for generals and their staff-officers . . . Here I met General J.E.B. Stuart for the first time, and was introduced to him, and to many others too numerous to name."

Just after the Black Horse Tavern you will cross Marsh Creek. A field stone bridge crossed the creek here in 1863. It was built in 1809 by William McClellan (builder of the Bream home and tavern).

At. 3.1 miles you will see the Christian and Elizabeth Byers farm on your right.

The farm consisted of about 120 acres and is one of the oldest in this area south of Gettysburg. During and after the battle, the house and barn (the latter now gone) was used as a Confederate hospital for about 100 wounded. The home was built about 1770, but has since been covered with siding — possibly hiding a log dwelling underneath.

At 4.1 miles the Lower Marsh Creek Presbyterian Church, built in 1790, is on your right.

The pastor of the church at the time of the battle, Rev. John R. Warner, witnessed much of the fighting and later became a popular battlefield guide. The church was used as a temporary Confederate field hospital, especially during the retreat.

After you have traveled a total of 6.8 miles, bear right onto Carroll Tract Road (77° 21' 49"W, 39° 47' 29"N). Pull into the parking lot along the road immediately to your right to pause here. Reset your odometer to 0.0. Carroll Tract Road was known as the Fairfield-Ortanna Road in 1863.

Tour Stop 1
The Initial Skirmish on the Fairfield-Ortanna Road

The town of Fairfield (named for the town of Fairfield in England), which we will visit after touring the battlefield, is just ahead on Rt. 116. After riding into Fairfield (from the other direction) about noon on July 3, 1863 with his 6th U.S. Cavalry, Maj. Samuel Starr sent details throughout the town to interview civilians about the Confederate wagon train said to be in the area. As related earlier, Lt. Christian Balder led a detachment out on the Fairfield-Ortanna Road here in hot pursuit.

Continue on Carroll Tract Road.

Within the first mile you will pass over some low ridges. In this area, Balder spotted wagons in the road ahead. Forming a line of battle atop one of these slight rises (we are unsure which), Balder ordered his men to charge the wagons. Note that in 1863, this was a dirt road lined with very stout and unusually high rail fences, so the cavalry was contained in the road. The charging troopers slammed into a picket line of a few dozen dismounted cavalrymen of Jones' Confederate Laurel Brigade (likely troopers of the 7th Virginia Cavalry). The Federals easily scattered them, but Balder's success was short-lived. After dispersing the Rebel pickets and pursuing them for a distance, Balder called a halt when he spotted a large column of Jones' men riding hell-bent toward them down the road ahead of you. Realizing that he was outnumbered, Balder ordered his men to turn around and gallop back to Fairfield and the safety of the rest of the regiment. The pursuing Virginians, unsure what supports the Federals had behind them, wisely pulled up rein and rode back to join the rest of their brigade.

After traveling exactly 2.0 miles on the Carroll-Tract Road, you will crest a high ridge.

Tour Stop 2
The Main Battlefield

Upon hearing of Balder's contact with Confederates, Starr rode his men out of town and onto this ridge, and formed a line of battle here. If you look to your left, off in the distance and along the bottom of the South Mountain ridge, you can see the rail line along which Capt. George Cram's column was riding. In order to view the entirety of the main battlefield, continue another .5 miles and turn right onto Knox Road. Pull over on the right side of the road, being careful of traffic, exit your vehicle, and walk back out to Carroll Tract Road.

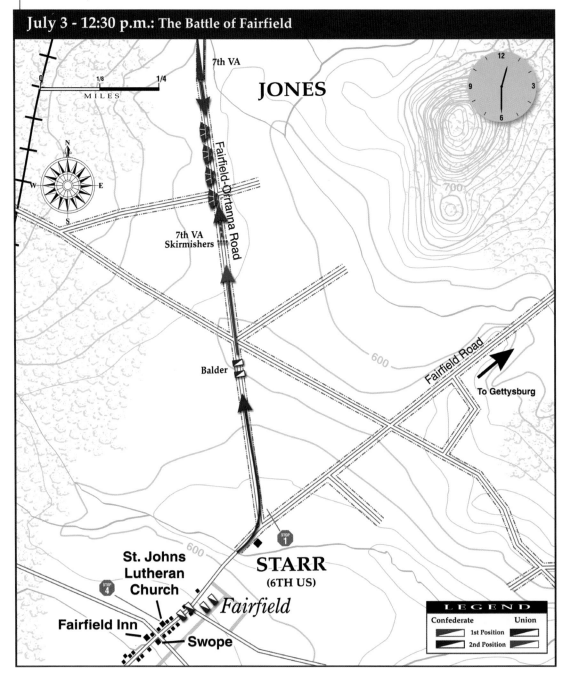

July 3 - 12:30 p.m.: The Battle of Fairfield

As you face the road, you can see the high ridge to your left that you passed over. The red brick home of farmer Benjamin Marshall is in front of you on the other side of the road. To your left on your side (east) of the road stood a small schoolhouse a little more than halfway to the ridge.

Once informed of the location of the wagons, accompanied by Southern cavalry in larger numbers than he may have expected, the stubborn Starr nevertheless determined to stay and fight. The mysterious stranger who initially reported the wagons and then guided the 6th U.S. Cavalry here had long since vanished. Starr galloped the regiment to the high ridge to your left, since he could see Confederate cavalry and wagons ahead in the road to your right. He deployed Lt. Tattnall Paulding's squadron dismounted along a fence line atop the ridge, to the east (your side of the road), while Balder's squadron remained mounted in the road in column. An apple orchard occupied much of the ridge on the western (far) side of the road. (Keep in mind that both sides of the road were lined with a stout wooden fence along its entire distance.)

From his position to your right opposite the Federals, Grumble Jones sized up Starr's obvious challenge. The veteran Confederate commander decided to immediately throw the hammer at him, and ordered his 7th Virginia Cavalry to attack. Drawing their sabers with a flourish and screaming the Rebel Yell, the Virginians raced down the road right in front of you from right to left, toward Starr at the top of the ridge. Their momentum was quickly extinguished when Starr's troopers opened a devastating fire from their single-shot carbines (mostly of the Sharps model). "They opened a galling fire on us, driving us back and killing and wounding a good many," admitted Lt. Col. Thomas Marshall, commander of the 7th Virginia. Several men and a number of horses fell in the road directly in your front.

When the 7th Virginia began falling back, its bugler sounded another charge, to no avail. Jones became livid as he watched his men being repulsed and refuse to charge a second time. He ordered Capt. Roger Preston Chew's battery of five cannon, which had just arrived along with the 6th

6th U.S. commander Maj. Samuel Starr. (LOC)

Virginia Cavalry, to deploy in the wheatfield to your immediate left. Chew's gunners lined up their five guns, loaded, and began hammering away at Starr's position on the ridge. Had you been standing on this spot that day, you would be right behind Chew's gunners.

Since he had no artillery with him, Starr could only trade carbine shots with Jones' cavalry in the distance while Chew's shells dropped among the Federals, the best shots blowing men and horses to bits. Knowing he could not hold his position long against enemy artillery and superior numbers of cavalry, Starr had only two options: pull his men out and retreat, or charge and hope the confusion of the 7th Virginia's repulse would allow him to break Jones' line. Since he was not one to give up the field easily, Starr decided on the latter option.

Aides rode up and down Starr's line to prepare for the charge. Paulding's squadron on the eastern side of the road was still dismounted, however, and the squadron under Lt. Adna R. Chaffee was dismounted and forming in the orchard on the western part of the ridge. Before the cavalrymen on foot could remount, the men in Balder's squadron, personally led by Starr, drew their sabers and galloped down the ridge toward Jones from your left to your right.

With the charge coming at them, the Southerners drew sabers and the 7th Virginia counter-

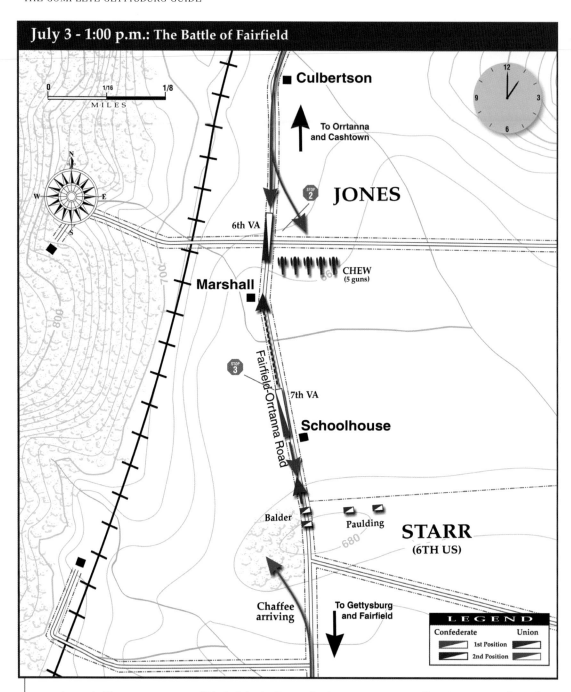

July 3 - 1:00 p.m.: The Battle of Fairfield

Culbertson

To Orrtanna
and Cashtown

JONES

6th VA

CHEW
(5 guns)

Marshall

Fairfield-Orrtanna Road

7th VA

Schoolhouse

Balder

Paulding

STARR
(6TH US)

Chaffee
arriving

To Gettysburg
and Fairfield

LEGEND

Confederate   Union

1st Position

2nd Position

MILES

0   1/16   1/8

charged. The two groups collided right in front of where you are standing. Jones, watching from behind his men, stood up in his stirrups and yelled to the commander of the 6th Virginia Cavalry, Maj. Cabell E. Flournoy, "Shall one damn regiment of Yankees whip my whole brigade?" When Jones ordered the 6th to join the charge, Flournoy led his troopers down the road and into the melee.

Some of the men of the 7th Virginia had torn down part of the fences along the road, so some Confederates were able to gallop into the fields on both sides. Several dozen troopers of the 11th Virginia Cavalry, commanded by Col. Lunsford Lomax, bolted into the assault. Some of Paulding's men had by this time mounted their horses and were now galloping down the road and through the fields along its east side to support Starr. Unfortunately for the Federals, many of Jones' men had flooded the fields along both sides of the road, and the Northern troopers soon found themselves surrounded by a wave of gray in front of where you are standing. A private of the 6th Virginia recalled, "The boys rode, sabre in hand, right into the Sixth Regulars, sabring [sic] right and left as they went. A great many of the enemy were knocked from their horses with the sabre, but succeeded in escaping through the tall wheat, which had not yet been harvested."

Attacked on three sides, Starr and Balder were ordered by several Confederates to surrender. Balder turned his horse's head south and attempted to blade his way out, but a pistol shot knocked him out of his saddle. Starr also flailed away with his saber, but was shot in the right arm. Lt. Robert Duncan of the 6th Virginia Cavalry spurred his horse next to Starr's mount, swung his saber, and sliced open the officer's scalp. Duncan went on to saber five more Federals. He ran his blade completely through one of the unlucky men, and twisted him off his horse.

Chaffee's two companies that had been posted dismounted on the ridge in the apple orchard fared no better. Troopers of the 7th and 11th Virginia Cavalry galloped up the ridge and ran them down, chasing them as they abandoned their horses and scattered between the apple trees. Lt. Joseph Bould, commanding one of the mounted squadrons, saw Chaffee's plight and ordered a counterattack into the orchard. One of Bould's troopers held the regimental standard of the 6th U.S. and was quickly targeted by the Confederates. Shot from several directions, the color bearer and the flag began to fall from the horse. Twenty-one-year-old Sgt. George Crawford Platt of the 6th U.S.'s Co. H instinctively grabbed the standard

The Benjamin Marshall house served as a hospital on July 3. (Stanley)

after cutting down one Confederate. The quick-thinking Platt tore it from the staff and stuffed it into his coat before ramming the flagstaff "through the first enemy that came before him." With a fresh saber wound of his own on his scalp, Platt cut a path out of the melee and galloped down the road toward Fairfield, saving his own life and the colors of his outfit.

Those of the regiment not killed, badly wounded, or captured ran from the maelstrom by hoof or foot. Most headed toward town, with Confederates in hot pursuit. Paulding and most of his men, however, were captured.

After hearing Chew's cannon, Capt. George Cram's squadron galloped off the railroad bed from the west and headed toward the fighting. Seeing that the rest of the regiment was surrounded or had scattered, Cram ordered a charge into what looked to be the enemy's exposed right flank. He and his squadron were quickly surrounded, however, and Cram was taken prisoner. Command of the squadron fell onto Lt. Nicholas Nolan, who yelled at Sgt. Martin Schwenk to beat a path through with his saber. Schwenk failed, but was able to rescue one of his captured officers by scooping him up to safety.

Jones' Confederates kept up a dogged pursuit of the escapees into the town, tracking them through yards and side streets as the frightened citizens of Fairfield scrambled for cover. The Federals dove into barns, doorways, and anywhere they could hide, while the Confederates ran down any bluecoats still on their horses or foolish enough to remain in the open. The Southerners gave up the chase about one mile south of the village.

Lt. Paulding, along with other prisoners of his companies, was corralled in the yard of the Marshall home in front of you. There, Paulding found the badly wounded Starr and Balder, as well as Chaffee, many more wounded, and the 6th U.S. Cavalry's surgeon, all gathered in the front yard. One trooper remembered "wash tubs full of bloody water about the yard, and strips of crimson cloth scattered over the grass." Paulding was marched down the road to your right to the Hugh Culbertson home, where he joined another 150 prisoners. More wounded were being treated there, too.

At the Fairfield fighting, Starr's command suffered more than fifty percent casualties: six killed outright, twenty-eight wounded, and 208 taken prisoner, for a total of 242. Most of the regiment's of-

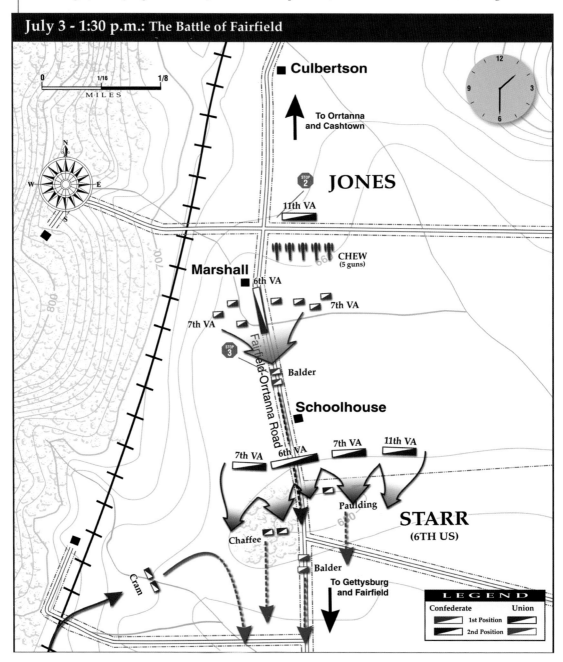

July 3 - 1:30 p.m.: The Battle of Fairfield

ficers were among the casualties. Jones' Brigade suffered fifty-eight killed and wounded. Neither the 11th Virginia Cavalry nor Chew's battery suffered any losses.

Early that evening, most of the Federal prisoners able to be moved were marched four miles northeast to the Confederate camps at Cashtown. With the Fairfield-Ortanna Road now clear, Jones moved his brigade into Fairfield and threw out pickets to scour the roads for any more Federals.

Starr and several other wounded officers were taken into Fairfield to be cared for by the surgeon and locals. Starr's arm was eventually amputated. Lieutenants Chaffee and Balder were also cared for in Fairfield. Chaffee's thigh wound was not serious, but Balder died a few days later from his wounds.

That night, those 6th U.S. Cavalry troopers fortunate enough to have escaped began to slowly stream back (many on borrowed horses) to the headquarters of the brigade near Emmitsburg. Those serving in the other regiments of the brigade, who had their own taste of hard fighting that day on the fields east of Gettysburg, listened as survivors recalled the Fairfield debacle. Lt. Henry Carpenter was in command of the remnant, barely enough troopers to flesh out a pair of small companies. "The 6th U.S. is cut to pieces," Pvt. Samuel Crockett of the 1st U.S. Cavalry noted in his diary. "There are less than a hundred of them left."

The regiment's forgettable days with Jones' Laurel Brigade were not over. During the retreat from Gettysburg, these same troopers faced each other at the July 7 Funkstown fight in Maryland. Only 200 troopers of the 6th U.S. Cavalry had been cobbled together by then, and they were once again overwhelmed by Jones' cavalry in a running fight covering five long and bloody miles. The 6th U.S. Cavalry lost another eighty-five casualties, most of them captured. "The Seventh Virginia Cavalry

A 1911 reunion of survivors of the 6th U.S. Cavalry gathered around the Marshall home. (Kevin Bream)

availed itself of the opportunity of setting old scores," Jones puffed in his Funkstown report, recalling the 7th Virginia's initial repulse by Starr at Fairfield. "Soon 66 bloody-headed prisoners were marched to the rear. . . . The day at Fairfield is nobly and fully avenged."

Starr healed and returned, less one arm, to the 6th U.S. Cavalry in November of 1863. He was later assigned to mustering and inspection duty until the war's end. He retired from the service in 1870 with the rank of colonel. He died in 1891 and was interred at Arlington. Lt. Adna Chaffee had a distinguished post-war career in the army and achieved the rank of major general during the Spanish-American War. His son, Maj. Gen. Adna Chaffee, Jr., was the first commander of the new U.S. Armored Corps (the descendant of horse cavalry) during World War II.

German-born Sgt. Martin Schwenk, who had tried to cut his way out of the worst fighting upon Lt. Nolan's order, was awarded the Medal of Honor in 1899 for rescuing one of his officers. For his valiant rescue of the 6th U.S. Cavalry's flag at Fairfield, Irish-born Sgt. George Platt, whom fellow trooper James McDowell called "the hero of the day," was awarded the Medal of Honor in 1895. During the war, Platt suffered a number of wounds including bullets in a leg, knee, and groin, as well as a saber cut to his head. He kept the regimental flag as a memento for the rest of his life. The George C. Platt Memorial Bridge in his hometown of Philadelphia was named in his honor.

The Culbertson house, a hospital for the 6th US Cavalry on July 3. (Stanley)

Return to your vehicle, carefully turn around, and return to Carroll Tract Road. If you wish to visit the Hugh Culbertson home, reset your odometer to 0.0, and turn right. After .2 miles, you will see the stone Culbertson home on your right (77° 22' 06"W, 39° 50' 02"N). The sign in the yard explains that this home served as a temporary field hospital for the 6th U.S. Cavalry after the battle.

If you visit the Culbertson home, carefully turn your vehicle around where possible, preferably at one of the cross roads ahead. Drive back to the Marshall home, which is on your right (77° 22' 07"W, 39° 49' 43"N). You may pause briefly here, traffic allowing, but please note this is private property.

In the front yard of the home is a plaque placed in 1909 by 6th U.S. Cavalry veterans to commemorate the battle of Fairfield. Several veterans' reunion gatherings were held here on the Marshall property. The large barn behind the home is a replacement of the original, which burned in 1900.

Drive .2 miles past the Marshall home, and on your right you will see a marker placed by the War Department for the Battle of Fairfield.

Tour Stop 3
War Department Marker of the Battle

This iron marker, which is a position marker for Jones' Confederate cavalry brigade, was placed in 1910-1911 by the War Department. From this position, you have a good view of the ridge ahead of you from which Starr launched his attack.

After another .2 miles, you will again pass over the ridge on which Starr and his men deployed.

On the left stood the fence line behind which the squadron of Lt. Paulding deployed. On the right stood the apple orchard in which Lt. Chaffee's squadron de-

In 1918, William Tipton took this photo of Jones' Brigade marker across from the schoolhouse on the Fairfield battlefield. (GNMP)

ployed. Off in the distance to the right is the ground over which Capt. Cram marched his squadron from the railroad bed to the defense of his comrades.

After another 2.1 miles you will be back at the intersection with Rt. 116. Turn right to enter the town of Fairfield and reset your odometer to 0.0. (As you drive, note that after approximately .1 miles, a large Confederate field hospital, after the battle of Gettysburg, stood to your right in what were mainly fields at that time. Many badly wounded Confederates were captured there by the Federal Army during the retreat from Gettysburg.)

Tour Stop 4
Sites of Interest in Fairfield

St. John's Lutheran Church

After a total of .3 miles, the St. John's Lutheran Church is on the right. Pull over to the right here. Built in 1854, this brick church (known then as the Evangelical Lutheran Church) served as a hospital for the wounded of both sides after the fight. Southern casualties were primarily from the 6th Virginia Cavalry. A War Department marker offers information about the area during the armies' retreat from the battle of Gettysburg, as does a sign placed by the Pennsylvania Historical and Museum Commission.

Fairfield Inn

A short distance ahead is the majestic Fairfield Inn, built in 1757. It is one of the nation's oldest, continuously operated inns. Originally the mansion house of Squire William Miller, the house and inn have hosted such famous individuals as Patrick Henry (a nephew of William and Isabella Henry Miller), Thaddeus Stevens, baseball Hall of Fame member Eddie Plank (a Gettysburg native), President Dwight D. Eisenhower and wife Mamie, as well as many Southern officers during the Gettysburg Campaign. (Initially, Fairfield was known as Millerstown.)

McKesson House

On the other side of the street is a two-story wood-sided dwelling built in 1801 called the "McKesson House." This was the 1863 home of Robert C. Swope. Maj. Samuel Starr of the 6th U.S. Cavalry was cared for here when his badly wounded arm was amputated. Twenty-one-year-old Rachel Elizabeth Blythe, a daughter of Hugh Culbertson (owner of the home on the Fairfield-Ortanna Road used as a hospital) helped care for Starr. Several others from the regiment were also hospitalized in the Swope home. There is a small plaque on the front of the house noting its significance.

To return to Gettysburg, turn around to travel east on Rt. 116. You will reach Gettysburg after about seven miles.

Additional reading

Eric. J. Wittenberg's *Gettysburg's Forgotten Cavalry Actions* (Gettysburg, Pa.: Thomas Publications, 1998) contains a detailed chapter on the battle of Fairfield. One of the earliest monographs devoted to this fascinating episode of the Gettysburg Campaign is an article by Paul Shevchuck in Issue No. 1 (July 1989) of the *Gettysburg Magazine*. J. David Petruzzi's article, "Annihilation of a Regiment," in the July 2007 issue of *America's Civil War* magazine contains the most recent scholarship on the combat and formed the basis for this tour.

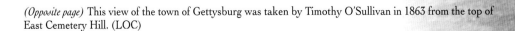

(Opposite page) This view of the town of Gettysburg was taken by Timothy O'Sullivan in 1863 from the top of East Cemetery Hill. (LOC)

Tour of Historical Sites in the Town of Gettysburg

"Sights and sounds . . . too horrible to describe"

*I*t is not unusual for many first-time visitors to Gettysburg, after driving into town, to ask locals, "Can you tell me where the battlefield is?" You can walk or drive from the town square in any direction and reach some part of the "battlefield," or you can just look around you. The town itself was as much of a battlefield as the land preserved by the National Park Service. During the late afternoon of July 1, the first day of the fight, approximately 20,000 soldiers of two Federal corps retreated through the town to the south and east, with thousands of Confederates hot on their heels. Fighting and skirmishing raged through the streets of the town while terrified citizens tried to stay out of the line of fire — the bravest among them slipping outside to help those who were wounded and those who were simply trying to find a place to hide.

On the second and third days of the battle, the town was in Confederate hands. Skirmish and sharpshooter fire whizzed through the streets, many of the deadly lead missiles hitting homes, fences, and anything else in the way. The sound of a bullet striking a brick wall first made an unearthly "thud" that rattled the citizens' ears, but by the third day small lead strikes went largely unnoticed. By this time, artillery projectiles fired by both sides crashed into homes (most of them inadvertently), severely damaging many structures. Some owners left the shells imbedded in their walls as a badge of honor and a curiosity for tourists to later admire. Given the titanic nature of the battle, it is something of a miracle that only one citizen, Virginia "Jennie" Wade, was killed during the three days by a bullet that struck her in her home.

Even on the morning of July 4, as Robert E. Lee prepared his army, his wounded, and his prisoners to leave the battlefield, sniping and sharpshooting continued throughout the town. One Southern officer threatened to shell the town itself. Thankfully, an intentional shelling of Gettysburg was not undertaken. Behind them, the armies left Gettysburg's blood-soaked soil, where thousands of wounded were left in the care of hundreds of citizens before the government could take full responsibility for their succor. Along the streets of the town and on outlying farms where the main fighting raged, the human wreckage of war was left for anyone who cared to view such gruesome sights. Thousands of bodies were either unburied or interred in hurried, shallow graves. Thousands of horses lay where they dropped. The stench was indescribable. The odors, airborne diseases, and accompanying vermin made many of the locals physically ill.

Gettysburg's modernity and development today belie those nearly unbearable July days and the months that followed. In addition to its battle history, Gettysburg, like so many other locales that date back to this nation's early period, carries a history of its own that also yearns to be appreciated. This walking tour of the town will take you to many of the most important and interesting sites of its history, battle-related and otherwise. Informational waysides are located at various spots in the town. To more fully appreciate the historical significance of this remarkable place, we encourage you to contact the Association of Licensed Town Guides for personalized tours. Information on the Association is included at the end of this tour.

Four of Gettysburg's main streets are laid out on the points of the compass: Carlisle Street to the north, York Street to the east, Baltimore Street to the south, and Chambersburg Street to the west. The town square (known as The Diamond in 1863, and Lincoln Square today) is the center of town. This tour begins at Lincoln Square, moves to the northern section, and continues clockwise. We advise you to park in the square or on an adjoining side street before beginning the tour, which is more enjoyable and educational if walked. Each numbered site is plotted on the accompanying map to assist you on foot. In addition, structures which feature a visible imbedded artillery shell are identified on the map by their corresponding letter.

This tour features only a few of the hundreds of interesting structures and sites to be experienced in this historic town, truly one of America's jewels – Gettysburg.

Note that many of the sites are private property, so please do not trespass or infringe on the rights of the owner or residents. Please walk safely — use crosswalks, obey traffic signals, and be cautious of vehicles.

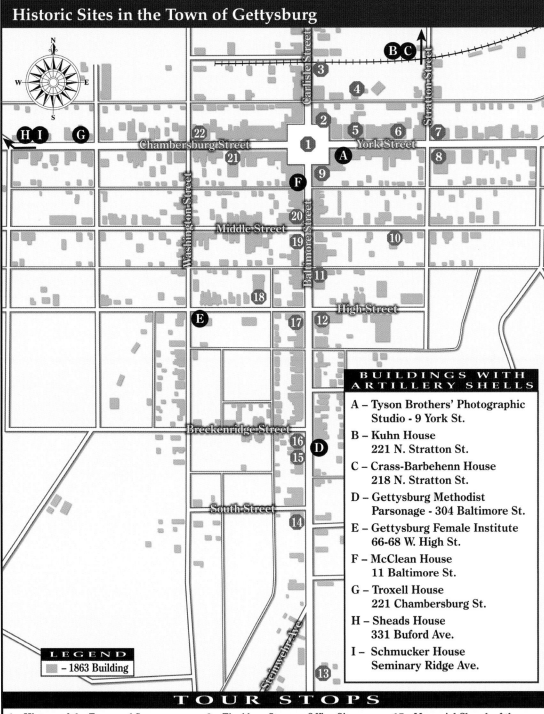

Historic Sites in the Town of Gettysburg

BUILDINGS WITH ARTILLERY SHELLS

A – Tyson Brothers' Photographic Studio - 9 York St.

B – Kuhn House
221 N. Stratton St.

C – Crass-Barbehenn House
218 N. Stratton St.

D – Gettysburg Methodist Parsonage - 304 Baltimore St.

E – Gettysburg Female Institute
66-68 W. High St.

F – McClean House
11 Baltimore St.

G – Troxell House
221 Chambersburg St.

H – Sheads House
331 Buford Ave.

I – Schmucker House
Seminary Ridge Ave.

LEGEND

– 1863 Building

TOUR STOPS

1 – History of the Town and Square
2 – McClellan House Site
3 – Hanover and Gettysburg Rail Station
4 – James Getty House Site
5 – Globe Inn Site
6 – Hoke-Codori House
7 – Plank's Garage
8 – St. James Lutheran Church
9 – Thaddeus Stevens Office Site
10 – Grand Army of the Republic Hall
11 – "Compiler" Newspaper Office Site
12 – Gettysburg Presbyterian Church
13 – Virginia "Jennie" Wade House
14 – Harvey S. Sweney House
15 – George W. Shriver House
16 – Tillie Pierce House
17 – Memorial Church of the Prince of Peace
18 – St. Francis Xavier Catholic Church
19 – Adams County Courthouse
20 – Fahnestock Dry Goods Store
21 – Christ Lutheran Church
22 – Eagle Hotel Site

The first courthouse sat in the middle of the Diamond until 1859, when it was relocated to its present location. (LOC)

The Square

Tour Stop 1
Brief History of the Town and The Square

Settlers first began building homes in the area that comprises today's Adams County in the 1730s. By 1741, the Marsh Creek Settlement (as it was then known) was home to approximately 150 families. The crossroads town of Gettysburg was founded on the 381-acre farm of Samuel Gettys, an early settler and tavern proprietor. In 1786, his middle son James laid out the town and streets. By 1795, thirty-three dwellings had been erected in the bustling town, and by 1806, when Gettysburg was incorporated as a borough, there were more than eighty homes.

In 1800, Gettysburg was named the county seat of newly created Adams County. A county prison and offices, newspaper, and county poorhouse followed. The original courthouse, a two-story building with a bell tower on top, stood in the middle of the square until it was removed in 1859. At the time of the battle, a 100-foot flagpole stood in the center. The pole was chopped down by Confederates from Lt. Gen. Richard Ewell's Corps when they briefly occupied the town on June 26, 1863.

"The Diamond" was the center of commercial and social activity for the town of Gettysburg. During the battle, it was a hub of activity for vastly different reasons. On the afternoon of July 1, the first day of battle, Federal soldiers from the 1st and 11th Corps were chased through the town by pursuing Confederates. Many of the Federals retreated through the square on their way to the heights east and south of town. Until the end of the battle, the square and most of the town was behind Southern lines.

Four Civil War era buildings remain in the square. Perhaps most recognizable is the large three-story Wills House (6 Lincoln Square) at the corner of the square and York Street (Rt. 30). The entrance to prominent Get-

The bed that Lincoln slept on is on display at the Wills House, which is owned by the National Park Service and is open to the public year-round. (Stanley)

tysburg attorney David Wills' law office was through the door on the square, and the York Street entrance led to the family's dwelling rooms. President Abraham Lincoln stayed here (and put the finishing touches on his Gettysburg Address) the night before the November 19, 1863, dedication of the Soldiers' National Cemetery. Today, the home is an impressive museum maintained by the National Park Service. It also houses the Association of Licensed Town Guides.

At the intersection with the square and Baltimore Street (Rt. 97) is the Stoever-Schick building (1-3-5 Baltimore Street), which following the battle housed the Christian Commission. In the backyard behind the building, an open-air commissary fed many famished soldiers. The three-story structure was built in 1817 and was owned at the time of the battle by Professor Martin Luther Stoever. It is the oldest structure on the square. The other two are the Maxwell Danner House at 8 Lincoln Square, and the Arnold Spangler House at 2-4-6 Baltimore Street.

. . . .

Northern Section

Tour Stop 2
Site of the McClellan House (present-day Gettysburg Hotel)

The present Gettysburg Hotel was built in the 1890s. Originally on this site was "Scott's Tavern," a smaller brick tavern and inn built by James Scott about 1797. It catered to stage route travelers between Gettysburg and York. William McClellan, a former New York sheriff, purchased it in 1810 and renamed it "Indian Queen." After 1846 it became known as the Franklin House, and then eventually the McClellan House. Daniel Webster is believed to have briefly stopped at the original tavern on a return trip from the West in 1833. In 1955, the hotel became a temporary White House while President Dwight D. Eisenhower was recovering from a heart attack in Gettysburg. The hotel was gutted by fire in 1983 and reopened in 1991.

Tour Stop 3
Hanover and Gettysburg Rail Station

The magnificently restored station building of the Hanover Junction, Hanover and Gettysburg Railroad is where President Lincoln arrived on November 18, 1863, for the dedication the following day of the Soldiers' National Cemetery. It was constructed in 1858 in Italianate Villa style. It was used as a field hos-

President Lincoln started his twenty-four and one-half hour journey in Gettysburg through the doors of the Hanover and Gettysburg Railroad Station, shown here in 1913. (GNMP)

pital on the first day of battle (July 1), with the first men carried inside belonging to Brig. Gen. John Buford's Federal cavalry. Many wounded from the Federal Iron Brigade were also treated here. The hospital was set up in the building as well as the passenger platform along the tracks. Following the battle, when train service was restored, the U.S. Sanitary Commission set up tents across the tracks from the rear platform to supervise the transportation of wounded.

This rare view of the James Gettys home is from a William Tipton stereoview taken in the late 1800s. (LOC)

Tour Stop 4
Site of James Gettys' Home

At this site along Race Horse Alley stood the home of James Gettys. The log and weatherboard structure was Gettys' home when he laid out the town in 1786. During the battle, it was the home of blacksmith Adam Doersom. The home was destroyed in a fire in 1880. This alley behind the Gettysburg Hotel is named Race Horse Alley because William McClellan, while owner of the hotel in the early 1800s, trained his racehorses here.

• • • • • • • • • • •

Eastern Section

Tour Stop 5
Site of the Globe Inn

The Globe Inn, owned at the time of the battle by Charles Wills, was one of Gettysburg's oldest taverns and hotels, although the construction date of the original two-story brick structure is uncertain. It was standing by 1798, and was then owned and operated by James Gettys. The oldest brick building in town, a third story was added sometime after 1864. The inn was long the unofficial headquarters of the Democratic Party in Gettysburg, and was frequented by Confederates during the battle.

Tour Stop 6
The Hoke-Codori House

Here on York Street is the Hoke-Codori House, built about 1788 by Michael Hoke. This dwelling has the distinction of being the oldest home within the original town limits of Gettysburg. During the battle it was owned by a local butcher named Nicholas Codori, who had purchased it in 1843. Because St. Francis Xavier Catholic Church was used to treat wounded for weeks after the battle, Catholic services were held here in his home.

Tour Stop 7
Plank's Garage (operated by Eddie Plank, Baseball Hall of Famer)

Baseball great Eddie Plank (known as "Gettysburg Eddie") owned and operated an auto garage here following his retirement from sports. Plank, a member of baseball's Hall of Fame, is buried in the town's Evergreen Cemetery.

Tour Stop 8
Saint James Lutheran Church (and site of original church)

The original church, built in 1848, stood here during the battle and served as a field hospital for many wounded. The old structure was demolished in 1911, and the present church before you was extensively damaged by fire in 1928, but was restored soon thereafter.

Tour Stop 9
Site of Thaddeus Stevens' Office

From 1824 to 1842, noted abolitionist Thaddeus Stevens had his law office on this site. He lived in Gettysburg from 1816 to 1842 before moving to Lancaster, Pennsylvania, after which time he was elected to the U.S. Congress. A prominent land speculator, Stevens owned the stone home along the Chambersburg Pike (occupied during the battle by widow Mary Thompson) said to have been used by Robert E. Lee as his headquarters during the battle. Stevens also owned the Caledonia Iron Furnace between Cashtown and Chambersburg, which was burned by Confederates on June 26, 1863, during Confederate General Ewell's advance toward the Susquehanna. His home was located on the site of the dwelling that stands today at 51 Chambersburg Street.

. . . .

Southern Section

Tour Stop 10
Grand Army of the Republic (GAR) Hall (originally Methodist Church)

Built in 1822, this was the first permanent Methodist Church in Gettysburg. It was used as a hospital during the battle. In 1880, the building was sold to the Cpl. Johnston H. Skelly post of the GAR. It is now owned by Historic Gettysburg-Adams County and used for community meetings, Sons of Union Veterans functions, and meetings of the Civil War Roundtable of Gettysburg.

This early 1900s image of the Gettysburg *Compiler* office just before it was torn down and the present brick building replaced it. Note "Penelope" in the middle foreground sticking out of the sidewalk. (ACHS)

Tour Stop 11
Site of the *Compiler* Newspaper Office

In 1863, this was the site of the office of the *Compiler*, one of Gettysburg's newspapers, as well as the home of its outspoken publisher Henry Stahle. The paper was the weekly voice of the area's Democratic Party. During the battle, Stahle took in a wounded Federal officer here and persuaded a Confederate surgeon to amputate the officer's badly wounded leg, thereby saving his life. General George Meade, commander of the Federal army, later allowed Stahle to be arrested for "helping" the Southerners to capture the officer during the battle — an unfounded charge concocted by local Republican dissenters. Note the breech of the cannon in the sidewalk here, nicknamed "Penelope." It was used to signal Democratic election victories until its barrel burst from an excessive powder charge in 1855. It was subsequently embedded at this location.

Tour Stop 12
Gettysburg Presbyterian Church

Like many churches, homes, and farms in and around the town, the Presbyterian Church served as a hospital beginning early in the battle, as well as for several weeks thereafter. This church was primarily the hospital of the Cavalry Corps of the Federal army. After the dedication of the Soldiers' National Cemetery on November 19, 1863, President Lincoln attended a patriotic meeting at this church; although the pews inside have been replaced, the one used by Lincoln remains. President Dwight D. Eisenhower and wife Mamie, who relocated to Gettysburg following his administration, were members of this church. The church's Eisenhower Lounge contains memorabilia of the late president. The structure, significantly modified since the war, was built in 1842.

Tour Stop 13
Virginia "Jennie" Wade House

Now a museum, this two-family home at 520 Baltimore Street was owned during the battle by John L. and Georgia Anna Wade McClellan. Jennie (actually called "Ginnie" by family and friends) was staying here, helping to care for the newly born son of her sister Georgia while Georgia's husband was serving in Co. E., 165th Pennsylvania Infantry. While preparing bread dough to bake for hungry soldiers on July 3, a Southern bullet penetrated two doors on the northern side of the home and struck Jennie in the back, killing her instantly. She was the only civilian killed during the battle. Jennie was initially buried in the garden behind the home. In January 1864, her remains were relocated to the German Reformed Church cemetery on Stratton Street. In November 1865, Jennie was finally buried in Evergreen Cemetery.

Tour Stop 14
The Harvey S. Sweney House

Known today as the "Farnsworth House," this popular restaurant and bed and breakfast was the wartime home of Harvey Sweney. The brick portion of the home was constructed in 1833, and the frame and log section in the rear is believed to date back to about 1810. Harvey's son John was briefly captured on June 26, 1863, while trying to escape with a horse when Confederates entered the town. When the battle began on July 1, the family of John T. Slentz, who rented the Edward McPherson farm along the Chambersburg Pike, found refuge here. The house was used for several days as a hospital for Federal soldiers wounded on the first day. Caught in the crossfire of the two opposing lines during the battle, the house was struck many times by bullets. Note the pockmarks in the bricks on the south wall, evidence of Federals attempting to shoot Confederate sharpshooters posted in the garret window above. An investigation in the 1970s speculates that the bullet that killed Jennie Wade may have been fired from the garret window.

The Harvey S. Sweney house on Baltimore Street. The back porch (now enclosed) and the small garret (attic) window were perches for Confederate sharpshooters. (Stanley)

Tour Stop 15
George W. Shriver House

Also a museum today, this home was owned during the battle by George Shriver and his wife Henrietta (known as "Hettie"). Built in 1860, the dwelling housed "Shriver's Saloon and Ten-Pin Alley" in the basement. At the time of the battle, George was serving in Co. C of the 1st Potomac Home Brigade Cavalry (a Federal unit raised in Maryland and known as "Cole's Cavalry"). Hettie and their two daughters fled the home on the afternoon of July 1, and Confederate sharpshooters occupied the attic shortly thereafter until the afternoon of July 3. Two of the Southerners were killed while posted in the garret window. George never saw his home again. He died in Andersonville Prison in Georgia in August 1864 after being captured during a skirmish near Winchester, Virginia eight months earlier.

Tour Stop 16
Tillie Pierce House

The James Pierce family lived here during the battle. When the fighting began, the family urged fifteen-year-old daughter Matilda ("Tillie") to leave town for safer environs at the home of Jacob Weikert at the base of Little Round Top. From there, Tillie brought food and water to Federal soldiers and assisted with the care of wounded. She finally returned home on July 7, appalled by the sights in town of the aftermath of the battle. Following the war, Tillie Pierce Alleman wrote a famous account called *At Gettysburg: Or What a Girl Saw and Heard at the Battle*. She died in 1914, just as another major war was breaking out overseas, and is buried in Trinity Lutheran Cemetery in Selinsgrove, Pennsylvania.

Tour Stop 17
Memorial Church of the Prince of Peace

Following the war, the Episcopal congregation in Gettysburg searched for a suitable church location. Beginning in 1867, services were conducted in the Court House and then the old Methodist Church on High Street (later the Grand Army of the Republic Hall). As the twenty-fifth anniversary of the battle drew near, the congregation publicized their new church project to be a sign of the "loving unity" that still existed between the North and South after the war, and that it would "embrace the memorials of both sides in rearing a lasting Temple to the Prince of Peace." The cornerstone of this impressive edifice that celebrates national reconciliation bears the date July 2, 1888, and was put in place by veterans. The church was completed twelve years later. Inside the bell tower are stones purchased and engraved during construction as a memorial to soldiers — many by their comrades, as well as memorial plaques.

Tour Stop 18
St. Francis Xavier Catholic Church

Here is another church that was employed as a hospital during and after the battle. Confederates used its cupola as an observation post. More than 250 wounded of both sides were treated here. An operating table was used just inside the main entrance. The church was constructed in 1852-53, and the current edifice was added in 1925. The memorial plaques on either side of the main entrance commemorate Fr. William Corby, a chaplain in the Federal Irish Brigade whose statue stands along Cemetery Ridge, and the Sisters of Charity (known as the "Angels of the Battlefield") of Emmitsburg, Maryland, for their work assisting the wounded. Inside the church on the right wall is a beautiful stained-glass panel depicting scenes following the battle.

The Adams County Courthouse as it appeared in 1913. Note the trolley tracks in the foreground. (GNMP)

Tour Stop 19
Adams County Courthouse

The new Courthouse was established here following the removal of the original building, which had stood in the center of the square until 1859. Late in the afternoon of June 26, 1863, soldiers of the 26th Pennsylvania Emergency militia (which included many local college and seminary students) and Robert Bell's Independent Adams County Cavalry, were paroled by Confederate Maj. Gen. Jubal A. Early following their capture during the Confederate occupation of the town. Early admonished the green recruits to return "home to their mothers."

Tour Stop 20
Fahnestock Dry Goods Store

During the first day of battle, Federal Maj. Gen. Oliver O. Howard (commanding the 11th Corps) used the roof of the Fahnestock Store as an observation post. It was also here that he learned of the death of the commander of the Federal 1st Corps, Maj. Gen. John F. Reynolds. The death of Reynolds left Howard temporarily in command of the field. Following the battle, the U.S. Sanitary Commission used this building to dispense needed supplies for wounded soldiers. The structure, greatly enlarged, was originally built as a house in 1810.

As you cross Middle Street, note that the Confederate line of battle ran east-west along Middle Street. As you continue along Baltimore Street, note that the procession leading from the square to the November 19, 1863, dedication of the Soldiers' National Cemetery used Baltimore Street before turning onto the Emmitsburg Road (today Steinwehr Avenue), to enter the cemetery from Taneytown Road.

After the battle, the U.S. Sanitary Commission used the Fahnestock Dry Goods store, captured here in July of 1863 by photographer Alexander Gardner. (LOC)

. . . .

Western Section

Tour Stop 21
Christ Lutheran Church (The College Lutheran Church)

Note the memorial in the shape of a podium and open book in the front steps. Near this spot on the afternoon of the first day of battle on July 1, Chaplain Horatio Stockton Howell of the 90th Pennsylvania Infantry was shot dead after refusing to surrender his sword to a Confederate soldier. The forty-two-year-old Howell had just attended to wounded Federal soldiers inside. The church, attended by many local students, was called "The College Church" at the time. Begun in 1835 and completed the following year, the church served as one of the earliest field hospitals on the first day of the battle.

Tour Stop 22
Site of the Eagle Hotel

A convenience store stands here now, but in 1863 the large Eagle Hotel was a fixture of Gettysburg. On June 30 and July 1 it served as the headquarters of Federal cavalry commander Brig. Gen. John Buford after he entered the town with his horsemen. A junction point on the stage route to

Chambersburg and Harrisburg, the original two-story hotel was built in the early 1830s, with a third floor added in 1857. Later, it was known as the Adams House when converted into apartments.

Gettysburg photographer William Tipton took this image of the Eagle Hotel in 1913. (ACHS)

There is much more to see and experience in the town beyond the sites in this tour. To fully experience the historical sites of the town of Gettysburg, contact the Association of Licensed Town Guides at (717) 339-6161 for a personalized guided tour. Specialized tours of Gettysburg's churches are also available seasonally from Historic Church Walking Tours Inc., which maintains a website at www.historicchurchwalkingtours.org. This tour is based in part on the tours given by both groups.

(Opposite page) Entrance to the Gettysburg Soldiers' National Cemetery taken in July, 1865 by William Morris Smith. (LOC)

Tour of the Soldiers' National Cemetery at Gettysburg

"And glory guards, with solemn round the bivouac of the dead."

Prominent Gettysburg attorney David Wills is often credited with the idea of originating and establishing a Soldiers' National Cemetery at Gettysburg. At least two others, however, earlier proposed the idea of burying the Federal dead in some special place on the battlefield.

Shortly after the Battle of Gettysburg, local attorney and Evergreen Cemetery President David McConaughy proposed that the Union dead be buried in a special section of Evergreen. By the end of July, about 100 had already been buried there, while thousands more were interred in shallow graves all over the field. Dr. Theodore Dimon, a New York surgeon caring for the wounded of his state, likewise proposed to McConaughy that a special cemetery be created on part of the battlefield.

Arguments soon ensued between McConaughy and Wills. McConaughy had attempted to persuade Pennsylvania governor Andrew Curtin to expand Evergreen with a soldiers' cemetery, but Wills wanted the state to purchase the land across the Baltimore Pike – today known as East Cemetery Hill – to create a separate cemetery. McConaughy, however, had already negotiated to buy the parcel from the owners, so Wills considered the establishment of a cemetery in the area where the large Pennsylvania Monument stands today.

Ultimately, Evergreen's board of directors agreed to sell the land immediately to the west of the town's burial ground, and soon the Soldiers' National Cemetery was established on twenty-two acres from six separate plots. Governor Curtin appointed Wills as his agent to oversee and coordinate the planning for the cemetery, and Wills hired well-known landscape gardener William Saunders of the U.S. Department of Agriculture to design the grounds.

Saunders determined that the dead should be grouped by state in a semicircle around a central monument. In order to give equity to each plot, no state was to be given more prominence than another, and the gravestones would be identical – nine inches high with the identification inscribed on the top. Early photographs of the cemetery show the headstones at this height, but over the years they have now become visible only at ground level.

Originally, Wills planned for an October 23, 1863 dedication ceremony, but the keynote orator, Edward Everett, was unavailable until November. November 19 was set as the day, and Wills also invited President Abraham Lincoln to attend and consecrate the new cemetery with "a few appropriate remarks."

In the meantime, re-interments of Federal dead from the battlefield began. Frederick W. Biesecker's bid of $1.59 per body was accepted to exhume the corpses, and

PROPOSALS
FOR THE REMOVAL OF THE DEAD ON THE
GETTYSBURG BATTLE-FIELD.

SEALED proposals will be received at my Office in the Borough of Gettysburg, until the 22d inst., at 12 o'clock, noon, for the following two contracts, viz:

1st. For disinterring the bodies on the Gettysburg Battle Field and at the Hospitals in the vicinity, and removing them to the Soldiers' Cemetery on the south side of the Borough of Gettysburg.
2d. For digging the graves, and burying the dead in the Cemetery.

☞ The specifications of work for each contract, to be strictly complied with by the Contractor, can be seen and examined at my office.

DAVID WILLS,
Agent for A. G. CURTIN, Governor of Pennsylvania.

Gettysburg, Oct. 15, 1863.

PRINTED AT THE "SENTINEL OFFICE," GETTYSBURG.

In October of 1863, proposals were accepted for the dis-interment and the reburials of the Union dead for the creation of the National Cemetery. (GNMP)

Samuel Weaver was hired to supervise. Not a single grave was opened unless Weaver was present, and he kept meticulous records of each grave. Free black workers exhumed each body, and they were buried in the National Cemetery in pine coffins. Pvt. Enoch M. Detty of the 73rd Ohio Infantry was the first to be buried, on October 28, in the new cemetery.

Although Weaver was convinced that no Southern soldiers were mistakenly transferred to the National Cemetery, research now indicates that at least four, and perhaps as many as nine, Confederate soldiers were misidentified as Federals. All of their gravesites will be visited in the tour.

James S. Townsend, Surveyor and Superintendent of Burials, saw to it that the dead were properly reburied in the new cemetery under Saunders' direction. Wooden headboards containing identification by Weaver initially marked each grave. When winter froze the ground, the work stopped until the spring thaw, and on March 19, 1864, Weaver declared that the task was complete. A total of 3,354 bodies had been re-interred along with 158 Massachusetts dead separately reburied by local contractor Solomon Powers.

The Soldiers' National Cemetery

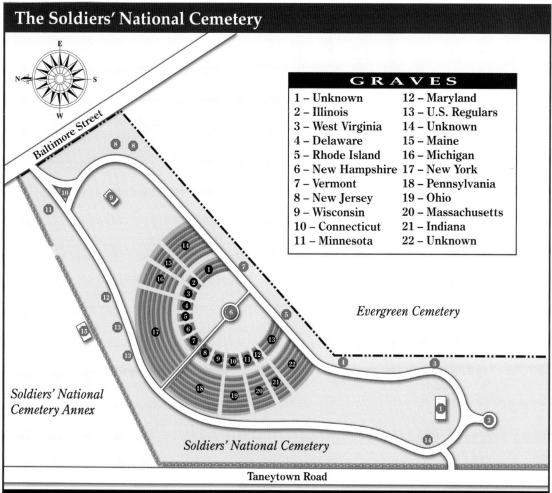

GRAVES

1 – Unknown	12 – Maryland
2 – Illinois	13 – U.S. Regulars
3 – West Virginia	14 – Unknown
4 – Delaware	15 – Maine
5 – Rhode Island	16 – Michigan
6 – New Hampshire	17 – New York
7 – Vermont	18 – Pennsylvania
8 – New Jersey	19 – Ohio
9 – Wisconsin	20 – Massachusetts
10 – Connecticut	21 – Indiana
11 – Minnesota	22 – Unknown

Evergreen Cemetery

Soldiers' National Cemetery Annex

Soldiers' National Cemetery

Taneytown Road

CEMETERY KEY

1 – Speaker's Rostrum	9 – New York State Monument
2 – Lincoln's Speech Memorial	10 – Maj. Gen. John Fulton Reynolds Monument
3 – Huntington's 1st Ohio Light Battery H	11 – 75th Pennsylvania Infantry
4 – 1st West Virginia Artillery, Battery C	12 – Gravesite of Capt. William E. Miller
5 – 1st U. S. Artillery, Battery H	13 – 61st Ohio Infantry Flank Marker
6 – Soldiers' National Monument	13 – 74th Pennsylvania Infantry Flank Marker
7 – 4th U. S. Artillery, Battery G	14 – 1st New Hampshire Battery
8 – Taft's 5th New York Independent Battery	15 – Friend to Friend Masonic Memorial
8 – Dilger's 1st Ohio Artillery, Battery I	

On November 19, 1863, the grand dedication ceremony took place. Although Everett gave the main address, Lincoln's short speech, known as the "Gettysburg Address," was immortalized. The speakers' platform was located in a high spot in adjoining Evergreen Cemetery and will be seen on this tour and visited in the tour of Evergreen Cemetery in this book.

Control of the National Cemetery was transferred to the War Department on May 1, 1872 and since August 10, 1933 has been administered by the National Park Service as a separate entity of the Gettysburg National Military Park. The cemetery today holds the remains of about 7,000 soldiers from several wars, along with many spouses.

The tour of the cemetery is divided into two sections. The first, Monuments and Sites of Interest, takes the visitor around the perimeter of the cemetery grounds to examine the monuments of Federal units stationed on Cemetery Hill during the battle, various memorials, and other points of interest. The second part, Gravesites of Interest, examines various gravesites within the State and National burial sections. If desired, if a visitor unfamiliar with the cemetery wishes to see it in its entirety with the shortest amount of walking necessary, simply go to the Gravesites of Interest section after Stop 6 at the Soldiers' National Monument. After viewing the various gravesites, the visitor may then resume the Monuments and Sites of Interest tour with Stop 7.

To tour the Soldiers' National Cemetery, park your vehicle at the cemetery parking lot along Taneytown Road. Carefully cross the road at the crosswalk and enter the gate.

. . . .

Tour I – Monuments and Sites of Interest

The tour follows the paved walking path, which circles the perimeter of the cemetery, in a counter-clockwise manner.
Inside the gate, bear to your right.

When the landscaping of the cemetery grounds was completed in 1869, the path was a walkway of chipped stone.

An early 1900s view of the Speaker's Rostrum in the Gettysburg National Cemetery. Note the Lincoln Speech Memorial in the distance. (LOC)

Tour Stop 1
The Speaker's Rostrum

Six U.S. Presidents have given Memorial Day addresses from the brick rostrum – Rutherford B. Hayes, Theodore Roosevelt, Calvin Coolidge, Herbert Hoover, Franklin D. Roosevelt, and Dwight D. Eisenhower. It was constructed in 1879, and serves as the platform from which various programs are conducted, including Remembrance Day events on November 19 of each year. Many dignitaries from across the globe have addressed large crowds over the years from the Rostrum.

Continue on the path, and to your right on a slight knoll is the Lincoln Speech Memorial.

Tour Stop 2
Lincoln Speech Memorial

Many visitors are under the impression that this memorial marks the spot from which President Lincoln delivered the Gettysburg Address. As stated earlier, the site of the speakers' platform at the dedication of the cemetery was likely in adjoining Evergreen Cemetery (that location will be pointed out shortly, and the visitor is taken to the actual spot in the Evergreen Cemetery Tour in this book). This memorial, constructed on January 24, 1912, is one of the few monuments in the world that specifically and exclusively commemorates a speech. Flanking a bust of Lincoln sculpted by Henry K. Bush-Brown (who also sculpted three equestrian monuments on the battlefield), an inscribed bronze tablet on the right side features Lincoln's Gettysburg Address, and on the left is the text of David Wills' letter inviting Lincoln to give "a few appropriate remarks" at the dedication on November 19, 1863. The stars above the plaque represent those states that remained loyal to the Union during the war. The monument was designed by Louis Henrick and cost a total of $5,000. Interestingly, the memorial was never formally dedicated – early disagreements over the proper location for the monument delayed its construction, so consequently there has never been a formal dedicatory ceremony.

In early November of 1863, David Wills sent an invitation to President Lincoln to come to the upcoming dedication ceremonies to make a few appropriate remarks. (LOC)

Behind the Lincoln Speech Memorial are some of the graves of 3,307 burials from post-Civil War conflicts; the rest are located in the northwest section of the cemetery. Although officially closed to burials in 1972, it is still open for the interment of dependents of veterans already interred here. You may wish to walk through this section, which receives very little visitation due to its more remote location.

Immediately to the left rear of the Lincoln Speech Memorial are two monuments, one for Hall's 2nd Maine Battery B and the other is of the 1st Massachusetts (McCartney's) Light Battery A.

Hall's Maine Battery, attached to the Federal 1st Corps, dedicated its first monument at its initial position on McPherson Ridge in 1889, and placed this marker at its July 2 position at least a year later. McCartney's Battery, attached to the 6th Corps, dedicated their monument here on October 8, 1885, the same day that most of the Bay State's monuments were dedicated at Gettysburg.

As you walk along the path, note the black iron fence to the right that separates the National Cemetery from the town's Evergreen Cemetery.

This fence, which originally partially enclosed Lafayette Square in Washington D.C. across from the White House at the time of the battle, was moved here in 1933 when the National Park Service was given responsibility for the National Cemetery.

Continue along the path and the next monument on your right is that of Huntington's 1st Ohio Light Battery H.

Tour Stop 3
1st Ohio Light Battery H Monument

Attached to the Artillery Reserve, this battery dedicated the monument (erected by the state of Ohio) on September 14, 1887, likewise the same day that many Buckeye veterans dedicated their monuments at Gettysburg.

The next monument on your right, and just before you reach the Gettysburg burials, is that of the 1st West Virginia Artillery, Battery C.

Tour Stop 4
1st West Virginia Artillery Battery C Monument

This monument was dedicated on September 28, 1898, and closely resembles the other West Virginia monuments placed on the battlefield.

As you walk further on the path, the semi-circle of Civil War graves begins on your left. The next marker to the right of the path is of the 1st U.S. Artillery, Battery H.

Tour Stop 5
1st U.S. Artillery Battery H Marker

This marker was erected during the placement of U.S. Regulars markers on the battlefield in 1907-08. Note the dent on one of the barrels – this particular tube is inscribed, "Revere Copper Co." and was manufactured at the business established by Paul Revere following the Revolutionary War. This cannon served at the battle and was damaged when struck by a Confederate shell. Note, also, that the tube has been installed upside down.

Continue along the path and on your left is the imposing Soldiers' National Monument.

Tour Stop 6
Soldiers' National Monument

First however, just in front of it you will see the Kentucky State Memorial, placed on November 19, 1975. Only a small disk identifies this marker of a border state during the war. It features an image of Lincoln's handwritten Gettysburg address, and one will often see pennies placed on it as tribute. It is fitting that Kentucky's memorial is here, as the state was not only the birthplace of Lincoln but of Confederate President Jefferson Davis as well.

During the dedication ceremonies of the cemetery in 1863, a large flagpole – not the speaker's stand – stood on the spot now occupied by the Soldiers' National Monument. The image of the flag-pole in photographs of the proceedings has assisted scholars in determining the actual location of the speaker's stand that day, which was in adjoining Evergreen Cemetery.

Dedicated on July 1, 1869, at a total cost of $50,000, the Soldiers' National Monument memorial-ized not just the Union victory in the war, but also the bravery and valor of fallen soldiers. The cornerstone for this monument was laid on July 4, 1865, the first Independence Day following the end of the war. The massive pedestal is made of bright white Westerly granite and supports the statue at the top called "The Genius of Liberty," who gazes upon the reposing dead with outstretched hand. Ringing the lower half of the monument are four allegorical figures, all carved in Italy at the studio of sculptor Randolph Rogers. They are:

"**War**" – represented by the resting soldier. The panels on both sides of his chair exhibit the modes of warfare, while his foot rests upon an artillery tube. He is relating his experiences for posterity to the female figure to his left, Clio.

"**History**" – represented by Clio, who is listening to War and recording the names of the dead and their deeds in her book. A stack of books, containing the record of martial history, is under her foot. To her right, the palm tree and pyramid symbolizes mankind's heritage, and the crumbling columns to her left symbolize the vanity of mankind's ambition.

"**Plenty**" – the third statue represents peace and prosperity that follows the cessation of war and the soldier's victory. The sheaf of wheat she holds, as well as the cornucopias represent the abundance of the land.

"**Peace**" – symbolized by the mechanic with the tools of his vocation, working to rebuild the nation.

Photographers Sumon & Murnane of York, PA., took this panoramic view of the Gettysburg National Cemetery in 1913. (LOC)

Return to the walking path and continue. The next marker on your right is that of the 4th U.S. Artillery, Battery G.

Tour Stop 7

4th U.S. Artillery Battery G Marker

This marker was placed during the period of 1907-08 when U.S. Regulars markers were placed on the field.

If you look through the gate in the fence to the right of the monument, note the rise of ground in adjoining Evergreen Cemetery. Atop it is a mausoleum ringed with tall, narrow trees. Evidence shows that the speakers' stand for the November 19, 1863 dedication stood about 100 feet to the left of that rise and nearer the fence. At the time, no fence separated the two cemeteries and the crowd filled the grounds of both. The speakers' stand faced the National Cemetery, in which the work of re-burying the battle dead continued during the ceremonies.

Continue on the path and as it begins to curve to the left, you will see two monuments on your right.

Tour Stop 8

5th New York Independent Battery and 1st Ohio Artillery Battery I Monuments

The New York State Monument overlooks her fallen sons on a crisp winter day. (Stanley)

The first commemorates Taft's 5th New York Independent Battery, and the second is a marker of Dilger's 1st Ohio Artillery, Battery I.

Taft's battery monument was placed in 1888, and Dilger's marker was dedicated on September 14, 1887, the same date that Ohio dedicated all of its monuments and markers on the field.

(Note that behind the monuments in the corner of the fencing along the Baltimore Pike is a comfort facility.)

To your left is the tall and imposing New York State Monument.

Tour Stop 9

New York State Monument

Fifty feet in height, the memorial was dedicated on July 2, 1893. It is second in size only to the Pennsylvania Monument along Hancock Avenue. The mourning figure at the top is actually crying as she gazes upon the dead of her state and extends a wreath to them.

Continue on the path and you will come to the portrait statue of Maj. Gen. John Fulton Reynolds, which stands in a triangle created in the walking path and the path to the Baltimore Pike entrance of the cemetery.

Tour Stop 10
General John F. Reynolds Portrait Statue

This is the first portrait statue erected on the battlefield. Sculpted by John Quincy Adams Ward, it was cast from bronze cannon barrels donated by Pennsylvania and dedicated on August 31, 1872. Reynolds, killed early on the morning of the first day of battle, was the highest ranking Union officer killed at Gettysburg.

Continue on the path as it curves to the left. The monument on your right is that of the 75th Pennsylvania Infantry.

Tour Stop 11
75th Pennsylvania Infantry Monument

It was placed in July 1886. The brick home that you see to the right of the monument, next to the Baltimore Pike gate, is the National Cemetery Lodge, which was the home of the National Cemetery superintendent.

Continue on the path and on your right you will see more gravestones of veterans from several wars who interred. Just as you reach the semicircular graves on your left, look to your right for the War Department grave marker of Capt. William E. Miller of Co. H of the 3rd Pennsylvania Cavalry.

Tour Stop 12
Grave of Capt. William E. Miller, 3rd Pennsylvania Cavalry and Medal of Honor Awardee

The stone, in the front row next to the path, is engraved with gold lettering and often has an American flag beside it. Along with Gen. Charles H. T. Collis (whose grave we will visit later), Miller is one of only two Medal of Honor awardees buried in the cemetery. While commanding a squadron of the 3rd Pennsylvania Cavalry of Brig. Gen. David McMurtrie Gregg's division at East Cavalry Field on the afternoon of July 3, Miller bravely charged his men – against orders – from Lott's Woods into a column of Confederate cavalry and routed a portion of it. He was also wounded during the charge. Instead of a court martial, Miller received the Medal of Honor for his action in July 1897. In 1877, Miller returned to the battlefield

The tombstone of Capt. William Miller is engraved in gold, a tribute bestowed upon Medal of Honor winners. (Stanley)

to visit the scene, and found his broken saber among the relics of the fight collected by farm owner John Rummel. Today, the regimental monument at East Cavalry Field sits near the spot from which Miller began his charge. After the war, Miller lived in Carlisle and served as a state senator, and died in 1919.

Continue along the path and you will see flank markers on your right for the 61st Ohio Infantry and the 74th Pennsylvania Infantry.

Tour Stop 13
61st Ohio Infantry and 74th Pennsylvania Infantry Flank Markers

The monuments of each of these regiments are on Howard Avenue, and these markers were placed on September 14, 1887 and July 2, 1888 respectively.

Follow the path and as it curves to the left around the Speakers' Rostrum, you will see on your left the monument of the 1st New Hampshire Battery.

Tour Stop 14
1st New Hampshire Battery Monument

This Reserve Artillery battery dedicated this monument on July 3, 1912.

You have returned to the cemetery gate at the Taneytown Road, and you may wish to take the next segment of the tour of Gettysburg battle gravesites that surround the Soldiers' National Monument.

· · · · · · · · · ·

Tour II - Gravesites of Note

Note the key on the map accompanying this tour that shows the sections of graves grouped by state, the U.S. Regulars, and unknown. They are numbered 1 through 22 and will assist you as you walk through the gravesites. Each tour stop that follows is also identified by the section in which it is located. At the head of each section you will see a stone that lists the state, Regulars, or unknown, as well as the number of bodies interred in the section.

To assist you in locating a particular gravesite, gravesites of note in a section are identified in a certain row and a certain number of graves from either the right or left in that row. Rows are counted from the front of the section, closest to the Soldiers' National Monument.

Around the perimeter of the semicircle of graves are plaques (cast and placed by the War Department) that feature excerpts from the poem *Bivouac of the Dead*, written in 1847 by Theodore O'Hara originally to commemorate the American dead of the Battle of Buena Vista during the Mexican War. Similar plaques can also be seen at several other national cemeteries. The full text can be found on page 204.

Enter the cemetery at the Taneytown Road gate and bear to the right on the walking path. The path will soon curve to the left, and as you come to the semicircular graves that surround the large Soldiers' National Monument, it is perhaps fitting that the first section of graves you see are for the unknown.

Cemetery Section 22
Unknown Dead Section

There are 979 graves in the cemetery of remains that are unidentified by name or the unit in which they served. The graves in this section, marked only by small numbered stones, are those for which no identification whatsoever could be found. There are three sections of exclusively unknown dead – the other two are Sections 1 and 14 on the other (north) side of the Soldiers' National Monument. Within most of the state and Regulars sections are many graves marked "Unknown" since they could not be identified by name.

Cemetery Section 13
Graves of Interest in the U.S. Regulars Section

In the second row, fifth from the left, is the gravesite of Lt. Christian Balder of the 6th U.S. Cavalry. Balder, a Prussian immigrant with six years' service in the army, was mortally wounded at the July 3 cavalry battle at Fairfield (see the tour of the Battle of Fairfield in this book). While being cared for at the

Fall leaves rest among the grave markers of the unknown soldiers in the Gettysburg National Cemetery. (Stanley)

Fairfield home of Robert C. Swope, Balder died a few days after the battle. In this section are several 6th U.S. Cavalry members who were killed at the battle or died of their wounds.

The only African-American buried in the semicircle of graves reposes under the second grave from the left in the front row. Pvt. Henry Gooden of Co. C, 127th Regiment of U.S. Colored Troops mustered into service on August 6, 1864, and survived the war. He died on August 3, 1876 in Carlisle, Pennsylvania and is buried in this plot.

Cemetery Section 12
Graves of Interest in the Maryland Section

In the first row, third from the left, is a grave identified as "M. F. Knott" of the 1st Maryland, Co. F. Burial records show him to be a member of the Federal 1st Potomac Home Brigade Infantry, but this is actually Pvt. Minion F. Knott of the Confederate 1st Maryland Infantry Battalion. Knott was wounded on July 3 at Gettysburg and died on August 24.

In the third row, second from the left, is the gravesite of Pvt. Richard Newton Gilson of the 1st Potomac Home Brigade of Cavalry, known as "Cole's Cavalry." Gilson is one of the several non-Gettysburg Battle dead buried in the state sections. Gilson died of wounds received during the pursuit of Maj. Gen. Jubal Early's army after the Battle of Monocacy the following year, on August 3, 1864, and was initially buried in Winchester, Virginia. In April 1890, Gilson's remains were re-interred in this plot.

Cemetery Section 21
Graves of Note in the Indiana Section

In the first row, the grave at far left is that of Cpl. William H. Story of Co. E of the 3rd Indiana Cavalry in Brig. Gen. John Buford's division (note the middle initial and company are inscribed incorrectly). Story was shot in the left chest on July 1 and died on July 10. Initially buried in the United Presbyterian Graveyard, according to records he was soon re-interred in Evergreen Cemetery in the soldiers' section. In May of 1877, Story's father had him reburied in this gravesite. Note that the stone is engraved with the misspelling "Cavelry" – this may be evidence that a later stonecutter was either inattentive or partially illiterate.

On the far right of this first row, the stone is simply inscribed with the initials "H. S. B." The soldier reposing here was later determined to be Cpl. Henry S. Brown of the 14th Indiana Infantry, killed on July 2.

In the fourth row, fifth from the left, you will see a grave inscribed "Levi Bulla." Private Bulla, however, survived the war and died in Kansas in the 1880s. The soldier buried here was found with Bulla's identification medal and was thus misidentified. Why this man possessed the medal is unknown. It is also unknown if Bulla ever came back to Gettysburg to visit "his" gravesite or if he even knew of it.

In the sixth row, third from the right is the grave of George Sylvester. Although inscribed here as a member of the 20th Indiana Infantry, no member with that name was killed at Gettysburg. This is likely the resting place of Cpl. George Sylvester of Co. A, 5th New Hampshire Infantry, killed on July 2 and likely later found in the same area as casualties from the 20th Indiana.

Cemetery Section 11
Marble Urn of the 1st Minnesota Infantry

At the head of the Minnesota section, note the marble urn. This urn, dedicated to the fallen of the 1st Minnesota Infantry and placed here in 1867, is the very first stone monument placed anywhere on the battlefield. The 1st Minnesota, the only regiment of the state to participate at Gettysburg, suffered losses of 68% during the battle (most of them on July 2 at the intense fighting at Cemetery Ridge during Longstreet's assault). A passage from Edward Everett's dedicatory speech is inscribed on the urn: "All time is the millennium of their glory."

Bivouac of the Dead

By Theodore O'Hara (1847)

The muffled drum's sad roll has beat
The soldier's last tattoo,
No more on life's parade shall meet
That brave and fallen few.

On Fame's eternal camping-ground
Their silent tents are spread,
And glory guards, with solemn round,
The bivouac of the dead.

No rumor of the foe's advance
Now swells upon the wind,
No troubled thought at midnight haunts
Of loved ones left behind.

No vision of the morrow's strife
The warriors dream alarms,
No braying horn, nor screaming fife
At dawn shall call to arms.

The neighing troop, the flashing blade,
The bugle's stirring blast,
The charge, the dreadful cannonade,
The din and shout are past.

Your own proud land's heroic soil
Shall be your fitter grave,
She claims from war his richest spoil,
The ashes of her brave.

Rest on, embalmed and sainted dead,
Dear as the blood ye gave,
No impious footstep here shall tread
The herbage of your grave.

Cemetery Section 20
Graves of Interest in the Ohio Section

In the Ohio section, fourth row, fourth from the right, is the grave of Pvt. George Nixon III of Co. B, 73rd Ohio Infantry. Many visitors to the cemetery seek out this gravesite of President Richard M. Nixon's great-grandfather. Forty-two-year-old Private Nixon was wounded in the right hip and side on July 2 while skirmishing near the Emmitsburg Road, and died on July 10 at the 11th Corps hospital located at the George Spangler farm south of the Granite Schoolhouse Road. Nixon was initially buried on Spangler's farm and was removed to this gravesite. His widow, taking care of their nine children, could not afford to have her husband's body returned home. A comrade who brought the badly wounded Nixon back to Union lines on the night of July 2 won the Medal of Honor for his heroism throughout the battle. Musician Richard Enderlin of the 73rd Ohio put down his bugle and shouldered a musket to fight alongside his men instead, and voluntarily crossed enemy lines to carry Nixon back to safety under a heavy fire. The German-born Enderlin was only twenty years old at the time, and died in 1930 at the age of eighty-seven. His medal was awarded in 1897. Richard Nixon, while vice-president, visited this grave in the 1950s.

In the last row, in the first grave on the right, rests the very first soldier to be interred in the Soldiers' National Cemetery. Pvt. Enoch M. Detty of Co. G, 73rd Ohio Infantry, wasn't technically a battle casualty, though – he died at Camp Letterman Hospital on October 26 of chronic diarrhea. Since Samuel Weaver's reburials in the new cemetery began two days later on October 28, twenty-four-year-old Detty was likely not initially buried in the cemetery at Camp Letterman, and instead this may have been his first and only burial.

Cemetery Section 10
Grave of Interest in the Connecticut Section

From 1893 to 1916, the Gettysburg Electric Trolley provided tours of the battlefield. This photo was taken in 1895 in front of the east gate of the National Cemetery. (ACHS)

There are possibly two (and perhaps even three) burials of Confederates in this small section. The first may be under the grave marked "--- Williams" in the second row, third from the left. The stone identifies this soldier as a member of Co. D of the 20th regiment, but no such last name appears on the muster rolls. Since he was exhumed from the area of Spangler's Spring, he may very well be Cpl. David Williams of Co. D, 20th North Carolina Infantry, killed in that area and otherwise unaccounted for.

A possible second burial of a Confederate may be found in the third row, fifth from the right under the stone engraved "S. Carter." Since the 15th Connecticut Infantry, as inscribed on the stone, was not at Gettysburg (and he cannot be found on muster rolls) this may be the gravesite of Lt. Sidney Carter of Co. A, 14th South Carolina Infantry, killed during the battle and otherwise unaccounted for.

The third possible Confederate burial is the first on the left in the second row. This grave is inscribed "William Gannells." This name does not appear in Federal or Confederate soldier records, but he may possibly be Cpl. William Cannell of Co. F, 16th Maine Infantry who was killed on July 1 – however, since $8.00 in Confederate currency was found on the body, he may be a Southerner instead.

Cemetery Section 9
Grave of Lt. Col. George H. Stevens, Wisconsin Section

In the Wisconsin section, in the first row and first on the left, is the grave of Lt. Col. George H. Stevens of the 2nd Wisconsin Infantry of the famed "Iron Brigade." Stevens is one of the two highest-ranking officers mortally wounded at the battle and buried here in the cemetery (the other is that of Lt. Col. Max A. Thoman in the New York section). Stevens was shot in the left side and bowels very early in the fighting on the morning of July 1, in the first enemy volley to hit the regiment at Herbst's Woods on McPherson Ridge.

Cemetery Section 18
Monument and Grave of Bvt. Maj. Gen. Charles H. T. Collis, Pennsylvania Section

At the head of the Pennsylvania section stands the impressive monument over the gravesite of Bvt. Maj. Gen. Charles Collis, former colonel of the 114th Pennsylvania Infantry (known as the "Collis Zouaves"). The Irish-born Collis was wounded at Chancellorsville in May 1863, and due to his recuperation was not with his regiment at Gettysburg. Collis was awarded the Medal of Honor for valor at the Battle of Fredericksburg for having "led his regiment in battle at a critical moment" when he seized the regiment's colors and led them in their baptism of fire, making him one of only two Medal of Honor awardees buried here. In 1900, Collis built a summer home in Gettysburg, and named it "Red Patch" in honor of the symbol of the 3rd Corps. The home still stands on the battlefield today along West Confederate Avenue just south of the Fairfield Road. Interestingly, the bust of Collis on this monument directly faces his Red Patch home. His primary post-war home was on Fifth Avenue in New York City. Collis died on May 11, 1902, and this monument was erected over his grave by friends and survivors of his regiment on May 13, 1906.

Cemetery Section 18
Graves of Note in the Pennsylvania Section

Here in the Pennsylvania section are several graves of interest.

First row, seventeenth from the right: This is the grave of Pvt. Thomas C. Hardy, a Pennsylvanian of the United States Marines – note that the stone is inscribed "U.S. Ship Savannah." Hardy died on November 8, 1888.

First row, thirty-first from the right: Note the grave of Pvt. William Tinsley of Co. F, 5th Pennsylvania Cavalry approximately in the middle of this row. Tinsley is one of the few buried here with his wife (Annie). Tinsley was not, however, a casualty of Gettysburg; in fact, he didn't even serve at Gettysburg, having not joined the regiment until August 1864, and he was buried here following his death in July 1908. The vast majority of the gravesites here in the first row, in fact, are those of Pennsylvania veterans who survived the war and chose to be buried here among their comrades.

First row, last on the left: This is the grave of Francis X. Weirick, who was actually a veteran of the Spanish American War, and who died in 1902 and chose to be buried here.

Second row, graves six through twelve from the right: Note that these graves are inscribed "Unknown Zouave." Most of these are the final resting places of soldiers of the 114th Pennsylvania Infantry (Collis' Zouaves) who were consumed by fire when the Joseph Sherfy barn burned to the ground on July 2. The wounded Zouaves had taken refuge in the barn but could not escape when shellfire ignited the structure. Collis, whose gravesite is at the head of the Pennsylvania section as discussed previously, made a post-war tradition of placing small American flags at the graves of these unfortunate unknowns of his regiment.

Third row, tenth through twelfth from the right: These three graves are the resting places of three members of the 18th Pennsylvania Cavalry of Brig. Gen. Judson Kilpatrick's division. All three were killed at the June 30 Battle of Hanover against Jeb Stuart's Confederate cavalry. Pvt. David W. Winans (stone is inscribed "Winning") was a member of Co. D, Pvt. Jacob Harvey was a member of Co. M, and Pvt. William Crawford was a member of Co. C.

Third row, forty-seventh from the right: This grave, in approximately the middle of this row, is inscribed "William Vosberg, 2 Div. Buford's Cav." The inscription is problematic in several respects; Brig. Gen. John Buford's cavalry, which consisted of three brigades, was the 1st Cavalry Division, and there is no William Vosberg (or similar name) on the rolls. The closest name is that of the surgeon of the 8th Illinois Cavalry of Buford's 1st Brigade, Hiram D. Vosberg, but he was not a casualty of the battle. Some historians have speculated that this is a member of the 17th Pennsylvania Cavalry of Buford's 2nd Brigade, which lost four men missing at Gettysburg.

Fourth row, twenty-fifth from the left: The "E. T. Green" that is buried here has been identified as Confederate Pvt. Eli T. Green, Co. E of the 14th Virginia Infantry. During Pickett's Charge, Green was shot in the right arm and hip. The arm was amputated, and he

Luminaries light up the gravesites of fallen Union soldiers in the Gettysburg National Cemetery during Remembrance Day celebrations. (Stanley)

died at Camp Letterman Hospital on August 15. Buried in the camp's cemetery in an unknown grave, the twenty-five-year-old saddler was mistakenly buried here as a member of the 14th Pennsylvania.

Fourth row, twenty-sixth from the right: Pvt. Green may have two Southern comrades in this row. This grave is marked simply "John Aker," but such a name does not appear in Federal records. This is possibly the grave of Pvt. James Akers of the 2nd Mississippi Infantry.

Fourth row, thirtieth from the right: This stone, inscribed "J. Graves" of Co. C of the 1st Regiment (there is no record of him), likely marks the Confederate grave of Sgt. Thomas Graves, Co. I of the 21st Georgia Infantry.

Sixth row, seventeenth from the left: This grave is identified as that of Cpl. Alfred Borden (stone is inscribed "Boyden") of Co. A, 149th Pennsylvania Infantry (Bucktails). Borden, however, survived the war. Since the body that reposes here was apparently identified by a letter on it, it seems that Borden had written this soldier and the body was subsequently misidentified.

Last row, sixth and seventh graves from the right: Similar to the Borden grave, these two plots evidence the example of misidentification by a letter. Both of these graves carry the name "Finnefrock," and many visitors suppose they were related. However, the "J. J. Finnefrock" in the sixth grave is more likely an unknown. These two bodies may possibly have been initially buried next to each other on the field, and a letter from a J. J. Finnefrock to Samuel somehow may have gotten attached to the second body. Other than Samuel, no one with this name killed at Gettysburg appears in the records. Samuel Finnefrock, of Co. B of the 142nd Pennsylvania Infantry, was mortally wounded on July 1.

Last row, eleventh from the right: This grave was originally identified as that of Pvt. Stephen Kelly, Co. E of the 91st Pennsylvania Infantry. Kelly, however, survived the war and died in Philadelphia in 1889. Found on this body was Kelly's knapsack bearing his name, which had been stolen just before the battle by an unidentified thief. The culprit, not Kelly, reposes here. Kelly is one of the few who could visit the cemetery to gaze upon "his" own grave – as well as the resting place of the apparent filcher.

Cemetery Section 2
Grave of Note in the Illinois Section

There is only one ground-level row of six graves here in the Illinois section. The third grave from the left is that of Pvt. David Diffenbaugh (incorrectly engraved Dieffeubaugh on the stone) of Co. G, 8th Illinois Cavalry. The 8th Illinois Cavalry served in Col. William Gamble's 1st Brigade of Brig. Gen. John Buford's 1st Cavalry Division, and a member of this regiment is generally credited with firing the "first shot" to open the battle. Prior to taking command of the brigade, Gamble commanded the 8th Illinois Cavalry, a unit he helped to raise at the start of the war. At Gettysburg, Diffenbaugh was detached from the regiment and served as one of Gamble's orderlies. Originally from Freeport, Illinois, Diffenbaugh is recorded to have been shot in the head and/or abdomen on July 1, and died the following day at a field hospital of the Federal 1st Corps. Diffenbaugh was the only member of the regiment killed at Gettysburg, and his name is likewise inscribed on the back of the regimental monument along South Reynolds Avenue on McPherson's Ridge.

The row of upright headstones here at the back of the section denotes the graves of Spanish-American War veterans. Two were residents of Tennessee, one from Missouri, and only one was from Illinois.

Cemetery Section 15
Graves of Note in the Maine Section

Those visitors interested in the July 2 saga of Col. Joshua L. Chamberlain's 20th Maine Infantry at Gettysburg will see several members of the regiment buried here. All are interred in rows two through five. Cemetery records show that all were killed or mortally wounded on July 2 during the fierce fighting on the southern slope of Little Round Top, and they were eventually exhumed from their battlefield gravesites on or near the Abraham Trostle farm and the John Weikert farm.

Cemetery Section 16
Graves of Note in the Michigan Section

In the first row, the first grave on the left is marked for Maj. Noah H. Ferry of Co. F of the 5th Michigan Cavalry. The 5th Michigan Cavalry served in the brigade of Brig. Gen. George Armstrong Custer along with the 1st, 6th, and 7th Michigan regiments. Ferry was killed during the massive cavalry battle at East Cavalry Field on July 3, and many of his brigade comrades killed or mortally wounded that day are buried here in the Michigan section. Ferry, however, does not repose here – and it appears he never did. Ferry is actually buried in Lake Forest Cemetery in Grand Haven, Michigan.

So why is his name inscribed here? While Ferry was rallying his men at the John Rummel Farm, he was shot through the head and killed instantly. His body was found on the field the following day, and was buried on one of the farms in the vicinity (perhaps at Rummel's or the Abraham Tawney farm on Low Dutch Road). Several days later, Rev. William Ferry recovered his son's remains and returned with the body to Michigan for burial. It may be that either no body was ever buried at this stone marked for Ferry, or another body, mistaken for Ferry, was buried here and is hence "unknown."

In the fourth row, the sixth grave from the right is engraved "John Nothing." This is actually the gravesite of Pvt. Jan Notting of Co. I, 5th Michigan Cavalry. Notting was also a casualty of the July 3 fighting at East Cavalry Field. He was wounded in the head and died that day, and his unfortunate epitaph is the result of bad recordkeeping or an inattentive stonecutter.

Graves of Interest in Outlying Section

After viewing the Michigan section, it is an opportune time to examine the graves that are outside the semicircle and behind the Michigan and New York sections.

In the front row of stones, there are two gravesites of note. A tall rectangular stone marks the grave of James Knox Polk Scott, who was a bugler in Co. H of the 1st Pennsylvania Reserve Cavalry. Known as "Colonel Scott," he planned to pen a three-volume history of the Battle of Gettysburg, but only the first volume was published (1927) before his death in 1933. Written in the quaint (and often quite humorous) style of the eighty-two-year-old former soldier, the volume is today prized by historians. Although he planned to attend West Point in 1861, the sixteen-year-old Scott instead joined the "Dunlap Creek Cavalry," which eventually became Co. H of the 1st Pennsylvania Reserve Cavalry. Captured in 1862, Scott was imprisoned at Belle Isle and Libby Prison, and was convalescing near Washington while his regiment participated in the Battle of Gettysburg. Scott's wife Beth Waring died in 1898, and when he was allotted this grave, he had his wife's remains removed to here. In 1914, Scott relocated to Gettysburg to study the battle and later gave tours of the field as a popular guide. In his book, Scott revealed that he kept himself "trim in health and morals by a daily pilgrimage" to this grave, and even included a photograph showing him standing beside this stone. Note that below his name, Scott had a shortened version of his name without the initial

James Scott visited his grave often after relocating to Gettysburg in 1914. (J.D. Petruzzi)

"K" engraved in parentheses. When he mustered into the service, an officer told him he had "too many names" and "kicked the 'Knox' out of the name I gave, leaving me to get along as well as I could as James P. Scott."

The second grave of note is that of Calvin Hamilton, who was a well-known and popular superintendent of the National Cemetery from 1891 (stone is incorrectly engraved 1889) until his death on March 11, 1914. A schoolteacher before the war, Hamilton was a member of Co. K of the 1st Regiment, Pennsylvania Reserve Corps, recruited primarily in Gettysburg. Hamilton was born near Gettysburg on November 29, 1841, and attended Pennsylvania (now Gettysburg) College before enlisting in September 1862. On the second day of the battle, while participating in a charge in the valley west of Little Round Top, Hamilton was shot in the right leg and recuperated at home after the battle. Standing with the help of crutches, he witnessed President Lincoln's address at the dedication of the cemetery on November 19, 1863 as one of the wounded soldiers in the area invited to the event. He continued to teach after the war, and spent thirty-four years in the Gettysburg school system. In 1891, Hamilton became the fifth superintendent of the National Cemetery – and the last one to have fought in the battle. In 1908, he began the tradition, which still continues to this day, of placing small American flags on the soldiers' graves on Memorial Day. Offered the job of supervising Arlington National Cemetery, Hamilton preferred to stay in Gettysburg and turned it down. He is buried here with his wife "Annie," whom he married in 1883.

You will also note a few government headstones here marked "Unknown." Some of these are for unidentified soldier remains that were found on the battlefield in more recent years.

Cemetery Section 4
Grave of Note in the Delaware Section

In the third row of this small section, the second grave from the right is inscribed only "Sergt. Seymore." Here reposes the Color Sergeant of Co. B, 1st Delaware Infantry, Sgt. Thomas Seymour. He suffered a horrible fate at Gettysburg; while holding his colors, he was cut in two by a shell and instantly killed, probably on July 2.

Cemetery Section 6
Graves of Note in the New Hampshire Section

In the first row, first grave on the left, you will find the resting place of Bartlett Brown. His stone is inscribed as being a member of this state, but he was actually a private in the 111th New York Infantry. Shot in the chest on July 3, Bartlett died soon after and was one of sixteen identified Federal burials behind the home of Jacob Swisher on the Taneytown Road. Curiously, although most of these burials were from the 3rd Division of the 2nd Corps in which the 111th New York served, somehow Brown's regimental identification was confused when he was later exhumed for transfer to the National Cemetery. Perhaps the writing on his temporary marker looked like "NH" instead of "NY" and he was thus mistakenly buried in this section instead of with his New York comrades. Brown's stone is often painted over with the correct unit designation.

Cemetery Section 17
Graves of Note in the New York Section

There are several gravesites of interest in the large New York section:

First row, twentieth from the left: This is the grave of Cpl. Cyrus W. James (incorrectly engraved as "Charles Jones") of Co. G, 9th New York Cavalry. Twenty-four-year-old James of Dunkirk, New York may very well have been the first Federal soldier killed at the Battle of Gettysburg on July 1. That unenviable distinction is often given to Pvt. Ferdinand Ushuer of Co. C., 12th Illinois Cavalry as well, but evidence shows that James may have been killed north of Gettysburg in early morning skirmishing near the Samuel Cobean farm along the Carlisle (Newville) Road – before the main skirmishing began with Confederate infantry near Marsh Creek on the Chambersburg Pike. James may have been killed in a short pre-dawn confrontation with troopers of the 35th Battalion Virginia Cavalry, 17th Virginia Cavalry, or other stragglers of Maj. Gen. Richard Ewell's Confederate corps who had passed through that area several days earlier. Ushuer, a member of Brig. Gen. John Buford's cavalry like James, was killed on the morning of July 1 near Herr Ridge by a shell fired from the Fredericksburg Artillery attached to Maj. Gen. Henry Heth's Confederate division soon after the start of the battle proper. James' body was perhaps first taken to the initial field hospital of Buford's division located at the railroad depot on Carlisle Street in town, but the location of his temporary battlefield burial is not known. Cyrus James' stone is often painted over with the correct name.

Third row, sixty-ninth from the right (approximately in the middle of the row): This grave carries the name of 1st Lt. J. Ross Horner of Co. K, 80th New York Infantry (the stone is marked "Regt. 20"). Horner, however, was killed on August 30, 1862 at the Battle of 2nd Manassas. It is highly doubtful that Horner would be buried here, so the body of an unknown – apparently carrying an article belonging to Horner and thus identified as him – is presumed to repose here.

Third row, graves twenty-seven through twenty-nine from the left: These three graves, all of the 5th New York Cavalry, hold the remains of troopers of Brig. Gen. Judson Kilpatrick's division killed at the June 30 Battle of Hanover with Jeb Stuart's cavalry. Pvt. John Lanegar served in Co. D, 1st Sgt. Selden Wales was in Co. A, and Lt. Alexander Gall was an adjutant on the staff of regimental commander Maj. John Hammond. During a mounted charge in the streets of Hanover against the 13th Virginia and 2nd North Carolina cavalry regiments, Sgt. Wales galloped ahead of his company. As he turned in the saddle to urge on his comrades, a Confederate bullet slammed into his heart and killed him instantly. During the same charge, Lt. Gall was shot in the left eye and the ball passed completely through his head, likewise killing him instantly.

Fifth row, sixty-eighth from the right (approximately in the middle of the row): Note that this stone is marked "Removed." This was the former gravesite of Capt. John N. Warner of Co. K of the 86th New York Infantry. He was killed instantly on July 2 during the fighting near Devil's Den and initially buried on the field. In January 1864, Warner was exhumed from this grave by his family and interred in the family plot in Woodhull, New York on January 26.

Sixth row, fourteenth from the right: Here rests a New York soldier whose grave is sought out by many visitors to the National Cemetery. Sgt. Amos Humiston of Co. C, 154th New York Infantry rests here under a stone that bears his name. He might instead, however, repose in the unknown section today had it not been for the fact that when his body was found, he was clutching a photograph of his three children but had no other identification on him. Thirty-three-year-old Humiston was mortally wounded on July 1 as the 11th Corps was routed through the town by Confederates. After the battle, the daughter of Graeffenburg tavern owner Benjamin Schriver discovered Humiston in a remote area along Stratton Street. The ambrotype of the children became a curiosity in his tavern, and by October many newspapers picked up the story. In early November, Humiston's wife Philinda read the story and when shown a copy of the photograph, identified them as their three children. She realized immediately that she had unknowingly been a widow for four months. Humiston's well-marked grave was opened and he was transferred here to the National Cemetery. In October 1866, a nearby brick building on Baltimore Street was converted to a home for orphans, and Philinda and her three children arrived in Gettysburg to take up residence there, with Philinda working on the staff. Several hundred children lived at the home throughout the decade, which still stands as a museum, until 1876 when it was closed. In 1993, a monument was funded and dedicated by residents of Gettysburg, Humiston's hometown of Portville, and descendants of soldiers of the 154th New York and placed near the spot where he was discovered. It is the only monument on the entire battlefield to exclusively commemorate an enlisted man.

Last row, sixty-second grave from the right (about the middle of the row): This is the gravesite of Cpl. Landrus (or Surrendus) A. Godfrey of Co. G, 9th New York Cavalry. The stone is engraved "L. A. Godfrey." Corporal Godfrey was one of the last mortally wounded casualties of General Buford's cavalry on the first day of battle, July 1. Late that afternoon, when the Federal 11th Corps hastily retreated through the town to this position (Cemetery Hill), some Confederate skirmishers hotly pursued them. A squadron of the 9th New York Cavalry rushed at them in the area of the intersection of the Emmitsburg Road and Baltimore Street, punishing the Southerners "severely" according to one of Buford's brigade commanders, Col. Thomas C. Devin. In the action, Godfrey was killed and Pvt. Franklin C. Cave of Co. I was mortally wounded. Godfrey was initially buried in the yard of James Pierce's home at the corner of Baltimore Street and Breckenridge Street.

Last row, sixty-first grave from the right: Bad recordkeeping has unfortunately altered the grave of this stone next to Godfrey. The inscription reads "Peter Junk," but this is the grave of Cpl. Peter Junck of Co. E, 119th New York Infantry, who was mortally wounded on July 1 and originally interred in the Associate Reformed Graveyard.

Last row, seventieth grave from the right: Eight graves to the left of Godfrey's grave lie the remains of one of the two highest-ranking officers mortally wounded at the battle and buried here (the other is Lt. Col. George H. Stevens in the Wisconsin section). This is the grave of Lt. Col. Max A. Thoman, commander of the 59th New York Infantry, whom his men called "Jack of Diamonds." A shell broke his right shoulder on July 2 during the fighting near the Copse of Trees, and Thoman died on July 11. His final request was to be buried on the field, and he was initially interred on Jacob Schwartz's farm near Rock Creek before being buried here among his fellow New Yorkers.

Last row, forty-eighth from the left: Under this stone engraved "John Biggs" rests the remains of Pvt. John C. Begg, who was one of several unfortunate casualties of accidents during the battle buried in the cemetery. A crewman of the 5th New York Light Battery, Begg was badly burned when a caisson limber exploded on July 2. He lingered at the 5th Corps field hospital until he died on July 7.

Cemetery Section 19
Graves of Interest in the Massachusetts Section

In the first row, eighth from the right, is a grave listed in cemetery records as that of S. Hindeman of the 15th Massachusetts Infantry. There is no record of such a name, however. This is more likely the resting place of a Confederate – Pvt. N. B. Hindman of Co. A, 13th Mississippi Infantry.

The grave of John T. Johnson is found in the third row, first on the right (grave is inscribed "J. L. Johnson"). Johnson is another of the several Confederates mistakenly buried in the National

Cemetery. He was actually a private in Co. K of the 11th Mississippi Infantry. About twenty years old, Johnson was wounded during Pickett's Charge on July 3, was captured, and died on August 4 at Camp Letterman hospital. When his marker was made at the cemetery at Camp Letterman, it was either mistakenly marked "11th Mass" or was later misread. His stone is often painted over with the correct unit, and sometimes a small Confederate flag flies here.

. . . .

Tour Stop 15
The Soldiers' National Cemetery Annex

Following your tour of the cemetery proper, you may wish to visit the Cemetery Annex, located on the other side of the stone wall to the southwest. This five-acre area was added to the cemetery in 1963 and features the "Friend to Friend Masonic Memorial." Sculpted by Ron Tunison, the memorial was commissioned by the Grand Lodge of Pennsylvania and dedicated on August 21, 1993. It shows Federal Captain Henry H. Bingham comforting the wounded Confederate Brig. Gen. Lewis A. Armistead at the eclipse of Pickett's Charge on July 3. Both Armistead and Bingham were Freemasons. The statuary depicts Armistead giving some personal effects, particularly his pocket watch, to Bingham to be sent to his family. Shot three times (but seemingly not mortally wounded) just after crossing the stone wall near the famed Bloody Angle, Armistead unexpectedly died on July 5 at a field hospital at the George Spangler farm.

Additional reading

Soldiers' National Cemetery – Gettysburg (Gettysburg, Pa: Thomas Publications, 1988) is a reprint of the 1865 Revised Report of the Select Committee Relative to the Soldiers' National Cemetery published by the Commonwealth of Pennsylvania. Along with interesting reports made at the time by the committee, it contains not only an early listing of interments but also an accounting of items that were found with the bodies when exhumed from other parts of the battlefield.

Indispensable to a study of the National Cemetery are two books by John W. Busey: *The Last Full Measure: Burials in the Soldiers' National Cemetery at Gettysburg*, David G. Martin, Ed. (Hightstown, N. J.: Longstreet House, 1988) and *These Honored Dead: The Union Casualties of Gettysburg* (Hightstown, N. J.: Longstreet House, 1996). The former, heavily consulted for parts of this tour, contains impressive scholarship on the identification of interments in the cemetery as well as a history of the grounds, and also identifies soldier interments in adjoining Evergreen Cemetery. The latter documents all known Federal casualties of the battle regardless of location of interment.

For a further study of the history of the cemetery as well as a useful guide, recommended is a volume by James Cole and Roy E. Frampton, *The Gettysburg National Cemetery: A History and Guide* (Hanover, Pa: The Sheridan Press, 1988).

An excellent article on the historiography of the cemetery was written by Blake Magner in *Gettysburg Magazine* (Issue Fourteen, January 1996) titled "The Gettysburg Soldiers' National Cemetery: Yesterday and Today."

(Opposite page) In late July of 1863, Alexander Gardner captured this image of the Evergreen Cemetery Gatehouse. Note the damage to the gatehouse and the artillery lunettes that still existed. (LOC)

Tour of Gettysburg's Evergreen Cemetery

"Remember me, when you pass . . . "

On November 29, 1853, a meeting of Gettysburg citizens was held at the all-purpose McConaughy's Hall (located at the present site of 18 Carlisle Street) to form a Cemetery Association and find suitable grounds for a public burying ground. Several small church, public, and private cemeteries existed in town and the surrounding area, but the citizens wanted a location for the dead of the borough to "repose together; as it ameliorates the prejudices arising from distinctions of sect, and rank, and class, and

. . . fosters feelings of brotherhood." Raffensperger's Hill west of town, about seventeen acres of land owned by George Shryock and Conrad Snyder, was selected by a committee chaired by McConaughy and purchased in 1854. The name "Ever Green Cemetery" was adopted, although by the 1880s the grounds were commonly referred to as "Evergreen Cemetery." The first interment there, on November 1 of that year, was Mary M., the wife of Daniel Beitler.

On September 1, 1855, the cornerstone for the cemetery gatehouse, now one of the most recognized landmarks at Gettysburg, was laid and dedicated. The gatehouse was constructed by prominent Gettysburg builder named George Chritzman (who is buried in the cemetery) at a cost of $1,025.00. It was designed by Philadelphia architect Stephen Decatur Button, who also designed the Alabama State Capitol in Montgomery. The gatehouse, then as now, serves as the cemetery office and the residence of the caretaker.

Evergreen Cemetery

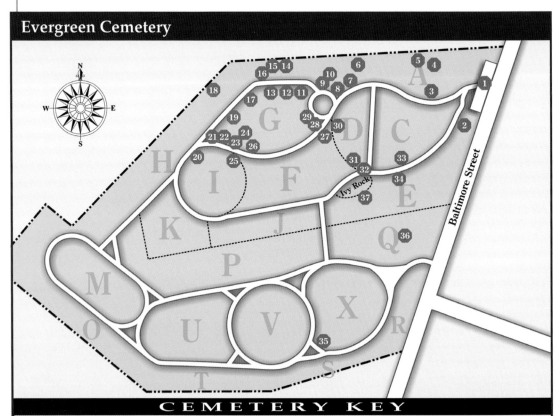

CEMETERY KEY

1 – Cemetery Gatehouse	13 – Samuel Weaver	26 – Harvey W. McKnight
2 – Gettysburg Civil War Women's Memorial	14 – Carrie S. Sheads	27 – Henry J. Stahle
3 – James Getty	15 – E. Salome "Sallie" Myers Stewart	28 – David McConaughy
4 – Oscar Shaw	16 – Esiah J. Culp	29 – Michael Jacobs
5 – Emmor B. Cope	17 – George Chritzman	30 – Edward McPherson
6 – Nov. 19, 1863 Speakers Platform Location	18 – William D. "Billie" Holtzworth	31 – John L. Burns
7 – Mary Virginia "Jennie" Wade	19 – Peter and Elizabeth Thorn	32 – Leander W. Walsh
8 – Samuel S. Schmucker	20 – David Wills	33 – Civil War Soldiers Section
9 – Solomon L. Powers	21 – Charles M. McCurdy	34 – William H. Tipton
10 – Allen Frazer	22 – David Kendlehart	35 – Edward S. Plank
11 – Frederick A. Huber	23 – Marianne C. Moore	36 – Samuel E. Cobean
12 – Johnston H. "Jack" Skelly	24 – Charles E. Goldsborough	37 – Old Re-Interments
	25 – Nesbitt Baugher	

Even though this tour is quite extensive and will guide you to the gravesites of many of Gettysburg's "notables," it is far from complete. If you walk through the older areas in this historic cemetery, you will discover the final resting places of many well-known names associated with the battle and Gettysburg's rich history who are not included on this tour.

. . . .

Tour Stop 1
The Evergreen Cemetery Gatehouse

Park your vehicle where convenient along the Baltimore Pike (Rt. 97) or in the lot across from the cemetery and walk to the gatehouse. Since the establishment of the cemetery, the eminence has been referred to as "Cemetery Hill," and the part of the hill on the east side of the pike, across from the gatehouse, is commonly called "East Cemetery Hill." A commanding view of the town, and much of what would become the Federal line during the battle of Gettysburg, is available from the highest terrain in the cemetery.

Completely renovated in 1999-2000, the gatehouse has been modified over the years. In 2000, the McConaughy History Room was established and added to the southern section. Analysis of the painted sections of the gatehouse was completed and the structure now features the colors that were present during the battle: dark barn red on the bricks, the white urn at the top, and dark brown cornice trim.

On February 9, 1856, German immigrant Peter Thorn was hired as caretaker of the cemetery. Peter, his wife Elizabeth, and their three sons, lived in the northern section while Elizabeth's parents, John and Catherine Masser, occupied the southern section. Note the water pump on the back porch of the northern side; it is assumed the original well was at this spot.

Tour Stop 2
The Gettysburg Civil War Women's Memorial

After walking through the gatehouse, about fifty feet to your left you will see a bronze sculpture. This is the Gettysburg Civil War Women's Memorial, sculpted by local artist Ron Tunison and dedicated on November 16, 2002. It depicts Elizabeth Thorn, six months pregnant during the battle as she afterward labored to bury fallen soldiers in the cemetery. Her caretaker husband Peter had joined the 138th Pennsylvania Infantry as a corporal the previous fall, so responsibilities at the cemetery fell to Elizabeth until the end of the war. The statue depicting the exhausted but equally determined woman honors all women who served in various capacities during the Civil War.

The Gettysburg Civil War Women's Monument, surrounded by magnificent fall colors, depicts a very pregnant and exhausted Elizabeth Thorn. (Stanley)

Elizabeth buried the first ninety-one dead soldiers from the battle (they were later removed for burial in the adjoining National Cemetery). In addition to the burden of her duties, she found her gatehouse home and grounds in complete disarray after the battle. Most of the gatehouse windows had been shot out, the water pump on the north side of the gatehouse was broken, and the few personal belongings still left in the house were covered with blood from wounded soldiers. The only dress Elizabeth had left was the one she had on, and she later stated that she "lived in that dress for six weeks." Throughout the cemetery, many of the gravestones had been laid on the ground by order of Maj. Gen. Oliver O. Howard when Federal Army headquarters were established here on the afternoon of July 1. His objective was not only to protect the markers, but to prevent them from becoming flying shrapnel if struck by enemy artillery. Several stones, however, had been damaged by shellfire. Fifteen dead horses lay in front of the gatehouse, and nineteen lay in the field southwest behind this statue. In the garden, just north of the gatehouse, sixteen soldiers and one black man had been buried.

Elizabeth's aged father helped dig many of the graves, but several friends who attempted to lend assistance left after only a few days, violently sick from the smell and sights of the repulsive duty. Until the gatehouse could be cleaned up and made habitable, the Federal Hospital Corps erected a tent nearby for Elizabeth and her parents to occupy.

On November 1, a short time before President Abraham Lincoln traveled to Gettysburg to help dedicate the National Cemetery, Elizabeth gave birth to a baby girl. She named the child Rosa Meade Thorn in honor of the Federal Army commander at Gettysburg. Elizabeth's labors during and after the battle nearly broke her health, which remained poor the rest of her life. She died in 1907.

Tour Stop 3
Grave of James Gettys (1759-1815), Founder of Gettysburg

Walk up the main pathway that leads directly behind the gatehouse to Section A of the cemetery. After about 180 feet from the gatehouse is the grave of James Gettys, the founder of Gettysburg. Gettys' tall grave monument faces the pathway and is next to it. In 1785, he purchased at a sheriff's sale 116 acres of his father's land here, then known as the "Marsh Creek Settlement." Gettys divided the land into lots and offered them for sale in January 1786. When Adams County was being created from the western section of York County, Gettys donated land for the jail and thus helped secure Gettysburg as the new county's seat.

A veteran of the Revolutionary War, Gettys later became a brigadier general in the local militia. He operated a tavern, served as burgess of Gettysburg, county sheriff, and in the Pennsylvania Legislature from 1807-1809. Gettys' wife Mary Todd was a cousin of President Lincoln's wife.

In March 1815, James, Mary, and his mother Isabella all died of fever the same week. The trio was initially buried in Black's Cemetery, an old Presbyterian burial ground three miles northwest of Gettysburg on Belmont Schoolhouse Road. Following the war in the summer of 1865, Gettys' son and namesake James returned to Gettysburg from Tennessee to relocate his parents' remains here, perhaps at least partially because of the famous battle in the town that bore his father's name. The monument placed over the grave in November of that year originally featured a cast iron sculpture of a reclining greyhound at its base on top of the cement pad in the ground (James Sr. was apparently fond of dogs). The dog was stolen in 1974 and never returned. An ornate wrought iron fence once encircled the plot (many such fences originally surrounded family plots in the cemetery). An urn once decorated the top of the monument, but was broken off long ago.

Tour Stop 4

Grave of Oscar Shaw (1887-1967), Singer and Actor

Walk from Gettys' grave to your right directly north. Just before reaching the iron fence that separates Evergreen from the National Cemetery, you will come to the grave of Oscar Shaw, a leading Broadway stage actor but probably best known for his appearance as Bob Adams in the 1929 Marx Brothers movie *The Cocoanuts*. Look carefully for this grave, as the stone is small and at ground level. Born in Philadelphia in 1887, Shaw studied at the University of Pennsylvania and gained notoriety in radio. He performed on various London stages and in several Broadway musicals. His wife Mary Louise Givler (stage name Louise Gale) also performed on Broadway.

The Shaws lived in Great Neck, New York, until their deaths, but maintained a summer home on the Biglerville Road north of Gettysburg at Keckler's Hill. Only the simple small ground-level stone marks their final resting place.

Tour Stop 5

Emmor Bradley Cope (1834-1927), U.S. Army Cartographer

E. B. Cope is one of the least known but influential in-dividuals in the early development of what is today known as the Gettysburg National Military Park. He served as a staff officer for Maj. Gen. Gouverneur K. Warren at Get-tysburg. Cope drew the first official U.S. Army map of the battlefield.

Cope was born in East Bradford, Pennsylvania in 1834, and worked as a mechanic for his father prior to the war. On June 4, 1861, he enlisted as a private in Co. A. of the 1st Pennsylvania Reserves (30th Pennsylvania Infantry) and soon made sergeant. As a result of his technical skills, he was transferred to the Topographical Engineers of the Army of the Potomac shortly after the Battle of Antietam. A week after Gettysburg, Cope was assigned to map the battlefield. Using his sketches of battle lines made in the saddle during the fighting, he crafted the valuable map known to scholars as "The Cope Map" (on right).

Promoted to captain in April 1864, Cope continued mapping battlefields in Virginia. Mustered out at the end of the war as major and brevet lieutenant colonel, Cope worked as a civil engineer until appointed the official en-gineer for the Gettysburg Battlefield Commission in July 1893 (he worked closely with historian John Bachelder). Cope marked the battle lines of both armies, designed the Army tablets and markers, and built battlefield roads, bridg-

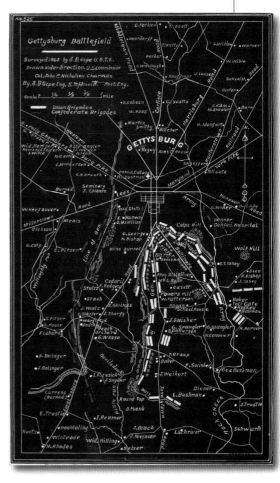

es, towers, and monuments. In 1922, he was appointed the first superintendent of the Gettysburg National Military Park and served in that capacity until his death in 1927 — the oldest employee of the U.S. Government at the age of 92. Cope reposes here with his wife Isabella (who died in 1903), an impressive black granite stone marking their graves.

Tour Stop 6

Site of the Speakers' Platform, November 19, 1863 Soldiers' National Cemetery Dedication

Research, including photographic evidence, indicates that the speakers' platform for the dedication of the adjoining Soldiers' National Cemetery was placed here on this high ground in Evergreen Cemetery facing the Soldiers' National Cemetery. This approximates the spot from which President Abraham Lincoln delivered his Gettysburg Address. A tall flagpole stood at the site where the Soldiers' National Monument now stands. No barrier stood between the two cemeteries at the time, and burials in the National Cemetery were still taking place during the dedication.

Mathew Brady captured this image of the dedication ceremonies of the National Cemetery. In this photo you can clearly see the flagpole where the Soldiers' National Monument now stands, the Evergreen Cemetery gatehouse, and just to the right, the speaker's platform. (LOC)

Tour Stop 7

Gravesite of Mary Virginia "Jennie" Wade (1843-1863), Only Civilian Killed during the Battle

One grave sought out by many visitors to Evergreen is that of "Jennie" Wade, the only Gettysburg civilian killed during the battle. She was hailed as a "heroine" as soon as stories of the battle surfaced following the fighting, and her remains endured two separate burials before being interred here in November 1865.

Jennie (actually known to her family as "Ginnie") was born in Gettysburg in 1843. As a child she worked in her father's tailoring business, until James Wade was declared insane in 1852. Jennie, along with her sisters and mother Mary, continued operating the business.

When the Confederates occupied most of the town on July 1, Wade left her Breckenridge Street home and sought refuge at the Baltimore Street home of her sister, Georgia Anna Wade McClellan, which was closer to the Federal lines. On the morning of July 3, while Jennie and her mother prepared bread dough in the kitchen of the home, a stray bullet penetrated two doors of the home and struck Jennie in the back, piercing her heart and killing her instantly.

Gettysburg resident Jennie Wade. (LOC)

She was initially buried in the garden in back of the McClellan home (in a coffin originally intended for a Confederate officer). In January 1864, her remains were relocated to the German Reformed Church cemetery on Stratton Street. In November 1865, Jennie was brought here to her final resting place.

Georgia McClellan moved west after the war and served as the president of the Iowa Woman's Relief Corps from 1897-1899. In 1900, the present grave monument (sculpted in Italy and paid for by the Corps) was erected, designed by Gettysburg resident Anna M. Miller. The flagpole was installed in 1910 and the flag flies day and night under a special provision that allows it to fly twenty-four hours per day for patriotic purposes (as does the flag at the grave of John Burns, which we will visit shortly). Two flags are donated each year by the Corps (note because of physical constraints, the flag actually flies over the nearby gravestone of Thaddeus F. Clay, a member of the 21st Pennsylvania Cavalry). When Georgia realized at the monument's dedication that it contained only Jennie's (inaccurate) nickname, she requested the bronze plaque featuring Jennie's full Christian name. It was installed on the monument in 1922. Jennie's parents are buried here under the low rectangular stone to the left of Jennie's monument.

Johnston Hastings "Jack" Skelly, a Union soldier who died on July 12, 1863, of wounds suffered at Winchester in June, is also interred in Evergreen. Some speculate that Wade and Skelly were engaged. We will also visit his gravesite during the tour.

Tour Stop 8
Gravesite of Samuel Simon Schmucker (1799-1873), Lutheran Seminary Professor

Samuel S. Schmucker, a well-known abolitionist, was one of the founders of the Lutheran Theological Seminary, Pennsylvania (later Gettysburg) College, as well as Evergreen Cemetery. During the battle, his home (located on the grounds of the Seminary) was ransacked by Confederates and he lost most of his library and personal possessions. The home was used also as a field hospital by both armies, but he was never compensated for damages.

Born the son of a Lutheran minister on February 28, 1799, in Hagerstown, Maryland, Schmucker graduated from the University of Pennsylvania in 1817 and studied theology at Princeton Theological Seminary. In 1820 he was ordained a minister and that year helped establish the General Synod of the Lutheran Church in America. He soon became one of the most influential, and often controversial, scholars in the Lutheran Church. He authored more than forty books and served as the president of Evergreen Cemetery in the year following the battle of Gettysburg. He died on July 25, 1873.

Schmucker served on the college's board of trustees for forty-one years, and in all that time is said to have missed only five meetings. The seminary's Schmucker Hall is named in his honor. Other members of his family repose behind his monument.

The gravesite of Solomon Powers in Evergreen Cemetery. (Stanley)

Tour Stop 9
Gravesite of Solomon Leland Powers (1804-1883), Gettysburg Stonecutter and Quarryman

Solomon Powers' quarry located just south of the cemetery provided the stone for the base of the Evergreen Cemetery Gatehouse, which was constructed in 1855.

Born in Croydon, New Hampshire, in 1804, Powers relocated to Baltimore, Maryland, in 1828 and met and married Ann Catherine Flemming in 1833. In 1838, the family moved to Gettysburg, where he opened one of the first stone quarries in the area, providing granite to a wide market. One of his earliest projects was the construction of a granite bridge over the "Tapeworm Railroad." Powers' Hill adjoining the quarry is a well-known landmark to many students of the battle. Nearly devoid of trees in 1863, the hill served the Union Army as an important signal station and artillery platform.

Located at the northeast corner of Washington and High Streets, Powers' home was inundated by casualties during the battle. His wife and five daughters nursed and comforted wounded soldiers from both armies during and after the fighting. When the National Cemetery was established, Massachusetts (unlike other states) contracted independently with Powers to have the state's dead relocated there. Powers helped transfer the remains of 158 Massachusetts soldiers. He is buried here with his wife Ann, who died in 1892.

Tour Stop 10
Unmarked Gravesite of Allen Frazer (1849-1863), Killed by Shell Burst on November 20, 1863

In the days and months following the battle, several citizens (mostly children) were badly wounded or killed while playing with discarded rifles and unexploded ordnance. Adults and children alike were attracted by the lure of the weapons and artifacts, and many attempted to extract the valuable iron from shell casings.

Fourteen-year-old Allen Frazer, who was living with the Solomon Powers family since the death of his parents, was one such victim. Russell M. Briggs of Philadelphia traveled to Gettysburg in November to remove the remains of a son killed in the battle (likely Cpl. George E. Briggs of the 72nd Pennsylvania Infantry) and to witness the cemetery's dedication. On November 20, the day after

Lincoln's address, Briggs attempted to open a shell on Powers' porch while young Frazer watched. The shell exploded, blowing off Briggs' hands and nearly cutting Frazer in two. Frazer was buried the following day here somewhere in the Powers plot. His grave is unmarked.

Tour Stop 11
Gravestone of Frederick A. Huber (1842-1862), Damaged during the Battle

Frederick Huber, a twenty-year-old sergeant in the 23rd Pennsylvania Infantry, died on May 31, 1862, of wounds received at the Battle of Fair Oaks. He was initially buried on the battlefield, but his father, Dr. Henry S. Huber, retrieved his remains and re-interred them here on June 13. The war followed Huber to his final resting place when the top part of his gravestone was damaged by a Confederate shell during the battle of Gettysburg. It was never repaired. Also interred here are his parents, Henry and Priscilla, as well as his brother John, who also served in the Union army.

Tour Stop 12
Gravesite of Johnston Hastings "Jack" Skelly Jr. (1841-1863), Union Soldier

Seven rows behind Huber's grave is the gravesite of Jack Skelly. Jennie Wade and Skelly were friends from childhood, but historians are uncertain whether they were engaged at the time Jennie was killed. Apparently, they wrote several letters to one another during the war. Only one letter — from Wade to Skelly in January 1863 — survives, but it does not indicate a romantic relationship.

Skelly was born in Gettysburg and worked as a stonecutter prior to the war. He served as a private in Co. E, 2nd Pennsylvania Infantry (a three-month unit) from April to July 1861, and in September enlisted as a corporal in Co. F, 87th Pennsylvania Infantry. Childhood friend John Wesley Culp had moved to Shepherdstown, Virginia, in 1856 with Jack's brother Charles to work as carriage makers. Charles returned to Gettysburg at the outbreak of the war to enlist with Jack, but Wesley remained behind and enlisted in Co. B of the 2nd Virginia Infantry on April 20, 1861. The regiment later became part of the famed "Stonewall Brigade." Wesley's brother William had enlisted with the Skellys in the Pennsylvania units. The Culp brothers fought on opposite sides during the June 1863 Second Battle of Winchester. The Culps emerged from the fighting unscathed, but Jack Skelly was wounded and captured near Carter's Woods on June 15. Charles remained with his brother and was eventually taken to Libby Prison until exchanged that August.

After a chance meeting with his wounded friend Jack, Wesley Culp arranged to have him moved to the Taylor House hospital in Winchester for better care. According to a legend in the Wade/Skelly story, Skelly gave a verbal message for Culp to pass along to the Skelly family should Wesley ever find himself back in Gettysburg. (Some speculate and debate whether any part of that "message" was meant for Jennie Wade.)

Culp did indeed find himself back in his native Gettysburg, and received permission on July 1 to visit his sisters. On the morning of July 2, Wesley Culp was killed instantly by a bullet while serving on his regiment's skirmish line. He fell on the Christian Benner farm, a parcel of land adjoining — but not actually on — the farm of his father's cousin, Henry Culp. He was buried on the battlefield, but attempts by his family to find the location were unsuccessful. Some speculate that Culp's body was secretly buried here in Evergreen Cemetery in an unmarked grave (see Tour Stop 16), but it is more likely that his remains were either never found or later removed to the "Gettysburg Dead" section of Hollywood Cemetery in Richmond, Virginia, during the exhumation of Confederate corpses following the war. Henry Kyd Douglas, an officer on the staff of Gen. Thomas J. "Stonewall" Jackson, wrote in his memoirs in 1899 that Culp was buried on the field "and sleeps there now."

Jack Skelly suffered for weeks from his agonizing wounds in the Winchester hospital before finally succumbing to them on July 12. Jennie Wade never knew that Skelly had been mortally wounded, and Skelly died without knowing that Jennie had been accidentally killed while baking bread. He was initially interred in a Winchester cemetery, but was relocated here in the fall of 1864. Skelly's parents and other family members are also buried here. Note the plaque in the ground in front of his stone, placed by the Gettysburg Sons of Union Veterans, G.A.R. Post #9, in 2003.

Tour Stop 13

Gravesite of Samuel Weaver (1811-1871), First Photographer in Gettysburg, Supervisor of the Removal of Union Dead to the National Cemetery

Five rows behind Skelly's grave rests Samuel Weaver. Although he established the first permanent photographic studio in Gettysburg on Chambersburg Street in May of 1852, Weaver is best known to students of the battle as the meticulous supervisor of the removal of Union dead to the newly established National Cemetery.

Weaver was a former "coach pedlar" who had little competition in the photographic business until the establishment of the Tyson Gallery in 1859. Following the battle of Gettysburg, however, Weaver's responsibilities took a more serious turn. Union dead from the battle had been buried all across the expansive battlefield, and scores of others from the sprawling campaign were interred at Hanover, Hunterstown, Fairfield, and other places. The government contracted with the winning bidder — Frederick W. Biesecker at $1.59 per body — to remove dead from the battlefield for interment in the new National Cemetery. Weaver was selected to supervise the exhumations, and James S. Townsend supervised the reburials.

From October 1863 to March 1864, Weaver supervised every exhumation of a Federal soldier, searched each corpse, and recorded every bit of useful information. His meticulous searches helped identify dozens of remains buried in hasty unmarked graves. As with any large undertaking under difficult conditions, mistakes were understandably made, but soldier identifications can be traced directly to Weaver's efforts. Of the 3,512 bodies relocated, Weaver was unable to identify 979.

Following Weaver's work with the National Cemetery, he also helped many Southern families locate the graves of their Confederate dead. While searching for Federal dead after the battle, he carefully recorded every identified Confederate grave. He may have had some affinity for Southerners since he had lived in Alabama from 1837-1839. In early 1871, he was contacted by the Ladies Memorial Association of Charleston to assist in the removal of South Carolina dead from the battlefield. Weaver agreed, but died before he could begin. Weaver also operated a freight business, and was with his train at York, Pennsylvania, while railcars were being separated. While leaning out the back of his car on February 10, 1871, a jolt from the locomotive threw him onto the track and the next car ran over his legs, cutting them off at the knees. Weaver bled to death quickly. He is interred here with his wife Elizabeth, who died in 1903. Their son George Weaver and his wife Lucilla are also buried here.

Tour Stop 14

Gravesite of Carrie S. Sheads (died 1884), Teacher, "The Angel of Oak Ridge Seminary"

Carrie Sheads is best known as the Gettysburg woman who on July 1, while the first day's battle swirled around her home west of town, saved the sword of a Federal colonel about to be captured by hiding it in the folds of her dress. Look for her grave in the back row of the large Sheads family plot.

During the battle, Carrie was the principal of the Oak Ridge Seminary for girls, located in her father Elias' home on the north side of the Chambersburg Pike west of town (the home still stands today at 331 Buford Avenue). As the fighting on July 1 rolled eastward toward and through town, Sheads' home became a makeshift hospital. Many Federal prisoners were also corralled for a time on her property. During the afternoon, when the Union line north of the pike was broken, Col. Charles Wheelock of the 97th New York Infantry burst into Sheads' home, where many of the wounded of his regiment sought refuge. Confederates on the colonel's heels demanded his surrender. Wheelock waved a white flag to protect his men, and walked down into Sheads' cellar to rest. Confederates found him and demanded his sword, but Wheelock rebuked them and attempted to break the blade. When one of the Southerners pulled a revolver, Carrie bravely stepped in and, secretly taking his sword, hid it in the folds of her dress. She then urged Wheelock to surrender to save his life. She later nursed the wounded of Wheelock's regiment, who were pleased to know that "their colonel's sword was safe." Carrie and her students nursed some 100 wounded in her home, earning the nickname "The Angel of Oak Ridge Seminary."

When the Confederates retreated after the battle, Wheelock was taken along with other prisoners on the march south along the Fairfield Road. On July 5, he escaped near the Monterey House and returned to Gettysburg and Sheads' home to reclaim his blade.

Private Asa Sleeth Hardman of the 3rd Indiana Cavalry, part of Buford's Federal cavalry division, fell wounded on the morning of July 1. Like so many others, he too sought refuge in the Sheads dwelling. He was captured, but following his exchange, returned to the Sheads home to ask for the hand of Carrie's sister Louisa in marriage.

The hand of war was very hard on the Sheads family. Besides the family's Gettysburg experience, all four of Carrie's brothers died as a result of the Civil War and are buried here in the family plot. Elias J., the oldest and a private in Co. F, 87th Pennsylvania Infantry, was killed on July 9, 1864, at the Battle of Monocacy near Frederick, Maryland. Jacob James Sheads, a private in the locally raised Co. B, 21st Pennsylvania Cavalry, expired on October 25, 1864 in a hospital at City Point, Virginia. Two other brothers — Robert E. of Co. A., 1st Pennsylvania Veteran Volunteers, and David M., like his brother Elias a member of Co. F, 87th Pennsylvania Infantry, were both discharged due to disability and died after the war as a direct result of their service. Robert was wounded at White Oak Swamp in Virginia on June 13, 1864, and finally died in October 1866. David died in June 1874. Note that a cousin buried here — Isaac Sheads of Co. F, 87th Pennsylvania Infantry — was killed at Cold Harbor on June 3, 1864.

Tour Stop 15

Gravesite of Elizabeth Salome "Sallie" Myers Stewart (1842-1922), Battlefield Nurse

Like so many houses in Gettysburg, Sallie Myers' home on Baltimore Street quickly became a hospital during the battle. Related to the Sheads family through her mother, Sallie's postwar experience was similar to that of Carrie Sheads' sister Louisa.

A local teacher, Sallie began nursing badly wounded soldiers at the St. Francis Xavier Roman Catholic Church on High Street on July 2. During her first visit to the church, she asked a soldier just inside the door if she could do anything for him. When he replied, "Nothing, I am going to die," she went outside and wept. The mortally wounded man, struck during the fighting on July 1, was Sgt. Alexander Stewart, 149th Pennsylvania Infantry. Undaunted, she returned and again spoke with the soldier. After talking about his family, Stewart asked Sallie to send them his dying message. He died on July 6, and Sallie contacted his family with the tragic news.

The following year, Stewart's widow, along with the dead soldier's younger brother Henry, visited Sallie Myers to thank her for all she had done to comfort Alexander. Sallie and Henry began courting and were married in 1867. Henry had also been wounded during the war. The couple moved to Jamestown, Pennsylvania, where Henry became pastor of the Presbyterian Church. Tragically, while Sallie was pregnant in September 1868, Henry died of complications from his wound. "One year ago today I left home a happy bride," she wrote in her diary on October 17. "This morning the cold snow is falling thick & fast upon my precious husband's grave." Ten days later Sallie gave birth to a boy. She named him Henry Alexander Stewart, in honor of the two most important men in her life.

Sallie Myers Stewart died in 1922 at the age of seventy-nine, after having been elected Treasurer of the National Association of Army Nurses, quite a distinction since she was not an enlisted nurse during the war. Although her husband Henry is interred in Jamestown, Sallie's gravestone pointedly states that the two were "reunited" upon her death.

Buried next to her is her son, Dr. Henry Alexander Stewart. Dr. Stewart was a highly respected physician in Gettysburg for many years, as well as a historian of the battle. He had attended Gettysburg College, then the Medical Department of the University of Pennsylvania in Philadelphia. After he graduated in 1892, he practiced in the office of Gettysburg's Dr. Walter O'Neal, and the following year began his own practice.

For many years, Dr. Stewart was a fixture of the landscape, often seen making house calls with his horse and buggy. When his famous and favorite horse "Dandy" died, he began using . . . an automobile. He was a pioneer in the use of X-ray machines, and in 1902 constructed and used the first such machine employed in the eastern United States outside of the major cities.

Long active in the Sons of Union Veterans of the Civil War, Dr. Stewart served as its state commander from 1920-1921. In 1935, he compiled a record of every Adams County Civil War soldier of record, and drew maps of the cemeteries in which they were interred, which included the positions of each grave. Until his death in 1956, Dr. Stewart always made sure that on Memorial Day, a flag was placed at the grave of every veteran buried in Adams County.

Tour Stop 16

Esiah Jesse Culp (1805-1861), Headstone Damaged during the Battle

A short distance south of Sallie Myers Stewart's grave is another headstone that was badly damaged by Confederate shellfire during the battle. This grave belongs to Esiah Jesse Culp, buried here in 1861. (Note the plaque affixed to the stone attests to the damage.) Esiah was the father of John Wesley Culp (discussed in Tour Stop 11), the Confederate soldier of the 2nd Virginia Infantry killed near his family farm on July 2. Some speculate that John Wesley Culp's remains, initially buried at the site of his death, were later secretly removed and buried here near his father, but this is unlikely.

Tour Stop 17

Gravesite of George Chritzman (1790-1871), Builder, Constructed the Evergreen Cemetery Gatehouse

George Chritzman was a prominent and successful builder in Gettysburg, and is best known for constructing the Evergreen Cemetery Gatehouse in 1855. The gatehouse is the most easily recognized Gettysburg structure associated with the battle.

The partnership of George Chritzman and his brother Henry produced several of the most lauded structures in town, including St. Francis Xavier Roman Catholic Church in 1852, the public school in 1857, and the President's House on the Pennsylvania (now Gettysburg) College campus in 1860. They also built a wooden covered bridge over Marsh Creek on the Emmitsburg Road in 1854, and two years later a similar bridge over Swift Run. During the war, Henry was captain of Gettysburg's Co. K, 101st Pennsylvania Infantry. George died in 1871 and is interred beside his wife Mary, who died eight years later.

Tour Stop 18

Gravesite of William "Billy" David Holtzworth (1843-1891), Early Battlefield Guide

One of the earliest and most knowledgeable guides on the Gettysburg battlefield was Billy Holtzworth, who escorted a number of famous personalities over the field. Presidents Ulysses S. Grant, Rutherford B. Hayes, and Grover Cleveland were led by him, as well as many generals such as Meade, Hancock, Sickles, Warren, Longstreet, Hampton, Hooker, Sheridan, and Sherman.

Born in Gettysburg on January 2, 1843, Holtzworth worked as an apprentice granite stonecutter, and enlisted in Gettysburg's Co. F, 87th Pennsylvania Infantry after serving for three months in a short-term unit. He was wounded twice during the war. Following his first wound as a corporal on June 13, 1863 at the battle of Winchester, Holtzworth was taken prisoner and, as he described, "cooped up" at Libby Prison and then Bell Isle for six weeks. He suffered his second wound as a sergeant at the Weldon Railroad near Petersburg, Virginia, on June 23, 1864, when he was shot through the left shoulder. Although his second wound paralyzed his arm, Holtzworth remained with his unit rsContinuing.

until the end of the war and was at Appomattox to witness Lee's surrender.

After the war he intently studied details of the Gettysburg battlefield, and was active as an officer in the Gettysburg Battlefield Memorial Association and the Grand Army of the Republic. In addition to being one of the first and most popular battlefield guides, Holtzworth also widely lectured about the battle across the country. Along with battlefield photographer William Tipton, he assisted artist Paul Philippoteaux in creating the Gettysburg Cyclorama painting, a 360-degree panorama of the scene of Pickett's Charge.

Holtzworth suffered several strokes toward the end of his life, and gave up guiding and lecturing. In 1887, he became the third superintendent of the Soldiers' National Cemetery at Gettysburg. When he died in 1891, he was buried — according to his wishes — in a plot very near the Soldiers' National Cemetery where he could rest near the annual programs taking place at the cemetery's rostrum. He is buried here with his wife Evaline Lindsay, whom he married in 1867 and who died in 1932.

Tour Stop 19
Gravesites of Peter (1826-1907) and Elizabeth (1832-1907) Thorn, Evergreen Cemetery Caretakers

Four months after the Evergreen Cemetery gatehouse was laid on September 1, 1855, Peter Thorn was appointed to be the first cemetery caretaker. Coincidentally, Peter and Elizabeth were married in Gettysburg on the day the cornerstone was laid. From 1856 to 1858, Peter built a home (still standing at 225 N. Washington Street) for himself and his bride, but never occupied it since the gatehouse, upon completion, was provided as a home for the caretaker free of rent.

Peter was born on July 24, 1826, in Rukershausen, Germany, and worked as a miner before sailing alone to America in 1852. Elizabeth Masser, born in Eigelsdorf, Germany on December 28, 1832, sailed to America with her parents in 1854. Before becoming caretaker, Peter also worked as a miner in Gettysburg, perhaps at a copper mine that existed on High Street in the vicinity where the St. Francis Xavier Catholic Church stands today. While Peter served as a corporal in the 138th Pennsylvania Infantry (his regiment was at Harpers Ferry and did not participate at Gettysburg), Elizabeth fulfilled the duties of caretaker. As previously recounted, with the help of her father and assistants, Elizabeth buried ninety-one dead soldiers of the battle, which were later removed to the National Cemetery. Other than the monthly caretaker salary of $13.00, she never received any compensation for the burdensome work. She was six months pregnant during the battle, and on November 1 gave birth to a daughter named Rosa Meade Thorn, in part in honor of the Federal commander at the battle. Rosa, one of two daughters, was never a healthy child. She died at the young age of fourteen in 1878 and is buried here beside her parents. Three of Peter and Elizabeth's four sons, Fred (with wife Saranda), George, and John (with wife Mia) are also buried here in the family plot.

Peter Thorn was wounded in the left arm at the Third Battle of Winchester in Virginia on September 19, 1864, and hospitalized for several weeks. He was present at Appomattox for Lee's surrender, and was mustered out of his regiment on June 23, 1865. He returned to Gettysburg and served as caretaker until 1874. From 1878 to 1884, Peter was the proprietor of the Wagon Hotel (later named the Battlefield Hotel), which stood at the junction of Baltimore Street and the Emmitsburg Road (Steinwehr Avenue today). He later purchased a home on West Middle Street and worked as a day laborer.

Peter died on January 8, 1907 at his home; Elizabeth followed him shortly thereafter that October. Her parents, John and Catherine, are buried about twenty-five feet to the left of the Thorns' headstones. (Note their last name is engraved "Maser" on the stones.)

Tour Stop 20
Gravesite of David Wills (1831-1894), Lawyer and Supervisor of the Establishment of the Soldiers' National Cemetery

Gettysburg attorney David Wills is perhaps best known as the influential resident who invited President Abraham Lincoln to speak at the dedication of the National Cemetery and give "a few appropriate remarks." He hosted the president in his home the night before the Gettysburg Address was delivered.

Wills was born north of Gettysburg on February 3, 1831, in Menallen Township, Adams County. He graduated from Pennsylvania (later Gettysburg) College in 1851. After serving as principal of a school in Cahaba, Alabama, he returned to Pennsylvania and studied law under Thaddeus Stevens in Lancaster. He was admitted to the county bar in 1854, opened a practice in Gettysburg, and served in various public offices in the town and county. In 1856, Wills married Catherine Jane "Jennie" Smyser of Norristown, who died in 1891 and is buried here beside her husband.

Following the battle, Wills was appointed agent for Pennsylvania Governor Andrew Curtin to purchase ground on Cemetery Hill to create a Soldiers' National Cemetery. Fellow attorney and president of the Evergreen Cemetery Association David McConaughy had already pursued the idea of establishing such a cemetery under the auspices of Evergreen. Animosity developed between the two men, and in the end it was Wills' effort that proved successful.

Wills invited President Lincoln to formally dedicate the grounds. Lincoln stayed in Wills' home on the southeast corner of the town square and York Street (which is still standing, owned by the National Park Service and open to the public) the night before his speech, where he may have put the finishing touches on his famous address in one of the bedrooms.

In 1874, Wills was elected president judge of the judicial district, was very active in the Presbyterian Church, and remained one of Gettysburg's most influential citizens. He died in 1894. There are many members of the Wills family buried in the plot.

Tour Stop 21
Gravesite of Charles McCurdy (1852-1938), Child Witness of the Battle

Ten years old at the time of the battle, Charles McCurdy was one of many of the town's children who watched parts of the battle and wrote about his experiences in 1929. His first experience with Confederate soldiers was on June 26, 1863, when Southerners entered town on their way toward the Susquehanna. Many sent young McCurdy on errands to procure food, but he decided not to comply.

On the evening of June 30 and again on the morning of July 1, McCurdy and several of his friends amused themselves by helping water horses from Buford's Federal cavalry division camped west of town. When the fighting started, McCurdy's group watched the spreading conflict until Confederate shells began falling in their vicinity and the boys ran home for safety. McCurdy's house was used as a Confederate hospital during the battle.

Tour Stop 22

Gravesite of David Kendlehart (1813-1891), Shoemaker and President of Gettysburg Borough Council during the Battle

Born in Gettysburg on December 30, 1813, Kendlehart followed his father's trade as a shoemaker. He owned and operated a shoe and boot store in Gettysburg for more than forty years. His home at 110 Baltimore Street still stands. One of Kendlehart's most famous employees was John Burns, who worked for Kendleart at the time of the battle (and whose grave we will also visit).

Apprenticed as a shoemaker since the age of twelve, Kendlehart married Eliza Ann Bowen in 1841. An avowed abolitionist, in at least one documented case Kendlehart assisted two captured fugitive slaves to escape a bounty hunter while traveling through Gettysburg prior to the war. He was president of the Gettysburg Borough Council when Maj. Gen. Jubal A. Early's Confederate division entered town on the afternoon of June 26 before continuing its march north. Early tried to use Kendlehart to requisition supplies for his men, including thousands of pounds of food and clothing. After meeting with his councilmen, however, Kendlehart informed the general that the town was unable to meet his requests. Early's men took whatever supplies they could find, camped that evening north of town, and marched for York the following morning.

Kendlehart died on April 30, 1891, and his wife Eliza Ann Bowen, buried here with him, died on March 17, 1902.

Tour Stop 23

Gravesite of Marianne Craig Moore (1887-1972), Poet

Marianne Moore was a Pulitzer Prize-winning poet of the 20th century and a cultural icon later in life. Although never a resident of Gettysburg, Moore is buried here with several members of her family approximately twenty feet to the right of the Kendlehart grave.

Moore was born on November 15, 1887, to John and Mary Moore in Kirkland, Missouri. She grew up in her grandfather's house since her father had been committed to a mental institution prior to her birth. Her grandfather, Dr. John R. Warner, had previously served as pastor of the Lower Marsh Creek Presbyterian Church near Fairfield, and the Great Conewago Presbyterian Church in Hunterstown. He was pastor in Hunterstown during the war years. His wife Jennie Craig, who died of typhoid fever shortly after the battle of Gettysburg, is buried here. Warner died in 1894 and was brought from Missouri to rest with his wife, firmly establishing the family plot in Evergreen Cemetery.

After Warner's death, Marianne, her brother John, and their mother Mary moved to Carlisle. Marianne graduated from Bryn Mawr College in 1909 and began writing stories and poems. In 1911, she began teaching English and other subjects to Indian students at the U.S. Industrial Indian School at the Carlisle Barracks. One of her students was Jim Thorpe, who was soon to become one of America's greatest athletes.

Marianne's poems were first published in 1915, and she quickly achieved wide acclaim. While living in New Jersey with her mother, Moore commuted to New York City. Soon her books of poetry were published, and several of them garnered major literary awards including the Pulitzer Prize for her 1951 *Collected Poems*. In 1955, David Wallace, a manager of the Ford Motor Company, asked Moore to suggest an "inspirational name" for a new car. She suggested several, but Ford ultimately christened the vehicle "Edsel."

Quite the sports fan, Moore threw out the first pitch on opening day at Yankee Stadium in 1968. She suffered a series of strokes shortly thereafter and died in 1972 in New York City. In 1990, the U.S. Postal Service honored Moore as one of America's greatest poets with her own postage stamp.

In 1947 while designing the present gravestone that marks her own and her mother's graves, Moore asked the stonecutter to leave the space you see below her name for the name of a husband in case she married; the fiercely independent poet remained single, and so the space remains blank.

Tour Stop 24

Gravesite of Charles Edward Goldsborough (1834-1913), U.S. Army Surgeon

Dr. Charles Goldsborough was a surgeon for the U.S. Army during the war, but two of his brothers served in the Confederate army. As happened many times in similar circumstances, the brothers met during the war under awkward circumstances.

Goldsborough, born in Frederick County, Maryland on December 16, 1834, studied medicine at the University of Maryland. In 1854, he opened an office in Hunterstown and married a local girl, Mary Neely, in 1857. Mary died in 1860, however, and Goldsborough enlisted as a surgeon with the 5th Maryland Infantry (U.S.) at Frederick.

On June 15, 1863, he was taken prisoner at the battle of Winchester in Virginia. His brother, Maj. William Goldsborough of the 2nd Maryland Infantry (C.S.A.), arranged to meet with Charles, who was later sent to Libby Prison in Richmond. There, Charles helped broker an exchange of 100 Federal doctors for the release of Confederate doctors held prisoner at Fort McHenry in Baltimore. Brother William, who marched with the Southerners into Pennsylvania, was wounded and captured at Gettysburg.

The following December, Dr. Goldsborough was sent to Fort Delaware where both William and another brother, Eugene, were held prisoner. Charles made his brothers as comfortable as possible until he was sent to administer to Federal forces in Virginia. On July 6, 1864, he was wounded at Petersburg and sent to Chesapeake Hospital. Following his recovery, Dr. Goldsborough was assigned to Lincoln Hospital in Washington until August 1865. He was released at the end of the war, but Eugene had died at Fort Delaware in February.

After the war, Dr. Goldsborough returned to Hunterstown and resumed his practice. On November 14, 1866, he married Alice E. McCreary, a daughter of Jesse McCreary, in front of whose home the July 2, 1863, cavalry battle at Hunterstown had begun. Alice's sister Martha was the mother of Eddie Plank, also known as "Gettysburg Eddie" and a member of the Baseball Hall of Fame (we will visit his grave later in the tour). Charles and Alice had ten children together, one of whom was named Eugene in honor of Charles' brother. Eugene died at the age of nineteen and is interred here in the family plot beneath the small obelisk monument.

Dr. Goldsborough died on October 13, 1913, and is buried here with his second wife Alice, who died in 1893.

Tour Stop 25

Gravesite of Lt. Nesbitt Baugher (1836-1862), Gettysburg's First Native Son Mortally Wounded during the War

Gettysburg's first native son-turned-soldier killed during battle in the Civil War was Nesbitt Baugher, first lieutenant of Co. B, 45th Illinois Infantry. Born in Gettysburg in 1836 and an 1853 graduate of Pennsylvania (later Gettysburg) College, he went on to become an attorney. In November 1857, Baugher moved to Illinois and worked as the editor of a newspaper in Galena until he enlisted in the fall of 1861. After being wounded an astonishing seven times at the battle of Shiloh in Tennessee while in command of his company, his father, Pennsylvania College president Dr. Henry Louis Baugher, visited him in a Quincy hospital. Convinced his son would survive, Dr. Baugher returned to Gettysburg. Nesbitt, however, died on May 16, 1862, and was brought home for burial with full military honors here in Evergreen five days later. He was twenty-five years old. Two of Nesbitt's cousins, Oscar and Charles Baugher (sons of his father's brother) served in the Confederate Army, and even visited Henry's sister during the battle.

Tour Stop 26

Gravesite of Harvey W. McKnight (1843-1914), Civil War Soldier and President of Pennsylvania (Gettysburg) College

Best known as the fourth president of Pennsylvania (now Gettysburg) College, Harvey McKnight was a militia soldier in the 26th Pennsylvania Emergency Militia when that unit was run out of Gettysburg on June 26, 1863, when Confederates entered town.

Nearby McKnightstown was founded by Harvey's father Thomas. Henry was born there on April 3, 1843, and attended the Chambersburg Academy and then Pennsylvania College in 1860. In 1862, he enlisted in Co. B, 138th Pennsylvania Infantry and the following year joined the 26th Militia. He was with this unit in Gettysburg when it was guarding the western part of town near Marsh Creek on the afternoon of June 26. The 26th Militia was routed by White's cavalry and fled north of town. Following the Gettysburg Campaign, McKnight enlisted in the 210th Pennsylvania Infantry and served as captain until war's end, when he returned to the college. He graduated from the Lutheran Theological Seminary in 1867, and in 1884 became president of Pennsylvania College, a position he held for twenty years.

Dr. McKnight died of throat cancer in 1914 and is buried here beside his wife Mary Welty, who died two years later.

Tour Stop 27

Gravesite of Henry John Stahle, Newspaper Editor

The editor of Gettysburg's *Compiler* for more than forty years and a staunch Democrat, Stahl was arrested by Federal commander Maj. Gen. George G. Meade shortly after the battle ended. An outspoken critic of President Lincoln and the war, Stahle had notified Confederate surgeons during the battle that a wounded Federal officer was hospitalized in his home. The surgeons saved the officer's life, but Stahle was arrested for furnishing information to the enemy. Sent to Ft. McHenry prison, Stahle claimed he was innocent and was released when the charges (perhaps facilitated by his political rival David McConaughy) were more political than treasonous.

Born in York, Pennsylvania in 1823, Stahle was the fourth of twelve children of John and Sara Stahle. After attending the York Academy, he apprenticed as a printer at a local newspaper. At the age of twenty-one he purchased the *Compiler* and during the war years, used it as a platform to launch editorials critical of Lincoln and the war.

As fate would have it, Stahle now reposes less than forty feet from his rival McConaughy, whose grave we will visit next. Stahle is buried beneath the smaller headstone next to the large obelisk in the plot. He died on May 12, 1892, and is buried here with his wife Louisa, who had died in 1879. Several members of his family are buried here, including a son who died within hours of his birth in 1853. Stahle's brother, James Alonzo, was a captain (and later colonel) in the 87th Pennsylvania Infantry. James is buried in Prospect Hill Cemetery in York.

Tour Stop 28

Gravesite of David McConaughy (1823-1902), Lawyer and Early Battlefield Preservationist

Overshadowed by the successes of political rival David Wills, McConaughy's efforts to establish a soldiers' cemetery and to save battlefield land are all but forgotten today. As early as 1862, McConaughy wished to establish a special cemetery for war dead, and after the battle of Gettysburg began purchasing land for such a purpose.

Born in Gettysburg on July 13, 1823, McConaughy was the great-great grandson of Irish immigrants who had settled in Pennsylvania as early as 1712. His father John died when he was only four years old and he was raised by foster parents. He attended Pennsylvania (later Gettysburg) College from 1834 to 1838, graduated from Washington (today Washington and Jefferson) College in 1840, and studied law under Thaddeus Stephens to become an attorney in 1845.

McConaughy helped to establish Evergreen Cemetery and served as its president from 1854 to 1863. At the start of the Civil War, he formed a company of home guard scouts in Gettysburg comprised of his law clients. He served as captain of this group, which he dubbed the "Adams Rifles." During every Confederate movement north during the war, McConaughy and his scouts strove to transmit information to the state capital. He was also likely the leader of the group of citizens that Brig. Gen. John Buford met with when that officer brought his Federal cavalry into Gettysburg the day before the battle on June 30, 1863.

Shortly after the battle ended McConaughy began purchasing land to bury those killed in the fighting, as well as to save areas of the battlefield, but it was David Wills who was ultimately appointed to oversee the creation of the Soldiers' National Cemetery. McConaughy was one of the influential forces in the creation of the Gettysburg Battlefield Memorial Association. He later served in the state legislature representing Adams and Franklin counties.

McConaughey died on January 14, 1902. He is buried here with both his first wife Catherine Arnold, who died along with their newborn daughter shortly after childbirth (note the headstone engraved "Dear Kate and our babe"), and his second wife Leana Mathews, who preceded him in death by one year. Also note the old gravestones of relatives in this plot — following the establishment of Evergreen Cemetery, McConaughy had these remains relocated here.

Tour Stop 29

Gravesite of Rev. Michael Jacobs (1808-1871), Professor and Scientist

Anyone who wants to know the weather conditions before, during, and after the battle of Gettysburg will be thankful for the efforts of Rev. Jacobs. Beginning in 1839 and continuing for decades thereafter, Jacobs recorded the weather conditions in Gettysburg three times each day. He also wrote one of the first comprehensive histories of the battle.

Jacobs was born in Waynesboro, Pennsylvania on January 18, 1808. He graduated from Jefferson College as the valedictorian of the class of 1828, and taught school in Maryland for one year. In 1829, he moved to Gettysburg where he became professor of mathematics and natural sciences at the Gettysburg Gymnasium. In 1832, he continued in that position when Pennsylvania (Gettysburg) College was organized, and remained there until 1865. About 1845, he developed a process for canning fruit and is regarded by many as the inventor of canned food.

Jacobs' daily readings of weather conditions (taken at 7:00 a.m., 2:00 p.m., and 9:00 p.m.) have been very helpful for historians studying the fighting. He published a book detailing both the battle and the campaign, and throughout his career wrote many articles on theology and science.

Dr. Jacobs died on July 22, 1871, at the age of sixty-nine. He is interred here at the large obelisk marker with his wife Julia, who died in 1892.

Tour Stop 30

Gravesite of Edward McPherson (1830-1895), Congressman, Owner of Farm Near Which the Battle of Gettysburg Began

"McPherson's Ridge" is best known to students of the battle as the area where the main fighting began on the morning of July 1, 1863. John Slentz and his family were renting Edward McPherson's farm west of Gettysburg at the time of the battle, but the property and terrain features have always been referred to as McPherson's.

Born in Gettysburg at the family farm on July 30, 1830, McPherson attended Pennsylvania (Gettysburg) College and graduated the valedictorian of the class of 1848. After studying law, he entered politics and was elected a congressman in 1859.

At the start of the Civil War, McPherson raised a company of the 1st Pennsylvania Reserves, and in September of 1862 served as an aide on Gen. John F. Reynolds' staff. As fate would have it, Reynolds was mortally wounded on the first day of the Battle of Gettysburg within sight of McPherson's farm.

He was a trustee of the college from 1861 until he died on December 14, 1895. Also buried here near the tall family obelisk monument is his wife Annie, who died in 1906. Many members of his family are interred here in the family plot, some of who were brought here from other burial grounds after the establishment of Evergreen Cemetery.

Tour Stop 31

Gravesite of John Lawrence Burns (1793-1872), Only Civilian to Fight in the Battle of Gettysburg

The second most sought-out grave in Evergreen Cemetery (Jennie Wade's is first) is the resting place of John Burns, the sixty-nine-year-old Gettysburg curmudgeon who walked into the fighting on July 1 and took up arms against the Confederates. Burns' gravesite, like Wade's, is marked with a flagpole.

The son of a Scottish father and English mother, Burns was born in Burlington, New Jersey on September 5, 1793 (although the stone is engraved 1794). Burns seems to have served for a short time in the War of 1812, but apparently saw no combat. This contradicts his later claims, and he does not appear to have served in either the Florida War or Mexican War. The legend that Burns experienced fighting prior to the Civil War notwithstanding, Gettysburg was almost certainly his first taste of combat.

He married Barbara Hagarman in 1820. Sometime after 1839, the childless couple adopted a child named Martha, who was born out of wedlock to a

Taken just days after the battle, John Burns poses for photographers outside his home on Chambersburg Street. (LOC)

woman who worked at the County Almshouse. John and his family lived in various places in and around Gettysburg prior to the war. He usually worked as a shoemaker (and held various odd jobs from time to time, including constable of Gettysburg), and in January 1863 purchased the home he had been renting at the intersection of West Street and the Chambersburg Pike.

On the morning of July 1, 1863, shortly after the battle of Gettysburg opened west of town, Burns left his home, crossed in front of the Lutheran Theological Seminary, and walked toward the fighting along McPherson Ridge. Eminel P. Halstead, one of Gen. Abner Doubleday's staffers, claimed to have met Burns at the time: "I met John Burns in the field east of the Seminary with an old [flintlock] musket on his shoulder . . . when near me he inquired, 'Which way are the rebels? Where are our troops?' I informed them they were just in front, that he would soon overtake them. He then said with much enthusiasm, 'I know how to fight, I have fit before!'"

Accounts vary widely, but Burns was probably a spectator that morning, watching from the Seminary grounds. After securing a new rifle, he started for the front again and encountered the 150th Pennsylvania Infantry near the Edward McPherson farm along the Chambersburg Pike. About an hour later, he joined the 7th Wisconsin Infantry at Herbst's Woods, close to where Federal Maj. Gen. John

F. Reynolds had been killed. Burns participated in some heavy fighting and was wounded as many as three times. A bullet in the leg finally felled him, and he spent the night on the field before making his way into town the next morning to the home of Alexander Riggs. From there, Burns was taken to his own home to recuperate.

Burns' legend soared after the battle, and he was hailed "The Hero of Gettysburg." After delivering his address at the dedication of the Soldiers' National Cemetery, President Abraham Lincoln asked to meet Burns. From David Wills' home on the town square, Lincoln and Burns walked together to the Presbyterian Church on Baltimore Street. The old man relished being photographed and interviewed, and poems and songs were written about the "patriot" who shouldered a gun to fight in the battle.

Irascible and jealous of the attention paid to Jennie Wade's story, Burns was not hesitant to defame her character in public, even taking to calling her a "she-rebel." He was only able to enjoy his fame for a few years before pneumonia took him on February 4, 1872. He was buried two days later beside Barbara (who had died in 1868) after an impressive procession through the cemetery that included several horse-drawn sleighs.

Burns' original headstone was vandalized and replaced by the present stone by Gettysburg's G.A.R. Post #9 in 1902. The flagstaff was erected in 1917 by a donation from John White Johnston of New York, who had intensely researched John Burns' life and family history. Regardless of his pre-Civil War military service, and in spite of his jealous temperament, the single-word inscription on his stone, earned on July 1, 1863, is well deserved: "Patriot."

Tour Stop 32

Gravesite of Pvt. Leander W. Welsh, First Federal Civil War Soldier Buried in Evergreen Cemetery

Just down the hill from Burns' grave is the resting place of Pvt. Leander Welsh of Co. E, 2nd Pennsylvania Infantry, which was recruited in Adams County. Welsh was the first Union soldier buried here in the cemetery. One of the county's earliest enlistees in this three-month unit, he died of typhoid fever at the Eagle Hotel (present site of a convenience store) in Gettysburg on June 20, 1861, and was buried the following day. He was only twenty years old. His grave is marked by a simple government headstone.

Tour Stop 33

Graves in the Civil War Soldiers Section

Here in the section set aside for Civil War soldiers, there are a number of interesting graves to point out.

Pvt. Hooper P. Caffey and Sgt. Mathew Goodson (Confederate) — Caffey, born in 1837, was a member of Co. H, 3rd Alabama Infantry. He was mortally wounded during Pickett's Charge and lingered until he died on September 13, 1863. Goodson, born in 1828, served in Co. A, 52nd North Carolina Infantry, was mortally wounded during the battle (date unknown) and died on July 12. Government headstones for both men are here alongside the rows of Federal soldiers, but neither Southerner is actually interred at this location. Several months after the end of the war, their bodies were discovered buried near the Jacob Schwartz farm, which was a Federal 2nd Corps hospital along White Run south of the cemetery. A large temporary cemetery for both Federal and Confederate dead had been established behind Schwartz's barn on what was called "Red Hill." Nearly 200 Confederates had been buried there. Goodson and Caffey were discovered somewhere near the farm by locals and re-interred side-by-side in January 1866 west of the present site of John Burns' grave. In the summer of 1867, however, Evergreen Cemetery lot owners were outraged when they learned that Confederate soldiers were buried on the grounds. In August, cemetery caretaker Peter Thorn was instructed to relocate the remains to a secluded area of the cemetery. He exhumed the men and reburied them as directed, but the exact location was never recorded. In 1989, cemetery superintendent Arthur L. Kennell had these two government headstones placed here alongside the soldiers killed in battle to memorialize the two Confederates who rest in graves that may never be found again. Goodson also has a memorial stone next to the grave of his wife, Catherine, at home in First Presbyterian Memorial Garden Cemetery in Cabarrus County, North Carolina.

Pvt. John W. Congdon, Co. A, 10th New York Cavalry — During the winter of 1861-62, the 10th New York Cavalry camped and drilled on grounds east of Gettysburg. Congdon, who had been sick in New York when his regiment departed for Gettysburg, boarded a train in December to rejoin his comrades. While the train approached the cavalrymen's camp, Congdon jumped up on the platform of his rail car to wave at his comrades. He seems not to have seen the wooden bridge over Rock Creek that the train was about to pass under, and his head struck a timber, knocking him off the train and into the creek. He was already dead when his friends reached him. Congdon was buried on December 29, 1861, just to the west of where the speakers' platform stood for the November 19, 1863, dedication of the Soldiers' National Cemetery. He was later reburied here to rest alongside comrades of his regiment who died of disease while camped here, as well as soldiers killed in battle.

Two stones marked "Unknown" — History can only speculate as to the identity of these graves. It is not even known whether they mark the resting places of Union or Confederate soldiers. They may be the graves of two unidentified remains (though not Caffey and Goodson) found on the battlefield. Unfortunately, the usually meticulous Evergreen Cemetery records do not mention these interments.

Cpl. Leroy (or Levi) S. Greenlee and Lt. Samuel Greenlee — Note these two stones that share a base. Cpl. Leroy S. Greenlee of Co. A., 140th Pennsylvania Infantry, was killed on July 2 and was buried here by his family. On May 28, 1864, his brother Samuel, a second lieutenant in Co. F, 1st Pennsylvania Reserve Cavalry, was killed at the Battle of Haw's Shop in Hanover County, Virginia (he had also been wounded in the cavalry battle at Brandy Station, Virginia, on June 9, 1863). Since the younger brother was buried here in Evergreen, their father brought Samuel's corpse here to Gettysburg to be buried beside Leroy. The younger Greenlee was twenty-one when he died, and Samuel was twenty-seven. Both were from Greene County, Pennsylvania.

Tour Stop 34

Gravesite of William H. Tipton (1850-1929), Battlefield Photographer

William Tipton is one of the most well known Gettysburg battlefield photographers of the postwar era. Because of Tipton's prolific photographic work, we have numerous views of the early battlefield, monuments, and visitors.

Tipton was born in Gettysburg on August 5, 1850, the eldest of eleven children of Solomon and Elizabeth Tipton. Local photographer Charles J. Tyson was impressed with Tipton's skill for drawing, and apprenticed the twelve-year-old in early 1863. Tipton assisted Tyson's firm while recording many views of the new battlefield, and in 1868 Tipton purchased Tyson's business. He photographed nearly every battlefield monument once it was in place, and captured dozens of views of the field and town.

Tipton served as burgess of Gettysburg, president of the town council, and represented Adams County in the state legislature. He also owned and operated "Tipton Park," a tourist stop and photographic studio in the vicinity of the comfort station presently located near Plum Run east of Devil's Den. His studio building was condemned, along with the Electric Railway that coursed nearby, and removed in the early 1900s.

Tipton died in 1929 and is buried beside his wife Mary E. Little, who predeceased him in 1921. Their daughter, Esther F. Tipton, is also interred here, as are Mary's parents. Esther has a government headstone because she served in the Army Nurse Corps during World War I. She died in 1958.

Tour Stop 35
Gravesite of Edward Stewart Plank (1875-1926), Member, Baseball Hall of Fame

Hall of Famer "Gettysburg Eddie" Plank. (ACHS)

The gravesite of "Gettysburg Eddie," one of the best pitchers in baseball, is sought out by many visitors to Evergreen Cemetery. Plank was born on August 31, 1875, the fourth of seven children of David S. Plank and his wife Martha E. McCreary. Martha was originally from nearby Hunterstown, and it was in front of her father's house that the July 2, 1863, cavalry Battle of Hunterstown began.

Plank was born on the family farm near Gettysburg and attended the Gettysburg Academy, a preparatory school for Gettysburg College. Although he never attended the college, Plank pitched on the school's baseball team. Connie Mack signed Plank to a major league contract with the Philadelphia Athletics, and he made his debut on May 13, 1901. While with the team, Plank won twenty or more games a season seven different times, and played in the World Series twice. He was known for his fastball and curve, but also for his penchant for talking to himself while on the mound and slowing down the game. Babe Ruth once said that Plank was the toughest pitcher he ever faced.

Plank played for the Athletics through the 1914 season, and the following year joined the St. Louis Terriers, reaching the twenty-win mark for an eighth time. In 1916 and 1917 he pitched for the St. Louis Browns and then retired (though he played semi-pro baseball for a few more years). He was the first left-handed pitcher to win 300 games, and still ranks very high among wins for southpaws. In 1999, Plank was ranked sixty-eighth of the top 100 greatest baseball players of the century by *The Sporting News*.

After retiring, Plank opened an auto garage in Gettysburg, and retired comfortably in 1923. On February 23, 1926, he suffered a stroke that paralyzed his left side, and slipped into unconsciousness. He died the following day at the age of fifty, with his wife, two brothers, and ten-year-old son Edward Jr. at his side. In 1946, Plank was inducted into the Hall of Fame. The urns on both sides of the Planks' headstone can often be found filled with baseballs in memory of "Gettysburg Eddie."

Plank is buried here beside his wife, Anna C. Myers, who died in 1955. Their son, Edward S. Plank Jr., served as a captain during World War II and is interred here in the family plot.

Tour Stop 36

Gravesite of Samuel Eichinger Cobean (1913-1951), Cartoonist

As you walk back toward the gatehouse after visiting Edward Plank's gravesite, you may wish to pay your respects to Samuel E. Cobean (his grave is about forty feet downhill from the large Funkhouser vault and marked by a small ground-level stone). An influence on generations of cartoonists, "Sam" Cobean was born in Gettysburg on December 28, 1913. He was the only child of a dentist named Dr. George Cobean and his wife Catharine Eichinger, who was a schoolteacher and artist.

In 1920, the Cobean family moved to Altoona, Pennsylvania, so that Sam's ill mother could receive better medical care. Catharine died two years later when Sam was only eight years old. After attending Altoona High School, Sam returned to Gettysburg and enrolled in the Gettysburg Academy. The following year, however, he and his father moved to Tulsa, Oklahoma, in an effort to improve his father's impaired health. There, he finished high school while working on the school's newspaper. Sam and his father returned to Altoona in 1931 and he enrolled in Gettysburg College. He later attended the University of Oklahoma and became a popular cartoonist. Disney Studios offered him a position and he dropped out of college to begin working on an animated feature called *Snow White and the Seven Dwarfs*.

In 1942 he married Anne McCool and began working as a cartoonist for the Screen Gems Writers in Hollywood. After being drafted into the Army in 1943, Sam worked on training films and drew patriotic cartoons that were widely distributed. His cartoons appeared in many popular magazines. It was Cobean who invented the "thought bubble," which shows a character's thoughts. It has become a staple of cartooning ever since.

On July 2, 1951, Cobean was driving to *The New Yorker* offices from his home in Watkins Glen, New York, when his sports car hit a tree. He was instantly killed. On July 5, the thirty-seven-year-old cartoonist was buried here beside his parents under this simple stone — a sharp contrast to the volume of artwork he offered the world.

Tour Stop 37

Old Re-interments and the "Ivy Rock" Area

As you begin walking to leave the cemetery, note the very old gravestones northwest of Cobean's gravesite (to your left as you walk toward the gatehouse). These are reburials from other Gettysburg area cemeteries. Many of the stones date back to the 1700s. Just north of this site is a noticeable rise or "hump" in the ground immediately south of John Burns' grave. This area was once covered with large boulders. Even though most were removed years ago, the area is still referred to as Ivy Rock.

You are encouraged to explore as much of the cemetery as you desire. Additionally, you may wish to visit the Veterans' Section at the western edge of Section U.

Additional Reading

The Evergreen Cemetery office offers a number of items about the cemetery and its history. A book by cemetery caretaker Brian A. Kennell offers invaluable information and was heavily consulted for this tour. *Beyond the Gatehouse: Gettysburg's Evergreen Cemetery* (Gettysburg, Pa: Evergreen Cemetery Association, 2000) is available at the office and local booksellers, and contains a good map of the cemetery. It is highly recommended.

(Opposite page) The P. Noel carving on a boulder located just above Devil's Den. (Stanley)

Stories in Stone:
Rock Carvings on the Gettysburg Battlefield

D evoted students of the Gettysburg battle and field are always searching for new information on the fighting, which usually comes in the form of heretofore unknown or ignored primary material that helps clarify and explain our understanding of the events that took place during that summer long ago in 1863. Visitors to the expansive national park usually visit the same handful of places each time they travel to Gettysburg, and so often miss out-of-the way locations well worth a few minutes of their

Tour Route of Rock Carvings on the Battlefield

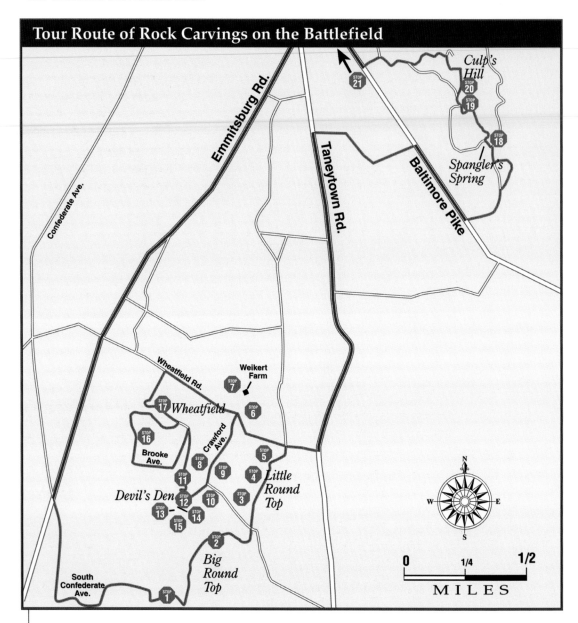

time. One of the best-kept secrets of Gettysburg is that primary "documents" reside on the battlefield itself in the form of rock carvings. Although some pre-date the battle, others were created between July 1-4, 1863, with the remaining examples carved into place by returning veterans. Many of the carvings survive and can be seen today, although time and erosion is taking its inevitable toll on this precious and unique aspect of the field. Debates — such as how many were carved by soldiers during the three-day engagement — continue to this day.

If you are fortunate enough to become familiar with the battlefield, you will undoubtedly develop the urge to move off the beaten path and seek out something new. Exploring away from the general tourist routes can be exciting — especially if you have a destination in mind. These rock carvings provide that type of satisfaction. And the lengthy hunt and the thrill of discovery will likely spur the desire for further research into their history, their origins, and more about the men who created them.

This chapter offers a detailed list and description of all of the known rock carvings scattered around the battlefield, together with how to find them (including Global Positioning coordinates) and various theories about their origins. A word of caution is in order. Some of the carvings are located in areas that can be difficult to reach and see, especially among the brush and weeds that grow tall and thick during the summer months. Make sure you are adequately dressed (proper footwear, leggings, etc.), prepared for the insects and pests of the field, and healthy enough before trying to reach some of the more obscure areas, and be careful and patient when climbing around the slippery and potentially dangerous rocks. Finally, children should be accompanied by watchful adults at all times.

To start the tour and the treasure hunt for these carvings, we will begin by driving on South Confederate Avenue (east of its intersection with the Emmitsburg Road) toward Big Round Top.

To reach South Confederate Avenue from the town square, turn right from the square onto Baltimore Street (Rt. 97). After .4 miles, turn right at the stop light onto Steinwehr Avenue (Rt. 15) and reset your odometer to 0.0. Continue straight and Steinwehr Avenue becomes the Emmitsburg Road (Rt. 15), which continues through the field of Pickett's Charge. After 2.6 miles, turn left onto South Confederate Avenue and reset your odometer to 0.0.

After .9 miles you will reach the small stone bridge over Plum Run and the first stop on the tour.

. . . .

Tour Stop 1
Dinosaur Footprints at Plum Run Bridge

Location: *(77° 14' 41"W, 39° 47' 05"N)*

History: Fossilized footprints of dinosaurs can be seen in the capstones used on the bridge across Plum Run along South Confederate Avenue. Although these are not rock carvings, they appear at the beginning of our journey and so are worth seeing.

LET'S FIND IT!
Park on the right side of the road just before you reach the bridge. If you examine the stones on the top of the right (southeast) side of the bridge, the fossilized dinosaur tracks appear in the stone sixth from the right. Atop the left (northwest) side of the bridge, they appear in the fifth stone from the right. If you do some detective work and look closely, you can also see other fossils in these capstones, one of which is a leaf.

To reach the next stop, continue along South Confederate Avenue for .3 miles until you reach the parking area on your left for the Big Round Top self-guided tour. Park your vehicle in one of the available spaces.

Tour Stop 2

Names and Symbols Carved on Big Round Top

Location: *(77° 14' 20"W, 39° 47' 11"N)*

History: Easily missed by visitors are a number of names, initials, and symbols carved on several boulders on the summit of Big Round Top. They may have been carved by a combination of locals, visitors, and veterans of the battle, and some may even pre-date the Civil War.

LET'S FIND THEM!

The summit is reached via a walking path that begins on the right side of South Confederate Avenue. Depending upon your age and health, the trek can be a considerable distance and elevation, so take your time walking to the top and take breaks as necessary.

All known carvings are on the tops of the rocks and boulders at the very

summit of the hill. As you stand at the highest point on the summit, walk carefully toward the large boulders at the northern edge (facing Little Round Top) that jut out over that side. Be very careful in this area – you will be standing on top of a steep cliff. On the flat tops of these boulders you will see carved names, such as "J. Noble," "J. Hinchliff," and "J. Crumlish." There are also initials such as "WHG" and "WHH." The names Hinchliff and Crumlish are rather unique; a John Crumlish served in the 1st Regiment of New York Engineers, but this unit was not at the battle. Likewise, soldiers named James Hinchliff served in Federal units that were not at Gettysburg. Without further documentation, it is impossible to determine the carvers' identities.

On top of some of the smaller rocks directly behind you are carved geo-

metric designs. They are difficult to discern, but one is in the shape of a star. Note, too, that some of the large boulders at the summit have drilled holes and foundation mounts that once held a tall observation tower on the summit of Big Round Top.

While here, examine the concrete base used as a foundation for the monument of the 41st Pennsylvania Infantry. In one corner are the handprints of one or more small children that were made in the wet concrete, just as kids today press their hands and feet in newly poured sidewalks and driveways. The prints are as old as the monument, which was placed here in September 1890.

Return to your vehicle, and once you have caught your breath from the long walk up and down Big Round Top, continue on South Confederate Avenue to the stop sign at the intersection with Wright Avenue (coming in from your right) and Warren Avenue (coming in from your left). Continue straight ahead and up the slope to the parking area on the left for a visit to Little Round Top. Park in an available space and walk on one of the paths that lead to the summit, which offers a famous and breathtaking view of the southern portion of the battlefield.

Tour Stop 3
Carving of Col. Strong Vincent's Wounding Site on Little Round Top

Location: *(77° 14' 13"W, 39° 47' 28"N)*

History: Little Round Top, one of the most popular areas of the battlefield and a favorite stop of photographers, contains several very interesting rock carvings. An inscription atop one of the large boulders near the summit identifies the rock upon which Col. Strong Vincent, a brigade commander in the Federal 5th Corps, stood as he rallied his men on July 2 and was mortally wounded in the groin by a musket ball. The inscription states: "Col. Strong Vincent fell here / Com 3rd. Brig. 1st Div. 5 Corps / July 2nd 1863." As was the case with many of the rocks scattered around the battlefield, creating the carving was a difficult task. This boulder is hard igneous volcanic rock, believed to be about 180 million years old.

This carving is one of the earliest — and perhaps the earliest — "monument" on the Gettysburg battlefield. The inscription was spotted as early as October 1864 by a journalist from Vincent's hometown of Erie, Pennsylvania, while touring the battlefield. During the decades following the battle, however, the inscription became covered with moss and other debris and was lost to history. In 1883, two aging former soldiers from New York were visiting Little Round Top with veterans from Vincent's 83rd Pennsylvania Infantry regiment. One of the New Yorkers was standing atop the boulder while the group watched the sun go down. When he spied what looked to be part of a carved inscription under his feet, he and the others excitedly began clearing away the debris. When they read the carving, Vincent's veterans began wondering aloud whether a small monument marking the site of Vincent's wounding farther south down the slope (to be discussed shortly) was wrongly placed.

LET'S FIND IT!

Along the summit of Little Round Top is an asphalt path for the convenience of visitors to this beautiful area and viewshed. The eminence was a maelstrom of fighting and death on the late afternoon and early evening of July 2 when Confederates attacked the Federals holding the rocky (and in some places wooded) slopes. Walk south on the path toward the large castle-style monument to the 44th/12th New York Infantry (which was designed by Gen. Daniel Butterfield, General Meade's chief of staff during the battle, and dedicated on July 3, 1893). There, you will find the "Vincent Boulder" on the left just before you reach the monument. The boulder is about four feet high with a rather flat top. This carving on top of the boulder is becoming more difficult to read with the passage of time, but you will often find the carving traced with white chalk or sometimes even paint. Children, unaware of the carving's existence, like to climb on top of this rock and so unintentionally assist in the carving's slow degradation.

Make sure and take note of the small marble slab mounted on a rock farther down the slope in the direction of the 83rd Pennsylvania Infantry monument

(which has a statue of Vincent atop it). The small slab was authorized in 1878 by the Strong Vincent Post G.A.R. (Grand Army of the Republic) of Erie, Pennsylvania. It was the first permanent marker on the battlefield outside of the Soldiers' National Cemetery. The present marker, however, is an exact replica of the original, which was badly damaged in the 1960s. It is said that this stone, originally placed by veterans to mark the spot where Vincent fell mortally wounded, may instead mark the location where Vincent was initially moved to safety before being removed behind Federal lines to a field hospital.

Additional reading: The only modern biography of Vincent, which includes sections about the rock carving and disputes regarding the possible locations of Vincent's wounding, is *What Death More Glorious: A Biography of General Strong Vincent* (Kearny, N.J.: Belle Grove Publishing, 1997) by James H. Nevins and William B. Styple.

To reach the next carving, walk north on the asphalt path until you reach the large and small monuments of the 91st Pennsylvania Infantry (just before reaching the waysides to the left of the path). The carving is in the boulder used as the base for the smaller 91st Pennsylvania monument on the right (east) side of the path.

Tour Stop 4

Carving of the Wounding Site of Gen. Stephen Weed and Lt. Charles Hazlett on Little Round Top

Location: *(77° 14' 11"W, 39° 47' 31"N)*

History: On the summit of Little Round Top in a boulder used as the base for the small 91st Pennsylvania Infantry monument is a carving most assume denotes the approximate location where Federal officers Brig. Gen. Stephen H. Weed and Lt. Charles Hazlett were shot on July 2. General Weed, commanding a brigade in the 5th Corps, took a bullet in the chest early in the evening that cut his spine and left him paralyzed and mortally wounded. According to some sources, these were Weed's last words: "I would rather die here than that the rebels should gain an inch of this ground." Lieutenant Hazlett, whose guns of Battery D, 5th U.S. Artillery, were being positioned on the crest, knelt over his close friend Weed to hear his words and comfort him. A Southern bullet struck Hazlett in the head and killed him instantly. He fell upon the chest of his dying comrade. Note that the 91st Pennsylvania's monument contains an inscription that it is in memory of Hazlett and Weed, and that the two officers "fell on this spot."

LET'S FIND IT!

On the east side of the paved walkway near the much larger monument of the 91st Pennsylvania Infantry, is the smaller monument to the same regiment located among the guns dedicated to Hazlett's battery. Behind this smaller monument on the boulder used as its base is the carving. Note that the carving, which is very faint and difficult to read, is in a semicircular shape. Some observers have postulated that this carving was done by the same hand that produced the Strong Vincent carving, since the letters appear similar in size and shape, and the word "commanding" is identically abbreviated in both examples. The carving reads as follows: "C. E. Hazlett Fell / Com'g Batt'y D U.S. Art'y in Battle / July 2nd 1863."

The next carving is in a boulder next to the small monument of the 91st Pennsylvania Infantry and the Weed/Hazlett carving.

Tour Stop 5
"U S" Carving on Little Round Top

History: On the top of a rock near the Weed and Hazlett carving is a visible carving of the letters "U S" with a circle below it. It may have been carved by a veteran.

LET'S FIND IT!

Locate the taller rock just to the right (north) of the boulder used for the Weed and Hazlett carving. On its rather flat top you will see the "U S" carving and circle. Other faded letters can be seen there as well if you look very closely.

Our next destination is the John T. Weikert farm on the north side of the Wheatfield Road. To reach it, return to your vehicle and proceed north to the stop sign at the intersection with the Wheatfield Road. Reset your odometer to 0.0. Turn left onto the Wheatfield Road.

Proceed .2 miles and turn right into the Weikert farm lane just before reaching Crawford Avenue. After driving about one-half of the distance to the Weikert farm house, pull over at the monument of the 93rd Pennsylvania Infantry, which is on your right side. Be careful not to block traffic on the lane, because even though the farm is owned by the National Park Service, the house is a private residence.

Tour Stop 6

Carved Initials and Foundation Debris of the 93rd Pennsylvania Infantry Monument on the John T. Weikert Farm Lane

Location: (77° 14' 15"W, 39° 47' 49"N)

History: The carved initials "L H M" appear just below the date on the front of the boulder used as a base for the 93rd Pennsylvania Infantry monument on the right side of the John T. Weikert farm lane. Here you will also find discarded stone originally used as the base for an earlier version of the monument.

LET'S FIND IT!

On the front of the boulder used as the base for the monument are the letters "L H M" carved into the face (research into the unit's roster has not turned up a member with those initials). Notice also that "3rd BRIG" is carved into one of the broken rocks resting on the ground a few feet to the left of the 93rd Pennsylvania monument, and "3rd DIV" is carved into a broken rock on the right. If you look closely, you will see similar carvings, which were professionally done, in other

broken rocks lying about. These designations initially appeared in this boulder when it was used as the base for the original smaller monument for the regiment that was placed here in 1884. That smaller monument, which now rests along Sedgwick Avenue across from the equestrian statue of Maj. Gen. John Sedgwick, is worth visiting to see the beautiful blue mosaic cross that adorns its front. When the newer and larger present monument of the 93rd Pennsylvania Infantry was installed on this boulder in 1888, the top of it (including the division and corps carving) had to be sheared off so the boulder would accept and support the new monument. Apparently, no effort was ever made to clean up the sheared pieces, and so they lie here now, scattered about on this hallowed ground for well over a century.

Our next carving is frequently sought out by many battlefield visitors. Tucked away in a quiet corner of a now serene field, it marks the initial burial location of a Federal officer killed on July 2. To reach it, continue toward the Weikert home and park your vehicle near the outbuilding to the left of the home, being careful not to block access to the building or the road.

Tour Stop 7

The "D.A. 140 P.V." Burial Location Carving of Capt. David Acheson, 140th Pennsylvania Infantry

Location: *(77° 14' 17"W, 39° 47' 54"N)*

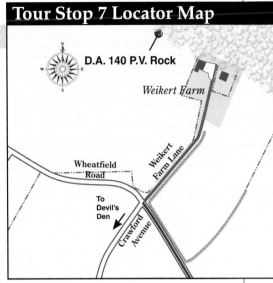

Tour Stop 7 Locator Map

D.A. 140 P.V. Rock

Weikert Farm

Wheatfield Road

Weikert Farm Lane

To Devil's Den

Crawford Avenue

History: One of the most famous rock carvings on the Gettysburg battlefield identifies the initial burial location of Capt. David Acheson of Company C of the 140th Pennsylvania Volunteer Infantry (of the Federal 2nd Corps). The carving is inscribed into a boulder where the twenty-three-year old Acheson was buried. The native of Washington, Pennsylvania, was killed with a shot to the chest on July 2 during the heavy fighting in the Bloody Wheatfield of farmer George Rose against Brig. Gen. Joseph B. Kershaw's Brigade of South Carolinians. While being carried to the rear by his comrades, Acheson was struck at least once more. His brother Alexander (known as "Sandie") reported that David had been struck three times. The next day (July 3) the captain's companions tried to locate and secure his body, but were driven back by Rebel skirmishers. On July 4, after the battle had ended and the Confederates had withdrawn, Acheson's remains were finally located. Like so many corpses, he had been robbed of most of his belongings. He was buried in a shallow grave near one of the large boulders just inside the tree line west of the John T. Weikert farm. With the help of a hatchet or some other sharp metal instrument, a soldier unknown to history crudely cut the initials "D.A." into the boulder at the head of the grave.

Todd and John Baird, cousins of Acheson's father, traveled from Washington shortly after the battle to find the body and bring it home for burial. Lt. James B. VanDyke, a member of Company D of Acheson's regiment, had witnessed the burial and led Todd Baird to the gravesite on July 13. (VanDyke had charge of a squad of men from the 140th Pennsylvania whose unfortunate task was to remain on the field to tend to the dead and wounded.) Acheson was disinterred, placed in a coffin, and taken home by wagon. He was buried in the family plot in Washington Cemetery (Section G) on July 15.

A soldier who served in Acheson's company may have later revisited his original burial spot and deepened the inscribed initials and added the regiment designation. It is also possible, however, that when the surviving veterans hired a Gettysburg stone cutter for the placement of their regimental monument west of the Wheatfield in 1881, they asked the cutter to deepen and revise Acheson's inscription.

LET'S FIND IT!

The Acheson boulder is located just inside the present-day tree line bordering the field on the west side of the John T. Weikert farm. To walk to the Acheson boulder, you need to either climb the fence along the left (west) side of the lane (you may see a footpath through the field at the eighth section of fence from the outbuilding), or walk into the field along the tree line behind the outbuilding.

Note that during the summer and fall, this field is often overgrown and/or very muddy. When you enter the field, you will see the tree line extending behind the home to the west. Follow the tree line westward until it ends and angles to the north. There are several boulders of various sizes in the ground near this angle in the tree line. Just inside the timber (about twenty-five feet) is a rounded boulder slightly larger than most of the others. The Acheson carving is on this boulder, and there often is an American flag beside it. The carving faces out toward the field, and since an eyewitness to Acheson's burial stated that the boulder was at the "head" of the grave, one can assume that Acheson was buried directly south of the boulder, immediately in front of the carving.

Additional reading: For an excellent small book about Acheson and the carving, see *Inscription at Gettysburg: In Memoriam to Captain David Acheson, Company C, 140th Pennsylvania Volunteers* (Gettysburg, Pa: Thomas Publications, 1991) by Sara Gould Walters, a Gettysburg Licensed Battlefield Guide. Information about Acheson and an excellent treatment of grave marking on the field can be found in Gregory Coco's *A Strange and Blighted Land—Gettysburg: The Aftermath of a Battle* (Gettysburg, Pa: Thomas Publications, 1995).

To visit the next several carvings, carefully turn your vehicle around to return to the Wheatfield Road. Turn right on the Wheatfield Road and take the first left onto Crawford Avenue. Proceed ahead until you reach the huge boulders of Devil's Den (note that at this point Crawford Avenue becomes Sickles Avenue). You may find it convenient to park your vehicle in one of the parking areas on the left side of the road just beyond where Warren Avenue enters from the left. From there, you will easily be able to walk to the next several stops.

To see the first carving, walk to the right (western) side of Sickles Avenue and angle to the north side of the boulders of Devil's Den until you come to the monument of the 4th Maine Infantry not far from the road.

Tour Stop 8
4th Maine Infantry Carving Near Devil's Den

Location: *(77° 14' 28"W, 39° 47' 30"N)*

History: The 4th Maine and corps insignia carving is one of three carvings on the battlefield that can be firmly attributed to veterans of the battle. It is near the regiment's monument slightly north of the rocks of Devil's Den; it is well carved by an experienced hand; and, it is believed to pre-date the regimental monument near it (dedicated on October 10, 1888). This carving was only recently re-discovered by Gettysburg Licensed Battlefield Guide Timothy Smith after the area was cleared of thick brush in 1993.

LET'S FIND IT!

If you stand several feet on the far side of the 4th Maine Infantry monument as you face Little Round Top, you can see the carving on a low boulder just a few feet northwest of the monument and near the park road. The boulder is inscribed "4th ME" and features the diamond insignia of the Federal 3rd Corps carved above it. Note the carving can be difficult to find when the boulder is covered with high brush or grass.

To see the next carving, walk back to Sickles Avenue and then walk north on the road to Warren Avenue. Walk to your right on Warren Avenue about thirty yards and you will see the monument of the 40th New York Infantry to your left just beyond meandering Plum Run.

Tour Stop 9

40th New York Infantry Carving in the "Valley of Death"

Location: *(77° 14'26"W, 39° 47'31"N)*

History: Also near the regimental monument, this carving features the regimental designation and the diamond-shaped insignia of the Federal 3rd Corps, and likely predates the monument (dedicated July 2, 1888). Like the 4th Maine carving, it was probably carved by, or under the direction of, a veteran or veterans of the regiment.

LET'S FIND IT!

The carving is in the low boulder right next to the monument on its south side, and can be difficult to see if covered by grass or brush.

To see the next spot, walk back to Sickles Avenue and walk along the avenue to your left toward Devil's Den. When you reach the first parking area on the left side of the road, you will see a path over a small footbridge that leads to the public convenience facility on the other side of Plum Run. As soon as you cross the bridge you will see the next boulder to your left front about forty yards distant in the direction of Little Round Top.

Tour Stop 10
The Trough Rock in the "Valley of Death"

Location: *(77° 14' 27"W, 39° 47' 29"N)*

History: Although not technically a "rock carving," this is an interesting man-made modification of a battlefield boulder. It is unknown whether this feature was created before or after the July 1863 engagement. Someone carved a "trough" into this large boulder in the Valley of Death close to where

the William H. Tipton photographic studio once stood. Along the left side of the groove appear metal clamps, suggesting that someone (perhaps Tipton or an early owner of the land) fashioned a pump to feed fresh water into the trough for animals to drink. In fact, an old photograph exists that shows a horse drinking from this trough. Plum Run is nearby and fresh water springs did and still exist in the area around this rock. Whether a farmer carved it for convenience before or after the battle, or whether it was created after the war for the use of battlefield visitors, is open to speculation.

LET'S FIND IT!

The "Trough Rock" is about five feet high, and the boulder's trough faces you as you walk to it. Upon examination you can easily see the metal clamps in the rock to the left of the trough.

The next two sites are atop Devil's Den. You may wish to walk to the top via one of the footpaths or along Sickles Avenue. For convenience later in the tour, you may wish to drive your vehicle to the top past the famous "Sharpshooter's Den" and park on the right side of the road. Note, however, that parking is more limited in that area. From there, you can easily walk to the next five sites.

The next rock carving is located on top of a low boulder just a few feet to the right of the left flank marker of Capt. James E. Smith's 4th New York Battery along Sickles Avenue, atop Devil's Den, just after the road straightens.

Tour Stop 11
The "P. NOEL" Carving at Devil's Den

Location: *(77° 14' 33"W, 39° 47' 30"N)*

History: This is a carving about which many stories, theories, and local cottage industry "ghost stories" have circulated. One story claims that the name was carved by a mourner who wished to mark the spot where a local young girl named Pauline Noel was accidentally thrown from a wagon and killed. A more nefarious (and some would argue less likely) version of the story claims that the carving was created by the ghostly finger of Noel's spirit, and that bad luck will befall anyone who traces the carving with a finger. However, no one named Pauline Noel ever lived or died in this area.

The most obvious origin of the carving is much less interesting. Research has shown that Gettysburg resident stonecutter Park Noel worked on the construction of several monuments on the battlefield. It is virtually certain he made the carving. Noel was born in 1867 in Gettysburg to William and Catharine Noel, and died in 1942 (he is buried in the town's Evergreen Cemetery). The carving is professionally done with actual stonecutting and carving tools, and displays the talent and certitude found on many monuments and gravestones sprinkled about the battlefield. Park likely made the carving in the late 1880s or early 1890s, when he was performing most of his work on monuments around the field.

LET'S FIND IT!

Once you locate the left flank marker (to the right of the monument as you face it) of Smith's 4th New York battery along Sickles Avenue, the carving is easily discernible next to it. Walk to the flank marker and you will see the carving in the rock beside it.

Additional reading: A very informative book on Devil's Den with a special section on the rock carvings in this area is *Devil's Den: A History and Guide* by Garry Adelman and Timothy Smith (Gettysburg, Pa: Thomas Publications, 1997). Several of the nearby carvings are also featured in the book.

From the P. Noel carving, carefully walk eastward to the top of the largest boulders of the Den. The next carving is atop the large boulder immediately south (to your right as you walk to it) of the small wooden footbridge that spans the crevice between the adjoining boulders.

Tour Stop 12

"J. Tipton" Carving at Devil's Den

Location: *(77° 14' 32"W, 39° 47' 28"N)*

History: J. Tipton, who carved his name on top of Devil's Den, has not been positively identified. He may have been a relative of famous Gettysburg photographer William Tipton. On the faces and tops of many of the Den's boulders, traces of chisel work — efforts to remove the plethora of graffiti in the area — can be easily seen. The Tipton carving, therefore, was likely done some time after 1894 when most of the cleanup work was completed.

LET'S FIND IT!

Examine the flat top of the large boulder immediately south of the small foot bridge. This is a difficult carving to see, and you may have to get down on your hands and knees to scan the top of this boulder to see it. Due to erosion and foot traffic on the boulders, the carving is very faint. You can also see many chisel marks on this boulder and other very faint carvings.

The next two carvings are very close to each other. To see them, walk south to Sickles Avenue and stand at the opening of the famous "Sharpshooter's Den." From there walk across the road and continue directly south to Benning's Brigade's iron marker in front of you. Continue down the hill past the marker, bearing slightly to the left, for about sixty paces (you should be able to discern a foot path here). You will see two large boulders ahead of you. The "Flag Rock" is the shortest of the pair.

Tour Stop 13

Carvings Atop the "Flag Rock" Near Devil's Den

Location: *(77° 14' 35"W, 39° 47' 26"N)*

History: A well-known collection of carvings regularly sought out by many Gettysburg visitors are found on what is commonly called the "Flag Rock" just south of Devil's Den. The large boulder features two carvings of American flags on its rather flat top. One carved flag is rather large and the other quite smaller. Also on top of the boulder are what appear to be the carved initials "UFS" and the date "1873." Other carvings are also visible on top of the boulder, but weather and erosion have made them nearly indiscernible.

LET'S FIND IT!

The carvings are on the very top of this boulder. Please note — if you decide to climb this boulder and the one at the next stop, do so carefully and only with assistance — especially if the boulder is wet. Only the most agile should attempt it with the utmost caution. Young children should never attempt to climb these high boulders. The carvings on the top are not very deep and are difficult to see, but easier to discern when you are standing on top of it during bright sunlight.

The next boulder that features a carving is the taller boulder about thirty feet north of the "Flag Rock" in the direction of Little Round Top.

Tour Stop 14

The "D. Forney 1849" Carving Atop the "Elephant Rock"

LET'S FIND IT!

About thirty feet north of the "Flag Rock" is a taller boulder that many observers note resembles an elephant when viewed from the area of the parking spaces along Sickles Avenue approaching Devil's Den. Using your imagination as you view the rock from that area, you may see what looks like an elephant's head facing to the left, with the trunk below and the rounded body to the right. Atop this rock is the carving "D. Forney 1849" with a diamond symbol to the right of

it. If the date of the carving is accurate, this is a very early pre-battle carving, and evidences the popularity of this area before the Civil War.

Research reveals that the carving is likely the handiwork of David Swope Forney. Born on January 9, 1828, Forney was one of three sons of Samuel and Eliza Swope Forney of Gettysburg. Samuel, known to locals as "Doctor Forney," operated a drug store in town. David was educated at Pennsylvania (now Gettysburg) College, and if he made the carving, it was done shortly after his graduation. The 1850 census listed Forney as "artist," and he became a very skillful portrait and landscape painter. Perhaps he spent a good deal of time atop the rock making sketches of the surrounding landscape. Forney moved to Virginia prior to the war to paint landscapes there, but soon bought large tracts of land in Pulaski and Wythe Counties after discovering and developing several successful zinc mines. The Falling Cliff mine in Wythe County, in fact, is still referred to today as "Forney's Mine." It is certain that he did not serve in the Confederate army (his name does not appear on any rolls), but he did remain in Virginia during and after the war. After dying in Virginia in 1911, his remains were brought back to Gettysburg, and he now reposes in Evergreen Cemetery. He and his wife, Mary J. Warden, had four children.

Use a great deal of caution if you decide to climb onto this high rock, and do so only with capable assistance.

The next carving, which is actually a man-made boundary stone denoting a tract of land owned by battlefield photographer William H. Tipton, can be a difficult one to find, especially in times of high foliage. Proper dress and footwear are necessary. To locate it, walk the foot path that leads from the "Elephant Rock" directly east and follow it when it turns south. When you reach the well-worn horse trail turn left and walk east (carefully) cross Plum Run. On the other side of the creek, walk the footpath to the right (south) along Plum Run about twenty yards and look for a low boulder on your left into which an iron spike has been driven.

Tour Stop 15
The William H. Tipton Boundary Stone

Location: *(77° 14' 36"W, 39° 47' 23"N)*

History: Gettysburg battlefield photographer William H. Tipton purchased thirteen acres in the Plum Run Valley after the battle and established a commercial operation known as Tipton Park. His photographic studio stood near where the comfort facility now stands (near the Trough Rock you visited earlier).

To reach the next destination, return to your vehicle and continue on Sickles Avenue past Devil's Den and take the first left onto Cross Avenue. Reset your odometer to 0.0. As it curves to the right, it becomes Brooke Avenue, proceed .4 miles. Park your car in front of the War Department plaque of Col. John R. Brooke's brigade (2nd Corps, 1st Division, 4th Brigade) on the right of the road.

Tour Stop 16

The Col. John R. Brooke Rock in Rose's Woods

Location: *(77° 14' 49"W, 39° 47' 42"N)*

History: Many of the most intrepid battlefield trampers seek out this "X" carving, which is situated on a large boulder in Rose's Woods. The carving and boulder mark the position that Col. John Rudder Brooke, a twenty-four-year-old brigade commander in Brig. Gen. John C. Caldwell's division, Federal 2nd Corps, took late on the afternoon of July 2 while launching a counterattack against two brigades of Lt. Gen. James Longstreet's Corps. Brooke's powerful attack pierced the center of Longstreet's line and advanced farther than any organized Federal troops on that part of the field on July 2. Although Brooke was forced to abandon his advanced position at the southwestern edge of George Rose's woods, his attack temporarily threw part of Longstreet's line into confusion and bought additional time for other Federal troops to reinforce the embattled sector on and around Little Round Top.

During the postwar years, Brooke regularly visited Gettysburg. During one visit on June 6, 1896, Brooke walked parts of the field with battlefield historian John Bachelder, who later recorded: "Behind the left center [of Brooke's brigade markers] there is a large rock marked with a cross. On this rock General Brooke took his position." It is assumed that Brooke carved the "X" into the boulder himself some time after the war. The location and existence of the carving was lost for nearly 100 years until 1994, when Gettysburg Licensed Battlefield Guide David L. Richards re-discovered the carving using only Bachelder's account as a guide.

is about five feet high. A lower broken part of the boulder rests in front of it. Brooke's "X" carving can be found at the top right edge of the boulder on its right (south) side as you approach it. If you closely examine among the cracks in the rock you will see the carving. It is only a few inches wide and rather faint, however, so it might take a few moments to locate.

Return to your vehicle and continue along Brooke Avenue (it will become de Trobriand Avenue) to the stop sign and turn left onto Sickles Avenue. Reset your odometer to 0.0. Proceed .1 miles on Sickles Avenue (you will pass the Wheatfield but not yet ascend "The Loop") and look for a boulder on the right side of the road in which is mounted a bronze plaque memorializing the service of the 32nd Massachusetts Infantry's surgeon A. Boylston Adams at the field hospital located here on July 2. Park on the right side of the road here.

Tour Stop 17
"P B" Initials Carved Into the Boulder near the Field Hospital Tablet of the 32nd Massachusetts on Sickles Avenue Near the Wheatfield

Location: *(77° 14' 41"W, 39° 47' 49"N)*

History: The initials "PB" appear on a boulder along Sickles Avenue fronting the rock-mounted plaque dedicated to the work done by surgeon Z. Boylston Adams at the initial field hospital of the 32nd Massachusetts Infantry on July 2.

LET'S FIND IT!

On the smaller boulder in front of the boulder-mounted plaque, along the road, you will see the initials "P B" carved into the face. Exactly what or whom they represent is unknown.

We will now proceed toward Culp's Hill, the right flank of the Federal Army during the battle. Continue on Sickles Avenue through "The Loop" until you reach the stop sign at the intersection with the Wheatfield Road. Reset your odometer to 0.0. Turn right.

Proceed .6 miles to the stop sign. Continue straight ahead and after another .2 miles you will come to the Taneytown Road (Rt. 143). Reset your odometer to 0.0.

Turn left onto the Taneytown Road and continue 1.4 miles and turn right onto Hunt Avenue. Reset your odometer to 0.0.

Drive .5 miles and you will come to the Baltimore Pike (Rt. 97). Reset your odometer to 0.0.

Turn right onto the Baltimore Pike, and proceed .3 miles and turn left onto Carman Avenue (there is a sign here that points to Culp's Hill). After another .3 miles, bear right onto Colgrove Avenue and reset your odometer to 0.0.

Continue .2 miles (it will become Slocum Avenue) and you will reach Spangler's Spring on your left, with Spangler's Meadow on your right. Pull ahead and park in a space available ahead of you in the spaces provided on the right side of Slocum Avenue.

Tour Stop 18
"A L Coble" Carving Near Spangler's Spring

Location: *(77° 13' 02"W, 39° 48' 55"N)*

History: A famous carving created by a battle veteran that some visitors seek out is that of Augustus Lucian Coble, Company E, 1st North Carolina Infantry, of George Steuart's Brigade, Edward Johnson's Division, Richard Ewell's Second Corps. It is also the only carving positively identified as having come from the hand of a Confederate soldier. A twenty-year-old private from Hartshorn in Alamance County, North Carolina, Coble served as one of the unit's color-bearers at Gettysburg. At the 50th Anniversary Reunion at Gettysburg in 1913, seventy-year-old Coble ventured out to the area east of Spangler's Spring here on Lower Culp's Hill (on the northeastern portion of the battlefield), to locate a notable spot where perhaps he held his regiment's colors during the battle. Apparently, he found it and decided to mark it. Coble died on April 28, 1928 at the age of eighty-five, and is buried beside his wife Letitia Caroline (Graves) Coble in St. Paul's Lutheran Church Cemetery in Burlington, North Carolina.

LET'S FIND IT!

From the parking spaces, walk to your right (east) along the tree line that borders Spangler's meadow (the large grassy area east of the parking area). The carving is in a large and easily detectable cluster of boulders about 100 feet from the parking area. The carving, which reads "A. L. Coble / 1st N. C. REG." can be difficult to locate. It is carved into the flat surface of the lower rock near where there is a large "cut" between two of the boulders. High grass and weeds can make this one difficult to see, but sometimes it is outlined with chalk, paint, or marked with a Confederate flag.

Reset your odometer to 0.0 and continue on Slocum Avenue. After .3 miles, along the right side of Slocum Avenue that leads to the summit of Culp's Hill (just before reaching the monument of the 29th Ohio Infantry) you will see a small boulder with the plaque of the 14th Brooklyn. Pull over and park on the right side of the road here.

Tour Stop 19

14th Brooklyn Dedication Carving on Culp's Hill

Location: *(77° 13' 10"W, 39° 49' 00"N)*

History: Only a boulder-mounted plaque notes the Culp's Hill service and location of the 14th Brooklyn (84th New York Infantry), placed on September 8, 1890. However, a bold carving in the boulder notes the year the small monument was dedicated.

LET'S FIND IT!

Examine the top of the boulder into which the plaque is mounted. Professionally and deeply carved into the boulder, rather than written into the language of the plaque, are these words: "Dedicated, A. D. 1890." The carving is in large letters and easily seen.

Continue on Slocum Avenue for another .1 miles. The monument of the 149th New York Infantry will be on your right. Pull over and park on the right side of the road here.

Tour Stop 20

Names Carved on Culp's Hill

Location: *(77° 13' 10"W, 39° 49' 04"N)*

History: On the boulder used as the base for the monument of the 149th New York Infantry (dedicated on September 18, 1892), carvings of names and dates appear. The foundation of this monument is a large flat rock at nearly ground level.

LET'S FIND IT!

Stand on the rock directly behind the monument, and you will be able to see some faint carvings. One is the date "1888" and the name "J E Thompson." On the boulder between this monument and the road appear the names "P. Socks" and "A. W. Lightner"

along with the date "1871." Note that the "G" and "N" in the latter name were carved backwards. Since the monument was not placed until 1892, these carvings pre-date that event.

The "P. Socks" carving was likely created by Peter Socks, who lived at the wartime property of James McAllister's Mill along Rock Creek. Andrew W. Lightner, a resident of the Isaac Lightner home along the Baltimore Pike, likely carved his name here. As we have seen along the tour, many locals carved their names in rocks throughout the battlefield before and after the battle, and even more probably await discovery.

To reach our final stop, we need to drive to the first day's battlefield west of town along the Chambersburg Pike (Rt. 30). Reset your odometer to 0.0.

Continue on Slocum Avenue, and after .1 miles turn left to continue on Slocum Avenue (do not continue straight to the summit of Culp's Hill). Reset your odometer to 0.0.

After .2 miles turn left and continue a short distance ahead to the intersection with the Baltimore Pike (Rt. 97). Reset your odometer to 0.0.

Turn right onto the Baltimore Pike, and proceed .8 miles until you reach the town square. Circle two-thirds of the way around the square and turn right onto Chambersburg Street (Rt. 30 West). Reset your odometer to 0.0.

Continue straight on Chambersburg Street, and after .2 miles bear right at the stop light onto Buford Avenue (it remains Rt. 30 West). After another .9 miles you will pass the McPherson Barn (the site of our final stop). Continue a short distance ahead and turn left onto Stone Avenue.

To visit the barn, you may park in one of two places for easy access. Immediately after turning onto Stone Avenue, you may pull into the parking lot of the old guide station on the right. You may climb the fence surrounding the McPherson property and walk to the barn. Since the property is part of the battlefield, you are permitted to walk the grounds. Please note that at times the field may be muddy and/or overgrown. Proceed with caution and utilize proper footwear.

The second best place to park requires that you drive to South Reynolds Avenue to your east and access the barn from that direction from the area of the monument erected to commemorate General Reynolds' mortal wound. To park there, follow Stone Avenue straight ahead, which becomes Meredith Avenue as it curves to the left, to the stop sign at the intersection with South Reynolds Avenue. Turn left here and drive a short distance ahead and park on the right side of the road across from the monument.

Walk to the left (west) side of the road toward the barn. You will need to climb over the wooden fence to walk the field to the barn.

Tour Stop 21

143rd Pennsylvania Infantry Soldier Initials on the McPherson Barn

Location: *(77° 15' 04"W, 39° 50' 12"N)*

History: On September 11, 1889, the monument of the 143rd Pennsylvania Infantry was dedicated on the south side of the Chambersburg Pike on the property of the wartime Edward McPherson farm (worked at the time of the battle by tenant farmer John Slentz and his family). The next day, two veterans of Co. F of the regiment walked to the famous barn, likely reminiscing along the way about their horrendous experiences during the early hours of July 1, 1863, on that very ground. (According to existing records, one of the men was captured on July 1.) Together, they decided to create a little monument of their own — adding (unwittingly) a whiff of mystery for later battlefield visitors who stumbled upon the carving of their initials and unit into one of the stones of the barn. On the south wall of the barn, the following was carved:

JCT 143 PV
SMG Sept 12 1889

Very few visitors have ever seen or even heard of this carving, which was "re-discovered" by Jesse Richards, son of Gettysburg Licensed Battlefield Guide David Richards, in March 2004. The younger Richards noticed the etching while examining the barn with his father. Who were these men? David promptly decided to find out. He researched the names in the unit and matched the carved initials with men whose names matched those initials. According to David, the carving was produced by Jonas C. Tubbs and Singleton M. Goss. Tubbs, a twenty-one-year-old private of Co. F, was captured on July 1. He was paroled at City Point, Virginia, promoted to corporal, and served until the end of the war. Goss, a drummer boy in Company F, was only sixteen or seventeen years old when he enlisted. He also served until the end of the war. Additional research into a list of attendees at the September 11, 1889, dedication of the regimental monument on "Pennsylvania Day" at Gettysburg proved that both Tubbs and Goss were in attendance. Tubbs died in 1909 and Goss lived until 1927.

Besides serving in the same company, both men knew one another prior to the war (they were born and raised near each other, just a few miles north of Shickshinny in the Ross and Union Township areas of Luzerne County, Pennsylvania). Both are buried in the same county in different cemeteries: Tubbs in Marvin's Cemetery near Muhlenberg, and Goss in Bethel Hill Cemetery in Ross Township.

LET'S FIND IT!

The carving is on the south wall (the wall that faces away from the Chambersburg Pike) and appears in the third stone above the top of the wooden vent on the right side of the wall, at about eye level for the average adult. Look carefully — the carving is hardly more than a scratching in the stone. If you closely examine the stones of this grand structure, you will be able to see many of the pockmarks left by bullets that struck the barn during the battle. The barn is believed to have been constructed as early as 1820 and has been refurbished several times since the war. The barn is all that remains of the wartime farm that included the home, a wagon shed, and several other outbuildings.

Almost certainly there are "undiscovered" carvings waiting to be found in rocks around the field, perhaps some of them created by veterans and early visitors. Undoubtedly, many may have been lost due to erosion, and hundreds were removed from the Devil's Den rocks during the cleanup process of the 1890s. Not only are there rock carvings to explore, but many of the

monuments have unique features like this New York monument (below left) on Culp's Hill. Note the lion's head and paw carved into the rocks of the fence.

The search and discovery of these carvings will take you to places on the field the vast majority of visitors never explore or see. Carvings by veterans, in particular, are a direct connection to the past.

Make the effort. Stand where these brave men stood and read their initials or observe their marks. By doing so, you help memorialize their deeds forever.

(Opposite page) The Tyson Brothers took this September 1863 photo of the tents at the Camp Letterman General Hospital. Note the fresh boughs of cedar, which were placed on each tent to ward off insects and help cleanse the air. (NARA)

Tour of Outlying Field Hospital Sites at Gettysburg

"Horror of horrors!"

D uring the heat of battle, the initial level of care wounded soldiers received was at a field dressing station, usually established by a regimental surgeon. Located just behind the fighting line, these stations offered a little protection in the form of a hill, ridge, barn, or tent. Medical personnel bandaged wounds and sometimes administered spirits to numb pain. If a soldier was unable to resume fighting, he was usually transferred by stretcher or ambulance wagon to a field hospital. Field hospitals were established

Tour Route of the Hospital Sites – Federal Hospitals

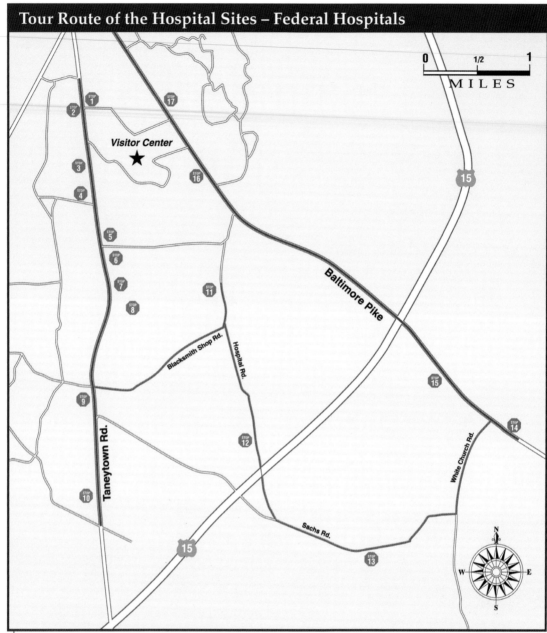

at the regimental, brigade, division, and even corps level. At the field hospital, staff had to decide who to treat, and in what order. Injured men were separated into three categories: slightly wounded, mortally wounded, and those requiring surgery. Surgical cases usually commanded the most immediate attention by surgeons, and typically consisted of amputations and the removal of bullets. The slightly wounded were cared for and allowed to rest, and the mortally wounded were made as comfortable as possible as they awaited death.

This tour of the most recognizable field hospitals sites surrounding Gettysburg is divided into two parts. Part I is the tour of Federal hospital sites, and Part II covers Confederate hospital sites. (Keep in mind that wounded from both sides were treated at virtually every site.) Both parts are subdivided into separate "corridors," which are areas along and near the major roads leading into and out of Gettysburg. The Hospital and Healthsystem Association of Pennsylvania marked many hospital sites in and around Gettysburg with a blue metal sign. (Tour stops that exhibit this sign note that after the name, like this: (HHAP).) Many other hospital sites on the battlefield and in the town are pointed out in other tours in this book.

Please keep in mind that many of the locations we will visit are privately-owned homes and properties. Do not trespass, and respect the privacy of the owners and residents.

The last site we will visit is the Camp Letterman General Hospital, which was established by the U.S. Army Medical Department after the battle to consolidate and care for the wounded who could not be quickly moved from the area because of the serious nature of their wounds.

To begin the tour, start at the exit for the parking lot for the Soldiers' National Cemetery on Taneytown Road. Turn right (south) onto Taneytown Road and set your odometer to 0.0.

. . . .

Part I. Federal Hospitals
Southern Corridor – Taneytown Road (Rt. 134) Hospitals

Tour Stop 1
Catherine Guinn Farm (HHAP)

"Katie" Guinn's two-story log home, which no longer exists, stood just a short distance on your left in an area used by the park for vehicle parking. The original home, built in 1776 by William Guinn, together with the large barn behind the home, served as both aid stations and hospitals on July 2 and 3 for Brig. Gen. Alexander Hays' division of Hancock's Federal 2nd Corps. During the battle, more than a dozen Confederate artillery rounds hit the home, which was only 100 yards behind the 2nd Corps' battle line. The damage made the feisty seventy-two-year-old Katie even more cantankerous than usual, and she was seen yelling at, slapping, and even chasing off Union soldiers milling about on her property. Several burials were recorded behind the home, including men of the 111th and 125th New York, and 8th Ohio Infantry regiments.

Continue less than .1 miles to the next site, which is on your right.

Tour Stop 2
Lydia Leister Farm (HHAP)

This tiny home of the widow of James Leister (who died in 1859) served as the headquarters of Army of the Potomac commander Maj. Gen. George G. Meade on July 2 and 3. Outbuildings as well as a large barn sat to the west of the home. Lydia Leister's property is within the boundaries of the Gettysburg National Military Park and is well maintained.

During the massive cannonade preceding the Pickett-Pettigrew-Trimble Charge of July 3, Meade and his staff vacated the home for safer environs farther south. The barn had already been used as an aid station and hospital, but wounded of both armies soon flooded into the little home. During the battle, both the barn and home were struck by Confederate artillery, and Leister claimed she lost "a heap" during the battle — her house was robbed, crops and hay lost, and all her fences were destroyed.

Continue .3 miles to the next site, which is on your right.

Tour Stop 3
Peter Frey Farm

Frey was a tenant farmer of this property, which is now within park boundaries. It served as an aid station and field hospital on July 2 and 3, mainly for Hancock's Federal 2nd Corps wounded. The stone section of the home is the original structure; the frame section was added later. During the battle, the home was hit several times by Confederate shells and the orchard and fences were completely destroyed. On July 3, Dr. Francis M. Wafer, a volunteer surgeon serving with the 108th New York Infantry, noted that the wounded of both armies covered a quarter of an acre on the property. More than 100 Federal soldiers and one Confederate were buried around the home. The barn was located north of the home along the road.

Continue .2 miles to the next site, which sits back slightly on Pleasonton Avenue. Turn right onto Pleasonton Avenue and the site is on your right.

Tour Stop 4
Jacob Hummelbaugh Farm (HHAP)

The Hummelbaugh farm (which is within park boundaries) served as the headquarters from July 4 to 6 for Maj. Gen. Alfred Pleasonton, the cavalry commander for the Army of the Potomac. It was one of the first aid stations and hospitals established for the Federal 2nd Corps on July 2, and also accommodated men of the 1st and 3rd Corps. On the first day of battle on July 1, Hummelbaugh suffered a great deal of damage at the hands of Federal 11th Corps men following the establishment of the Union line atop Cemetery Ridge just to the west of his home. Men from an artillery unit stole his bay horse, and many bushels of fruits and vegetables were also appropriated, along with sheets, quilts, sundry household items, and chickens. By July 3, his house and barn (which was east of the home) were filled with wounded. On the night of July 2, a Federal officer spotted huge piles of amputated limbs outside the first floor windows. Many soldiers from both armies were buried around the house and barn.

Did You Know?

The most well-known officer treated at the Jacob Hummelbaugh farm was the mortally wounded Confederate Maj. Gen. William Barksdale, who fell on the afternoon of July 2 while leading his brigade into action during Longstreet's assault on the Federal left. The fiery Southern commander was carried here later that day but died sometime during the night. He was temporarily buried in the yard alongside a Pennsylvania soldier. Barksdale was later removed and now lies in an unmarked grave in the family plot at Greenwood Cemetery in Jackson, Mississippi.

To continue to the next site, carefully turn around and return to the Taneytown Road. Turn right, reset your odometer to 0.0, and the site is .1 miles on your left.

Tour Stop 5
William Patterson Farm (HHAP)

Forty-year-old Patterson and his wife Lydia owned seventy-five acres, with a barn on the west side of the Taneytown Road across from his home. Both structures served as field hospitals on the first day, and later for the 3rd Division of the Federal 2nd Corps. Several Confederate artillery shells landed on the property during the battle. A shell fired from the two Southern signal guns that triggered the July 3 artillery barrage exploded in Patterson's barn. The shrapnel tore an arm off of a young black boy, the servant of a New York officer. At least ten Union soldiers were buried on the farm. For a few days following the battle, Maj. Gen. Marsena R. Patrick, provost marshal of the Army of the Potomac, made his headquarters here.

Continue .2 miles to the next site, which is on your left.

Tour Stop 6
Michael Frey Farm (HHAP)

The small farm property of Michael and Sarah Frey served as a field hospital during the battle, probably for Maj. Gen. Daniel Sickles' Federal 3rd Corps, from July 2 to 4. It may also have been a spot where the ambulances of the 2nd Corps were parked and collected to receive their wounded. On the final day of the battle, the Artillery Reserve of the Army of the Potomac (about 100 guns) was gathered in the fields just north of this home. Frey's property probably served as headquarters for the commander of the Reserve, Brig. Gen. Robert O. Tyler. Frey's barn sat just north of the home along the road.

Continue .1 miles to the next site, which is on your left.

Tour Stop 7
Jacob Swisher Farm

Following the battle, the graves of sixteen soldiers, most of them members of Brig. Gen. Alexander Hays' 3rd Division, Federal 2nd Corps, were found directly behind Swisher's home. Companies D and K of the 6th New York Cavalry had acted as headquarters guard for the Corps, which accounted for the burial of two troopers of the regiment there. Swisher's barn was directly north of the home, set back slightly from the road.

Continue .1 miles to the next site, which is on your left.

Tour Stop 8
The Sarah Patterson Farm (HHAP)

Patterson's farm served as the hospital for Brig. Gen. John Gibbon's 2nd Division of the Federal 2nd Corps. Surgeon Justin Dwinell, in charge of the hospital, later wrote that some 500 wounded occupied Patterson's barn and surrounding grounds on the night of July 2, along with wounded from the 3rd Corps and unidentified Confederates. The barn may be the original, but the home is likely a post-battle structure. According to an early map of burials, the dead were interred in three long trenches immediately south of the home.

Continue .6 miles to the next site, which is on your right.

Tour Stop 9
Leonard Bricker Farm (HHAP)

Bricker's stone house, along with his barn that sat across the Taneytown Road and slightly to the south, served as an aid station and hospital for both the Federal 3rd and 5th Corps. Several Federal burials were identified near the house.

Continue .2 miles to the next site, which is on your right.

Tour Stop 10
Jacob Weikert Farm (HHAP)

The well preserved Weikert house and barn served as a hospital for the Federal 2nd, 3rd, and 5th Corps until July 5, and is one of the most well known hospital sites of the battle. The eight-room house, large bank barn, and carriage house were all used by hospital staff and wounded. Dr. Clinton Wagner, chief surgeon of the 2nd Division, 5th Corps, selected the 102-acre Weikert property for a hospital on July 2. Weikert, described by a Michigan officer as a "mean Dutchman," fled to his cellar with his family on the afternoon of July 2, taking the hand crank of his water well with him, and leaving the wounded in his yard begging for the water they could not get. Lt. Ziba Graham found Weikert in the cellar with his hand crank and demanded he turn it over. When the Dutchman refused, Graham threatened to shoot him and Weikert wisely surrendered it. The victorious officer began drawing water for the wounded, many of whom were Confederates.

Many years after the battle, Wagner wrote about seeing three of the farm's most famous patients lying dead on the front porch of the home that evening: Brig. Gen. Stephen H. Weed, Col. Patrick H. O'Rorke, and 1st Lt. Charles Hazlett. All three were casualties of the July 2 Federal defense of Little Round Top. Hazlett was temporarily buried at the east end of the garden, probably near the road. By that night, about 750 wounded were being cared for on the property, including patients from Maj. Gen. Lafayette McLaws' Confederate division.

By the morning of July 3, seventeen hospital tents encircled the home. In them were seventy-five of the most serious cases, with 100 other wounded suffering under tent flies. The barn was jammed with wounded. Nearly 1,000 injured men from both armies were being tended to on the Weikert property. Medical staff dumped piles of amputated limbs across the road that eventually towered as tall as the fence. When the artillery bombardment began that afternoon and shells began dropping on the property (some of which hit the unfortunate wounded), the patients were evacuated farther south to the Lewis A. Bushman farm. After the battle, Weikert sought reimbursement for most of his household items (which were completely destroyed) as well as for his crops, fences, and timber.

To continue to the next site, carefully turn your vehicle around to drive north on the Taneytown Road. While passing the Jacob Weikert Farm, reset your odometer to 0.0. After .5 miles, turn right onto Blacksmith Shop Road. Continue 1.0 mile to the site, which is on your left. Because of the long driveway leading up to the home, most of the buildings are difficult to see from the road.

• • • • • • • • • •

Southern Corridor – Baltimore Pike (Rt. 97) Hospitals

Tour Stop 11
George Spangler Farm (HHAP)

George Spangler's large 156-acre farm is also one of the most well known hospital sites because Confederate General Lewis A. Armistead died here. Two stone markers at the entrance to the home identify it as a Federal 11th Corps hospital as well as the location where Armistead received his final care.

Forty-eight-year-old George Spangler and his wife Elizabeth Brinkerhoff Spangler owned the farm during the battle. Late on July 1, the Federal 11th Corps established its hospital here, and several hundred wounded were treated on the grounds. During and after the battle, more than 2,000 men were cared for at this site, including roughly 100 Confederates.

Hundreds of hospital tents were erected on these grounds during the early days following the battle, and the barn and other outbuildings were filled to capacity. "The wounded are so numerous that some have yet to lie out in the open air," wrote one of the injured soldiers. Maj. Gen. Carl Schurz, commander of a division in the 11th Corps, visited the site on July 4 during a rainstorm. "I saw long rows of men lying under the eaves of the buildings, the water pouring down on their bodies in streams. Most of the operating-tables were placed in the open," he wrote. "There stood the

This 1890s view of the George Spangler farm was taken by local photographer William Tipton. (GNMP)

surgeons, their sleeves rolled up . . . their bare arms as well as their linen aprons smeared with blood. . . . [One surgeon] put down his knife, exclaiming that his hand had grown unsteady, and that this was too much for human endurance, hysterical tears running down his face."

On the evening of July 3, General Armistead was carried here after he fell wounded within the "Angle" during Pickett's Charge. He was treated in the summer kitchen of the home for bullet wounds in his leg and shoulder. Although his injuries were not thought to be life-threatening, he expired on July 5.

According to an early map of interments, there were four long burial trenches immediately south of the home.

To visit the next site, carefully turn your vehicle around to go back on Blacksmith Shop Road. After .2 miles past the George Spangler Farm, turn left onto Hospital Road. Continue .5 miles to the site, which is on your left.

Tour Stop 12
George Bushman Farm (HHAP)

This farm, owned in 1863 by fifty-three-year-old George Bushman and his wife Anna, was the hospital during the battle of Maj. Gen. Henry Slocum's Federal 12th Corps. From July 2 to early August, about 1,200 wounded were cared for here, including about 125 Confederates. The oldest (northern) section of the stone home was built around 1800, and the entire house was completed prior to the war. The large barn that stood here was located just across the driveway fronting the home, and was filled with wounded. (Note the stone marker that designates this site as the 12th Corps hospital.) The initial field hospital of the Corps was located to the rear of Powers' Hill, but Confederate shelling forced it to be moved here late on July 2. According to a medical attendant, the hospital's cemetery, divided into two sections for Federal and Confederate dead, was located east of the house.

Continue .3 miles and turn left onto Sachs Road. After .7 miles the next site is on your right.

Tour Stop 13
Michael Trostle Farm (HHAP)

Officially, this farm (which may have been owned at the time of the battle by John Trostle, possibly Michael's son) served as the hospital for the Federal 6th Corps under Maj. Gen. John Sedgwick. Because that corps was held in reserve during the battle and was not heavily engaged at Gettysburg, there were few casualties to service. The 2nd, 3rd, and 5th Corps used this farm to treat their more numerous wounded.

Several hundred wounded were treated here, including more than a dozen Confederates. Fifty-eight identified Federal burials were found on the property, as well as eleven Confederate burials. The Federal bodies were later removed, most of them to the Soldiers' National Cemetery.

Continue .6 miles and turn left onto White Church Road. Continue .5 miles and turn right onto the Baltimore Pike (Rt. 97). After .1 miles the next site is on your left.

Tour Stop 14
Isaac Lightner Farm (HHAP)

Fifty-three-year-old Isaac Lightner and his wife Barbara owned this 115-acre farm during the battle. From 1857 to 1860, Lightner served as sheriff of Adams County. His three-story brick home, completed in 1862, was nearly new when the armies reached Gettysburg. Although the sign designates this as an 11th Corps hospital, the farm actually served as the hospital of the 2nd Division, Federal 1st Corps (and possibly the 1st Division as well), beginning on July 1. Lightner's large wooden barn, like virtually every other structure in and around Gettysburg, was filled with wounded, and stood in the rear of the home with the main door facing the Baltimore Pike.

In a postwar claim for damages, Lightner noted that all of his buildings were occupied for the treatment of wounded, most of his hay had been used for bedding, and many of his fence rails had been burned. Tents of wounded filled his property until the hospital was closed on July 20.

To visit the next site, carefully turn your vehicle around to drive north on the Baltimore Pike. After .4 miles past the Isaac Lightner Farm, the next site is on your left.

Tour Stop 15
Daniel Sheaffer Farm (HHAP)

Many students of the battle are aware of Federal 3rd Corps commander Maj. Gen. Daniel Sickles' controversial actions on July 2, and that his right leg was amputated after it was badly wounded by an artillery shell. No one knows with certainty where his limb was removed; even Sickles' later account is ambiguous. What we do know is that Sickles spent the evening of July 2 in the Daniel Sheaffer home before being taken away on the morning of July 3 for Washington.

After General Sickles' leg was mangled by a Southern 12-pound round solid shot, the limb was amputated at either a field hospital closer to the battlefield or here on the Sheaffer property, where amputations were performed in the barnyard. The barn, which was constructed of logs, stood behind the present carriage house building. Elizabeth Thorn, the caretaker of the town's Evergreen Cemetery, and her sons spent two days at the home after fleeing their cemetery gatehouse dwelling in the midst of the battle.

This brick home was built about 1780 by Nicholas Mark, and is one of the oldest brick dwellings in Adams County. It served as a tavern for a time during its early years. Sheaffer purchased the 69-acre farm from Josiah Benner about 1845. During the battle, Sheaffer, his wife Lydia Baublitz Sheaffer, and several of their children lived here. The family apparently vacated the home by July 2 for safer environs to the south. The property was overrun by soldiers and used as a field hospital by several units, including men from the 3rd and 12th Corps. Bloodstains still clearly visible on second-story floorboards in the home stand witness that the house, in addition to the barn and outbuildings, was occupied by wounded men.

Continue 1.7 miles to the next site, which is on your left.

Tour Stop 16
Nathaniel Lightner Farm (HHAP)

Nathaniel Lightner's stately and well-kept stone home is all that remains of this farm. Lightner's wooden barn stood north of the home along the road. Hospital staff from the Federal 6th and 12th Corps, and perhaps some from the 1st and 11th Corps earlier during the battle, used the buildings to care for the wounded.

On July 1, the first day of the battle, Lightner had gone into Gettysburg to purchase whiskey and other supplies. After the fighting raged through the town, Lightner finally made his way back to his home late in the afternoon. "Horror of horrors!" he later wrote. "I saw my yard full of soldiers. Under an apple tree I found the surgeons with a man stretched out on our dining table and cutting and sawing a leg off, and on the grass there lay a pile of limbs. I went around to the kitchen door and looked in. . . . The floor was covered with wounded men." Lightner's wife and children had been forced out of the home and took refuge in the stables.

Wounded occupied the house for weeks after the battle, forcing the family to live in their carpentry shop building until the last soldier was removed. Following a period when Lightner's entire family was chronically ill, he completely gutted the home in 1872 and "made the house new from cellar to garret." After the battle, Lightner and his family gathered up many souvenirs from the battlefield to sell in order to defray the costs of repairing his wrecked farm. Lightner was arrested for his deeds by military authorities. Capt. H. B. Blood, "the meanest man in the world, came down to gather up Government property, and he had me arrested," Lightner explained in 1893. "He put me to considerable expense, but my neighbors got me off after a few days. That arrest is the only thing of it all that made me mad, and I am mad about it yet."

Many dead were buried on Lightner's property. A veteran who returned in 1897 and spoke with the aging farmer was told that many bodies were still on his property. Intentionally or otherwise, Lightner had failed to notify authorities of their existence so they could be removed to the Soldiers' National Cemetery or claimed by family members. One of those interred on the property was twenty-nine-year-old Pvt. Augustus Konig (or Koenig) of Co. B, 1st Minnesota Infantry, who fell mortally wounded on July 2 while repelling an attack against lower Cemetery Ridge. The private, who was nicknamed "Beer Keg" by his comrades because the former brewer was (fittingly) shaped like a beer barrel, died on July 3.

Continue .3 miles to the next site, which is on the right.

Tour Stop 17
Henry Spangler Farm (HHAP)

Henry Spangler and his wife Sarah occupied this 230-acre farm, which was owned at the time of the battle by Henry's father Abraham. The battlefield feature known as Spangler's Spring is about .3 miles to the rear (southeast) of the farm.

Originally a log home built in 1744 stood on the property. The house was enlarged in 1819 with the addition of a fieldstone structure on the north side. The large barn was used as a hospital by the 2nd Division, Federal 12th Corps, from July 1 to July 4, when it was moved to the George and Anna Bushman farm. The barn and other outbuildings are now gone. Several Confederates, including a lieutenant colonel from an Alabama regiment, were also treated here. Seventy-eight identified Federal burials were found on the property, as well as five Confederates, indicating that large numbers of men were treated here.

To continue with the tour to Confederate hospital sites, continue north on the Baltimore Pike (it will become Baltimore Street) approximately 1.7 miles to the stop light at the intersection with Middle Street (one block south of the square). Turn right onto Middle Street and reset your odometer to 0.0. Continue .3 miles to the next site, which is on your right.

• • • • • • • • • • •

Part II. Confederate Hospitals
Eastern Corridor Hospitals

Tour Stop 18
Henry Culp Farm (HHAP)

This beautiful property is owned by the National Park Service. Because of its proximity to the eastern edge of town and Culp's Hill, the house and outbuildings served as a large hospital for Maj. Gen. Jubal Early's Confederate division of Lt. Gen. Richard Ewell's Second Corps. Col. Isaac E. Avery of the 6th North Carolina Infantry was mortally wounded in the back of the neck during the July 2 attack on Cemetery Hill. The temporary brigade commander (of Brig. Gen. Robert Hoke's Brigade)

Tour Route of the Hospital Sites – Confederate Hospitals

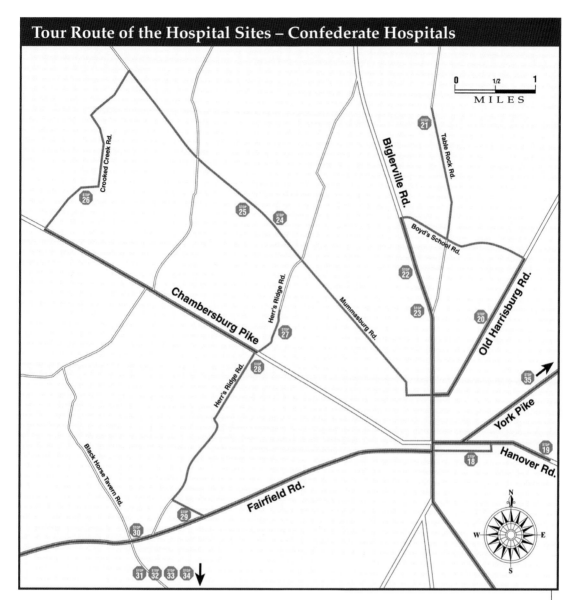

was carried here a short time after he fell. The thirty-four-year-old Avery, son of a distinguished North Carolina family, was tall and weighed more than 200 pounds. After the bullet knocked him off his horse (in the area where the Gettysburg High School stadium now stands), he lay on the ground, pulled out a pencil and a piece of paper, and began writing. The note, one of the most famous of the entire war, was to his friend, Maj. Samuel Tate: "Major – Tell my father I died with my face to the enemy – I. E. Avery." He died at the Culp property on July 3 and his body was carried in a wagon on the long Confederate retreat to Virginia following the battle.

> *To visit the next site, continue for another .2 miles and turn left onto 6th Street. After .1 miles, turn right onto Hanover Street (Rt. 116). Continue .7 miles (it becomes the Hanover Road) and the site is on your left.*

Tour Stop 19
Daniel Lady Farm (HHAP)

The well-preserved circa 1835 stone home of Daniel and Rebecca Lady, which sits on 140 acres, currently serves as the

headquarters of the Gettysburg Battlefield Preservation Association. The house served as a hospital primarily for General Ewell's wounded Confederate artillerymen. A fruit orchard stood to the left of the barn in 1863. Soldiers made several carvings in the interior of the German-style barn and the house and barn were heavily damaged by Union artillery fire from Powers' Hill; the carvings and damage can still be seen today.

In his claim for damages, Lady stated that upon his return after the battle, "wounded soldiers were in the house and dead bodies [were] lying around which [we] were obliged to bury." Many Confederates were buried in the garden and yard. In addition to treating the wounded, evidence suggests that the

The Daniel Lady barn (above) was used as a hospital for wounded Confederates from Ewell's Second Corps. Soldiers carved their initials into a beam in the barn (right). (Stanley)

farm may have served for a short time as the headquarters for General Ewell and possibly for Brig. Gen. John B. Gordon. There is also evidence that General Robert E. Lee may have used or stayed for a time at the home on the night of July 1.

> *To visit the next site, carefully turn your vehicle around to return west on the Hanover Road (Rt. 116). As you pass the Lady Farm, reset your odometer to 0.0. Continue 1.3 miles to the town square and turn right onto Carlisle Street. Continue .4 miles and bear right to follow Business Rt. 15 (the Old Harrisburg Road). Continue .9 miles to the site, which is on your left.*

• • • • • • • • • •

Northern Corridor Hospitals

Tour Stop 20
Josiah Benner Farm (HHAP)

Five hundred acres on this site were sold in 1776 to John Reid, which he called "Spring Garden." The stone springhouse, which stands behind the home, was noted for some of the cleanest and coldest water in the county. The home is well preserved, although the upper front porch is a postwar addition. One account states that General Ewell rested here on July 1 and (according to other accounts) bathed the stump of his leg that had been amputated less than a year earlier in the cool spring water. The farm may have served as an early field hospital for Maj. Gen. Jubal A. Early's Division of Ewell's Second Corps.

Federal Brig. Gen. Francis C. Barlow, the commander of a division in the 11th Corps who was grievously wounded north of town on July 1, was captured and carried to the Josiah Benner farm by a few of his fellow prisoners. He was placed in an upstairs bedroom and eventually treated by Confederate surgeons, who told Barlow the wound was mortal. Barlow survived, however, and was later treated by Federal doctors after the Confederates retreated from the battlefield.

Lt. Theodore A. Dodge of the 119th New York Infantry was also wounded on July 1 and was carried to a bed in the Benner home after being captured. The Benner property was caught in an artillery crossfire, and Dodge claimed that three shells hit the home (one remains embedded in a wall today). One shell set the house on fire (it was quickly extinguished) and another hit above Dodge's room, showering him with bits of ceiling plaster. Dodge was also recovered by Federals and taken from the home by ambulance on July 4.

Continue on Business Rt. 15 for .6 miles, then turn left onto Boyds School Road. Continue for .7 miles and turn right onto Table Rock Road. Continue for 1.1 miles to the next site, which is on your left.

Tour Stop 21
Jacob Kime Farm (HHAP)

This farm, worked during the battle by Jacob and Elizabeth Kime, was owned by Josiah Bringham. The home originally consisted of a two-story log structure built in the early 1800s. The old home, significantly altered since the war, lies buried under several alterations. The present barn was built in 1876 to replace a similar structure that existed at the time of the battle.

The property was apparently used as a field hospital by Brig. Gen. John Gordon's Brigade since records show the burials here were all members from the 34th, 38th, and 61st Georgia Infantry.

Did You Know?

Capt. William L. McLeod, a twenty-two-year-old 34th Georgia Infantry officer, was mortally wounded on July 1 and subsequently buried under one of Kime's peach trees by his slave, Moses. In 1865, Moses and John R. Prescott (the deceased's brother-in-law) traveled back to Kime's farm all the way from Emanuel County, Georgia, to retrieve the remains. According to at least one account, his distraught mother could not then bear to rebury his corpse. William was the first member of the immediate family to die, and the newly established family cemetery had yet to be used. Mrs. McLeod decided her son would be buried there when another family member died. His coffin was kept in the family parlor, where his mother regularly put flowers on it for the next seven years. As fate would have it, the next family member to die was John Prescott — the same man who had dug up his brother-in-law in 1865. A joint funeral was held, and the two were buried together in the family cemetery.

To visit the next site, carefully turn your vehicle around to return south on Table Rock Road. When passing the Jacob Kime Farm, reset your odometer to 0.0. Continue 1.1 miles, and at the stop sign turn right onto Boyds School Road. Continue .5 miles and turn left onto the Biglerville Road. Continue .5 miles to the site, which is on your right.

Tour Stop 22
Samuel Cobean Farm (HHAP)

During the battle, this 136-acre farm was owned by widower Samuel Cobean. His wife Eliza Jane McCollough died prior to the war, but a niece lived here and kept house for him. Both of Cobean's sons were serving in a Pennsylvania regiment in Virginia during the battle. The house was built in 1805, and today the farm serves as a utility property for the National Park Service.

The property has an interesting battle history that begins early on the morning of July 1. Behind the home at the top of a knoll overlooking the Newville (Carlisle) Road was a picket post manned by members of the 9th New York Cavalry, part of Col. Thomas Devin's brigade, Brig. Gen. John Buford's Federal cavalry division. Buford had placed the vedettes of his brigades in a wide arc west and north of the town to watch for the expected advance of Confederates. Shortly after daybreak, firing broke out in the area of the knoll between the New York troopers and Confederates in the Carlisle Road (who may have been infantry or cavalry stragglers from Ewell's Corps that had advanced through Gettysburg five days earlier on the march north toward Harrisburg). Cpl. Cyrus W. James of the 9th New York Cavalry, who was killed during this exchange, is widely regarded as the first Federal to die that morning. A native of Dunkirk, New York, James was initially buried in a private yard in Gettysburg but lies today in the Soldiers' National Cemetery. This encounter took place before the official "first shot" of the battle along the Chambersburg Pike between Buford's dismounted cavalry and the head of Maj. Gen. Henry Heth's Division, which was marching east from Cashtown.

When the battle began in earnest later that morning, Federal cavalrymen warned Samuel Cobean to leave his property. He refused, but moved into the basement when Confederates from Ewell's Corps took possession of the farm. The home was struck several times by artillery shells, many of Cobean's possessions were confiscated, and all of his cattle were slaughtered for food. According to one of Cobean's granddaughters Maj. Gen. Isaac Trimble, who was wounded on July 3 during Pickett's Charge, had his leg amputated in the Cobean parlor. Trimble was moved to the Robert McCurdy home and was later treated at the hospital at the Lutheran Theological Seminary until he was fit enough to be sent to a military prison in Baltimore, Maryland.

Continue .1 miles south to the next site, which is on your left.

Tour Stop 23
William Ross Farm (HHAP)

This 114-acre farm was owned by forty-one-year-old William and his wife Sarah. The barn has been removed, and the existing house may not be the original one. Since a member of the 12th Alabama Infantry was buried here, the property may have been used as a field hospital by at least part of Maj. Gen. Robert Rodes' Division of Ewell's Corps, among others. To support Ross' 1868 damage claim, one of his neighbors affirmed that he saw many wounded Confederates in the home, and most of his crops — at least fifteen acres — were destroyed. Interestingly, the small shed that now stands behind the home was used by returning veterans during the seventy-fifth anniversary of the battle in 1938. At that time, the shed stood near the Eternal Peace Light Memorial on Oak Hill.

Continue south 1.0 mile, then turn right onto Lincoln Avenue. Continue .2 miles and turn right onto College Avenue (the Mummasburg Road). Continue 1.7 miles to the site, which is on your right.

. . . .

Northwestern Corridor Hospitals

Tour Stop 24
David Shriver Farm (HHAP)

This old stone house (with a wooden addition) marked the site of the 150-acre Shriver farm in 1863, which was owned by David Shriver and his wife Susan (or Susannah). Their daughter Mary was married to John S. Forney in 1862, who owned the farm on the south side of the Mummasburg Road across from the location of the Eternal Peace Light Memorial (on the property where the monument of the 17th Pennsylvania Cavalry is located). The Forney buildings were also used as a Confederate field hospital; they fell into ruin and were removed in the early 1900s.

More than 800 wounded Confederates were found on the Shriver Farm after the battle, mostly from Col. Edward O'Neal's Brigade, Rodes' Division, Ewell's Second Corps. A "Dr. Hayes" was in charge of this large hospital. There were many burials on the property, and eleven remains were located in the 1870s, but by that late date only five of them were still marked. The barn, which stood directly across the road from the home, and other outbuildings were filled with wounded. The Shriver's property was used as a hospital for more than one month after the end of the battle. Shriver received from the Federal government a grand total of $242.00 in compensation for the heavy damages he sustained.

Continue .3 miles to the next site, which is on your left.

Tour Stop 25
Jacob Hankey Farm (HHAP)

> ### Did You Know?
> On June 30, 1863, the day before the start of the battle, a Confederate from Louisiana was discovered hiding in David Shriver's barn. He was probably a member of either Early's Division or Maj. Gen. Edward Johnson's Division, both part of Ewell's Corps. In all probability, the exhausted and sick man ended up there after being left behind when Ewell's men marched through Gettysburg on June 26. Dr. John W. C. O'Neal of Gettysburg attempted to treat him, but the Southerner died and was buried somewhere along the roadside. It is not clear whether his body has ever been located.

Jacob Hankey died in 1860, and his farm was being run in 1863 by his heirs, probably by his eldest son David. The farm of more than 230 acres consisted of land on both sides of the road. Like the Shriver Farm, this property was also a large hospital for Rodes' Division of Ewell's Corps. Many Confederate burials were found here, including thirty-nine identified graves. Dr. Charles Krauth, forced out of his home on the campus of the Lutheran Theological Seminary on July 1, cautiously walked with his family through the Confederate lines to Hankey's farm. He later wrote that more than 1,000 wounded Southerners were on the farm by the end of the battle.

The barn here dates back to the war, but the house is of later construction. The original home stood where a stone well exists today along the road in front of the newer home. The old well was part of the front porch of the original home. Maj. Charles Blacknall of the 23rd North Carolina Infantry recalled the importance of the well. Shot in the mouth on July 1, Blacknall was taken to Hankey's farm. "The place is well remembered from the fact that there was a well on the front porch. The demand for drinking water was so much greater than the supply," he recalled. "The well in the Hankey porch was soon pumped dry by thirsty soldiers. But still they came working the pump, jarring the house and adding to the tortures of the suffering officers inside." Blacknall placed a soldier named Coghill to guard the pump, who nearly had to bayonet the parched men while waiting for the well to fill again.

Continue 1.8 miles and turn left onto Crooked Creek Road. Continue 1.4 miles to the next site, which is on your left.

· · · · · · · · · · ·

Western Corridor Hospitals

Tour Stop 26
Christian Shank Farm (HHAP)

This large 300-acre farm sat squarely in the middle of the advance of the Confederates from late June until the start of the battle, and was behind Robert E. Lee's lines once the battle began. Christian Shank, as well as relatives John Shank and Daniel Shank, owned farms along this crossroads that connected the villages of Seven Stars and Mummasburg. Confederates camped on the surrounding fields and on many farms in the area, dismantled outbuildings for firewood and hospital supplies, and destroyed crops. More than 100 Confederate graves dotted the fields in this area well into the 1870s.

Continue .5 miles and turn left on the Chambersburg Pike (Rt. 30 East). Continue 2.2 miles and turn left at the stoplight onto Herr's Ridge Road. Continue .2 miles to the next site, which is on your right.

Tour Stop 27
Michael Crist Farm (HHAP)

Michael Crist purchased his farm of 141 acres just a few months before the battle. Both the stone house and large barn were used as field hospital buildings, possibly by the division of Maj. Gen. William Dorsey Pender, part of Lt. Gen. A. P. Hill's Third Corps. When the battle began, Crist's family and farmhand John Allewelt left the property with their horses, but Michael Crist stayed behind. Most of his fences and crops were destroyed. There were at least two burials on the property, one of a Georgian and the other a member of the 13th North Carolina Infantry, Brig. Gen. Alfred Scales' Brigade, Pender's Division.

To visit the next site, carefully turn your vehicle around to return .2 miles to the Chambersburg Pike (Rt. 30). At the stoplight turn right, then turn immediately left to continue on Herr's Ridge Road. Pull over to the right to examine the next site, which is on your immediate left.

Tour Stop 28
Frederick Herr's Tavern

Thomas Sweeney built this tavern in 1815. Shortly after it was erected, some sources allege, its basement was used for a counterfeiting operation. Frederick Herr purchased the tavern and ninety-five-acre farm in 1828 and ran a successful food, beverage, and lodging house. (Supposedly, he continued the counterfeiting business in the basement and operated a brothel on the upper floor.) Prior to the war, Herr's tavern was a safe stop on the Underground Railroad that assisted escaped slaves on their journey north.

Beginning on July 1, the tavern, directly behind the center of the Confederate line, served as a temporary field hospital. Six burials of members of the 11th and 26th North Carolina Infantry and the 33rd Virginia Infantry were found here after the battle, which indicates it was at least used in part by A. P. Hill's Corps. Bloodstains have also been found on the second-story floor. There have been several additions to the buildings since the war to support the current commercial operation.

To visit the next site, continue .6 miles to the stop sign. Continue straight on Herr's Ridge Road. Drive another .6 miles and turn left onto Fairplay Road. Pause here if traffic allows. Be very careful. Ahead to your right is the Adam Butt home described in the next stop. The ruins of the original barn foundation are to the right of the home. Continue .3 miles on Fairplay Road to the next site, which is on your right at the intersection of Fairplay Road and the Fairfield Road (Rt. 116).

Tour Stop 29
Adam Butt Schoolhouse (HHAP)

Near the time of the battle, Adam Butt purchased the one-room schoolhouse that stood on this property (the present brick residential building integrates the old structure). The previous owner was Samuel Herbst. Butt's home and farm, where he lived with his wife Nancy and four children, is the home you were able to see when you turned onto Fairplay Road.

According to Butt's 1868 claim for damages, both his farm and schoolhouse property were used by Confederate hospital staff for several weeks. Since this property on the Fairfield Road stood along one of the routes of the retreat of Lee's army following the battle, it and many other properties in the area were used as hospitals for quite some time after July 3. Several Confederate brigades used the Butt property, including Brig. Gens. Cadmus Wilcox's and Ambrose Wright's brigades, both of Hill's Corps.

To continue, turn right onto the Fairfield Road (Rt. 116) and continue .6 miles to the next site, which is on your right.

Tour Stop 30
Francis Bream's "Black Horse Tavern" and Farm (HHAP)

Francis Bream, born in 1806, was the first sheriff of Adams County. In 1843, he purchased this property, which consisted of a fieldstone home and tavern, a very large barn, and more than 400 acres of farmland. All the buildings, including the smaller outbuildings, were used by Lt. Gen. James Longstreet's First Corps for several weeks after the fighting ended. Some seventy identified graves were found on the property, with most of the men members of the divisions of Maj. Gens. Lafayette McLaws, John B. Hood, and George E. Pickett. Bream claimed more than $7,000 worth of damages to his devastated farm and buildings, but he was never compensated.

If you wish to visit a seldom-seen and very old area cemetery that was part of Bream's property (and in which a Confederate officer was initially buried), turn right onto Black Horse Tavern Road just ahead. Continue for .1 miles, and on your right is the colonial-era McClelland Family Cemetery. (If you do not visit the cemetery, skip to the end of this section for further driving instructions.)

The McClelland Cemetery, located behind Black Horse Tavern, holds the remains of two Revolutionary War soldiers. After the battle, at least one Confederate was interred here until 1871. (Stanley)

Maintained by the Gettysburg chapter of the Daughters of the American Revolution, the cemetery sits on the hillside and is surrounded by an old stone wall.

At least one Confederate was buried in this cemetery until his removal in 1871. Col. William Davie DeSaussure, an 1838 graduate of South Carolina College, became an attorney but joined the army as a captain during the Mexican War. Afterward he served in state government and in 1855 was commissioned a captain in the 1st U.S. Dragoons (cavalry). When South Carolina seceded from the Union in December 1860, he resigned his commission and the following year became colonel of the 15th South Carolina Infantry. On the afternoon of July 2, 1863 he was leading his regiment against the Federal left flank on the George Rose farm when a bullet pierced his chest. He died soon thereafter. His corpse was carried to Bream's property and buried in the center of the McClelland Cemetery. In 1871, his remains were shipped south for interment in Richmond's Hollywood Cemetery. His remains were removed a third time and reinterred in the First Presbyterian Church Cemetery in Richland County, South Carolina near his home.

There are two Revolutionary War soldiers also buried here, along with many early Adams County residents. Unfortunately, most of the gravestones are disintegrating and impossible to read. Following your visit to the cemetery, to return to the tour, carefully turn your vehicle around and return to the Fairfield Road. You will need to then turn left onto the Fairfield Road, then take the first right to continue on Black Horse Tavern Road. Reset your odometer to 0.0 and follow the directions below.

If you did not visit the cemetery, turn left onto Black Horse Tavern Road across from this site and reset your odometer to 0.0. Continue .2 miles to Plank Road. Turn right onto Plank Road and drive .3 miles to the next site, which is on your right.

Tour Stop 31
John F. Currens Farm (HHAP)

In addition to the area of Bream's Tavern and farm, Pickett's Division of Longstreet's Corps also used this nearby home of John Currens and his wife Elizabeth. The original home was a two-story log dwelling that has been incorporated into the present home (remodeling of the structure uncovered many of the logs). In his claim for damages filed in 1868, Currens claimed that 500 panels of his snake fence were destroyed, in addition to damages to his crops and orchards. Both the home and large barn were used to treat the wounded. Several graves on the property were exhumed during the summer of 1872, and the remains shipped south to Richmond, for interment in Hollywood Cemetery.

Continue .5 miles to the next site, which is on your left. Please note, however, that the road beyond this distance (about .1 miles) to the home is a private road. Please respect the wishes of the property owner and do not drive or walk past the privacy signs.

Tour Stop 32
John S. Crawford Farm (HHAP)

Basil Biggs, a forty-three-year-old black American, lived on and farmed this 289-acre property, which was owned by Gettysburg attorney John Crawford. With him were his wife, Mary J. Jackson, and their five children. (A few years before the war, the family lived on and farmed the now-famous Edward McPherson farm along the Chambersburg Pike west of town.) Biggs, who was also a veterinarian, assisted runaway slaves escaping along the Underground Railroad in their bid for freedom. When the fighting began on July 1, Biggs escaped to York on a borrowed horse.

The site consisted of a stone home, large barn, and other outbuildings. Following the battle, Biggs was one of several laborers contracted to work under Samuel Weaver to exhume the graves of Federal soldiers on and around the battlefield and rebury them in the new Soldiers' National Cemetery. Biggs, however, had plenty of corpses to deal with on his own tenant farm. Nearly fifty identified graves of Confederates were found near his stone home and large barn. The property was one of the primary hospitals used by McLaws' Division, part of Longstreet's Corps, and particularly by the brigades of Brig. Gens. William Barksdale and Paul J. Semmes (both Barksdale and Semmes were mortally wounded during the fighting on July 2).

In his damage claim, Crawford attested that not only had all the buildings been used by wounded, but the dining room was employed for amputations. All of the corn, oats, and wheat were destroyed, as well as most of the fencing. Basil lost $1,500 of his own property. Following the war, Biggs became a property owner by purchasing the Peter Frey farm on the road to Taneytown. He died in 1906 at the age of eighty-seven.

One of the graves found on Crawford's farm had a curious twist. Pvt. Radford G. Gunn of the 17th Mississippi Infantry was mortally wounded near Joseph Sherfy's Peach Orchard during Longstreet's assault on July 2. He died on July 27. His grave was marked with a headboard unlike any other found on the battlefield. A professionally engraved silver plate was tacked onto the board that declared, "Oh God preserve his body for friends." Presumably, Gunn carried this plate with him during his service for just such a use, and his surviving comrades knew about it. Today Gunn, who was a farmer in Egypt in Chickasaw County prior to enlisting in May 1862, rests in Richmond's Hollywood Cemetery.

The Crawford home, which overlooks a closed ford on Marsh Creek, is now called "Farm at the Ford."

To visit the next site, carefully turn your vehicle around to return on Plank Road. After .5 miles from the Crawford farm, a hospital sign marks the next site, which is on your left.

Tour Stop 33
Francis Bream's Mill and William E. Myers House (HHAP)

By the time of the battle, Francis Bream had owned the mill that stood behind the hospital sign here along Marsh Creek for more than fifteen years. All traces of the mill, which was known as "Mineral Mills," are long gone, having burned to the ground in 1896. The most famous Confederate treated here was Brig. Gen. James L. Kemper, commander of a brigade in Pickett's Division, Longstreet's Corps. He was painfully wounded during Pickett's Charge on July 3 when a bullet hit him in the upper thigh-groin area. The main building of the flour mill was a large three-story wooden structure. There was also a saw mill, blacksmith shop, and other outbuildings on the seventy-acre property.

William E. Myers operated the mill during the war. Twenty-seven-year-old Myers lived on the property in a two-story log home, which may have stood where the old home to the right of the hospital sign now stands. The primary Confederate unit to use the Mill property as a hospital, including Myers' home, was Pickett's Division.

Continue .4 miles and turn right onto Black Horse Tavern Road. Continue 1.4 miles and turn right onto Pumping Station Road. Continue .2 miles and turn left onto Roberta Way. Continue .2 miles and turn right at the "T" to the next site, which is .2 miles on your right.

Tour Stop 34
John Socks (Sachs) Mill and Samuel Pitzer's Schoolhouse (HHAP)

The stately home here belonged to John Socks (or Sachs), who operated a mill near this location. This property and the nearby farm of Samuel Pitzer (which can be easily viewed from Confederate Avenue to the west near the Virginia Memorial) were likely used as hospitals. At least twenty-one Confederate graves were found in areas surrounding Socks', Pitzer's, and the adjoining farm of S. A. Felix directly to the north of this location. A one-room schoolhouse also stood on Pitzer's property, which several sources state was used by General Longstreet as his headquarters during the battle. Both the school and Felix's buildings are now gone. As Maj. Gen. John B. Hood (one of Longstreet's division commanders) was being carried past the schoolhouse in an ambulance following his wounding on July 2, a Federal artillery shell struck the canvas roof of his carriage. A witness to the event recalled that the badly wounded general "merely looked up" after the shell tore off the top of the wagon.

To visit the final stop, the site of Camp Letterman General Hospital, carefully turn your vehicle around and drive .2 miles and turn left onto Roberta Way. Continue .2 miles and turn right onto Pumping Station Road. Continue another 1.1 miles and turn left onto Business Rt. 15 (the Emmitsburg Road) and drive 2.3 miles to the Gettysburg town square. From the square, turn right onto York Street (Rt. 30 East). After .1 miles, bear left at the

"Y" to continue on the York Road. After another 1.3 miles you will see the stone marker for Camp Letterman General Hospital on your right. There is space here to carefully pull off (be mindful of traffic) and examine the marker, which was placed here in 1914. The entrance lane to the hospital camp began just on the far side of the marker.

To visit the hospital site (which has been consumed by commercial development), continue ahead to a place where you can safely turn around and return west on the York Road. After .1 miles past the hospital marker, turn left onto Natural Springs Road. Turn left into the second entrance, which is the first entry lane into the large parking lot for the commercial strip building you can see ahead. Follow the lane to the far side of the parking lot where you see wayside markers.

• • • • • • • • • • •

Tour Stop 35
Camp Letterman General Hospital Site

The wayside markers here describe Camp Letterman General Hospital, which was established on July 20 on this land that was part of the George Wolf farm. Shortly after the battle, the Medical Department of the Army realized that the establishment of a large medical facility would help care for the thousands of wounded left behind by both armies and reduce the burdens on area families. Federal doctor Henry Janes, placed in charge of the more than sixty field hospitals in and around Gettysburg, reported that the hospitals contained more than 20,000 wounded, including nearly 5,500 injured Confederates.

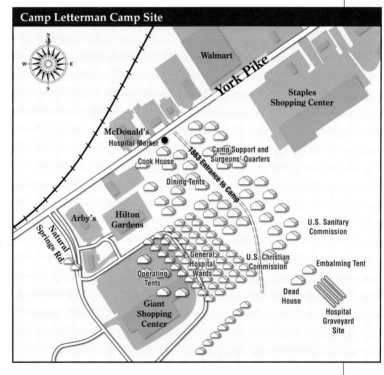

Jonathan Letterman, Medical Director of the Army of the Potomac, was able to send the vast majority of the wounded to established military hospitals, but 4,217 were too badly injured to travel and needed to be treated locally. The site here was chosen by Janes, as well as two other medical inspectors from the department, since the ground was high, dry, and exposed to fresh breezes. The nearby railroad also facilitated the transportation of prisoners and supplies.

Called "Wolf's Woods," the site had been used by locals as a picnic spot for many years prior to the battle. It contained a spring, and wells were also dug to supply the camp with ample fresh water. Once established, the hospital (under the supervision of Dr. Cyrus Chamberlain) was clean, efficient, and well managed. As can be seen on the accompanying map, several rows of tents housed the wounded, and a cook house was erected near the road. A cemetery was established just south of the camp, immediately behind the current commercial strip building.

At its peak, the camp contained more than 400 hospital tents, each holding up to ten patients. On August 30, there were about 1,600 patients here, but by late October only 300 remained. On November 10 there were 100 patients. By November 20, the last of the wounded were removed and the hospital was closed. Many of the dead buried in the cemetery were claimed by family, and the rest of the Federal dead were removed to the Soldiers' National Cemetery upon its establishment (including, by accident, a Confederate or two).

As can be seen on the map, nearly all of the acreage of the hospital camp has been developed and so forever lost.

> *To return to Gettysburg, exit the parking lot and return to the York Road. Turn left onto the York Road (Rt. 30 West) and after 1.3 miles you will return to the square.*

Additional reading

For detailed information regarding nearly every identified hospital site of the battle, readers are encouraged to refer to the late Gregory A. Coco's *A Vast Sea of Misery: A History and Guide to the Union and Confederate Field Hospitals at Gettysburg, July 1 – November 20, 1863* (Gettysburg, Pa.: Thomas Publications, 1988). Coco did more research into the hospital sites and casualties of the battle than any other historian, and his book was heavily consulted for this tour. Several other books by Coco on related subjects will also be of interest, and will be found in the bibliography of this book.

Bibliography

Primary Sources

Newspapers

Atlanta Journal
Baltimore American
Baltimore Evening Sun
Brooklyn Daily Eagle
Charlotte Observer
The Compiler (Gettysburg, PA)
Franklin Repository (Chambersburg, PA)
Gettysburg Times
The National Tribune
New York Herald

New York Times
Philadelphia Inquirer
Philadelphia Weekly Times
Richmond Dispatch
Richmond Times-Dispatch
St. Mary's Beacon (St. Mary's County, MD)
The Star Sentinel (Gettysburg, PA)
Vevay Reveille (Vevay, IN)

. . . .

Periodicals

Journal of the U.S. Cavalry Association

Maine Bugle

. . . .

Manuscript Sources

Linda K. Cleveland Collection, Straban Township, Pennsylvania:

"Hunterstown, Pennsylvania: A Small but Significantly Historical Village," by Linda K. Cleveland, June 2008, unpublished manuscript

"The Jesse McCreary Home, Hunterstown, Pennsylvania," by Linda K. Cleveland, June 2008, unpublished manuscript

"The Tate Blacksmith Shop, Hunterstown, PA, and President Washington's Visit," by Linda K. Cleveland, March 2007, unpublished manuscript

Gettysburg National Military Park Archives, Gettysburg Pennsylvania:

William G. Delony letters of July 4 & 7, 1863

"History of Hunterstown" unpublished manuscript

Historical Society of Pennsylvania, Philadelphia, Pennsylvania:

Samuel Penniman Bates Papers

Library of Congress, Manuscripts Division, Washington, D.C.:

The Gregg Collection, David McMurtrie Gregg Papers, Container 3
"Brevet Major General David McMurtrie Gregg" by David M. Gregg, 1934, unpublished manuscript

National Archives, Washington, D.C.:
Record Group 94, Muster Rolls
"Military History of Brevet Major-General Thomas C. Devin"

"Military History of Major-General Alfred Pleasonton"

U.S. Army General's Report of Civil War Service, M1098.

United States Army Heritage and Education Center, Carlisle, Pennsylvania:

Civil War Miscellaneous Collection
Eugene Blackford Memoir

Gregory A. Coco Collection

George A. Custer Papers

Harrisburg Civil War Round Table Collection

University of Virginia, Alderman Library, Charlottesville, Virginia:

Fitzhugh Lee Papers

Virginia Historical Society, Richmond, Virginia:

Henry B. McClellan Papers

J.E.B. Stuart Papers

Articles

Beale, George W. "A Soldier's Account of the Gettysburg Campaign." *Southern Historical Society Papers* 11 (July 1881): 320-27.

Calef, John H. "Gettysburg Notes: The Opening Gun." *Journal of the Military Services Institution of the United States* (January/February 1907): 40-58.

CEG. "The Hunterstown Fight." *The National Tribune*, October 10, 1901.

Clark, Stephen A. "Farnsworth's Death." *The National Tribune*, December 3, 1891.

Cochran, L. L. "The Tenth Georgia Regiment at Gettysburg: Graphic Description of America's Grandest Tragedy." *Atlanta Journal*, February 23, 1901.

Colley, Thomas W. "Brigadier General William E. Jones." *Confederate Veteran* 6 (1898): 267.

"General Stuart's Expedition into Pennsylvania." *Southern Historical Society Papers* 14 (1886): 480-84.

Green, N. H. "Cavalry Fight at Hunterstown." *The National Tribune*, May 31, 1923.

Heth, Henry. "Letter from Major-General Henry Heth, of A. P. Hill's Corps." *Southern Historical Society Papers* 4 (1898): 151-60.

Hunt, Henry J. "The Third Day at Gettysburg," included in Robert U. Johnson and Clarence C. Buel, *Battles and Leaders of the Civil War*. 4 vols. New York: Century Printing Co., 188-1904. 3:188.

Imboden, John D. "Lee at Gettysburg." *Galaxy Magazine* (April, 1871): 511-513.

Jackson, Henry E. Untitled letter. *Confederate Veteran* 7 (1899): 415.

Lane, James H. "Twenty-Eighth North Carolina Infantry." *Charlotte Observer*, February 17, 1895.

Lochren, William. "The First Minnesota at Gettysburg." *In Glimpses of the Nation's Struggle: A Series of Papers Read before the Minnesota Commandery of the Military Order of the Loyal Legion of the United States.* 1893.

Love, William A. "Mississippi at Gettysburg." *Publications of the Mississippi Historical Society* 9 (1906).

Matthews, H. H. "The Pelham-Breathed Battery, Part XII: The Raid into Maryland, Hanover and Carlisle, Pa., Up to and including Gettysburg." *St. Mary's Beacon*, April 20, 1905.

Matoon, G. W. "Custer's Fight at Hunterstown." *The National Tribune*, November 21, 1901.

McClellan, Henry B. "Stuart at Gettysburg." *Philadelphia Weekly Times*, October 6, 1877.

Mosby, John S. "General Stuart at Gettysburg." *Philadelphia Weekly Times*, December 15, 1877.

Parsons, Henry C. "Gettysburg: The Campaign was a Chapter of Accidents." *The National Tribune*, August 7, 1890.

Paul, E. A. "Operations of Our Cavalry – The Michigan Cavalry Brigade." *New York Times*, August 6, 1863.

Pennypacker, Samuel W. "Six Weeks in Uniform: Being the Record of a Term in the Military Service of the United States in the Gettysburg Campaign of 1863." In *Historical and Biographical Sketches*. Philadelphia, Pa.: R. A. Tripple, 1883.

Pleasonton, Alfred. "The Campaign of Gettysburg," included in Alexander K. McClure, ed. *The Annals of the War: Written by Leading Participants North & South.* Philadelphia, Pa.: The Times Publishing Co., 1878: 447-459.

Schurz, Carl. "The Battle of Gettysburg." *McClure's*, Vol. 29, July 1907.

Toms, George W. "Kilpatrick's Cavalry at the Battle of Gettysburg." *The National Tribune,* September 17, 1885.

Wolf, Hazel C., ed. "Campaigning with the First Minnesota: A Civil War Diary." *Minnesota History* 25, No. 4 (December 1944): 342-61.

· · · · · · · · · · ·

Books

Alexander, Edward Porter. *Fighting for the Confederacy: The Personal Recollections of General Edward Porter Alexander*. Gary W. Gallagher, ed. Chapel Hill: University of North Carolina Press, 1989.

——. *Military Memoirs of a Confederate*. New York: Charles Scribner's Sons, 1907.

Baines, Charles H. *A History of the Philadelphia Brigade*. Philadelphia, Pa.: J.B. Lippincott & Co., 1876.

Beale, George W. *A Lieutenant of Cavalry in Lee's Army*. Boston: Gorham Press, 1918.

Beale, Richard L. T. *History of the Ninth Virginia Cavalry in the War Between the States*. Richmond, Va.: B. F. Johnson Publishing Co., 1899.

Benedict, George Greenville. *Army life in Virginia: Letters from the Twelfth Vermont Regiment and Personal Experiences of Volunteer Service in the War for the Union, 1862-63*. Burlington, Free Press Assoc., 1895.

Best, Issac O. *History of the 121st New York Infantry*. Chicago, Ill.: Jason H. Smith, 1921.

Biddle, Chapman. *The First Day of the Battle of Gettysburg – An Address Delivered Before the Historical Society of Pennsylvania, On the 8th of March, 1880*. Philadelphia, Pa.: J. B. Lippincott & Co., 1880.

Bigelow, John. *The Peach Orchard, Gettysburg, July 2, 1863*. Minneapolis, MN: Kimball-Storer Co., 1910.

Blackford, William W. *War Years with Jeb Stuart*. New York: Charles Scribner's Sons, 1945.

Brooke-Rawle, William, ed. *History of the Third Pennsylvania Cavalry in the American Civil War of 1861-1865*. Philadelphia, Pa.: Franklin Printing Co., 1905.

Brooke-Rawle, William. *The Right Flank at Gettysburg: An Account of the Operations of General Gregg's Cavalry Command*. Philadelphia, Pa.: Privately published, 1878.

Brown, J. Willard. *The Signal Corps in the War of the Rebellion*. Boston, Mass.: U.S. Veteran Signal Corps Association, 1896.

Buehler, Fannie J. *Recollections of the Rebel Invasion and One Woman's Experience During the Battle of Gettysburg*. Gettysburg, Pa.: Star and Sentinel Print, 1900.

Caldwell, J. F. J. *The History of a Brigade of South Carolinians, Known First as "Gregg's" and Subsequently as "McGowan's Brigade."* Philadelphia, Pa.: King & Baird, 1866.

Casler, John O. *Four Years in the Stonewall Brigade*. Guthrie, OK.: Privately published, 1893.

Cheney, Newell, comp. *History of the Ninth Regiment, New York Volunteer Cavalry, War of 1861 to 1865*. Poland Center, N.Y.: Martin Merz & Son, 1901.

Clark, Stan Jr., comp. *Bayonet! Forward: My Reminiscences by Joshua Lawrence Chamberlain*. Gettysburg, Pa.: Stan Clark Military Books, 1994.

Confederate Reminiscences and Letters 1861 to 1865. 10 vols. Atlanta, GA.: Georgia Division, United Daughters of the Confederacy, 1994-2001.

Cooke, John Esten. *Wearing of the Gray: Being Personal Portraits, Scenes & Adventures of the War*. New York: E. B. Treat & Co., 1867.

Cozzens, Peter, ed. *Battles & Leaders of the Civil War, Volume 5*. Chicago, Ill.: University of Illinois Press, 2002.

——. *Battles & Leaders of the Civil War, Volume 6*. Chicago, Ill.: University of Illinois Press, 2004.

Cozzens, Peter and Robert I. Girardi, ed. *The New Annals of the Civil War*. Mechanicsburg, Pa.: Stackpole Books, 2004.

Curtis, Orson B. *History of the Twenty-Fourth Michigan of the Iron Brigade, Known as the Detroit and Wayne County Regiment*. Detroit, MI.: Winn & Hammond, 1891.

Doubleday, Abner. *Chancellorsville and Gettysburg*. New York: Charles Scribner's Sons, 1882.

Douglas, Henry Kyd. *I Rode With Stonewall*. Chapel Hill, N.C.: The University of North Carolina Press, 1940.

Garnett, Theodore Sanford. *Riding with Stuart: Reminiscences of an Aide-de-Camp*. Robert J. Trout, ed. Shippensburg, Pa.: White Mane, 1994.

Gettysburg Battle Field Commission of Michigan. Michigan at Gettysburg, July 1st, 2nd and 3rd, 1863. Detroit, Mich.: Winn & Hammond, 1889.

Gettysburg Battle-field Commission of New Jersey. State of New Jersey: Final Report of the Gettysburg Battle-field Commission, 1891. Trenton, N.J.: John L. Murphy Publishing Company, 1891.

Gillespie, Samuel L. *A History of Company A, First Ohio Cavalry, 1861-1865*. Washington Court House, Ohio: Press of Ohio State Register, 1898.

Goldsborough, W.W. *The Maryland Line in the Confederate Army, 1861-1865*. Baltimore, Md.: Press of Guggenheimer, Weil & Co., 1900.

Gregg, David M. *The Second Cavalry Division of the Army of the Potomac in the Gettysburg Campaign*. Philadelphia: Privately published, 1907.

Haden, Benjamin J. *Reminiscences of J.E.B. Stuart's Cavalry*. Charlottesville, Va.: Progress Publishing Co., 1912.

Hard, Abner N. *History of the Eighth Cavalry Regiment, Illinois Volunteers During the Great Rebellion*. Aurora, Ill.: Privately published, 1868.

History of Adams County, Pennsylvania. Chicago, Ill.: Warner, Beers & Co., 1886 (Reprint by Adams County Historical Society, Gettysburg, Pa., 1992).

Hoke, Jacob. *The Great Invasion of 1863, or General Lee in Pennsylvania*. Dayton, OH: W. J. Shuey, 1887.

Holcombe, Return I. *History of the First Regiment Minnesota Volunteer Infantry*. Stillwater, Minn.: Easton & Masterman Printers, 1916.

Horner, John B., ed. *The Letters of Major Robert Bell*. Gettysburg, Pa.: Horner Enterprises, 2005.

Howard, Wiley C. *Sketch of Cobb Legion Cavalry and Some Scenes and Incidents Remembered*. Atlanta, Ga.: Atlanta Camp 159, Sons of Confederate Veterans, 1901.

Husby, Karla J. and Eric J. Wittenberg, eds. *Under Custer's Command: The Civil War Journal of James Henry Avery*. Dulles, Va.: Brassey's Inc., 2000.

Ide, Horace K. *History of the 1st Vermont Cavalry Volunteers in the War of the Great Rebellion*. Elliot W. Hoffman, ed. Baltimore, Md.: Butternut & Blue, 2000.

Isham, Asa B. *An Historical Sketch of the Seventh Regiment Michigan Volunteer Cavalry*. New York: Town Topics Publishing Company, 1893.

Jackson, H. Nelson, comp. *Dedication of the Statue to Brevet Major-General William Wells*. Privately published, 1914.

Jacobs, Michael. *Notes on the Rebel Invasion of Maryland and Pennsylvania and the Battle of Gettysburg, July 1st, 2d, 3d, 1863*. Philadelphia, Pa.: J.B. Lippincott, 1863.

Johnson, Robert U. and Clarence C. Buel, ed. *Battles and Leaders of the Civil War. 4 vols.* New York: The Century Co., 1888-1904.

Jones, Terry L., ed. *Campbell Brown's Civil War: With Ewell and the Army of Northern Virginia*. Baton Rouge, La.: Louisiana State University Press, 2001.

Kidd, James H. *Personal Recollections of a Cavalryman with Custer's Michigan Brigade in the Civil War*. Ionia, Mich.: Sentinel Printing Co., 1908.

Ladd, David L. and Audrey J., eds. *The Bachelder Papers: Gettysburg In Their Own Words*. 3 volumes including maps. Dayton, Ohio: Morningside Press, 1995.

Lang, Theodore F. *Loyal West Virginia from 1861-1865*. Baltimore, Md.: The Deutsch Publishing Co., 1895.

Lee, William O., comp. *Personal and Historical Sketches and Facial History of an by Members of the Seventh Regiment Michigan Volunteer Cavalry 1862-1865*. Detroit, Mich.: 7th Michigan Cavalry Assoc., 1902.

Longstreet, James. *From Manassas to Appomattox: Memoirs of the Civil War in America*. Philadelphia: J. B. Lippincott Co., 1896.

Mahan, Dennis Hart. *Advanced-Guard, Outpost, and Detachment Service of Troops, with the Essential Principals of Strategy, and Grand Tactics*. New York: John Wiley, 1863.

Marshall, Charles. *An Aide-de-Camp of Lee*. Sir Frederick Maurice, ed. Boston, Little, Brown & Co., 1927.

McClure, Alexander K., ed. *The Annals of the War: Written by Leading Participants North & South*. Philadelphia, Pa.: Philadelphia Weekly Times Publishing, 1878.

McLean, James L., Jr. and Judy W. McLean, comp. *Gettysburg Sources*. 3 vols. Baltimore, Md.: Butternut and Blue, 1986-1990.

McClellan, Henry B. *The Life and Campaigns of Major General J. E. B. Stuart*. Boston: Houghton-Mifflin, 1895.

McDonald, William M. *A History of the Laurel Brigade, Originally Ashby's Cavalry*. Baltimore, Md.: Sun Job Printing Office, 1907.

Michigan Monument Commission. *Michigan at Gettysburg: July 1, 2, 3, 1863*. Detroit, Mich.: Winn & Hammond, 1889.

Morrison, James L., ed. *The Memoirs of Henry Heth*. Westport, Conn.: Greenwood Press, 1974.

Myers, Frank M. *The Comanches: A History of White's Battalion, Virginia Cavalry*. Baltimore, Md.: Piet & Co., 1871.

New York Monuments Commission. *New York at Gettysburg*. 3 vols. Albany, N.Y.: J. B. Lyon Co., 1902.

Nicholson, John P., comp. *Pennsylvania at Gettysburg: Ceremonies at the Dedication of the Monuments Erected by the Commonwealth of Pennsylvania to Mark the Positions of the Pennsylvania Commands Engaged in the Battle*. 4 vols. Harrisburg, Pa.: B. Singerly, 1893.

Norton, Henry. *A Sketch of the 8th N.Y. Cavalry, Unwritten History of the Rebellion*. Privately published, 1888.

Norton, Oliver Willcox. *The Attack and Defense of Little Round Top, Gettysburg, July 2, 1863*. Privately published, 1913.

Pennypacker, Samuel Whitaker. *The Autobiography of a Pennsylvanian: Samuel Whitaker Pennypacker*. Philadelphia, Pa.: The John C. Winston Company, 1918.

Pickerill, W. N. *History of the Third Indiana Cavalry*. Indianapolis, IN: Aetna Printing Co., 1906.

Preston, Noble D. *History of the Tenth Regiment of Cavalry New York State Volunteers*. New York: D. Appleton & Co., 1892.

Robertson, John, comp. *Michigan in the War*. Lansing, Mich.: W. S. George & Co., 1882.

Scott, James K. P. *The Stories of the Battles at Gettysburg*. Harrisburg, Pa.: The Telegraph Press, 1927.

Skelly, Daniel Alexander. *A Boy's Experiences During the Battle of Gettysburg*. Gettysburg, Pa.: Privately published, 1932.

Sorrel, G. Moxley. *Recollections of a Confederate Staff Officer*. New York: Neal Pub. Co., 1905.

Taylor, Walter H. *Four Years With General Lee*. New York: D. Appleton, 1877.

Tobie, Edward P. *History of the First Maine Cavalry, 1861-1865*. Boston, Mass.: Press of Emory & Hughes, 1887.

Tooms, Samuel. *New Jersey Troops in the Gettysburg Campaign, From June 5 to July 31, 1863*. Orange, N.J.: Evening Mail Publishing House, 1888.

Tremain, Henry Edwin. *Two Days of War: A Gettysburg Narrative and Other Excursions*. New York: Bonnell, Silver and Bowers, 1905.

United States War Department. *The War of the Rebellion: A Compilation of the Official Records of the Union and Confederate Armies*. 70 vols. in 128 parts. Washington, D.C.: Government Printing Office, 1880-1901.

Walker, Francis Amasa. *History of the Second Army Corps in the Army of the Potomac*. New York: Charles Scribner's Sons, 1886.

Weaver, T. C. *Third Indiana Cavalry: A Brief Account of the Actions In Which They Took Part*. Greenwood, IN: Privately published, 1919.

Wittenberg, Eric J., ed. *At Custer's Side: The Civil War Writings of James Harvey Kidd*. Kent, Ohio: The Kent State University Press, 2000.

———. *One of Custer's Wolverines: The Civil War Letters of Bvt. Brig. Gen. James H. Kidd, Sixth Michigan Cavalry*. Kent, Ohio: The Kent State University Press, 1999.

· · · · · · · · · ·

Secondary Sources
Articles

Adelman, Garry E. "Hazlett's Battery at Gettysburg." *Gettysburg Magazine* 21 (July 1999): 64-73.

Alexander, Ted. "Gettysburg Cavalry Operations, June 27 – July 3, 1863." *Blue&Gray Magazine* Vol. 6, No. 1 (October 1988): 8-41.

Barnett, Bert. "Union Artillery on July 3." In *Programs of the Sixth Annual Gettysburg Seminar*. Gettysburg, Pa.: Gettysburg National Military Park (1998): 205-246.

Black, Linda G. "War Comes to Professor Michael Jacobs." *Gettysburg Magazine* 6 (January 1992): 99-105.

Burger, T.W. "First to Fall." *Civil War Times Illustrated*, Vol. 39, No. 4 (August 2000): 32-38.

Campbell, Eric A. "A Field Made Glorious: Cemetery Hill: From Battlefield to Sacred Ground." *Gettysburg Magazine* 15 (July 1996): 107-128.

Chapman, John M. "Comanches on the War Path: The 35th Battalion Virginia Cavalry in the Gettysburg Campaign." *Civil War Regiments*, Vol. 6, No. 3 (1999): 1-30.

Clouser, Jeff. "Stories of the Stones." *Civil War Times Illustrated*, Vol. 37, No. 4 (August 1998): 32-36.

Cooksey, Paul Clark. "Around the Flank: Longstreet's July 2 Attack at Gettysburg." *Gettysburg Magazine* 29 (July 2003): 94-105.

———. "Of Hooves and Shoes: Two Controversies at Gettysburg." *Gettysburg Magazine* 36 (January 2007): 116-124.

———. "They Died as if on Dress Parade: The Annihilation of Iverson's Brigade at Gettysburg and the Battle of Oak Ridge." *Gettysburg Magazine* 20 (January 1999) 89-112.

——. "Up the Emmitsburg Road: Gen. Robert E. Lee's Plan for the Attack on July 2 on the Union Left Flank." *Gettysburg Magazine* 26 (January 2002): 45-52.

Deppen, John. "Old and Valued Friends: Generals Lewis Armistead and Winfield Scott Hancock." *Gettysburg Magazine* 34 (January 2006): 41-50.

Dreese, Michael A. "Ordeal in the Lutheran Theological Seminary: The Recollections of First Lt. Jeremiah Hoffman, 142nd Pennsylvania Volunteers." *Gettysburg Magazine* 23 (July 2000), 100-110.

Dougherty, James J. "A History of the McPherson Farm at Gettysburg." *Gettysburg Magazine* 26 (January 2002): 20-44.

Downs, David B. "His Left was Worth a Glance: Meade and the Union Left on July 2, 1863." *Gettysburg Magazine* 7 (July 1992): 29-40.

Elmore, Thomas L. "Torrid Heat and Blinding Rain: A Meteorological and Astronomical Chronology of the Gettysburg Campaign." *Gettysburg Magazine* 13 (July 1995): 7-21.

Fennell, Charlie. "George Greene's Defense of Culp's Hill." *Blue&Gray Magazine*, Vol. 20, No. 2 (2002): 6-14.

Gorman, Paul R. "J.E.B. Stuart and Gettysburg." *Gettysburg Magazine* 1 (July 1989): 86-92.

Grogan, Michael S. "Buford's Valiant Stand at Gettysburg." *Military History* (June 1997): 62-68.

Haines, Douglas Craig. "Before the Setting of Another Sun: The Advance of Ewell's Corps June 18 through June 29." *Gettysburg Magazine* 33 (July 2005): 7-26.

——. "Lee's Advance Along the Cashtown Road." *Gettysburg Magazine* 23 (July 2000): 6-29.

——. "R. S. Ewell's Command June 29 – July 1, 1863." *Gettysburg Magazine* 9 (July 1993): 17-32.

Hartwig, D. Scott. "The 11th Army Corps on July 1, 1863 – The Unlucky 11th." *Gettysburg Magazine* 2 (January 1990): 33-49.

——. "The Fate of a Country: The Repulse of Longstreet's Assault by the Army of the Potomac." In *Programs of the Sixth Annual Gettysburg Seminar*. Gettysburg, Pa.: Gettysburg National Military Park (1998): 247-289.

——. "Guts and Good Leadership: The Action at the Railroad Cut, July 1, 1863." *Gettysburg Magazine* 1 (July 1989): 5-14.

——. "I Have Never Seen the Like Before: Herbst Woods, July 1, 1863." In *Papers of the Tenth Gettysburg National Military Park Seminar*. Gettysburg, Pa.: Gettysburg National Military Park (2005): 155-196.

——. "Never Have I Seen Such a Charge: Pender's Light Division at Gettysburg, July 1." In *Programs of the Seventh Annual Gettysburg Seminar*. Gettysburg, Pa.: Gettysburg National Military Park (2000): 37-60.

Hassler, William W. "Harry Heth: Lee's Hard-Luck General." *Civil War Times Illustrated*, Vol. 5, No. 4 (July 1966): 12-20.

Heiser, John S. "The High Water Mark of an Army: The Army of Northern Virginia in the Gettysburg Campaign." In *Programs of the Seventh Annual Gettysburg Seminar*. Gettysburg, Pa.: Gettysburg National Military Park (2000): 1-17.

Hempel, Katherine. "Gone and Nearly Forgotten: David McConaughy, the Man Behind the Soldiers' National Cemetery and the Gettysburg National Military Park." *Gettysburg Magazine* 34 (January 2006): 86-97.

Herdegen, Lance J. "Old Soldiers and War Talk – the Controversy Over the Opening Infantry Fight at Gettysburg." *Gettysburg Magazine* 2 (January 1990): 15-24.

Hintz, Kalina Ingham. "Dinna Forget: The Gettysburg Monuments to General John F. Reynolds." *Gettysburg Magazine* 31 (July 2004): 88-111.

——. "When the General Fell: The Monumental Death of John F. Reynolds." *Blue&Gray Magazine*, Vol. 22, No. 2 (2005): 24-28.

King, G. Wayne. "General Judson Kilpatrick." *New Jersey History* 91 (Spring 1973): 35-52.

Krolick, Marshall D. "Forgotten Field: The Cavalry Battle East of Gettysburg on July 3, 1863." *Gettysburg Magazine* 4 (January 1991): 75-88.

Kross, Gary. "Gettysburg Vignettes – Action on the Eastern Flank." *Blue&Gray Magazine*, Vol. 14, No. 5 (1997): 6-22/47-65.

——. "Gettysburg Vignettes – Attack from the West." *Blue&Gray Magazine*, Vol. 17, No. 5 (2000): 6-22/44-65.

——. "Gettysburg Vignettes – To Die Like Soldiers." *Blue&Gray Magazine*, Vol. 15, No. 5 (1998): 6-25/50-65.

Krumweide, John F. "A July Afternoon on McPherson's Ridge." *Gettysburg Magazine* 21 (July 1999): 21-44.

Kushlan, James P. "Behind the Lines: A Note from the Editor – The Puddingstone." *Civil War Times Illustrated*, Vol. 37, No. 3 (August 1998): 4.

Ladd, David L. and Audrey J. Ladd. "Stuart's and Gregg's Cavalry Engagement, July 3, 1863." *Gettysburg Magazine* 16 (January 1997): 95-110.

Latschar, Terry. "My Brave Texans, Forward and Take Those Heights!: Jerome Bonapart Robertson and the Texas Brigade." In *Programs of the Ninth Gettysburg National Military Park Seminar*. Gettysburg, Pa.: Gettysburg National Military Park (2002): 122-142.

Longacre, Edward G. "Judson Kilpatrick." *Civil War Times Illustrated*, Vol. 10, No. 1 (April 1971): 24-33.

Magner, Blake A. "The Gettysburg Soldiers' National Cemetery: Yesterday and Today." *Gettysburg Magazine* 14 (January 1996): 102-112.

Martin, James L. "Dreaming the Confederacy: The Lost Cause, the Mind of the South, and the Confederate Memorials at Gettysburg." *Gettysburg Magazine* 34 (January 2006): 98-127.

Martz, Jason A. "It Was Not a Happy Time: What the Civilians of Gettysburg Saw and Heard During the Battle." *Gettysburg Magazine* 18 (January 1988): 114-128.

Murray, R. L. "Cowan's, Cushing's and Rorty's Batteries in Action During the Pickett-Pettigrew-Trimble Charge." *Gettysburg Magazine* 35 (July 2006): 39-53.

Musto, R. J. "The Treatment of the Wounded at Gettysburg: Jonathan Letterman: The Father of Modern Battlefield Medicine." *Gettysburg Magazine* 37 (July 2007): 120-127.

Nye, Wilbur Sturtevant. "The Affair at Hunterstown." *Civil War Times Illustrated* (February 1971): 29-30.

O'Brien, Kevin E. "Glory Enough for All: Lt. William Brooke-Rawle and the 3rd Pennsylvania Cavalry at Gettysburg." *Gettysburg Magazine* 13 (July 1995): 89-107.

——. "Valley of the Shadow of Death: Col. Strong Vincent and the Eighty-Third Pennsylvania Infantry at Little Round Top." *Gettysburg Magazine* 7 (July 1992): 41-49.

Orr, Timothy J. "On Such Slender Threads Does the Fate of Nations Depend: The Second United States Sharpshooters Defend the Union Left." In *Papers of the 2006 Gettysburg National Military Park Seminar*. Gettysburg, Pa.: Gettysburg National Military Park (2008): 121-146.

Patterson, Gerald A. "George E. Pickett: A Personality Profile." *Civil War Times Illustrated*, Vol. 5, No. 2 (May 1966): 19-24.

Petruzzi, J. David. "The Fleeting Fame of Alfred Pleasonton." *America's Civil War*, Vol. 19, No. 1 (March 2005), 42-49.

——. "He Rides Over Everything in Sight." *America's Civil War*, Vol. 20, No. 1 (March 2006), 42-49.

——. "John Buford: By the Book." *America's Civil War*, Vol. 19, No. 3 (July 2005), 26-34.

——. "Opening the Ball at Gettysburg: The Shot That Rang for Fifty Years." *America's Civil War*, Vol. 20, No. 3, July 2006.

——. "Six Weeks in the Saddle." *America's Civil War*, Vol. 21, No. 3 (July 2008), 26-37.

Phipps, Michael. "Walking Point: John Buford on the Road to Gettysburg." In *Papers of the Tenth Gettysburg National Military Park Seminar*. Gettysburg, Pa.: Gettysburg National Military Park (2005): 129-142.

Powell, David. "Stuart's Ride: Lee, Stuart, and the Confederate Cavalry in the Gettysburg Campaign." *Gettysburg Magazine* 20 (January 1999): 27-43.

Richards, David L. "The Brooke-Richards Rock." *Blue&Gray Magazine*, Vol. 20, No. 2 (2002): 59.

——. "Two Veterans Leave Their Mark." *Blue&Gray Magazine*, Vol. 22, No. 2 (2005): 53.

Richter, Edward G. J. "The Removal of the Confederate Dead from Gettysburg." *Gettysburg Magazine* 2 (January 1990): 113-122.

Sanders, Steve. "Enduring Tales of Gettysburg: The Death of Reynolds." *Gettysburg Magazine* 14 (January 1996): 27-36.

Schaefer, Thomas. "If You Seek His Monument – Look Around: E.B. Cope and the Gettysburg National Military Park." In *Programs of the Fifth Annual Gettysburg Seminar*. Gettysburg, Pa.: Gettysburg National Military Park (1996): 107-133.

Shevchuck, Paul M. "The Fight for Brinkerhoff's Ridge, July 2, 1863." *Gettysburg Magazine* 2 (January 1990): 61-73.

——. "The 1st Texas Infantry and the Repulse of Farnsworth's Charge." *Gettysburg Magazine* 2 (January 1990): 81-90.

——. "The Battle of Hunterstown, Pennsylvania, July 2, 1863." *Gettysburg Magazine* 1 (July 1989): 93-104.

Shultz, David and Richard Rollins. "The Most Accurate Fire Ever Witnessed: Federal Horse Artillery in the Pennsylvania Campaign." *Gettysburg Magazine* 33 (July 2005): 44-79.

Smith, Carlton. "Honor-Duty-Courage: The 5th Army Corps During the Gettysburg Campaign." In *Programs of the Sixth Annual Gettysburg Seminar*. Gettysburg, Pa.: Gettysburg National Military Park (1998): 173-204.

Smith, Timothy H. "The Story of Albertus McCreary: A Boy's Experience of the Battle." *Gettysburg Magazine* 17 (July 1997): 118-128.

——. "The Strange Tale of Ephraim Wisler." *Blue&Gray Magazine* Vol. 21, No. 1 (2003): 15.

——. "These Were Days of Horror: The Gettysburg Civilians." In *Programs of the Fifth Annual Gettysburg Seminar*. Gettysburg, Pa.: Gettysburg National Military Park (1996): 81-90.

Snell, Mark A. "A Hell of a Damned Fool: Judson Kilpatrick, Farnsworth's Charge, and the Hard Hand of History." In *Programs of the Ninth Gettysburg National Military Park Seminar*. Gettysburg, Pa.: Gettysburg National Military Park (2002): 181-194.

Taylor, Michael W. "North Carolina in the Pickett-Pettigrew-Trimble Charge at Gettysburg." *Gettysburg Magazine* 8 (January 1993): 67-93.

Timble, Tony. "Harrison: Spying for Longstreet at Gettysburg." *Gettysburg Magazine* 17 (July 1997): 17-19.

Vermilyea, Peter C. "The Professor and the Major: A Gettysburg Controversy." *Gettysburg Magazine* 37 (July 2007): 16-23.

Wert, Jeffry D. "All the Powers of Hell Were Waked to Madness." *America's Civil War Magazine*, Vol. 15, No. 3 (July 2002): 42-48.

Wilson Jr., Clyde N. "The Most Promising Young Man of the South: James J. Pettigrew." *Civil War Times Illustrated*, Vol. 11, No. 10 (February 1973): 12-23.

Winschel, Terry. "The Jeff Davis Legion at Gettysburg." *Gettysburg Magazine* 12 (July 1995): 68-82.

Wittenberg, Eric J. "Merritt's Regulars on South Cavalry Field: Oh, What Could Have Been." *Gettysburg Magazine* 16 (January 1997): 111-123.

——. "The Truth About the Withdrawal of Brig. Gen. John Buford's Cavalry, July 2, 1863. *Gettysburg Magazine* 37 (July 2007): 71-82.

Wright, Steven J. "Don't Let Me Bleed to Death: The Wounding of Maj. Gen. Winfield Scott Hancock." *Gettysburg Magazine* 6 (January 1992): 87-92.

Woods, James A. "Orphans in the Storm: The 115th Pennsylvania and 8th New Jersey in the Fight for the Wheatfield and Stony Hill." *Gettysburg Magazine* 29 (July 2003): 106-120.

Books and Pamphlets

Adelman, Garry E. *The Early Gettysburg Battlefield: Selected Photographs from the Gettysburg National Military Park Commission Reports, 1895-1904.* Gettysburg, Pa.: Thomas Publications, 2001.

——. *Little Round Top: A Detailed Tour Guide.* Gettysburg, Pa.: Thomas Publications, 2000.

Adelman, Garry E., John Richter and Timothy Smith, comp. *99 Historic Photographs of Culp's Hill, Gettysburg Pa.* Gettysburg, Pa.: The Center for Civil War Photography, 2003.

Adelman, Garry E. and Timothy H. Smith. *Devil's Den: A History and Guide.* Gettysburg, Pa.: Thomas Publications, 1997.

——. *The Myth of Little Round Top, Gettysburg, Pa.* Gettysburg, Pa.: Thomas Publications, 2003.

Allardice, Bruce S. *More Generals in Gray.* Baton Rouge: Louisiana State University Press, 1995.

Annual Reports of the Gettysburg National Military Park Commission to the Secretary of War, 1893-1904. Washington, D.C.: Government Printing Office, 1905.

Archer, John M. *Culp's Hill at Gettysburg: The Mountain Trembled.* Gettysburg, Pa.: Thomas Publications, 2002.

——. *The Hour Was One of Horror: East Cemetery Hill at Gettysburg.* Gettysburg, Pa.: 1997.

Bates, Samuel P. *The Battle of Gettysburg.* Philadelphia, Pa.: T.H. Davis & Co., 1875.

——. *Martial Deeds of Pennsylvania.* Philadelphia, Pa.: T.H. Davis & Co., 1875.

Bennett, Gerald R. *Days of Uncertainty and Dread: The Ordeal Endured by the Citizens at Gettysburg.* Littlestown, Pa.: Privately published, 1997.

Beyer, W. F. and O. F. Keydel, ed. *Deeds of Valor: How America's Civil War Heroes Won the Congressional Medal of Honor.* 2 vols. Detroit, MI: Perrien-Keydel Co., 1901.

Bloom, Robert L. *We Never Expected a Battle: The Civilians at Gettysburg, 1863.* Gettysburg, Pa.: The Adams County Historical Society, 1988.

Boatner, Mark M., III. *Civil War Dictionary.* New York: David McKay Co., 1959.

Boritt, Gabor S., ed. *The Gettysburg Nobody Knows.* New York: Oxford University Press, 1997.

Brennan, Patrick. *To Die Game: Gen. J.E.B. Stuart, CSA.* Gettysburg, Pa.: Farnsworth House Military Impressions, 1998.

Brown, Kent Masterson. *Cushing of Gettysburg: The Story of a Union Artillery Commander.* Lexington, KY: The University Press of Kentucky, 1993.

Busey, John W. *The Last Full Measure: Burials in the Soldiers' National Cemetery at Gettysburg.* Hightstown, N.J.: Longstreet House, 1988.

——. *These Honored Dead: The Union Casualties at Gettysburg.* Hightstown, N.J.: Longstreet House, 1996.

Busey, John W. and David G. Martin. *Regimental Strengths and Losses at Gettysburg.* Hightstown, N.J.: Longstreet House, 1986.

Carmichael, Peter S. *William R. J. Pegram: Lee's Young Artillerist.* Charlottesville, Va.: University Press of Virginia, 1995.

Cisco, Walter Brian. *Wade Hampton: Confederate Warrior, Conservative Statesman.* Washington, D.C.: Brassey's, Inc., 2004.

Clark, Walter, ed. *Histories of the Several Regiments and Battalions from North Carolina in the Great War, 1861-1865.* 5 vols. Goldsboro, N.C.: Nash Brothers, 1901.

Coco, Gregory A. *Gettysburg's Confederate Dead.* Gettysburg, Pa.: Thomas Publications, 2003.

——. *A Strange and Blighted Land - Gettysburg: The Aftermath of a Battle.* Gettysburg, Pa.: Thomas Publications, 1995.

——. *A Vast Sea of Misery: A History and Guide to the Union and Confederate Field Hospitals at Gettysburg, July 1 - November 20, 1863.* Gettysburg, Pa.: Thomas Publications, 1998.

Coddington, Edwin B. *The Gettysburg Campaign: A Study in Command.* New York: Charles Scribner's Sons, 1968.

Coffin, Howard. *Full Duty: Vermonters in the Civil War.* Woodstock, Vt.: The Countryman Press, Inc. 1993.

Cole, James and Roy E. Frampton. *The Gettysburg National Cemetery: A History and Guide.* Hanover, Pa.: Sheridan, 1988.

Collins, Darrell L. *Major General Robert E. Rodes of the Army of Northern Virginia, A Biography.* New York: Savas Beatie, 2008.

Commonwealth of Pennsylvania. *Report of the Select Committee Relative to the Soldiers' National Cemetery.* Harrisburg, Pa.: Singerly & Myers, State Printers, 1865.

Davis, Burke. *Jeb Stuart: The Last Cavalier.* New York: Rinehart, 1957.

Dawson, John Harper. *Wildcat Cavalry: A Synoptic History of the Seventeenth Virginia Cavalry Regiment of the Jenkins-McCausland Brigade in the War Between the States.* Dayton, OH: Morningside House, Inc., 1982.

Desjardin, Thomas A. *Legends of Gettysburg: Separating Fact From Fiction.* Gettysburg, Pa.: Friends of the National Parks at Gettysburg, Inc., 1996.

——. *The Monuments at Gettysburg.* Gettysburg, Pa.: Friends of the National Parks at Gettysburg, Inc., 1997.

——. *Stand Firm Ye Boys From Maine: The 20th Maine and the Gettysburg Campaign.* Gettysburg, Pa.: Thomas Publications, 1995.

Divine, John E. *35th Battalion Virginia Cavalry.* Lynchburg, Va.: H. E. Howard Co., 1985.

Dougherty, James J. *Stone's Brigade and the Fight for the McPherson Farm, Battle of Gettysburg, July 1, 1863.* New York: Da Capo Press, 2001.

Dreese, Michael A. *The Hospital on Seminary Ridge and the Battle of Gettysburg.* Jefferson, N.C.: McFarland & Company, Inc., 2002.

Eicher, John H. and David J. Eicher. *Civil War High Commands.* Stanford, Ca.: Stanford University Press, 2001.

Flagel, Thomas R. and Ken Allers, Jr. *The History Buff's Guide to Gettysburg*. Nashville, TN: Cumberland House Publishing, Inc., 2006.

Frankfort, Dennis. *Gettysburg Battle Lands: Protection and Preservation*. Gettysburg, Pa.: Friends of the National Parks at Gettysburg, Inc., 1999.

Frassanito, William A. *Early Photography at Gettysburg*. Gettysburg, Pa.: Thomas Publications, 1995.

——. *Gettysburg: A Journey in Time*. New York: Charles Scribner's Sons, 1975.

——. *The Gettysburg Bicentennial Album*. Gettysburg, Pa.: The Gettysburg Bicentennial Committee, 1987.

——. *The Gettysburg Then & Now Companion*. Gettysburg, Pa.: Thomas Publications, 1997.

——. *Gettysburg Then & Now: Touring the Battlefield With Old Photos, 1863-1889*. Gettysburg, Pa.: Thomas Publications, 1996.

Gambone, A. M. *Hancock at Gettysburg...And Beyond*. Baltimore, Md.: Butternut and Blue, 1997.

Gottfried, Bradley M. *The Maps of Gettysburg: An Atlas of the Gettysburg Campaign, June 3 - July 13, 1863*. New York: Savas Beatie, 2007.

——. *Roads to Gettysburg: Lee's Invasion of the North, 1863*. Shippensburg, Pa.: White Mane Books, 2001.

Gragg, Rod. *Covered With Glory: The 26th North Carolina Infantry at the Battle of Gettysburg*. New York: Harper Collins, 2000.

Grimm, Herbert L., Paul L. Roy and George Rose. *Human Interest Stories of the Three Days' Battles at Gettysburg*. Gettysburg, Pa.: Tem Inc., 1995.

Harris, Nelson. *17th Virginia Cavalry*. Lynchburg, Va.: H.E. Howard, Inc., 1994.

Harrison, Kathy Georg, comp. *The Location of the Monuments, Markers, and Tablets on Gettysburg Battlefield*. Gettysburg, Pa.: Thomas Publications, 1993.

Hassler, Warren W., Jr. *Crisis at the Crossroads: The First Day at Gettysburg*. Tuscaloosa, Ala.: University of Alabama Press, 1970.

Hawthorne, Frederick W. *Gettysburg: Stories of Men and Monuments as Told by Battlefield Guides*. Gettysburg, Pa.: The Association of Licensed Battlefield Guides, 1988.

Holland, Lynwood M. *Pierce Young: The Warwick of the South*. Athens, Ga.: University of Georgia Press, 1964.

Hopkins, Donald A. *The Little Jeff: The Jeff Davis Legion, Cavalry, Army of Northern Virginia*. Shippensburg, Pa.: White Mane, 1999.

Jorgenson, Jay. *Gettysburg's Bloody Wheatfield*. Shippensburg, Pa.: White Mane Books, 2002.

——. *The Wheatfield at Gettysburg: A Walking Tour*. Gettysburg, Pa.: Thomas Publications, 2002.

Kennell, Brian A. *Beyond the Gatehouse: Gettysburg's Evergreen Cemetery*. Gettysburg, Pa.: Evergreen Cemetery Association, 2000.

Kesterson, Brian Stuart. *Campaigning With the 17th Virginia Cavalry Night Hawks at Monocacy*. Washington, WV: Nighthawk Press, 2005.

Kirshner, Ralph. *The Class of 1861: Custer, Ames, and Their Classmates after West Point*. Carbondale, Ill.: Southern Illinois University Press, 1999.

Krick, Robert K. *The Gettysburg Death Roster: The Confederate Dead at Gettysburg*. Dayton, Ohio: Morningside Press, 1985.

Lambert, Dobbie Edward. *Grumble: The W. E. Jones Brigade 1863-64*. Wahiawa, Hi.: Lambert Enterprises, Inc., 1992.

Large, George R. *Battle of Gettysburg: The Official History by the Gettysburg National Military Park Commission*. Shippensburg, Pa.: Burd Street Press, 1999.

Longacre, Edward G. *The Cavalry at Gettysburg: A Tactical Study of Mounted Operations During the Civil War's Pivotal Campaign, 9 June - 14 July 1863*. Rutherford, N. J.: Fairleigh-Dickinson University Press, 1986.

——. *Custer and His Wolverines: The Michigan Cavalry Brigade, 1861-1865*. Conshohocken, Pa.: Combined Publishing, 1997.

——. *General John Buford: A Military Biography*. Conshohocken, Pa.: Combined Books, 1995.

——. *Gentleman and Soldier: A Biography of Wade Hampton III*. Nashville, Tenn.: Rutledge Hill, 2003.

Martin, David G. *Confederate Monuments at Gettysburg*. Conshohocken, Pa.: Combined Books, Inc., 1995.

——. *Gettysburg: July 1 (Completely Revised Edition)*. Conshohocken, Pa.: Combined Books, 1996.

Martin, Samuel J. *Kill-Cavalry: The Life of Union General Hugh Judson Kilpatrick*. Mechanicsburg, Pa.: Stackpole Books, 2000.

Mingus, Scott Sr. *Flames Beyond the Susquehanna: The Gordon Expedition, June 1863*. Columbus, Ohio: Ironclad Publishing, 2008.

——. *Human Interest Stories of the Gettysburg Campaign*. Orrtanna, Pa.: Colecraft Industries, 2006.

——. *Human Interest Stories of the Gettysburg Campaign, Volume II*. Orrtanna, Pa.: Colecraft Industries, 2007.

Murray, R. L., ed. *New Yorkers in the Civil War: A Historic Journal, Volume 3*. Wolcott, N.Y.: Benedum Books, 2004.

——. *New York's Officers at Gettysburg: Biographies of New York's Highest Ranking Commanders at Gettysburg*. Wolcott, N.Y.: Benedum Books, 2003.

Nevins, James H. and William B. Styple. *What Death More Glorious: A Biography of General Strong Vincent*. Kearny, N.J.: Belle Grove Publishing Co., 1997.

Newton, George W. *Silent Sentinels: A Reference Guide to the Artillery at Gettysburg*. New York: Savas Beatie, 2005.

Newton, Steven H. *McPherson's Ridge: The First Battle for the High Ground, July 1, 1863*. Cambridge, Mass.: DaCapo Press, 2002.

Nichols, Edward J. *Toward Gettysburg: A Biography of General John F. Reynolds*. University Park, Pa.: The Pennsylvania State University Press, 1958.

Nofi, Albert A. *The Gettysburg Campaign, June - July 1863*. New York: Gallery Books, 1986.

Nye, Wilbur Sturtevant. *Here Come the Rebels!* Baton Rouge, La.: Louisiana State University Press, 1965.

Penny, Morris M. and J. Gary Laine. *Struggle for the Round Tops: Law's Alabama Brigade at the Battle of Gettysburg*. Shippensburg, Pa.: Burd Street Press, 1999.

Pfanz, Harry W. *Gettysburg: Culp's Hill and Cemetery Hill*. Chapel Hill, N.C.: University of North Carolian Press, 1993.

——. *Gettysburg: The First Day*. Chapel Hill, N.C.: The University of North Carolina Press, 2001.

——. *Gettysburg: The Second Day*. Chapel Hill, N.C.: The University of North Carolina Press, 1987.

Phipps, Michael. *Come On You Wolverines!: Custer at Gettysburg*. Gettysburg, Pa.: Farnsworth House Military Impressions, 1995.

—— and John S. Peterson. *The Devil's to Pay: Gen. John Buford, USA*. Gettysburg, Pa.: Farnsworth Military Impressions, 1995.

Phisterer, Frederick. *New York in the War of the Rebellion, 1861-1865*. Albany, N.Y.: J. B. Lyon Co., 1907.

Pitts, Calista. *Gettysburg Addresses*. Gettysburg, Pa.: Thomas Publications, 2000.

Platt, Barbara L. *This is Holy Ground: A History of the Gettysburg Battlefield*. Harrisburg, Pa.: Huggins Printing, 2001.

Priest, John Michael. *Into the Fight: Pickett's Charge at Gettysburg*. Shippensburg, Pa.: White Mane Books, 1998.

Raus, Edmund J., Jr. *A Generation on the March: The Union Army at Gettysburg*. Gettysburg, Pa.: Thomas Publications, 1998.

Ray, Fred L. *Shock Troops of the Confederacy: The Sharpshooter Battalions of the Army of Northern Virginia*. Asheville, N.C.: CFS Press, 2006.

Reardon, Carol. *Pickett's Charge in History & Memory*. Chapel Hill, N.C.: The University of North Carolina Press, 1997.

Ristine, James D. *Gettysburg: Vintage Postcard Views of America's Greatest Battlefield*. Charleston, S.C.: Arcadia Publishing, 1999.

Robertson, John. *Michigan in the War*. Lansing, Mich.: W. S. George & Co., 1882.

Rummel, George A., III. *Cavalry on the Roads to Gettysburg: Kilpatrick at Hanover and Hunterstown*. Shippensburg, Pa.: White Mane, 2000.

——. *72 Days at Gettysburg: Organization of the 10th Regiment, New York Volunteer Cavalry*. Shippensburg, Pa.: White Mane, 1997.

Salmon, John S. *Historic Photos of Gettysburg*. Nashville, TN: Turner Publishing Company, 2007.

Sauers, Richard A. *Gettysburg: The Meade-Sickles Controversy*. Washington, D.C.: Brassey's, Inc., 2003.

Schildt, John W. *Roads to Gettysburg*. Parsons, W.V.: McClain Printing Co., 1978.

Sears, Stephen W. *Gettysburg*. Boston, Mass.: Houghton Mifflin Co., 2003.

Sharpe, Michael. *Historical Maps of Civil War Battlefields*. London, England: PRC Publishing Ltd., 2000.

Shue, Richard S. *Morning at Willoughby Run: The Opening Battle at Gettysburg*. Gettysburg, Pa.: Thomas Publications, 1998.

Shultz, David and David Wieck. *The Battle Between the Farm Lanes: Hancock Saves the Union Center, Gettysburg, July 2, 1863*. Columbus, Ohio: Ironclad Publishing, Inc., 2006.

Slade, Jim and John Alexander. *Firestorm at Gettysburg: Civilian Voices, June-November, 1863*. Atglen, Pa.: Schiffer Publishing, Inc., 1998.

Smith, Timothy H., comp. *Farms at Gettysburg: The Fields of Battle - Selected Images from the Adams County Historical Society*. Gettysburg, Pa.: Thomas Publications, 2007.

——. *Gettysburg's Battlefield Photographer - William H. Tipton*. Gettysburg, Pa.: Thomas Publications, 2005.

——. *In the Eye of the Storm: The Farnsworth House and the Battle of Gettysburg*. Gettysburg, Pa.: Farnsworth Military Impressions, 2008.

——. *John Burns: The Hero of Gettysburg*. Gettysburg, Pa.: Thomas Publications, 2000.

——. *The Story of Lee's Headquarters, Gettysburg, Pennsylvania*. Gettysburg, Pa.: Thomas Publications, 1995.

Stackpole, Edward J. *They Met at Gettysburg*. Harrisburg, Pa.: Eagle Books, 1956.

Stewart, George R. *Pickett's Charge: A Microhistory of the Final Attack at Gettysburg, July 3, 1863*. Boston, Mass.: Houghton Mifflin, 1959.

Styple, William B., ed. *Generals in Bronze: Interviewing the Commanders of the Civil War*. Kearny, N.J.: Belle Grove Publishing Company, 2005.

Trudeau, Noah Andre. *Gettysburg: A Testing of Courage*. New York: Harper Collins, 2002.

Walters, Sara Gould. *Inscription at Gettysburg: In Memoriam to Captain David Acheson, Company C, 140th Pennsylvania Volunteers*. Gettysburg, Pa.: Thomas Publications, 1991.

Warner, Ezra J. *Generals in Blue: The Lives of the Union Commanders*. Baton Rouge, La.: Louisiana State University Press, 1964.

——. *Generals in Gray: The Lives of the Confederate Commanders*. Baton Rouge, La.: Louisiana State University Press, 1959.

Wasel, Bob and Sarah Richardson, comp. *The Gettysburg You Never Knew*. Privately published, 1996.

——. *More Gettysburg You Never Knew*. Privately published, 1997.

Wachsmuth, C. Wayne. *Ewell's Approach*. Gettysburg, Pa.: Friends of the National Parks at Gettysburg, Inc., 1998.

Wert, Jeffry D. *Cavalryman of the Lost Cause: A Biography of J.E.B. Stuart*. New York: Simon & Schuster, 2008.

——. *Gettysburg: Day Three*. New York: Simon & Schuster, 2001.

Wert, J. Howard. *A Complete Hand-Book of the Monuments and Indications and Guide to the Positions on the Gettysburg Battle-Field*. Harrisburg, Pa.: R. M. Sturgeon & Co., 1886.

Wheeler, Richard. *Gettysburg 1863: Campaign of Endless Echoes*. New York: Plume, 1999.

——. *Witness to Gettysburg*. New York: Harper & Row, 1987.

Williams, T. P. *The Mississippi Brigade of Brig. Gen. Joseph R. Davis: A Geographical Account of Its Campaigns and a Biographical Account of Its Personalities, 1861-1865*. Dayton, Ohio: Morningside House, Inc. 1999.

Wills, Garry. *Lincoln at Gettysburg: The Words that Remade America*. New York: Simon & Schuster, 1992.

Wittenberg, Eric J. Gettysburg's Forgotten Cavalry Actions. Gettysburg, Pa.: Thomas Publications, 1998.

——. *Protecting the Flank: The Battles for Brinkerhoff's Ridge and East Cavalry Field, Gettysburg, Pennsylvania*. Celina, Ohio: Ironclad Publishing, 2002.

Wittenberg, Eric J. and J. David Petruzzi. *Plenty of Blame to Go Around: Jeb Stuart's Controversial Ride to Gettysburg*. New York: Savas Beatie, 2006.

Wittenberg, Eric J., J. David Petruzzi, and Michael F. Nugent. *One Continuous Fight: The Retreat from Gettysburg and the Pursuit of Lee's Army of Northern Virginia, July 4 - 14, 1863*. New York: Savas Beatie, 2008.

* * * * * * * * * *

Map Sets

Friends of the National Parks at Gettysburg Map Set, Developed and Produced by Thomas A. Desjardin. Gettysburg, Pa.: Friends of the National Parks at Gettysburg, Inc., 1998.

Gettysburg Battlefield in One Volume. Olean, NY: McElfresh Map Co., 1994.

Gettysburg National Military Park, Pennsylvania, Civil War Battlefield Series. Aurora, CO: Trailhead Graphics, Inc., 2000.

Map of Adams County, Pennsylvania, From Actual Survey by G. M. Hopkins, 1858. M. S. & E. Converse, Publishers, Philadelphia Pa.

A Theater Map of the Gettysburg Campaign 1863. Olean, NY: McElfresh Map Co., 2003.

J. David Petruzzi

J. David Petruzzi is widely recognized as one of the country's leading experts on the Gettysburg campaign in general, and cavalry operations in particular. He is the author (with Eric Wittenberg) of the bestsellers *Plenty of Blame to Go Around: Jeb Stuart's Controversial Ride to Gettysburg* (Savas Beatie, 2006) and (with Wittenberg and Michael Nugent) *One Continuous Fight: The Retreat From Gettysburg and the Pursuit of Lee's Army of Northern Virginia, July 4-14, 1863* (Savas Beatie, 2008). J.D. is a regular contributor to *America's Civil War* magazine, and has published in a wide variety of periodicals including *Gettysburg Magazine*, *Civil War Times*, *Blue & Gray*, and *Zouave* magazine. He has appeared as a main character in two Civil War documentaries, and served as historical advisor on these productions. J.D. is a popular speaker on the Civil War Roundtable circuit, regularly conducts tour of Civil War battlefields and related sites, and maintains the popular blog "Hoofbeats and Cold Steel" (http://jdpetruzzi. blogspot.com). His personal website is http://jdpetruzzi.com.

J.D. is a member of the Civil War Preservation Trust and an active supporter of battlefield preservation. An avid golfer and outdoorsman, he lives with his wife Karen in Brockway, Pennsylvania, where he runs his own insurance agency. They have one child, a daughter named Ashley.

Steven Stanley

Steven Stanley is a graphic artist specializing in historical map design and battlefield photography. His maps, considered among the best in historical cartography, have been a longtime staple of the Civil War Preservation Trust and have helped raised millions of dollars for the Trust through their preservation appeals and interpretation projects. Steve's maps have appeared in *Hallowed Ground* and *America's Civil War* magazines, and in *In the Footsteps of Grant and Lee: The Wilderness Through Cold Harbor* by Gordon Rhea. His work has been commissioned by various historical preservation organizations and agencies that include the National Park Service, the Shenandoah Valley Battlefield Foundation, the Tennessee Civil War Preservation Association, and the Army Reserve, Office of the Historian. Steve is a past board member of the Central Virginia Battlefields Trust, and is a founding board member of the Richmond Battlefields Association and the Friends of Cedar Mountain Battlefield. He has been a student of the Civil War for all his adult life, with a special zeal for the preservation and natural beauty of battlefields. Steve enjoys the unique perspectives and opportunities provided by the specialized study of historical sites through photography and cartography.

Steven is also a member of the Civil War Preservation Trust and an active supporter of battlefield preservation. He loves exploring Civil War battlefields whether on foot or bike, especially the Gettysburg battlefield. He and Kyrstie live in Gettysburg, Pennsylvania. He has two lovely daughters living in Florida and Virginia.